THE TRIPTYCH OF THE KINGDOM

THE TRIPTYCH OF THE KINGDOM

A HANDBOOK OF THE CATHOLIC FAITH

BY

DR. N. G. M. VAN DOORNIK
REV. S. JELSMA
REV. A. VAN DE LISDONK

Translated from the Dutch

EDITED BY
REV. JOHN GREENWOOD

SANDS & CO. (PUBLISHERS) LTD.
15 King Street, Covent Garden, W.C.2
and at 76 Cambridge Street, Glasgow

Nihil obstat:
Hubertus Richards, S.T.L., L.S.S.
Censor deputatus

Imprimatur:
E. Morrogh Bernard,
Vic. Gen.

Westmonasterii, die 10a Novembris, 1953.

First published March 1954

MADE AND PRINTED IN GREAT BRITAIN
BY NORTHUMBERLAND PRESS LIMITED
GATESHEAD ON TYNE

CONTENTS

EDITOR'S NOTE

THE authors of this Course of Instructions on the Catholic Faith are working in Holland under the auspices of the Una Sancta movement. Consequently their approach is based on actual experience of convert work and is tempered with much understanding of the problems of the non-Catholic position. "Una Sancta House" in the Hague, of which Dr. van Doornik is the Superior, counts its converts at more than 250 per year.

The Una Sancta movement approaches convert making psychologically. The enquirer without involving himself in any obligation, may call at an ordinary house comfortably furnished and chat over his problems with a layman or a priest. If he wishes to have a full course of instructions he or she may continue with them at this establishment. Where exactly the same ideas are used but a shop is substituted for a house, the institution is called the Open Door.

The success achieved by these new means is quite phenomenal and it is fitting that priests engaged on a work of such importance should give us the fruit of their learning in a concise course.

FOREWORD

We should like, first of all, to write a few introductory words for our non-Catholic readers.

Naturally enough, we do not know your personal reasons for reading this book; we can only presume that you find sufficient interest in Catholicism to warrant your going into it deeper. In the course of your life you have had probably some limited contacts with the Catholic Church. May be, you have noticed something characteristic about our churches, or our priests. Perhaps you have read books or seen films depicting the deeper realities of Catholic life. Or again, in visiting the homes of Catholic friends, you have found a crucifix or holy picture displayed in a prominent position. It is quite possible that you have been to Mass with a Catholic, and still more possible that you understood very little about the ceremony.

When you were at school, some mention may have been made of the conflict between Catholics and Protestants, especially during the Reformation period. This included the mis-deeds of Queen Mary and her burning of Archbishop Cranmer, or the part played by Catholics in the Gun-Powder Plot, or again the massacre of the French Huguenots. The Spanish Inquisition may have been another topic of discussion.

You may have had another chance of making contact with the Faith by travelling abroad through Catholic countries. Towards the end of the war many people in the Forces were billeted in Catholic households, living for quite a time with these families.

It may be even that you are friendly with a Catholic boy or girl, and are seriously thinking of future marriage, and in this case you wish to know more of your affianced's religion.

All these influences have given you some idea of the Catholic Church, although you would be the first to admit that it is a vague knowledge. At the back of your mind odd questions arise on Papal Infallibility, Confession, the Mass, Indulgences. Since much that you have heard on these subjects appears rather strange, and some of Catholic teaching quite unacceptable, you are probably hoping that this book may help to explain things more clearly.

Most of our readers, however, will make use of this book as a manual of religious instruction. They have already a leaning towards the Church and stand on the threshold, waiting only for a clear personal conviction of her truth before entering.

It is for these readers in particular that we write the following pages. A personal conviction that the Church possesses the truth, is the one and only reason why one should become a Catholic; it cannot be merely a question of some whim or feeling, however refined, nor for the sake of a girl-friend. This is obvious when one takes into account that each one of us has a settled outlook on life, which cannot be changed arbitrarily, even when we love somebody dearly. This love may be indeed an inducement to change one's religion, but will not diminish the difficulties involved. There are a good many wrong ideas current about this, unfortunately even among Catholics. How could one merely forget, or slur over one's present conviction and adopt a whole set of new ones, just in order to get married?

We do not wish to deny that a change of outlook may be simulated, but from our experience, we also know that by far the greater number of young people sooner give up having instructions than feign new beliefs they do not accept. The difficulties in the beginning can be considerable. These may come from one's surroundings, or from the need to change old customs and views. In non-Catholic circles there exists sometimes strong anti-Catholic feeling, which need not always be attributed to anti-Papalism. Parents who are themselves convinced Protestants, quite understandably consider the conversion of their child from the family religion, as an apostacy. This in spite of the fact that a Protestant should always have the right to investigate freely. In principle one cannot blame a person if he tries to understand another's way of thinking, even if there is a likelihood that, as a result, he too may adopt that way of thought.

Thus, frequently, a certain tension develops between parents and children, causing much distress, and considerably hampering the process of instruction. Indeed, this process begins right from the very first talk, when something stirs in the soul. This is because anyone who begins having instruction from a priest will be bound to change some of his ideas, even though he does not ultimately become a Catholic. It is impossible to come into contact with an institution like the Catholic Church without altering, and in some cases completely abandoning, one's old views. The experience is rather like a journey abroad through foreign lands; the result very often is a broadening of one's outlook. So, in a somewhat similar manner, a trip through the Catholic world, with its two-thousand-year-old development and culture, will cause one to change some old ideas, abandon some prejudices, and admit that some opinions were pure fantasy. One soon finds out that a Catholic does not kneel before a statue of Our Lady as a pagan before an idol; that he does not pay to have his sins forgiven; that the Pope is capable of sinning; that Indulgences cannot be sold, etc.

It becomes quite clear that one knows very little about Catholicism. And why? Well, think for a moment, who were your informants? Were they experts teaching on behalf of the Church, or were they those of another faith who themselves relied only on hearsay? There is no need to tell you what sort of information on religious matters you will get at the office or from behind the shop counter. Almost any nonsense can pass muster, because there is no expert to contradict it. And we must not forget, that not all Catholics are well enough instructed to know all the answers.

In such a way you may have built up gradually a picture of the Catholic Church which bears no relation to reality. Instead, to get a true idea, you must see the whole of Catholic doctrine and practice, you must study the Church's rich liturgy and centuries' old culture; then you can form an opinion. It will take some months to get this right perspective. The ideal attitude is to be open to the truth, to be prepared to listen and to try to understand impartially, neither determined to 'believe at all costs' nor, on the other hand, to 'deny in any case'. The best way to commence is to have some preliminary instructions, without involving yourself in any obligations.

The first few months can be the most difficult, and it happens sometimes that even those who are sympathetic to begin with, suffer a reaction and find everything unacceptable.

Added to all this, there may be an unconscious struggle with a former conviction which dies hard, whilst the opposition from family and friends grows even more pronounced. A quite natural reaction sets in making one doubt whether the Faith is worth all this trouble.

On the other hand, however, the Catholic Church exercises an undoubted fascination. One begins already to find that the basis for everything is much sounder than one had supposed; the teaching hangs together so logically. The Bible and Christ Himself have much more significance among Catholics than one had imagined as a Protestant, and beneath the surface of mere external appearances and routine there lurk astonishing depths. One feels sometimes a slight sensation of dizziness and resistance; one is afraid of being caught unawares; and above all, one does not wish to let oneself go unrestrainedly. Those who seek for the truth are never fanciful dreamers. They always fear that they may be hallucinated, and consequently shun all suggestion. Their great weapon is suspicion, with which they defend themselves against priests and new ideas, against arguments, ceremonies and rites however impressive. Of course, not all have this deep resistance, although one does come across people who will hold on like grim death to an old conviction for as long as they possibly can; and who pray God on their knees that He will not send them along the road to that despicable, backward, arrogant Church.

And yet, in spite of all this, the Church remains an attraction. She is ancient and she is one; her interpretation of the Bible sometimes throws a remarkably new light on texts which were meaningless before. The past rises up to bear witness—great thinkers emerge from the dim ages of old, one discovers cathedrals and abbeys, libraries and museums full of the most wonderful Catholic culture. . . . Did one just pass by all this before? It is bewildering and also a little humiliating to realize that one had ignored a world full of beauty and truth through prejudice and bigotry. These prejudices now stand before one, meaningless and empty, silent and foolish, like exposed traitors. The old customs and beliefs, the familiar *milieu* so dear to one, begin to lose their glamour, leaving one ill at ease in one's former environment. One no longer has an outlook on things like the others, no longer joins in as before, not even for the sake of a sweetheart's tears. Over against all this stands the Catholic Church majestic but still strange.

This is the period of crisis through which the majority pass. They know that they can never go back, and that the past is empty, but as yet they have no positive assurance to fill the gap.

(Cf the 2 Vols of the 'Road to Damascus'. Each chapter is an account of the conversion of some prominent person to Catholicism).

One ought to realize how important it is at this stage to persevere. On no account should one give up. Just because everything seems topsy-turvy, one's judgment is not clear and objective, and therefore it is imperative to *go on.* Then comes a period of calm. It is usually at this juncture that people who have never prayed before, for whom Christ was nothing more than a name, begin to wonder how they lived peacefully enough up till now, without once thinking about the real reason for their existence. Indeed, they have passed hundreds of churches, listened to religious programmes on the wireless, even seen other people praying, suffering and dying, without ever once reflecting on the problems of life and death, and never going down on their knees to pray.

Now comes the time when a person *really kneels down to pray.* It is with a certain fear, a feeling of smallness that one really speaks for the first time in one's life, to the Maker of all things. Anyone who has learned to pray as a child on his mother's knee, can scarcely imagine the difficulties others encounter when they turn to an unknown God, an invisible Being, who does not even seem to reply. It is by an almost palpable grace from God that this difficulty is overcome, resulting in a contact between the convert and God, hitherto quite unknown. To an outsider, this in itself can be strangely moving.

All this is only the general outline. Each case is different, and one does not find two enquirers who come into the Church by exactly the same path. Education, former beliefs, character, temperament, circumstances, all have an influence upon the individual process. When you read the accounts written by converts to Catholicism, you will be struck by the variety of difficulties encountered and the equally marvellous solutions found for them. Whoever finds truth and peace of mind in Catholicism will look back upon these difficulties with a feeling of real deliverance. The fight was not over trifles, it was over a radical change of attitude, opinion and outlook, influencing the whole of one's life intimately. One becomes a different person, and—as you will perhaps agree with me later on—a better person.

We do not wish to replace the teacher instructing you—indeed we cannot—but may we be allowed to offer a little advice. When you go to a priest first of all, it should not be with the intention of becoming a Catholic, straight away. Your tentative purpose should be to get to know Catholicism better. Only when you can accept the teaching absolutely implicitly and with complete surrender, are you justified in conscience in taking the step which leads to your entering the Church. During instructions you remain completely free. No priest will try to force you. The Church is not concerned with quantity, only with quality. You may of course have been told differently. It would not surprise us if at some time or other you had believed that priests were out to catch guileless souls in their nets. In fact, no priest may in conscience baptize an adult who does not believe and who does not wish to be baptized. What is asked of you is an honest, straightforward attitude, an open mind, free from fear and suspicion, ready to listen. And in this frame of mind only should you read the following pages.

May we add now a word or two for Catholic Youth. This book is written for non-Catholic *catechumens* and is equally suitable for Catholic young people. This may sound rather strange, and so here is the explanation.

The non-Catholic comes to the Catholic Faith after a struggle with problems which have greatly shaken his former philosophy of life. He has become estranged from what was once so dear to him, and what he once held for certainty has crumpled up helplessly. Darkness precedes light, and only by suffering is new joy born.

The young Catholic just out of his adolescence stands before a similar task. One need not regard the fact too tragically, but it still remains true that many come to see the Faith differently. When one was a child, one accepted everything that was told by parents and clergy without criticism. The more marvellous the stories, the more eagerly were they listened to.

Without requiring any proof one lived in the happy conviction that one had been born into the true Church, and that one was privileged above other children who blindly clung to their protestant faith. But there comes the day when one's critical sense awakens—the realization dawns upon one that non-Catholics also believe that they possess the truth. How can that be? You are sure that they are wrong. But why? In the end this worrying question may arise in your mind: "Every religion maintains that it is the true one. Why should the Catholic religion be the true one—the precise religion to which *I* belong?" Is that just a coincidence? Certainly faith is a gift of God and can stand many an impact, nevertheless you would undoubtedly like to know how to ward off those attackers who regard Catholicism as merely homogeneous with every other religion, if indeed they do not place it below them as out-of-date and childishly naïve.

Again, some young person may be brought suddenly into contact with a non-Catholic who is in the same condition, but whose mind is already open to Catholicism. The same questions arise and the same answers are given by both, and this eventually results in a mutual enkindling of faith—not now, however, as a matter of childlike acceptance, but as a matter of personal religious conviction. But this entails that the spiritual development of a person should match his mental development. When young students have to solve their own religious problems, with no more than their lower-school knowledge of the Catechism to help them, it is obvious that such knowledge will be inadequate. And it may be that the more fully developed and educated man turns away, disappointed, from a Faith which has no better answers to the problems of life, without realizing that he has, in reality, only been discussing all these matters with the child still within him.

The Catholic Faith has indeed many more answers to life's questions than those officially printed in the Catechism. Further she can prove all these answers historically, philosophically and theologically, in such a way that not only the student but the professor finds himself becoming interested. One must however be fair. If a person sets out to solve a problem in connection with the psychology of the chimpanzee, he does not look it up in "The Young Animal Lover"; and in order to form a personal opinion as to the religious background of the Reformation, one should not begin by upsetting the nursery in search of a "Brief National History".

It would be palpably foolish to try and find the answers to your religious difficulties with no more than the insufficient religious knowledge which you remember from your school-days, to fall back upon. In such circumstances a conflict must inevitably follow, and if you begin a debate with an educated Humanist, or a non-Catholic college friend, you will be forced into giving confused answers, or into having to reply sheepishly: "I am sorry, but I really do not know. You will have to ask a priest that."

It is a sad, yet in some ways a consoling sign, that many Catholic people are ashamed of their lack of knowledge of the dogma of their Faith.

Those who are just entering upon life and leaving behind them the peace of the home or the schoolroom, may well feel almost giddy on encountering the chaos of religious opinions, trends and philosophies, which greet them out in the world. At the office, behind the counter, at the club, they face questions which are baffling. Because they are known to be Catholics, a number of obsolete controversies, which nevertheless have a bearing upon modern life, are sure to be brought up. Any intelligent former pupil of a Catholic school may still be able to save the situation. But what about the others?

Gradually real misgivings may come to increase that unpleasant uneasiness of which they are aware in the depths of their consciousness. If they do not try to get guidance at this stage, even greater dangers threaten. You have only to look round to see the leakage in the big cities; it may even be found among those who perhaps sat next to you at the Catechism class, excellent boys and girls, and who may have left school with the highest marks for religious knowledge.

The whole point is that this lapse could have been prevented if only the general knowledge of religion had been made into a personal matter and used to fit personal circumstances. High marks indicate so little how far knowledge has been genuinely absorbed and become coherent in a person's mind. That which is not first properly assimilated is never really digested. Let us however take courage, for the moment, for development is never more favourable than when a deficiency is most painfully felt.

That is the cheering fact in the attitude of many of the younger generation: they realize that the knowledge which they have of the Faith is insufficient. They want to know *why* they are justified in believing; they want to know *what* precisely they have to believe and what not; they want most of all to grasp the congruity and consistency of the whole thing.

We have tried to answer such questions in this book, and especially we have tried to bring out clearly that consistency. Our Faith is not just a collection of disconnected dogmas which have each in turn to be proved. One main line runs quietly and steadily through the whole of the teaching of the Catholic Church. God did not come down to earth in order to instruct us in logic, and the Gospels are very little concerned with systemizations, but it is an occasion for happiness to realize that man did at least discover in God's revelation, something of that mighty unity which is contained in it.

This unity of Catholic teaching is the result of the work of many theologians who, over a period of nearly two thousand years, have studied God's word and have discovered and explained the connection and inter-relation of all its various parts. It is unjustifiable for any educated Catholic not to make an effort to assimilate the main principles of this great survey and record. Only so does one gain real insight into one's faith, and the radiance of this unity shines on to all the separate details, and throws just the right light on to all the different truths of dogma.

From the point of view of Apologetics, this unity is of the greatest importance. As long as one is still in the stage where one has to look up, so to speak, an alphabetical list of answers to worrying questions, the thing is apt to remain a mere patchwork of meaningless expressions. But when one is able to take in the whole subject at a glance, and to know just where the difficulty lies, the problem can be much more thoroughly and effectively tackled.

Such matters as indulgences, purgatory, veneration of the saints, and so on, which—if we believe our opponents—are among the most important points of revelation, will then take their proper place: important certainly, for nothing in our Faith is unimportant, but still not in the first rank.

But even more important than the *defence* of the Faith is the *living* of it. It is our sincere desire that the study of this book should rouse a feeling of gratitude in the heart of every Catholic reader for the great gift of Faith, and a loving gift of self to Him who is represented in the centre panel of our Triptych as the predominant figure: Jesus Christ.

THE AUTHORS

INTRODUCTORY CHAPTER

In this chapter we propose to consider the world in which we live and to ask two questions: "What is God?" and "Must Man serve God?"

§ 1. *What is God?*

ON SOME SILENT NIGHT under a starry sky, most people have experienced a sensation of mysterious awe towards the Power who governs the universe. On such an occasion the world of men seems to be very far away, and it is as though one entered into contact with a Being of an altogether different order. Many are the questions which are asked in regard to this Being, whom we call God. These are the sort of remarks one hears from the young people of to-day.

"What is God? Who is God? What does He look like? Is he a Power—or is He only a thought, an idea? Who is this God to whom we pray? *What* is It? The whole thing is a mystery." Or again:

"God . . . and Men. These are the things upon which, as a thinking person, I know I ought to reflect. Yet, when I begin to do so, they expand into problems of almost giddy dimensions. Who *is* God? Why should there *be* a God? Why does He act in one particular way and no other?"

Most probably you also have asked yourself the question: "What is God?" If we wish to go into the matter seriously, the best way is surely to observe His work, His creation, as closely as we can, and then, from thinking about this world, to rise towards the Maker of it, and so to try to understand more about Him.

God, indeed, is not a man with hands and feet like the rest of us. I assume that the pictures from your Children's Bible have gradually been replaced in your mind by a truer representation of the Deity. A child cannot think otherwise than in pictures, but the adult has grasped that God has no real resemblance to childhood's imagery, but exists without bodily form, apart from the material world, as a pure spirit. We understand by the expression pure spirit, not ethereal matter, not a transparent body, but a Being without matter or form, who is a pure thinking and willing Power.

God is thus an infinite Spirit who has created the universe by His omnipotent will. One could appropriately say: " He thought it into existence." It is most important that this should be properly understood. It may well happen that a child has always pictured God as a great King, who literally has His throne upon the clouds, and that later on he discards this idea as childish, without, however, definitely replacing it by a more correct view of the Almighty. If so, it would not be the first time that a person had lost his faith in God because he thought—quite wrongly—that those who believe in God connect their belief with absurd and childish representations. The intelligent believer knows quite well that God is a Being so infinitely exalted that He cannot be pictured. Even when he calls God a *Person,* this does not mean a *man,* but an independent Being, who is distinct from this visible world, and exists as an omnipotent Spirit of whom we can only formulate a vague and imperfect idea.

It is true that the way God is imagined differs considerably with different people, but it does not follow from this that God Himself is subject to change. He remains eternally the same, but man tries over and over again to grasp His essence in one comprehensive vision. We must understand that God is necessarily a mystery. He is infinite while our intellect is finite and limited. We *cannot* fathom Him. One might even say that a religion which has no mysteries, which pretends to be able to explain everything absolutely clearly, must be false for the reason that God cannot clearly be explained. We have to prepare ourselves for this when we grow to know Him better; we grow dizzy as we try to gaze into the depths of God's Being and there remains nothing for our poor intellect to do but to surrender itself to Him.

He and I are the two poles round which (for me at least) the world turns. Without Him, the fact of my being cannot be explained. My existence cries out for a cause, and the name of that cause is God.

Who is God?

We spoke before of a silent night under a starry sky. We are apt to reflect more deeply at night because the noisy everyday life is for the moment stilled, and in solitude we come face to face, as it were, with the universe. Sometimes, perhaps, you have gazed into the fathomless depths of that universe and meditated upon the innumerable problems which it involves. Is space limited? Is this small globe alone inhabited by people? Who can say? What however becomes clearer in one's mind is the immense power and greatness of He who has brought forth all these wonders. I will not worry you with fantastic figures which, in any case, we are unable completely to grasp, but even the light years have to be reckoned in millions, and the entire age of the sun is in comparison so short that it plays no really important part in the interminable evolution of matter.

This is a thought which scarcely touches us in the course of our daily life. One is at one's office, one's business, performing mechanically the thousand and one duties of ordinary existence, and seldom pausing to realize that one is a part of God's magnificent creation. And yet Man stands, as it were, poised between the impenetrable vastness of the universe and the equally baffling minuteness of the elements from which that universe has been built up: the cell, the atom.

What strikes us in both cases is the *structure* of the whole. This creative Power has exhibited a sense of order. Now that His work is complete, we can reconstruct its laws; the dead, inert matter, once set in motion, remains in motion, and under identical circumstances constantly produces identical reactions. We find neither caprice nor arbitrariness. When one goes deeply enough into the subject, one invariably finds that the Maker of the Universe has restricted, within certain fixed laws, the forces which cause matter to move. The Divine Power has not only created this Matter and this Force, but controls them and is Master of the Universe.

One is, of course, very familiar with the word finality. One understands by it that every substance tends towards a definite purpose which arises from its nature, and necessarily attains that purpose unless prevented by some superior power. When hydrogen and oxygen are mixed in the well-known ratio and under the usual conditions, they necessarily result in water. Under normal conditions a blade of grass, and not anything else, will proceed from a grass-seed. Ever since bees have existed they have gathered honey and stored it in honeycombs; and the fertile cell necessarily develops, without any exterior interference, into a human being. The microscopic cell already contains within itself all the forces which—God alone knows how—will enable the Matter to achieve its purpose.

God has foreseen: He has built up orderly structures and had a purpose in view. As beings become more complex He allows them to fulfil their purpose by less mechanical means. Take, for example, the shape of the receptacle which the bee chooses in which to store its honey. Few even technical minds would have discovered the economical structure of the hexagonal honeycomb. Either the bee is a mathematical genius or some other Being has thought it out for her.

Whatever this divine Power may be which has built up the universe, it has shown itself at all events to be infinitely great, infinitely purposeful, and that It can think both ingeniously and synthetically.

Further It has dealt with Man in a very remarkable way. There exists between Man and creation a relationship of which the result is *beauty*. The swaying woods, the roaring seas, the driving clouds, do not only strive after the attainment of their object, but also inspire Man with an indescribable sensation of happiness, a thrill of sheer loveliness. If this Power can cause Man to be moved to such a degree, It must Itself know beauty in its deepest sense. It has also created happiness which, in this world, is the sole prerogative of Man. The animal knows satisfaction, but happiness is reserved to that being which is distinguished from every other kind of being by the possession of understanding and freewill.

Man, as a person, strives for complete happiness. If, then, Man is not to be the exception (we need not enlarge here upon a subject which will be more fully dealt with later on) complete happiness must exist for him too. This world cannot bestow it—but who can possibly prove that this creative Power has exhausted itself with *our* world?

It has not only prescribed laws for matter and energy, but Man also carries within his heart a law to which he knows that he is subject. The law bids him to do good and refrain from evil. It is quite possible, of course, that one man will regard as good something of which another will disapprove, but that does not alter the fact that every man, when he does regard a thing as wrong, finds within himself a law which tells him: "Thou shalt not!" The fact of this law indicates a lawgiver who is thus definitely expressing an intention and purpose.

He does not suggest, He does not merely request, but He gives the positive command: "Thou shalt not!" He acts with authority and insists on being obeyed, and the remarkable thing about this interior voice is that it continues to make itself heard even when we will not listen to it.

If, therefore, we summarize what the existing universe has taught us about the Maker of it, we shall come to the conclusion that there must exist also a Being with unlimited power, who has planned everything with a marvellous sense of order and beauty, and whose laws of creation are designed in each case to attain a definite end. The material world is itself subject to those laws of nature and is thus impelled towards the achievement of this same ultimate purpose.

Man alone has complete freedom to resist the laws engraved in his heart, and consequently never entirely achieves his aim in this life. In the following chapters we shall see over and over again how these two human characteristics, liberty and final end, are connected.

This idea of God, as we have sketched it here, is to be found, in a more or less pure form, with most nations. The mysterious power of that great Being is almost universally acknowledged, and produces, even in the case of uncivilized tribes, that sense of religious awe and dependence which is regarded by many, although incorrectly so, as the very essence of religion.

If we follow the history of Mankind, we shall find that this idea of God was very specially developed in the case of a small nation which existed in the midst of a pagan culture where religion had degenerated into polytheism. From about the time 2000 B.C. the Jewish people showed such a remarkable grasp of the greatness and eminence of God that it is well worth touching on here.

With them God was adored as the highest Majesty, the Lord of Glory, the supreme Ruler of the world and the eternal King. The psalms and the prophets extolled His greatness in the most poetical language. Their idea of justice, mercy, goodness and love also far exceeded that of any other nation: the whole of creation is seen but as a reflection of God's beauty. Rarely indeed has the greatness and sanctity of the Almighty been more graphically described than in the Book of Job.

"Strip, then, and enter the lists; it is My turn to ask questions now, thine to answer them. From what vantage-point wast thou watching, when I laid the foundations of the earth? Tell me, whence comes this sure knowledge of thine? Tell me, since thou art so wise, was it thou or I designed earth's plan, measuring it out with the line? How comes its base to stand so firm, who laid its corner-stone? To me, that day, all the morning stars sang together, all the powers of heaven uttered their joyful praise. Was it thou or I shut in the sea behind bars? No sooner had it broken forth from the womb than I dressed it in swaddling-clothes of dark mist, set it within bounds of my own choosing, made fast with bolt and bar; Thus far thou shalt come, said I, and no further; here let thy swelling waves spend their force.

Dost thou, a mortal, take command of the day's breaking, and shew the dawn its appointed post, twitching away earth's coverlet, scaring away the ill-doers? The dawn, that stamps its image on the clay of earth; stands there, flung over it like a garment, taking away from the ill-doers the darkness that is their light, so that all their power goes for nothing."[1]

But no one has shown Man a deeper, holier and more adorable picture of God than Christ Himself. With the Jews, God is depicted as the strict Ruler, the just avenger of evil. With Christ, His main characteristic is love. Later on we shall discuss the conception of God as presented to us by Jesus: that is, the Christian conception. We hope to be able to show that the mystery of the Divine Being is dealt with by Him in so profound, so all-embracing a manner, that it could only have been possible to One who was Himself beholding that Divine Being unceasingly.

§ 2. *Must Man serve God?*

The whole world and our entire life is guided by a wise and loving Power whom we call God. The question for us is whether there ought to exist, in our own particular case, a personal relationship between this God and us, or whether it is sufficient for us to accept the fact of His existence and then continue with our ordinary daily life? Is it sufficient to imagine Him as somewhere far away beyond the stars, or must He have a place in our mind, our will and in our heart?

There will probably not be many who will answer this question in the negative; nevertheless it is a fact that there are very

[1] Job 38, 3-15.

many who have never really entered into personal contact with God. He remains for them little more than a distant thought, whose Name only comes to their lips in a moment of danger or of anger. They have never really prayed—except perhaps when in peril of immediate death during a raid, or in an air-raid shelter.

There is no excuse for this attitude. God has an absolute right to be honoured as the supreme Authority, to be worshipped as Ruler, to be served as Creator and obeyed as Lawgiver.

Some readers may suggest that it would be sufficient to lead a good life without specifically thinking of God. This needs further discussion as it is a matter of real importance.

Well then, let us begin by agreeing with you: it is sufficient to live a good life. But what does one understand by a good life? Does it merely mean not to kill, not to steal, and in general to observe the rules of polite society? Would that be sufficient to justify one in the eyes of the great Sovereign, who has created and continues to keep in existence this universe, of which one is also a part? Do you not think that this great Sovereign, who after all is a Person, expects that one should sometimes think of Him, invoke His holy name, render homage and gratitude to Him for all His wonderful gifts?

Might not this also be reckoned as part of a good life? Might not the correct attitude towards God be regarded as even more important than the correct attitude towards one's neighbour, one's creditor, one's customer or charge-man about which one is so careful? Is it, in short, possible to live a good life while ungratefully and discourteously turning one's back upon one's Creator? A man, whom we shall again mention very frequently in the following pages, once said with supreme wisdom that the first and greatest commandment was: "Thou shalt love the Lord thy God with thy whole heart, with thy whole soul, and with all thy strength."

It is quite possible, of course, to agree with all this in principle and in theory, and yet, as it were, to find oneself unable to enter into personal contact with God. He is a Spirit; we can neither see nor hear Him, and He never seems to give us a sign that He does indeed understand. One who has never experienced a sense of personal relationship with God faces a difficulty which can probably only be overcome by competent guidance and help such as no book can give. Usually, however, the difficulties are of a practical nature and do not actually arise on account of principles. In the rush and anxiety of life one has no time to think of God: family cares, the hurry of business, the almost unceasing noise and activity around one, all combine to stifle any faintly-awakened thought of Him. When one is still young, in particular, and life is full of the promise of happiness, it seems easy enough to manage without the Deity. It is incomprehensible, indeed, to a believer, that so many intellectual young people seem never to have given a serious thought to the problem of religion.

Without religion, life is reduced to an utterly aimless state of existence. As long as a person remains strong and energetic, it is possible that he will scarcely notice the spiritual emptiness of his life; but when suffering touches him, when he loses those dear to him, and there comes to him at last a realization of his own impotence and wretchedness; when he is seized by a longing for happiness—then, sometimes, in one surging effort, spirit will rise above matter in an attempt to find and understand the essence of life itself. It is not perhaps quite so strange as it may sound that, when in danger of sudden death, the word "God" leaps to the lips of many an atheist. It is the result of the subconscious conviction that God can still help where all earthly help has failed.

But, one may ask, is it not cowardly only to call upon the Creator when one is in need? One does not think much of a friend who, when he is short of money, is perpetually upon one's doorstep, yet passes by in prosperity, without so much as a greeting.

In this connection, it is interesting, although perhaps a little humiliating, to reflect how readily this urge for God finds expression with more primitive peoples than ourselves. In the case of the Incas, the Sumerians, the Greeks and the Egyptians, for instance, as soon as their culture began to develop it pointed towards God, and the beauty and grace of their architecture found its culmination in the church or the temple. It has always been the way that as Man bows towards the ground, church spires and minarets rise up towards heaven, as twin symbols of dependence and power. Just as truth, morality and beauty are an integral part of culture, so also religion is bound up with it in such a way that, without religion, both Man and culture inevitably deteriorate. He who is nothing more than a business man, a scientist, an artist, or whatever his profession may be, misses the plenitude and the richness of life, and breaks his ties with his Maker just as the spider breaks the thread from which he hangs.

From all this we may draw the conclusion that the worship of God is a duty, and a duty without the performance of which no man can live either fully or worthily. But, let us hasten to add, it is very much more than a duty: it is a wealth, a support, a happiness, enriching life beyond all measure, and in the absence of which existence is—although perhaps not always consciously so—one-sided, sterile and aimless.

The Catholic Catechism begins with this question: "Who made you?" and then: "Why did God make you?" A simple enough question but strangely unanswerable for one who has no religion. Usually we shall find that he has never seriously considered it. There are so many other questions connected with life, that the most important question of all, regarding life itself, has never been asked.

For what purpose were we born? To found a family? To have a successful career? To become a man of note or an accomplished woman of the world?

If so, when this aim is achieved, there remains nothing more to be done: life henceforth becomes aimless, and the person who has reached middle-age, stands as a tree whose ultimate fruits have been gathered, and which now only awaits the axe.

Has life, indeed, no deeper meaning than this? And is Man no more than a link in the process of reproduction, with his mother set on one side of him and his child on the other? Of all our achievements, of our very selves, is there to remain no more than a fleeting memory?

What is the true purpose of our existence? If the final aim of life is not connected with class, with profession, with race or rank—and it is not—then it must necessarily be with something which is common to Mankind and which rises superior to life itself.

We saw in the previous chapter that God created the world with a definite purpose. Being in Himself infinitely perfect, it follows that He cannot pursue any end which is outside Himself. His ultimate purpose cannot be other than Himself because, since He is infinite perfection, everything must necessarily be centred in Him. Creatures may pursue first one aim and then another, but their End can only be in the very ocean of God's essence. The stars and the flowers, the loveliness of woods and insects, the mountains and valleys, are no more than the heralds of His power, and cannot do otherwise than proclaim His greatness and wisdom.

But Man, who was made after God's own image, occupies a quite unique position in Creation. It is not sufficient for him to be satisfied with the mere fact of existence. He must *consciously* orientate his life towards his Creator: that is to say must live according to his Creator's intention and His expressed commands.

Only then does Man grasp the meaning of life; only then does he grasp also the answer to that question: "Why did God make me?"

He made us in order that we *might Serve Him.*

This idea gives unity and purpose to the whole of life. It then is no longer just a series of unimportant details, but has one definite line and intention running through it. We are constrained by one over-riding aim which unites all our actions. The theme of life will no longer be merely prosperity, career, or the happiness of a home, but all these concentrated in one supreme motive: *the service of God.*

As long as one has no particular religion, this service of God will necessarily have to consist mainly in prayer and in following the law of one's conscience. But very few of us will not remember, even if only from days of long ago, the words of the Lord's Prayer:

> Our Father, who art in heaven, hallowed be thy name; thy Kingdom come; thy will be done on earth as it is in Heaven. Give us this day our daily bread; and forgive us our trespasses, as we forgive them that trespass against us. And lead us not into temptation. But deliver us from evil. Amen.

Begin and end the day by saying this prayer slowly and with emphasis—and it may perhaps help you to continue praying in your own words. To pray is to speak to God. Speak to Him then about your worries, your work, your failures and sins; about those whom you love and the ideals which you strive for; speak to Him with simplicity and confidence, and ask Him especially that you may have light to find the truth, and grace and strength to follow the truth when found.

The Catechism also indicates the second purpose of Man: that is, perfect happiness. But here we are over-stepping the bounds of the cosmos and of ordinary life, and shall therefore leave the subject, in order to return to it more fully later on.

PART I

THE FOUNDATION OF THE CHURCH

CHAPTER I

THE ANTECEDENTS OF CHRISTIANITY

SYNOPSIS

In the previous chapter we spoke of the nature of God and of our duty to serve Him. It might be argued, perhaps, that it is sufficient to serve Him according to the natural law which He has put into the heart of every man, were it not for the fact that He has gone far beyond this, and has Himself revealed to us most precisely the manner in which He wishes to be served.

God has personally intervened, and has shown Man a form of divine worship which has thus superseded all others. This form of worship, or religion, is called Christianity because it was first founded by Jesus Christ Himself, and He made Himself the living example of it. This religion is now continued, in visible form on earth, by the Roman Catholic Church.

Readers holding different views will, naturally enough, not accept these statements without further evidence, and will no doubt ask for proof:

1. That Jesus Christ is, in fact, the true Messenger of God;
2. That His doctrine is now actually to be found, and has been continuously preserved, in the Catholic Church.

Only when they are satisfied as to the answers to these two questions, will they put the third:

3. What, then, *is* the doctrine of the Roman Catholic Church?

We shall endeavour to answer these questions satisfactorily. The first will be dealt with in the first and second chapters, and the second in Chapter III. The remainder of the book will be devoted to the answer to the third question.

IN THE WHOLE of the first part of this book we shall find ourselves upon historical ground. This does not, however, necessarily mean that all the events with which we have to deal can be explained in a purely natural manner. In the history of Mankind, such extraordinary things have happened that it is only possible to conclude that some power has intervened which is not natural but supernatural. "*This,*" we exclaim, "is God speaking."

The most wonderful occurrence of all was the appearance upon earth of God's own Messenger, Jesus Christ, and the marvellous way in which His coming was prepared beforehand. In this chapter we are going to deal with this preparation, and so treat successively of the election of the Jewish people as the Chosen Race, and the prophecies of the Jewish prophets.

The story of the life and mission of Jesus Christ has a long antecedent history. There is no question here of a man who, like so many million others, just came for a while and disappeared. Just as He has been remembered and talked of for centuries after His death, so He was spoken of and looked for centuries before His birth. His history is, as a matter of fact, as long as the history of Mankind itself, and we shall find the whole account in the Bible.

The Bible is a book, or rather a collection of books, which one can buy in any bookshop: indeed, one can safely say that it is the most widely read book in the world. A number of writers have incorporated in it accounts of the various periods and incidents of the long history of God's dealings with men, and of Man's response to God. The complete work is called the Bible (from the Greek *ta biblia*) which means *the* book, for the simple reason that there is no other writing in existence which can in any way be compared with Holy Scripture.

In spite of the centuries which have elapsed since it was compiled, we are still able to read it in its original form, because the continuity of its text has been faithfully preserved. The printed copies now in circulation, are taken from the old hand-written scripts in Greek and Hebrew. The Hebraic parts of the Bible, which were composed before the birth of Christ (that is to say, all the Old Testament) date from the Massorah, which is the textual tradition by which Jewish scholars compiled an official register of its words, consonants, vowels and accents. As far back as the first century before Christ, copyists and revisers were trained and employed to fix the Hebrew text.

By arranging the various handwritings according to so-called groups, the textual critics can assess the relative value of these different groups, and we may safely conclude that, as far as the essence of the contents is concerned, the primitive wording of the Bible has been most carefully preserved, and that the editions published nowadays do indeed give us the original rendering of it.

In the year 1947 wandering Bedouins found in a cave to the north of the Dead Sea, nine documents hidden in earthen jars. These manuscripts contained various Hebrew texts, among others a complete text of Isaias which, according to American explorers, is dated about 100 years before Christ. Great importance is attached to this book, since it is apparently about a thousand years older than the one now in use.

We are not at the moment considering the Bible as a book inspired by God, but as a written source of history, in which, as it is commonly agreed by all scholars whether Christian or otherwise, the Messianic texts, dating from before Christ, have been collectively dealt with.

As we have already said, the first part of the Bible is concerned with the period before the advent of Christ. We read of the creation of heaven and earth, and of how God breathed life into Man, made after His own image. We are told how Adam, whose destiny it was to find his supreme happiness in the service and the friendship of God, consciously fell, and so broke the close ties which bound him to his Creator. We follow all the tragedy of the separation of the human race from God with the entrance of sin into the world, and of the weary inheritance of evil which has since fallen upon Mankind.

Once the harmony of the original relationship with God had been disturbed, and Man had become detached from the divine friendship, his own interior balance was also, as it were, affected, and he continued progressively to lose contact with God. Even his purely human knowledge about his Creator began to grow dim, and men found themselves following after other gods. Succeeding generations finally degenerated into idolators who worshipped such human elements as fire, or the sun and stars. This was the moment at which God Himself chose to intervene.

§ 1. *The Chosen People*

God decided to choose a small nation whose mission it should be to maintain belief in the one Almighty God. In the city of Ur in Chaldea was found the man selected as the instrument for the fulfilment of this promise. God called him Abraham which means the Father of Many. (Genesis 12, 1-3).[1] So Abraham set out on the journey the Lord had commanded him, and came to the land of Chanaan, on the east coast of the Mediterranean.

It is with Abraham that the history of the Jewish people, properly speaking, begins, and the importance of his place in God's plan for the human race can hardly be over-stressed. It was his belief in the great God, whom he called Jahve which continued to burn like a flame in the Jewish nation during thousands of years, and was still burning undimmed at the time of the coming of the Messiah. It became, indeed, the starting-point of the mission of Jesus Christ, the Redeemer.

Thus God became the God of Abraham and of the Jewish people whom He called His Chosen People. You may well ask why His choice should fall upon them in particular? To such a question there seems no positive answer. As a nation they were insignificant and relatively of no importance, although individually they were undoubtedly gifted and had many good qualities. One thing, however, emerges clearly: by the help of God's grace, the Jews succeeded in fulfilling their divinely appointed mission. Just as Abraham's faith was severely tested, so also it was only at the cost of great trials and sufferings that his descendants were able to preserve the treasure of their faith in the Almighty.

It was in Abraham that God's plan for Mankind first took concrete form. He was already growing old, with a wife embittered by the loneliness of a childless woman, when God promised him the heir who was to be the first of a great and fruitful people, as innumerable as the stars of heaven or the grains of sand lying along the shores of the Mediterranean Sea.

And Abraham believed: he believed in spite of the human improbability of the prophecy, the cynical smile of a disillusioned wife, and the hidden insinuations of his friends. He continued to believe in spite of the lapse of time, the fear of the future sacrifice demanded of him, and the apparent negation of the prediction by reality. He believed for one reason only—the best of all—that God had promised. There was no token or symbol to help him, only the remembrance of the divine pledge. His faith was as barren and naked as a rock—

[1] The reader should be familiar with at least a summary of the Old Testament. If he is not, the omission should be repaired at this point if possible.

but as firm. It even remained unshaken when, after the birth of the promised son, Isaac, the life of the child was demanded of him by God. Without a thought of the mighty people yet to be, and the future generations, the divine demand would have been complied with, had not God Himself intervened and forbade the completion of the sacrifice which He had only intended as a final test of Abraham's faith.

Thus he indeed became the father of a great people. Isaac was born, and begot Jacob, and Jacob begot the twelve sons who were to give their names to the twelve tribes of Israel. It may perhaps appear to us a hesitating and almost reckless beginning to the story of the world's redemption. What strange destiny was to grow out of it? Egypt, the land of exile, seemed at one moment to be the end of all plans for a great people, until the advent of Moses who, after his encounter with the Egyptian, fled into the desert, and so ultimately met his Lord in the midst of the flaming bush. With that meeting came certainty.

"I am the God thy father worshipped, the God of Abraham, and Isaac, and Jacob." And then: "God said to Moses, I am the God who IS; thou shalt tell the Israelites, the GOD WHO IS has sent me to you."[2] After this there follows the long and detailed story of the liberation of the Jews from out of Egypt, with all the miracles of the Red Sea and the forty years of adventurous wandering in the desert. The great nation which the one-time little family of Abraham has now become, takes possession at last of the Promised Land, and all the lines of destiny begin to converge towards the coming of the great Messiah. During the whole of this history the Chosen People, now grown and multiplied beyond all measure according to the prophecy, remained docile in the hands of God.

The nation flourished. First of all it drew up a Code of Laws; then appointed kings to govern it. There were battles with the Philistines, and under David and Solomon the little State took firm root. Jerusalem became the site of an imposing temple in honour of Jahve, for faith in God and in the coming of the Messiah remained the real and underlying strength of this people.

Faith is, indeed, the only key to the story of the Old Testament. We find the prophets appealing constantly and with tremendous force to the Chosen of God to remain true to

[2] Ex. 3, 6 and 14-15.

their traditions. In the later years of decay, when the State was torn by disunion, and the Jewish religion threatened by the invading civilization of the Gentiles, the prophets were multiplied, and their warnings grew more and more terrible. But above and beyond all the vicissitudes and the disasters of the Jewish destiny, the faith that took birth in Abraham, remained alive in his descendants. Even during the tragic period of the Babylonian exile, and in the battle of the Maccabean brothers for Israel's independence, it was the promises of Jahve which strengthened the courage of the people, and inspired the pen and the lips of David and the prophets.

This faith, which binds together the whole Old Testament history, finally joins and binds it to the story of Christ's redemption of the world. He it is who assumes the faith of Abraham, Moses, Gedeon, Jephte, David, Isaias and Daniel, and fulfils at last all their hopes. Finally Paul, the apostle, writing to the Hebrews, gathers up the meaning of the succeeding books of the Old Testament, in one magnificent exposition of their significance.

> "He to whom the name of Abraham was given showed faith when he left his home, obediently, for the country which was to be his inheritance; left it without knowing where his journey would take him. Faith taught him to live as a stranger in the land he had been promised for his own. . . . It was faith that enabled Sara to conceive offspring, although she was past the age of child-bearing; she believed that God would be faithful to His word. . . . Here is one man . . . and from him springs a race whose numbers rival the stars of heaven. . . . It was faith they lived by, all of them, and in faith they died; for them, the promises were not fulfilled, but they looked forward to them and welcomed them at a distance, owning themselves no better than strangers and exiles on earth. . . . Abraham showed faith, when he was put to the test, by offering up Isaac. He was ready to offer up an only son, this man . . . who has received the assurance, 'It is through Isaac that thy posterity shall be traced'. It was by faith that Isaac, in blessing Jacob and Esau, foretold what was to come; by faith that Jacob, on his death bed, made reverence to the top of Joseph's staff, as he blessed his two sons in turn; by faith that Joseph, when he too came to the end of his life,

gave orders for the removal of his bones. The parents of Moses showed faith . . . by hiding their child away for three months . . . and Moses showed faith, when he grew up, by refusing to pass for the son of Pharoah's daughter . . . all the wealth of Egypt could not so enrich him as the despised lot of God's anointed; he had eyes, you see, for nothing but the promised reward. It was in faith that he left Egypt behind, defying the royal anger . . . in faith that they crossed the Red Sea as if it had been dry land . . . Faith pulled down the walls of Jericho, after seven days spent in marching round them. . . . What need is there to say more? Time will fail me if I try to go through all the history of Gedeon, of Barac, of Samson, of Jephte, of David and Samuel and the prophets. Theirs was the faith which subdued kingdoms . . . men whom the world was unworthy to contain. . . . One and all gave proof of their faith, yet they never saw the promise fulfilled."[3]

This, then, is what we learn from the books of the Old Covenant. They are the history and the sayings of a people who fought for an unshakable belief in God and in the Messiah whom they awaited from God.

§ 2. *The Prophecies concerning the Messiah*

The prophets played a most important role in the religious and social life of the Jewish people. They preached the authentic conception of God, explained and upheld the ten commandments explicitly laid down for the Jews, and gave solemn warnings against the dangers of idolatry and immorality. While they preached penance and often threatened chastisement, nevertheless they accompanied their warnings with wonderful hopes of a glorious reward. They were essentially the prophets of the future, and so kept the divine expectations of the people alive.

Over and over again they opened out vistas of a marvellous future era, in which once more God would dwell among His people and would redeem them from all that had caused them to drift away, and so held Him distant from them. By these means the prophets kept constantly before the minds of the Jews a picture of the promised Messiah to which they could

[3] Heb. 2, 8-40.

turn hopefully in times of trouble. They themselves called this predicted Saviour the Messiah, or Masjiah, as it is written in Hebrew, which signifies Anointed; for they readily imagined Him as a sovereign anointed by God in the same way as David and Solomon.

The actual prophecies concerning Him, that is the so-called Messianic prophecies, were never meant to foretell in precise detail the story of the coming Christ. The prophets visualized the future as timeless and ageless, much as we view eternity, or the stars in the firmament regardless of the varying distances which separate them from us and from each other. Their object was twofold: to keep alive in the hearts of the Chosen People the hope of redemption and of salvation, and to foretell enough about the promised Redeemer to ensure His being instantly recognized at His advent.

At the very instant when the need for a Saviour arose, as a consequence of Man's sin in the Garden of Paradise, His coming was foretold by God Himself in the words which He spoke to the devil who had tempted Man to sin:

> "And I will establish a feud between thee and the woman, between thy offspring and hers; she is to crush thy head, while thou dost lie in wait at her heels."[4]

In the far distant future, the fight between good and evil was to burst into fresh flame, and in this new battle the tempter was to be overwhelmed and crushed by the child born of a woman. The prophets were destined gradually to elucidate the meaning of these words to succeeding generations.

After the revelation to Abraham that: "In thee all the races of the world shall find a blessing";[5] the dying Jacob announced:

> "But thou, Juda, shalt win the praise of thy brethren; with thy hand on the necks of thy enemies, thou shalt be reverenced by thy father's sons. . . . Juda shall not want a branch from his stem, a prince drawn from his stock, until the day when He comes who is to be sent to us, He, the hope of nations."[6]

When, after years of wandering through the desert in the plains of Moab, which is now called Transjordan, the Jews

[4] Gen 3, 15. [5] Gen. 12, 3. [6] Gen. 49, 10-12.

came within sight of their own former native country, the prophet Balaam, come to curse but forced instead to bless, rendered into unmistakable, if somewhat hesitating phrases, his vision of the coming Messiah.

"Thus speaks Balaam, the son of Beor, thus speaks the man who has seen with the eyes blindfolded; thus speaks the man who has looked on a vision sent from God, who has fallen into a trance and learned to see aright. My vision is not of this time, it is not of the things that meet my eyes. I see a star that rises out of Jacob, a stem that springs from Israel's root."[7]

It all sounds a trifle mysterious, and there are no details as yet; nevertheless the pedigree of the future Saviour is slowly beginning to be traced: from Abraham through Jacob (who was also called Israel) to Juda. The next link in this ancestral chain is forged for us by the prophet Nathan, sent by God Himself with a message to King David:

"Henceforth my people are to have a settled home, taking root in it and remaining in undisturbed possession of it . . . and this too the Lord promises, that He will grant thy line continuance. So, when thy days are ended, and thou art laid to rest beside thy fathers, I will grant thee for successor a son of thy own body, established firmly on his throne. I will prolong for ever his royal dynasty. . . . Through the ages, far as thy thought can reach, dynasty and royalty both shall endure; thy throne shall remain for ever unshaken."[8]

Except for the actual genealogy of the descent, and the immense importance and enduring quality of the work to be performed by the future Messiah, not much in the way of detail is communicated to the Jews. But the importance of the Messianic mission is once again stressed in Psalm 2 where, according to the poet, God speaks as follows:

"Thou art My Son, the Lord's word came to me; I have begotten thee this day. Ask thy will of Me, and thou shalt have the nations for thy patrimony; the very ends of the world for thy domain."[9]

[7] Num. 24, 15-17. [8] II Kings 9, 11-16. [9] Ps. 2, 7-8.

It would appear also that the coming Redeemer is not only intended to bring salvation to the Jewish people, but to men of all nations, and that the boundaries of his activity, both as to time and to space, are to be without limit, for in Psalm 71 we read:

"Ageless as sun or moon He shall endure; kindly as the rain that drops on the meadow grass, as the showers that water the earth . . . All kings must needs bring their homage, all nations serve Him . . . For ever let His name be used in blessing, a name to endure while the sun gives light; in Him all the tribes of the earth shall be enriched, all the nations shall extol Him."[10]

After this we learn something of the actual qualities of the Redeemer Himself, and of the functions which God intends Him to fulfil. In Psalm 109 Jahve speaks to the promised Messiah: "Sit here at My right hand while I make thy enemies a footstool under thy feet." Thus He is to be a judge: seated at the right hand of God He will mete out justice to His enemies. But further than this He will also be a priest: "The Lord has sworn an oath there is no retracting, thou art a priest for ever in the line of Melchisedech", as we read in the same psalm.

It is interesting to note that we see this priestly figure of Melchisedech appearing also in the life of Abraham, who, as a token of his gratitude, offers to God a sacrifice of bread and wine. The expected Messiah is therefore to be a priest of the same exalted line.

It is when we reach the eighth century before Christ, that we first hear the voice of the prophet Isaias. To him is reserved the wonderful mission of announcing the virgin birth, and the divine origin of the future Redeemer, more explicitly than ever before. When the vacillating King Achaz will not accept God's offer of a sign from heaven, Isaias turns on him with the fierce:

"Cannot you be content with trying the patience of men? Must you try my God's patience too? Sign you ask none, but sign the Lord will give you. Maid shall be brought to bed of a son, that shall be called Emmanuel."[11]

[10] Ps. 71, 5-17. [11] Is. 7, 13-14.

The name Emmanuel frequently recurs in the prophecies of Isaias, while the portrait he draws for us is sketched in with lines which grow increasingly sharp and clear.

"For our sakes a child is born, to our race a son is given, whose shoulder will bear the sceptre of princely power. What name shall be given Him? Peerless among counsellors, the mighty God, Father of the world to come, the Prince of Peace. Ever wider shall His dominion spread, endlessly at peace; He will sit on David's kingly throne, to give it lasting foundations of justice and right; so tenderly He loves us, the Lord of Hosts."[12]

Then, for the first time, we hear something of the spiritual qualities of the Messiah, who is to spring forth from the rod of Jesse:

"From the stock of Jesse a scion shall burgeon yet; out of his roots a flower shall spring. One shall be born, on whom the spirit of the Lord will rest; a spirit wise and discerning, a spirit prudent and strong, a spirit of knowledge and of piety, and ever fear of the Lord shall fill His Heart."[13]

A contemporary of Isaias, the prophet Micheas, was also filled with this sense of ardent expectation. He it is who first mentions Bethlehem as the birthplace of the Redeemer:

"Bethlehem-Ephrata! Least do they reckon thee among all the clans of Juda? Nay, it is from thee I look to find a prince that shall rule over Israel. Whence comes He? From the first beginning, from ages untold! Enabled by the Lord His God, confident in that mighty protection, stands He, our Shepherd, and safely folds His flock; fame of Him now reaches to the world's end."[14]

Thus it is obvious that Micheas now adds Shepherd to the other functions of the Saviour.

Jeremias lived about a century later than these two, Isaias and Micheas, and was the tragic witness of the fall of the Kingdom of Juda. He repeats, in magnificent phrases, what had already been foretold by former prophets, with special

[12] Is. 9, 6-7. [13] Is. 11, 1-2-3. [14] Mich. 5, 2-5.

emphasis however upon the wisdom and the justice of the Messiah.

"Nay, a time is coming, the Lord says, when I will raise up, from the stock of David, a faithful scion at last. The land shall have a king to reign over it, and reign over it wisely, giving just sentence and due award. When that time comes, Juda shall find deliverance, none shall disturb Israel's rest; and the name given to this king shall be, The Lord vindicates us."[15]

Ezechiel, following on Jeremias, equally compares the Redeemer with King David, but adds no fresh features to the already existing picture of the Messiah.

It is not until the sixth century before Christ that the prophet Zacharias first makes his appearance, after the exile of the Jews. Speaking of the Redeemer to come, he lights up for us one small incident which is to take place later:

"Glad news for thee, widowed Sion; cry out for happiness, Jerusalem forlorn! See where thy king comes to greet thee, a trusty deliverer; see how lowly he rides, mounted on an ass, patient colt of patient dam! Chariots of thine, Ephraim, horses of thine, Jerusalem, shall be done away, bow of the warrior be unstrung; peace this king shall impose on the world, reigning from sea to sea, from Euphrates to the world's end."[16]

The Messiah is thus evidently not to be a ruthless conqueror, who builds his empire on the foundations of violence and political strength. His is no kingship of blood and tears. He is not only just and holy, but also essentially simple. He will come riding on no finely caparisoned horse, but sitting humbly upon an ass, the national beast of burden, will one day enter the capital city of His kingdom.

Once again let us listen to Isaias as he speaks to us of the Servant of God, who is to be lowly, detached from the passing things of this world, and with soul and body attuned to suffering:

"And now, here is my servant, to whom I grant protec-

[15] Jer. 23, 5-6. [16] Zach. 9, 9-10.

tion, the man of my choice, greatly beloved. My spirit rests upon Him, and He will proclaim right order among the Gentiles. He will not be contentious or a lover of faction; none shall hear His voice in the streets. He will not snap the staff that is already crushed, or put out the wick that still smoulders; but at last He will establish right order unfailingly. Not with sternness, not with violence; to set up right order on earth, that is His mission. He has a law to give; in the far-off islands men wait for it eagerly."[17]

We have purposely returned to the prophecy of Isaias, because in the second part of his book he speaks of the Messiah in language which is unique among all the prophets. The Redeemer is here shown us in very lovable and human guise, as one who comes to suffer and to serve. He is indeed to be a wonderful prophet, filled with "the spirit of Jahve", but a prophet who does not conceal His obedient submission to the great God of His own people.

"Listen, remote islands; pay heed to me, nations from far away. Ere ever I was born, the Lord sent me his summons, kept me in mind already, when I lay in my mother's womb. Word of mine is sword of His, ready sharpened, under cover of His hand; arrow He has chosen out carefully, hidden yet in His quiver. Thou art my servant, He whispers, Thou art the Israel I claim for My own."

We understand from this that the Messiah is to receive His mission directly from Jahve, who will give strength and clearness to His words so that they are like a sharp sword. Nevertheless the Jews will not listen to His warnings:

"To me, all my labour seemed useless, my strength worn out in vain; His to judge me, He, my God, must reward my work as He would."[18]

The result, however, of this spiritual deafness on the part of the Chosen People, appears to be only a marvellous extension of the scope of the mission of the future Messiah.

"I have appointed Thee to be the light of the Gentiles,

[17] Is. 42, 1-4. [18] Is. 49, 1-4.

in Thee I will send out my salvation to the furthest corners of the earth."[19]

The fact that men may turn a deaf ear to the Redeemer, need not necessarily arise from either laxity or indolence. The presence of enemies may be the cause. And so Isaias, at this point, changes his theme from the mission of the Messiah through His preaching, to the mission of the Messiah through His suffering and passion. His is to be the fate of many other prophets; but here there will be no flinching. He will not attempt to ward off pain: rather will He go out to meet and challenge it.

> "I offered My body defenceless to the men who would smite Me, My cheeks to all who plucked at My beard; I did not turn away My face when they reviled Me and spat upon Me."[20]

There are still more details of this voluntary passion to be learnt from Isaias:

> "A victim? Yet He Himself bows to the stroke, no word comes from Him. Sheep led away to the slaughter-house, lamb that stands dumb while it is shorn; no word from Him."[21]

But there is no question of the holocaust which is here depicted being only a gesture: no more than a dramatic demonstration of the patience and heroic fortitude of one man. The principal point stressed is that this suffering, this death, are to be endured and offered for us—it is we who are to benefit by His bitter sorrow.

> "Our weakness, and it was He who carried the weight of it, our miseries, and it was He who bore them. . . . All the while it was for our sins He was wounded, it was guilt of ours crushed Him down; on Him the punishment fell that brought us peace, by His bruises we were healed."[22]

The ultimate result of all this suffering, and the marvellous fruit of the death of the Redeemer, are to be shown in a renewed equity between men:

[19] Is. 49, 6. [20] Is. 50, 6. [21] Is. 53, 7. [22] Is. 53, 4-5.

"The Just One, My Servant, many shall He claim for His own, win their acquittal, on His shoulders bearing their guilt."[23]

Thus God will have mercy upon men and restore them once more to His grace, for the sake of His Servant, the Messiah, to come.

The picture of the Passion, so exquisitely drawn by Isaias, we shall also find as the motif of Psalm 21, the opening words of which were, according to the Gospel story, used by the dying Christ Himself: " My God, my God, look upon me; why hast Thou forsaken me? "

This Psalm consists of two parts which will be found to correspond more or less with each other (Verses 2-22 and 23-31) while the first verse can be considered as the heading, or title, to it.

The commencement is an impassioned and sorrowful appeal to God for deliverance and protection from surrounding enemies. The second half is a song of heartfelt and humble gratitude for the assistance rendered. In the final verses there is a note of triumphant thanksgiving for the conversion of even the most distant nations, and for a world turned back once more to the worship of its God.

" But I, poor worm, have no manhood left; I am a byword to all, the laughing-stock of the rabble. All those who catch sight of me fall to mocking; mouthing out insults, while they toss their heads in scorn, he Committed himself to the Lord, why does not the Lord come to his rescue and set His favourite free? What hand but Thine drew me out from my mother's womb? Who else was my refuge when I hung at the breast? From the hour of my birth, Thou art my guardian; since I left my mother's womb, Thou art my God. Do not leave me now, when trouble is close at hand, when I have none to help me. My enemies are all about me, hemming me in, packed close as a herd of oxen, strong as bulls; so might a lion threaten me with its jaws, roaring for its prey. I am spent as spilt water, all my bones out of joint, my heart turned to molten wax within me; my strength has shrivelled up, like clay in the baking, and my tongue sticks fast in my mouth; Thou hast laid me in the

[23] Is. 53, 11.

dust, to die. Prowling about me like a pack of dogs, their wicked conspiracy hedges me in; they have torn holes in my hands and feet; they mark every bone in my body, as they stand there watching me, gazing at me. They divide my spoils among them, cast lots for my garments."

Then follow the verses of praise and gratitude. Many striking details of the future Passion are foreshadowed in this psalm: the loneliness of the Man of Sorrows, mocked and scorned, surrounded on all sides by bitter enemies; the immensity of the suffering of the crucifixion which is likened to the complete pouring out of water, so that even the last reserves of strength are exhausted; the thirst which makes the very tongue stick to the jaws; the parting of His garments.

In this connection it is interesting to note that there is a passage in the second part of the Book of Zacharias, which only reveals its complete meaning when taken in conjunction with the prophecies of Isaias regarding the sufferings of the Servant of Jehovah. The wording of this prophecy, indeed, gives an altogether wider perspective to the death of Christ, by surrounding Him in His apparent loneliness by many who are to mourn over Him and regard Him as the first of a new generation of men:

> ". . . towards me they shall look; me whom they have pierced through. Lament for Him they must, and grieve bitterly; never was such lament for an only son, grief so bitter over first-born dead. . . . When that day comes, clansmen of David and citizens of Jerusalem shall have a fountain flowing openly, of guilt to rid them, and of defilement."[24]

Finally we arrive at the last of the Messianic prophecies handed down to us in the Old Testament, which are to be found in the Book of Daniel. This prophet lived at the period of the exile of the Jews in Babylon, that is to say about six centuries before the birth of Christ. In the year 605 B.C. Daniel was taken, presumably as a Jewish captive, to the city of Babylon where, as a boy, he was educated at the court of the victorious king.

In a dream or a vision of the night, this Daniel saw four

[24] Zach. 12, 10-14; 13, 1.

terrible beasts rising from the sea. A celestial court, sitting in judgment, condemned the four monsters—one of them being killed and the other three losing their power. The symbolism of all this is somewhat obscure but in any case not very important. But suddenly, in his dream, another figure made its appearance which, if we have carefully followed the former prophecies, we shall recognize as having all the characteristics of the expected Messiah.

"Then I saw in my dream, how one came riding on the clouds of heaven, that was yet a son of man; came to where the Judge sat, crowned with age, and was ushered into his presence. With that, power was given him, and glory, and sovereignty, obey him all must, men of every race, and tribe, and tongue; such a reign as his lasts for ever, such power, as his the ages cannot diminish."[25]

Here is already to be seen, as it were, on the far horizons of Time, the second coming of Christ and the Day of Judgment. His kingdom will continue throughout endless ages. Nevertheless, everything points to the establishment also of an actual kingdom upon earth, a kingdom in which all nations and all peoples will be gathered together under His sovereignty to serve Him as King.

In the ninth chapter of the same Book we find still another of the prophecies of Daniel, usually known as Daniel's Prophecy of the Weeks'.

"It is ordained that this people of thine, that holy city of thine, should wait seventy weeks before guilt is done away, sin ended, wrong righted; before God's everlasting favour is restored, and the visions and the prophecies come true, and he who is all holiness receives his anointing. Be assured of this, and mark it well; a period of seven weeks must go by, and another period of sixty-two weeks, between the order to rebuild Jerusalem and the coming of Christ to be your leader. Street and wall will be built again, though in a time of distress; and then sixty-two weeks must pass before the Christ is done to death; the people will disown him and have none of him. Then the army of an invading leader will destroy both city and sanctuary, so that his taking away

[25] Dan. 7, 13-14.

will mean utter destruction; only a ruin is to be left when that war is ended. High covenant he shall make, before another week is done, and with folks a many; but when that week has run half its course, offering and burnt-sacrifice shall be none; in the temple all shall be defilement and desolation, and until all is over, all is fulfilled, that desolation shall continue."[26]

Although in this prophecy very exact numbers are given, its precise meaning is far from clear at first sight. Many Christian commentators have tried to discover from its calculations, the exact time of the coming of the Messiah. Other Bible interpreters, equally scholarly, are frankly sceptical as to such a possibility.

One may perhaps assume that the 'weeks' (or periods of seven years) were taken from the decree of the Persian king Artaxerxes I who lived 458 B.C. This decree, which deals with the rebuilding of the temple of Jerusalem, will be found in the seventh chapter of the first Book of Esdras. According to this method of calculation, the year A.D. 29 would be the year in which "holocausts and meat-offerings ceased", that is to say were no longer acceptable to God, as shown by the rending of the veil of the temple. (Matthew 27. 51.) This year, A.D. 29, would thus coincide more or less with the year of the crucifixion of Our Lord.

By the Catholic Church, however, the question of the correctness of this computation has always been left open, its conclusions being neither ruled out nor universally accepted. In any case the only matter of paramount importance is dealt with in the 24th verse of this ninth chapter of Daniel, in which the advent of the Messiah is unequivocally prophesied, and in which all other prophecies relating to His coming are, as it were, gathered together in one phrase "and the visions and the prophecies come true".

St. Paul's Epistle to the Hebrews begins with the words: "In old days, God spoke to our fathers in many ways and by many means, through the prophets." As we have said before, St. Paul was not given to exaggeration, and indeed over and over again, and in the most varied circumstances, the prophets were used to translate the messages of God to the world. In the Old Testament the dominating note of all these messages

[26] Dan. 9, 24-27.

was a certain hidden hope and expectation: the Messiah, the Redeemer, was to be looked for. Different lights, from as many different angles, were shed upon the figure of the promised Saviour, and each prophet had his own, fresh vision to proclaim.

The purpose of His coming, the manner of His appearance, the effect of His work and mission on earth, the circumstances in which it would be carried out—all these were dealt with successively. Let us try to introduce some sort of order and sequence into this welter of detail, and so, if we can, shortly summarize the most important conclusions of the various prophecies:

1. The Messiah is to oppose some enemy of Mankind (the devil, sin, evil) and to gain a complete victory.
2. This victory is to be a very great blessing not only to Abraham, Isaac and Jacob, the first Fathers of the Jewish nation, but also to their descendants. In fact, *all nations* are to participate in this divine blessing.
3. In the later prophecies the idea of kingship is further connected with this theme of victory. The Redeemer is to be a Monarch who, in accordance with the ancient Eastern conceptions of kingship, will be the Saviour of His people, the great military leader, dealing out justice, protecting and assisting the poor, and generally seeing to the welfare of His subjects.
4. Thus it necessarily follows that the Redeemer will be of royal birth, descended from the family of David, in the city of David, Bethlehem. At the time of His birth the monarchy will have lost much of its glory and earthly splendour as part of the Jewish State, but He will re-establish it in all its former brilliance for ever and ever.
5. The new King will be unlike all others. He will not establish His kingdom by means of earthly power and violence. On the contrary, Himself a Man of mysterious divine origin, filled with the spirit of God, it is as a teacher and a prophet that He will first address Himself to the Jewish people, and then, finally, since He is unable to touch and convert the hardness of their hearts, to the whole of Mankind.
6. In addition to the sublimity of the doctrine which He preaches, His chief service to Mankind will be that of

His bitter passion and lonely death. This passion will be brought about by His own people, but He will bear it with superhuman patience, and without resisting in word or in deed. He will be dragged before a Court, condemned to death by an unjust sentence, and then voluntarily offer His life to God as a holocaust and propitiation for the sins of all men. It is above all in this supreme generosity and readiness to offer Himself as a sacrifice, that He shows forth His *priesthood.*

7. Finally, notwithstanding the seeming defeat of the circumstances of His death, He emerges as the complete victor; from the seed of His incomparable sacrifice will grow and flourish an everlasting and eternal Kingdom of God which, by its supernatural power, will draw into its orbit innumerable races and people, who will be joined to Him for ever as one nation in the presence of God.

CHAPTER II

THE MESSIAH

SYNOPSIS

I. God has created us and is Lord of all mankind, therefore we are obliged to serve Him.
Now it should be sufficient to live according to the natural law which God has put into our hearts.
Instead of this, however, He has revealed that He desires to be served in a particular way, as we are now about to prove.

II. There exists a book, the Bible, the text of which is over two thousand years old and has been authentically handed down to us. From this book it is clear that the Jewish people themselves were convinced that they had been chosen by God to prepare the way for the future Messiah. Furthermore, many actual prophecies concerning that Messiah are contained in this same book.

III. We shall now endeavour to prove that a Man was indeed born in whom all these prophecies were fulfilled, and who confirmed by miracles His divine mission. This Man was Jesus of Nazareth.

HAVE THESE PROPHETICAL STATEMENTS BEEN IN FACT FULFILLED?

ONE MUST REMEMBER that it is not very difficult to awaken in a people the expectation of salvation: to predict the future appearance of some wonderful man who will usher in a new era of greatness, peace and justice. God's own marvellous intervention is only clearly recognizable when such a man does indeed enter history and proves indisputably that all these prophecies have in fact been fulfilled in *Him*.

We are now going to show that Jesus Christ has in truth done this. As, however, it is a necessary preliminary that the authenticity of the Book in which the story of His life is told must first be absolutely established, we shall proceed to devote a somewhat extensive chapter to the subject of its origin and composition.

(This is perhaps the point at which the student should read

some Life of Our Lord, or one of the Gospels: preferably the Gospel of St. Luke.)

§ 1. *The Historical Reliability of the Gospels*

When the voice of the last prophet had faded into silence, and the whole Jewish people were waiting in tense expectation for the coming of the promised Messiah, in the little town of Bethlehem, during the reign of Augustus, Roman Emperor and Ruler of Palestine, a Child was born who at His circumcision received the name of Jesus.

Both Matthew and Luke tell us a wonderful story as to this Child, and of how His birth was foretold to His future Mother, who was to remain a virgin, nine months beforehand by the great Archangel Gabriel himself, sent as a direct messenger from the court of Heaven. Of how also wise astrologers from the East, saw a strange star shining in the sky, sign of the birth of a great monarch, and following it came to the stable where He and His Mother had taken refuge. Word reaching King Herod through these three Wise Men of the birth of a king in Israel, he suspected the presence of the Messiah, but the foster-father of the Child, Joseph, receiving a warning dream, fled to Egypt with the Mother and Infant before the vengeance of Herod could take effect.

A strange and wonderful tale, but in olden days, we must remember, wonderful tales were habitually told of the doings of great men. And so we should pass by these testimonies of St. Luke without paying too much attention to them, if only the Child had afterwards stayed quietly at Nazareth with His parents when they returned from Egypt: had followed the respectable trade of His foster-father and remained a carpenter all His life: had listened peacefully to the discourses, and prayed with the villagers in the synagogue, and in the evenings had joined in the conversation of the other men. If He had, in short, followed the normal, daily round of life—an honest, pious citizen, maybe even the good father of a family.

Instead of that, what happened? This man of the Gospel tales set out from His home, and went preaching the Kingdom of God up and down the towns and villages of Judea and Galilee; and further, in this Kingdom of God which He taught, He boldly placed Himself as the central figure. He called

Himself openly the Messiah, the Son of God, whose coming had been so long foretold by the prophets. He worked miracles and died on the cross, so that many believed in Him. It was reported that He had risen from the dead, and His disciples stoutly maintained that He would one day return to judge the world.

Since then, no one has been able to pass Him by with indifference. One way or the other He demands a decision for life: to be for Him or against Him means for us either eternal salvation and happiness, or eternal rejection.

Therefore it is of the utmost importance that we should know whether this man, who placed Himself completely above everyday affairs, and wished to be regarded as Lord of all things, both in the material world and in the interior life of the soul, actually did exist and form part of the world's history. Did He in truth ever live? Are there reliable sources from which this can be irrefutably proved? Is there really no possibility of fraud or illusion in the matter? How, in fact, can we know and be sure about Jesus?

More than a century ago a number of German and French scholars, who did not know what to make of the Bible-portrait of this wonderful, God-like Christ, decided among themselves that, as a reality, the Jesus of the Gospels had never existed. This view, however, did not long prevail, and it is no longer held to any great extent even in the scientific world. There are too many genuine documents, too much information from historical sources confirming the existence and work of Jesus of Nazareth, for any real doubt to be entertained. The only question which still arises is as to whether, in addition to the Christian, there are also non-Christian—that is to say pagan or Jewish—sources of information which attest to His life on earth? And, further to this, are those Christian sources of information which we undoubtedly do possess, altogether trustworthy?

We propose to consider both these questions.

I. NON-CHRISTIAN SOURCES

1. *Roman Testimonies*

As in the Roman Empire there existed innumerable religious sects, it is extremely remarkable that the two most famous historians of the time, Tacitus and Suetonius, mention both Christ Himself and the early Christians.

The evidence of Tacitus. About A.D. 116 Tacitus, writing in his usual short, laconic style, mentioned in his Annals that Nero was fiercely persecuting a certain sect of people known as Christians, who were hated by the Romans on account of their general crimes and delinquencies. In order to evade the suspicion that he, Nero, had set fire to Rome, he was openly accusing the Christians of the outrage. Then, somewhat scornfully and almost as an afterthought Tacitus adds: "The founder of this sect, named Christ, was executed by the procurator, Pontius Pilate, during the reign of Tiberius. Although, however, this pernicious superstition (*exitiabilis superstitio*) was momentarily subdued, it again broke out, not only in Judea, where the mischief had first arisen, but also in the city of Rome where, as a matter of course, all the scandalous things of the world find a meeting-place and are approved."

Without allowing ourselves to become unduly excited over the vexed question of the sources from which Tacitus may have drawn his information—protocols belonging to the Senate; information given by the pro-Consul Pliny with whom he was on friendly terms; and so on—two facts undoubtedly emerge. First, that there is no question in this case of a Christian insertion or interpolation, and second, that Tacitus both knew and recorded, as it had also been known before his time in the most cultivated Roman circles, that a definite Christian movement was in existence, dating back to a certain man named Christ. (Annals 15. 44.)

The Evidence of Suetonius. Suetonius, confidential secretary at the Court of Hadrian I (117-138) deals with the Christians in two passages of his Lives of the Caesars (Nero 16 and Claudius 26). In his biography of Nero he disdainfully alludes to "Christians who adhere to a new and pernicious superstition" *(genus hominum superstitionis novae ac maleficae).*

When it comes to the life of the Emperor Claudius, he states that the latter expelled the Jews from Rome because they were continually creating a stir *impulsore Chresto* or "at Christ's instigation".

These are probably the disturbances also mentioned in the Acts of the Apostles: "Paul left Athens after this, and went to Corinth. Here he met a Jew named Aquila, born in Pontus, who, with his wife Priscilla, had lately come from Italy, where Claudius decreed that all Jews should leave Rome." (Acts. 18, 1-2.)

With reference to the use of these words by Suetonius, the question arises as to who this 'Chrestos' may have been? Suetonius himself seems to have believed him to be a Jew working in Rome. All kinds of theories have been advanced, the most widely held to-day being that, while there was undoubted mention of Jesus Christ, Suetonius, who did not personally make enquiries as to the identity of the originator of the Movement which caused such excitement in the Jewish colony, simply copied some police-report in which Christ, instead of the Christians, was mentioned as being the cause of the trouble. The spelling 'Chrestos' presents no difficulty; this was the common pronunciation of the name at the time. At all events, it is obvious from these various references, that in about the year A.D. 50 there were Christians in Rome who were engaged in active propaganda among the Jews.

The Evidence of Pliny, the Younger. Pliny was a pro-Consul for the province of Bithynia—a wise and serious man and a scrupulously careful administrator. In the year A.D. 112-113 he wrote a detailed letter about the Christians to the Emperor Trajan. Accusations as to their way of living had reached him, and he made detailed and precise enquiries, without however discovering anything wrong. During the course of the investigations, a number of apostates, some of whom had turned their backs on Christianity for as long as twenty years, testified that these people were in the habit of meeting together on fixed days, long before daybreak, in order to sing hymns in honour of Christ whom they regarded as a God *(quasi-Deo)*.

Meanwhile, the priests belonging to the Jewish religion were complaining that their temples were becoming deserted and the vendors of sacrificial-meat were being ruined, so quickly had Christianity spread. What course, therefore, should he, Pliny, follow? So we see that Christianity already existed in Asia Minor, and that these Christians themselves believed that their founder was Christ. On the evidence of these documents alone, it would be difficult to deny that Christ had ever existed.

2. *Jewish Evidence*

The Evidence of Flavius Josephus (A.D. 37-100). Born of one of the aristocratic-priestly families, and thoroughly grounded in both religion and law, this Josephus wrote some important historical books, notably on the 'Jewish War', a chronicle of the last revolt in Judea which was quelled by Titus, and 'Jewish Antiquities', a history of the Jewish People. Exceedingly careful of his personal prestige and standing, he was obviously anxious to flatter the Romans, and in addition this Pharisee was something of an opportunist. Nevertheless we find, in his 'Jewish Antiquities' a remarkable statement about Christ: "There was at that time a wise man, Jesus—if, that is to say, one may call him a man. For he worked miracles and was a teacher of men, who accepted the truth which he taught joyfully. He drew many Jews after him and also many Gentiles. This was the Messiah. And although Pilate, by reason of an accusation brought against him by our elders, sentenced him to the cross, those who had loved him before did not cease to love him. On the third day after his death he appeared to them again, living. The prophets sent by God had foretold this, and a thousand other amazing things of him. Even up to our day the generations of those people who were called Christians after him, have never died out."

For more than three centuries a fierce discussion has raged over this extract. Is it possible that Flavius Josephus—a Jew —wrote such a testimony? It does not fit in very well either with that which precedes or with that which follows it. It is noticeable that apologists of the second and third centuries never refer to it. It is not impossible that the original passage of Flavius Josephus was corrected by some Christian copyist of the third century. A few Catholic historians suggest a complete interpolation at some later date.

Yet Flavius must have heard Jesus spoken of, and this is confirmed by the fact that he mentions elsewhere St. John the Baptist, and James called the brother of Jesus; although the following addition: "who is named Christ" is again, however, of a later date. He probably says nothing about Christ because he is a Pharisee and a friend of the Romans. He wrote for the Roman public at large, for the glorification of his own people and, in such a framework, a long explanation about Messianism and Messianic activities, and particularly the story of an excitable personage who had managed to deceive and stir up a group of uncultured men, would have been quite out of place.

II. CHRISTIAN SOURCES

The revelations of God—the secrets of the life of God and of our life in connection with Him—we learn principally from the twenty-seven books of the New Testament. Jesus Christ Himself wrote nothing, and He gave no orders to others to write. He preached, and He added discourses to explain His preaching. In this way began a tradition which has endured. But from the very first He set the minds of His disciples at rest: that which they preached, both the doctrine and the rules of life which they passed on to others, were under the sure protection of His Spirit, that is to say of the Holy Ghost, who "will in His turn make everything plain, and recall to your minds everything I have said to you".

Nevertheless, a desire was beginning to make itself felt for the firm assurance of the written word, and the Holy Ghost inspired some of those who had listened to Christ's own discourses, and others who had often heard them repeated by His disciples, to write down these recollections. It was again the same Holy Ghost who led the apostles, and later the bishops of the newly established Church, to acknowledge these writings, usually without any hesitation, as God's own word emanating either from the apostles themselves or from their disciples. These were joined on to the Books of the Old Testament, and men began to speak of the *Canon*—a list of books, constituting a fixed norm or rule of life.

Thus the spoken word preceded the written Scripture, and the New Testament came into existence in the Church.

On reflection it is clear that the most reliable information about Jesus would be likely to be found within the circle of His own listeners and disciples, that is to say supposing that those who composed that circle were trustworthy, had a sound judgment, and were able to give an honest report. That which these first witnesses preached is to be found mainly in the four gospels: they form the core of the record of the original preaching of the apostles.

But, faced with this, the modern man is inclined to shake

his head doubtfully, accustomed as he is to learn everything from the written or printed word. He perceives—and this causes his hesitation—that the printed gospels, the few books now available, are in the end only the partial rendering of a *verbal* Christian teaching and preaching. All that the apostles and the disciples remembered of the words and expressions used by Christ they handed on, and these words lingered in the minds and hearts of their listeners. This is a case of the authority of what Papias calls: "the living word". The crucial question for us therefore is as to whether this word has any real authority? Is memory a safe storehouse: a reliable criterion of truth?

In order to find the right answer one has perhaps to put the question somewhat differently: was *their* memory a safe storehouse, able to hold and keep the truth unchanged and intact?

Jewish education always implied a special training of the memory. The pupils' only way of learning was by listening to and remembering what was said by the teacher. No other method of study then existed. Jeremias, for instance, did not write down his prophecies beforehand but, living in the midst of the reality, this sensitive, quiet poet reacted very strongly to the passing impressions made on him by circumstances and events. Immediately, he expressed, in sober although spontaneous words, touched with the warmth of real zeal, all that he had thus perceived. Men listened to him, his words were repeated, and only after twenty-two years of oral tradition were they written down at last.

It is exactly the same with regard to the *Mishna,* that most important part of the *Talmud* having reference to the Law: it is no more than a hard core of verbal instruction transmitted into writing. The Rabbis themselves maintained that a good pupil might be likened to a cistern from which not a drop of water escaped. In the same way the words of Christ, reproduced for us in the gospels, were seized upon and stored up in those strongly guarded memories which, we must recollect, in those days still retained their full vigour and had not as yet been vitiated by a welter of news and propaganda forced upon the attention from every part of the world.

The method of learning and memorizing then in vogue depended largely upon what might be called teaching expedients, which formed the basis of its reliability, such as the use of regularly spaced tone-variations, often in strophic form;

of chanted refrains; of strongly worded phrases; parallelism and antithesis. They were sometimes even accompanied by rhythmical movements and dancing. Examples of this are to be found in the gospels: for instance, in the Sermon on the Mount, with its alternating benedictions and maledictions; many of the maxims of the Proverbs; and forcible phrases such as: "Ask, and the gift will come; seek, and you shall find; knock, and the door shall be opened to you. Everyone that asks will receive; that seeks, will find; that knocks, will have the door opened to him."[1] Or again in the Magnificat, that wonderful hymn of the thanksgiving of the Virgin Mary, in which, quite spontaneously, she expressed her gratitude and joy by means of the scriptural quotations and allusions which came so readily to her mind.

In this way, the teaching of Jesus, and the preaching of His apostles—even, here, and there, the original expressions used by them—could be kept intact, and verbal tradition be correctly preserved and reproduced in writing.

The Christian sources of information which are of interest to us are identical with these *Canonical Books,* regarded by the Church as inspired: that is to say, the four Gospels, the Acts of the Apostles, and the Epistles written by the various apostles.

A. *The Four Gospels*

In four short books we find one and the same gospel, which is no less than the message brought to earth for us by Christ: the good news of which He Himself was the living representative, and with which is bound up our everlasting salvation and happiness. The Gospel stands for Jesus Christ Himself—a divine gift, and the gift which He brought us in the name of God.

1. *Origin of the Gospel*

How did this Gospel—this fourfold message of the Kingdom of God—first begin? Passing over for the moment the general differences between Matthew and Mark and Luke and John, we might perhaps speak of a double birth which, in the end, is but the birth of one.

[1] Matt. 7, 7.

The Gospel emanated from the living tradition of the first Christian community, but bears in its fourfold rendering the very distinct traces of individual, personal work. What exactly was the purpose of the Evangelists? Especially of the Synoptics? Did each set out to write an original, historical account, and produce, on the pretext of the study of original sources, some private conception of his own of Christ and His work? Quite the contrary. What each obviously had in mind was quietly and concisely to gather up and arrange in order all the various traditions concerning Jesus, which had already been spread about among the faithful as stories told by Peter and the other apostles, or as statements and reminiscences gathered from His Mother.

An apostle, or some follower of the apostles, would speak of Christ: his aim was certainly not the mere dry-as-dust statement of facts, nor the equally dry refutation of error. His whole endeavour was *to preach Jesus.* Those who listened wanted to feel in their hearts that glorious, divine Christ—it was *He* whom they wished to hear speaking; they longed to feel how He loved them, how He suffered and died for them; they wanted to be comforted again by the hope of His glorious return—perhaps very near. Because of this they asked for details; they repeated to themselves His own words and phrases. That is how the story of the life and work of Jesus was first told, and was preached in words by the apostles, and the teaching carried out in their own lives and conduct.

But, on the other hand, each apostle contributed his own personal thoughts and memories of the life of Christ: it is not at all impossible that certain fixed renderings, certain definite narratives, passed unchanged from mouth to mouth.

The Evangelists drew on this great fund of oral instruction, of already well-known tradition: they arranged and wrote down the narratives: they authenticated and co-ordinated all the information regarding Jesus that was already extant in the Primitive Church. Quite possibly, of course, they made some additional researches of their own, but in the main, both as regards matter and even sometimes manner, they kept to the recognized preaching of the apostles. Their only desire was to bear faithful witness to the first, genuine tradition.

Here, then, is already a very firm basis of reliability for the gospel stories. We are in the presence of a community of earnest and fervent young Christians who, needless to say, were in a position to check immediately whether the written word corresponded with the apostolic preaching; who were extremely susceptible to every word and act of their Redeemer, who had grown to be a living reality in their hearts, coming as they did under the immediate influence of the actual companions of His life on earth. A writer would have met with but scant success had he attempted to put forward his truths in any but the traditional way "in Christ Jesus", and in agreement with "the sound principles which are the principles of our Lord Jesus Christ, the doctrine which accords with holiness".[2]

As a criterion, therefore, of the validity of these Gospels as part of the Canon of Scripture, that is to say as part of those books now accepted as the standard or rule of Faith by the Christian Church, we have, over and above the soundness of the doctrine contained in them, the fact that they were accepted as such by the first Christians themselves. In addition to this there is also the fact, which is most essential, that each has behind it the authority of an apostle: the written testimony is directly connected with a disciple of the Master. It was to emphasize this that the formulas were first introduced: "The Holy Gospel according to Matthew: according to Mark; according to Luke; according to John."

2. *The Origin of the four separate Gospels*

To the early Christians the four Gospels formed in reality but one. In the fourth century St. Augustine speaks of the four books of the one Gospel. This unity is particularly noticeable in the first three: the Gospel according to Matthew, Mark and Luke. From the eighteenth century on, these have been known as the synoptic Gospels, after the Greek word synopsis, which means "clearly arranged together" and their authors are recognized as synoptics.

a. *The Synoptics*

All of them followed more or less the same plan when describing the life of Our Lord: there is a certain mutual conformity, which nowhere degenerates into plagiarism or mere monotonous repetition of the same thing. Their personalities remain quite distinct throughout, and in this way they bring a pleasant sensa-

[2] I Cor. 4, 17; I Tim. 6, 3.

tion of variety to the circle of their readers. A separate consideration of the work of these three authors will be found to confirm this statement.

1. The Gospel according to *Matthew*

Originally written about the years 50-55 in the popular Jewish or Aramaic language, which fact is vouched for by both Bishop Papias, a pupil of St. John, and also Irenaeus of Lyon who lived in the second century—this Gospel was already, by the end of the first century, being quoted in Greek only. The identity of the adapter of this translation, now in general use in the Church, was not however known to St. Jerome in the fifth century. The author was obviously a Jew—and yet he had not been uninfluenced by Greek culture. A strong tradition in the Church identifies him with Levi, the son of Alfeus, whom Jesus called to follow Him from the custom-house. A publican was able to write; he would be exact in recording facts quietly and without comment. The story in this Gospel is logically constructed and follows a definite scheme, perhaps a trifle monotonously and without much effect of light and shade. Such would have been the calm, reasoned manner of writing to which he would be accustomed.

Further to this, Matthew knew for whom he was writing, and why he followed this particular arrangement of facts. He had his own compatriots constantly in mind, the Jewish Christians, and this was already noted and commented on by both Eusebius and Origen in their day. It was for this reason that he wrote in a language which only the Jews understood, and followed the typical Jewish literary style. We can note his parallelism, his comparisons, his occasional rhythmic phrasing; the way in which he begins and ends a series of ideas with one sole idea in identical wording: "Blessed are the poor in spirit; the Kingdom of Heaven is theirs. . . . Blessed are those who suffer persecution in the cause of right; the Kingdom of Heaven is theirs." (Matt. 5. 1-7.)

Typical Jewish expressions recur frequently; holy city, holy place, house of Israel; and he refers no less than thirty-two times to the 'kingdom of heaven', whereas the other Evangelists preferably speak of the 'kingdom of God'. We shall also notice that he never explained Jewish customs and conditions of life, since his allusions to them were already familiar to his readers.

The five well-known discourses: Christ's Sermon on the Mount;[3] His Instruction to the Apostles;[4] the Parables;[5] His Instruction to His Disciples;[6] and His Sermon upon the Judgment to come;[7] round which all the facts which he related are

[3] Matt. 5. [4] Matt. 10, 5-42. [5] Matt. 13.
[6] Matt. 18, 3-35. [7] Matt. 23, 2-25.

grouped, as well as the story of the events themselves, have only one predominating aim in view: to stress the great truth that Jesus is the Messiah, the Son of David predicted by the prophets, and that He was sent to the lost sheep of the House of Israel. In a continuous undertone of melancholy there runs the theme, also expressed by John, that He came to His own and His own received Him not. So it is that he ends his book of the Gospel with Christ's promise to all nations.

At the same time it is noticeable how Matthew sets out to show that the preaching of Jesus follows on from the Old Testament and is the completion of it. He expressly mentions that Christ was sent to the Jews in particular:[8] the Jews remain the Children of the Kingdom, and Jerusalem is still the Holy City,[9] for Christ is King of the Jews and the Son of David. He points out, with far greater emphasis than the other Evangelists, that in Jesus all the Messianic expectations are fulfilled.

But, even while the Gospel of Jesus follows on from the Old Covenant, this is above all a case of *new* tidings. It is Matthew who, in an unrelenting, uncompromising way, especially in Chapter 23, attacks the spirit of the Pharisees and their manner of interpreting the Law.

He further emphasizes the universality of the Kingdom of God; the ideal of fellowship with the poor and the oppressed; the new interior life of the Faithful, banded together in one Church, acknowledging one Authority. This occasional lapse into Apologetics in no way detracts from the historical value of the book, and we shall consider it again later.

The talent of Luke is perhaps missing in this writer as are also the spiritual flights of John: still, he consistently gives the impression of an exact and honest witness who is writing down accurately what he has seen and heard. This is essentially the Gospel of the Messiah: written by Matthew who, like one of the angels at the Crib, very faithfully bears witness to the glad tidings which he carries within him. We seem to see him, calm and imperturbable, as he moves his pen up and down across the pages, sketching in all the details about Christ which still linger in his memory, and with which the Holy Ghost inspires him.

2. The Gospel according to *Mark*

John Mark, who was the cousin of Barnabas, and who so frequently accompanied Paul on his journeys, was described by Peter as his son and was with him in Rome. He wrote the second Gospel between the years A.D. 55-62. Moving as he did in the circle of the

[8] Matt. 10, 5-6.

[9] Matt. 8, 12 and 4, 5.

most prominent apostles, it follows that he must repeatedly have heard Christ spoken of, and thus learned many wonderful and intimate details of the Master. Perhaps he had even seen Jesus with his own eyes, for might he not well be that young man who, he tells us, had followed Christ to Gethsemane on the night of His arrest, and who finally, when all the disciples had fled and the soldiers laid hold of him, fled also, leaving his linen shirt in their hands. [10]

This Mark is evidently no Scribe or man of letters, but a simple fellow with but a modest education. He writes Greek badly and with constant lapses into phrases betraying his Jewish origin. But he tells his tale in a fresh and virile style—perhaps one might say in the popular-realistic style. It may be that some of the older authors, such as Papias, Irenaeus, Clement of Alexandria, and Origen, are right when they maintain that he was the mouthpiece of Peter, and noted down with extreme care, but not necessarily in the right order, all that Jesus had said and done, as far as Peter could remember. "For he himself had never heard Jesus speak nor followed him; but it was Peter whom he followed later on. The latter taught as circumstances might require at the moment, but not consecutively, nor following the precise order of Christ's words. Therefore Mark was quite correct in merely writing down incidents as he recollected them, and his only preoccupation was neither to omit nor to misinterpret anything which he had learned."

In this Gospel therefore it is only natural that Peter should be given the most prominent place. Twenty-two of the seventy-two verses of Chapter 14, which contains the story of Christ's Passion, have to do with Peter: Peter who denied Christ; whom Christ called Satan because he attempted to hold Him back from His appointed task; who was present during the Transfiguration on Mount Tabor.

Somewhere about the year A.D. 61 Mark was in Rome, where Peter was preaching Christ to the people, and to the small community of Christians. Peter asked Mark to set down these marvellous stories, which Mark did without any pretension to scientific knowledge and without any logically prepared plan. Yet undoubtedly he had a particular circle of readers in mind as he wrote, and was writing with a definite purpose.

It was not for the Jews that he committed his information to paper—we may know that by the fact that his explanations of Jewish customs and phrases would have been superfluous for them; for every Jew knew that the Jordan was a river, and the reason for which he had to wash his hands before each meal. It is most

[10] Mark 14, 51.

probable that he was addressing himself to the *Christians in Rome*, that is, to the converted Gentiles.

He lays special emphasis upon their vocation or calling; for their sake he willingly makes use of Latin expressions; and it is no doubt the reason why his Gospel opens with the words: "The beginning of the Gospel of Jesus Christ, the Son of God." He was anxious to demonstrate to these people, who only a few years before were still offering sacrifices to their pagan deities, that Jesus was in truth the Son of the Living God. And he principally tells them of the miracles which the Divine Master worked. Jesus is Lord of inanimate Nature: He heals the sick; He raises from the dead; and (here we can almost see the former idolater earnestly shaking his head as he drives home his point) He has complete authority over evil spirits. Without exception everyone must acknowledge that Christ is Master and God—even the very devils. And so it was that Mark wrote the Gospel of the Son of God, beginning with John the Baptist who, with the voice of a lion, proclaimed His coming, up and down the desert, and ending with the cry of the Roman centurion: "Verily, this Man was the Son of God."

3. The Gospel according to *Luke*

Towards the year A.D. 60 Luke, the Physician, put together a third Gospel in which he reproduced all that he had learned from his collaborator and travelling companion, Paul. Born at Antioch, he was converted to Christianity in early manhood. St. Paul had a natural affinity with a cultured man of letters such as was this young Greek, and so begged him to accompany him upon his third missionary journey, and thence on to Rome. The tradition which has come down to us from St. Irenaeus is brief and tersely worded: "Luke, the companion of Paul, wrote down the Gospel which the latter preached."

The beginning of his Gospel indicates that his purpose was to give, above all, an objective-historical account. He thus thought it necessary to record once more from the beginning—after very precise research-work—all that had been handed down by the first disciples and ministers of the Church. He drew his information from many different sources and the result is eminently satisfactory. He has assimilated and co-ordinated much material of which there is no trace to be found in the Gospels of either Matthew or Mark: for instance, the wonderful account of the great journey upon which the Apostles set out (Luke 9.) and of the childhood of Christ. Of the twenty-four chapters of his Gospel there is only one which does not offer us fresh information. He also tries to put the details of his Narrative into chronological order, even though we may get the occasional impression that he sets down a parable, or one of Our Lord's addresses, at some particular point or another, not so much for the reason that they actually belong there, as that they have to be got in sooner or later. We also find that he sometimes intentionally deviates from precise chronological sequence in order to give us, without pause, a complete story or argument. In addition to this, he has taken pains to insert his events into the general framework of the political and ecclesiastical history of the Palestine of those days.

The sources from which he drew his information are not mentioned, but no doubt he borrowed much from Paul's preaching. In Rome and in Antioch he may also have come into contact with Peter, and in Jerusalem he probably met James the Less. It is of course not impossible that he learned direct from Our Lady some of the memories of the childhood and youth of her Son which she had kept in her heart.

Reading his Gospel in Greek, we notice that his literary construction is strong, powerful and excellently put together; indeed the first sentence of his book is considered to be a model of the best Greek style, worthy in every way of the classics. His vocabulary is larger than that of Mark, and as far as possible he avoids the use of unusual words. He is said to have been a man of both taste and talent, good at telling a story, and possessing the psychological gift of observation.

For whom was his Gospel intended? Most probably for former pagans who had become Christians. He elucidated Jewish terms and explained Jewish customs in the same way as did Mark. He omitted what would not interest heathens—as, for instance, the explanation of the Law in the Beatitudes. He was careful to soften down anything which might give offence to such converts, or which might sound harsh to them. For instance, Matthew says quietly in the Beatitudes: "If you greet none but your brethren, what are you doing more than others? Will not the *very heathen* do as much?"[11] Luke writes: "What credit is it to you, if you do good to those who do good to you? Even *sinners* do as much."[12]

And, finally, his Gospel is of an explicitly wide and *universal character*. The Christ which he depicts is "the light which shall give revelation to the Gentiles",[13] and if the Jews themselves are blind and refuse to see this light and accept this salvation, "others will come from the east and the west, the north and the south, to take their ease in the Kingdom of God".[14] We also notice that, according to him, the last word spoken by Jesus Christ was a promise that "repentance and remission of sins should be

[11] Matt. 5, 47.
[12] Luke 6, 33.
[13] Luke 2, 32.
[14] Luke 13, 29.

preached in His name to all nations, beginning with Jerusalem".[15]

The Christ of his Gospel is the Good Samaritan, who runs to meet the prodigal son and embraces him; who defends from the Pharisees the unknown sinner weeping at His feet; and takes the Good Thief with Him into paradise. From His lips come the beautiful parables of God's loving care. And the only word spoken upon the cross which Luke has recorded is: "Father, forgive them; they do not know what it is they are doing."[16]

He is anxious to stress to these first Christians to be converted from paganism, the real meaning and truth of the doctrine taught them, and to make them understand how merciful is God to sinners. His central idea is the redemption of all men without distinction of race or class, but he has given us no dogmatic exposition of the subject such as came from the pen of his master, Paul. He allows the facts to speak for themselves.

We can say that Luke wrote the Gospel of the Merciful Redeemer, and the symbol of the winged calf, by which the writers and painters of the Middle Ages always represented him, finds its *raison d'être* in his opening words, which tell of the offering of Zachary—but it is a symbol which is quite inadequate to convey the richness and the warmth of love by which his writing is inspired.

It is always the one Gospel of Christ which is conveyed to us through these three separate channels. Any unprejudiced person who reads the three books through, cannot fail to be struck by the conformity of the general plan which underlies them all, and to notice how, in the main, the framework of the events is identical. The stories correspond, often indeed being placed in the same sequence, and occasionally one is even struck by the similarity of the reflections made and the words used.

And yet what differences! How many strange divergences which cannot be entirely explained by the varying personalities or literary skill of the authors. Why, for instance, does Mark speak of that Gentile woman, a Syrophenician by birth, who gave such a magnificent answer to Christ when He demurred at taking the children's bread and throwing it to the dogs: "The dogs eat of the crumbs the children leave, underneath the table": while Luke in his Gospel, written for pagans, does not refer to this touching little incident at all.

According to Matthew and Luke, again, Our Lord instructed His apostles to take nothing with them when journeying; neither staff, nor wallet nor bread nor money, no second coat nor spare shoes; but Mark, on the contrary, distinctly states that "He gave them instructions to take a staff for their journey and nothing more."

[15] Luke 24, 46-47.

[16] Luke 23, 34.

It has been calculated that, according to the number of verses, Matthew can claim almost one third, Mark about one tenth and Luke rather more than a third, as each his own separate and individual contribution to the general Gospel narrative.

It is a case of striking similarities, and yet, in these very similarities so many variations and, on the whole, so many different renderings to be found among the three, that serious search has been made—and is still being made—for the fundamental cause of such divergences. We can only call it the problem of the Synoptics and for the moment leave it at that.

There is obviously great interdependence: it is possible that there were other written documents which preceded these gospels: in any case there was all the original verbal tradition and preaching. However the matter may be regarded, it must be conceded that the authors themselves had no scruple in making their writings resemble the fountain-head from which they are all obviously drawn, which inclines one to attribute the variations, at all events in part, to the fact that these gospels were intended for different circles of readers, as well as to the individual style of each evangelist. The divergences are not of such a fundamental character that a definite choice between them ever becomes necessary; it is perhaps more that the breath of the Holy Spirit, as it stirred and quickened their minds with its inspiration, yet left untouched their personal attractions and inclinations.

Another possible solution is offered by some students of the Scriptures. The Apostles preached the Kingdom of God in Jerusalem and Palestine, in Rome and Antioch. From the Palestine preaching there came into being the Gospel written in the Aramaic language by Matthew, an eye-witness, now unfortunately lost; then, much later, what was mainly the Catechesis of Peter was reproduced by Mark in Rome; and finally Luke noted down Paul's preaching at Antioch, but was influenced at the same time by other witnesses of the teaching of Christ, and possibly also made use of the work of Mark and of a primitive Greek translation of Matthew—now lost. After this we find a new Greek version of Matthew, which is the one in present use, but which appears to bear traces of the influence of both Mark and Luke.

The minor differences which we have established, taken in conjunction with the conformity in all essentials, surely point to a greater historical reliability than any mere mechanical copying could guarantee us?

b. *John*

After these three Gospels we come to that other and last Gospel which is attributed by the Church to St. John, and which immediately strikes us by a noticeable difference in its tone, and in the manner in which it is written, both as regards its descriptions and even the facts related themselves. In dealing with this Gospel, we shall consider the differences between it and those of Matthew, Mark and Luke in both the apparent aim and scheme of construction, and thus find a reply to the question as to whether the author had any intention of writing, strictly speaking, history at all.

The difference between his work and the others is to be found equally in the facts related and the manner of relating them.

He does not deal with *important facts* such as the youth of Christ, His baptism, the temptation in the desert, His transfiguration, or the Holy Eucharist; in short with practically everything which took place in Galilee. Instead he relates events which one finds nowhere else. These appear to have been enacted during a period of two or three years, whereas the three Synoptics assume only one year for them.

He develops his story about Jesus mainly in conversations and discourses, to which both miracles and facts are subordinated. In these conversations we find ourselves listening to the thoughts of a mystic, who quietly pursues the theme of his contemplation, and continually ascends to the inmost secrets of the life of God and the divinity of Christ. The miracles are only related in order to support that supreme truth to which he unceasingly leads us, by first one path and then another, that is to say, to the fact that Jesus is the Son of God, the light of the world, the Incarnate Word.

The complete salvation to be found in Christ is expressed by images and figures of speech not easily understood except in conjunction with the Old Testament and Judaism; but which nevertheless outline very sharply how abundant that salvation is for all who believe in Him. For Christ is the Light which triumphs over the darkness of the world and sin; the Bread which satisfies hunger for ever; the Water which quenches even the deepest thirst; the Vine which is covered with living branches; and the Good Shepherd who gives His life for His sheep. He is the fulfilment of the deepest desires of Man, but the necessary condition for the attainment of this happiness is belief in Him as Redeemer.

In his style of writing the author shows a delicate sensitiveness to human existence in general—its contrasts and its tensions.

In his considerations he does not dwell upon so many subjects as the synoptics, who speak of the law of Christ and its requirements and contrast it with the ancient law; of the principles of the Pharisees compared with the Kingdom of Heaven and all the various properties and characteristics of the latter, accompanied by much practical information as to Jesus' Person, His Mission, His Passion and His Death. On the contrary, this evangelist seems to be inspired and held by the one great reality: God, and Jesus Christ whom He has sent to us. To know Him is the only path to true and eternal life.

The explanation of these differences resolves itself very simply into this: that John deliberately wished to write another Gospel in which he took it for granted that the other three were already known. Therefore he shows us Jesus in quite another way—but he does not show us another Jesus. He always bears this aim in mind: to bring us, by his writing, to that complete and profound belief which carries with it eternal life, that is to say, the belief that Jesus Christ is indeed the Son of God. He wishes us to share in his own contemplation of Christ and in his own experience of Christ; he wishes to testify to the only truth which exists for him. His profound desire is not only to point out that Jesus is the Messiah and the Son of God, but to bring home to us that highest revelation of all, the tangible love of God made manifest in Christ. For him that is the very core of the Christian life: the encounter of man's heart and spirit with Christ by faith. He continually stresses his main idea: Faith, Life, Christ, Son of God.

Therefore, out of the life of Jesus, he selects chiefly those words and deeds which tell us the most clearly that He is the Son of God and the bestower of eternal life on all who believe. For example, in relating the years of the Ministry, he particularly mentions the miracle of the multiplication of the loaves, because this offers an excellent opportunity of making clear to us the thoughts of the Messiah upon the sources of eternal life. On the other hand, he omits the incident of the institution of the Holy Eucharist as being already sufficiently well known from the other Gospels.

For this reason also he records the conversations which deal *indirectly* with the personality of Christ; which demonstrate His likeness to the Father; and the mission of the Holy Ghost in completing His own work on earth. In the case of the Synoptics, on the contrary, one has more or less to draw one's individual conclusions about the personality of Christ from the general story of His life on earth.

To prove the truth of what he says he appeals to the testimony of St. John the Baptist and to that of Christ Himself, the holiness of whose life, and whose miracles, can but confirm his words.

It is obvious that this Gospel presupposes readers who already have considerable knowledge of the history and teaching of Jesus Christ; who are already formed in the interior life; and who realize the meaning of conversion, and of surrender to God by love and faith. The Christians to whom he addressed himself were presumably not of Jewish but of pagan origin, as would appear from the explanations which he gives of Aramaic words and of Jewish customs and feasts; as also from certain geographical allusions, and from the manner in which he repeatedly refers to the Jews as a body of men hostile to Christ.

From the Gospel itself it would appear that the author is a Jew who is writing in a foreign tongue. His Greek is simple, rather poor, and monotonous. He has only a very limited vocabulary at his disposal. Typically Jewish turns of phrase are frequent, and his use of antithesis and parallelism point to the old Jewish method of instruction. He dwells on the Old Testament as one who loves and has grown up with it.

His very detailed descriptions, and the exact chronology, point to the work of an actual witness of the events, which he implies moreover by such phrases as: "we have seen His glory". No wonder that some person—perhaps one of his followers—added at the end of this Gospel: "It is the same disciple that bears witness of all this and has written the story of it; and we know well that his witness is truthful."[17] Most probably the author was present at the Last Supper. He knows every detail of it, as for instance Christ's wonderful farewell address. He is the disciple whom Jesus loved and who stood at the foot of the cross with the Mother of the Saviour, and who ran with Peter to the tomb so early on Easter morning. From the Synoptics we know that three of the disciples enjoyed a privileged position: Peter, James and John. The author of this Gospel definitely draws a distinction between himself and Peter, so it was not the latter; James was already dead long before the Gospel appeared, somewhere about the year A.D. 100.

Therefore tradition, and through it the Church, speaks of John, son of the fisherman Zebedee, as being the author of what we may call the Gospel of the Word. It was with a practical intention that he wrote down what he had witnessed with his own eyes, and what he had been allowed to know and to love of the Word of Life. He did not merely content himself with expressing his own personal reflections and individual views: he formally testified to the truth of what he wrote: "He who saw it has borne his witness; and his witness is worthy of trust. He tells what he knows to be the truth, that you, like him, may learn to believe."[18] Yet in spite of the avowed historical intention of the book, this eagle—who for half an hour had known the silence of Heaven when the seventh seal had been broken by the Lamb—rose above all the vicissitudes and changing events of time and history to the pure knowledge and experience that God is Love.

[17] John 21, 24.

[18] John 29, 35.

3. *Historical Value of the Gospels*

The preceding consideration of the four Evangelists and their respective Gospels undoubtedly leaves us with the impression that they recorded what had actually happened; and although they had no formal intention of writing history in the modern sense of the word, yet nevertheless they meant to share their knowledge of historical facts with the Faithful.

We may, in short, summarize this question, in its relation to modern ideas and conceptions, in this way: Is it possible that, under the very eyes of contemporaries of Jesus Himself, the Apostles and their followers could have either written or said anything but the pure historical truth about His life and teaching?

To put such a question is to answer it in the negative, and the more so because, as we have already seen, these Gospels are the accumulated deposit of all the oral teaching and preaching which had preceded them. At the same time the Christians of the Primitive Church did undoubtedly apply a selective process, rejecting what we now call the *apocryphal* writings of the second century, such as the proto-Gospel of James, the Arabic Gospel of the Childhood of Christ, the various Gospels of the Hebrews and Egyptians, as well as the Gospels of the Ebionites by Peter, Matthew, Philip, etc., while accepting the four recognized versions of the Gospel which we have been discussing.

That which at first sight might lead to a doubt as to the historical reliability of even these four Gospels—that is to say, the general similarity of the texts combined with the marked differences in certain parts, and the purely external and systematic way in which the facts are presented:—offer us, in reality, the surest guarantee that here we have to do with an early apostolic and Christian tradition, and that the unusual way of dealing with their subject adopted by all the Evangelists, is neither more nor less than a meticulous loyalty to that tradition. They left apparent inequalities and contradictions to look after themselves, while they closely followed the current usage of the Early Church.

One may sum up shortly as follows: Two of the Gospels were written by eye-witnesses, Matthew and John; they were actually present on most of the occasions described and had themselves heard the words of Our Lord. The other two Evangelists, Luke and Mark, were the pupils and companions of the Apostles, and thus continually influenced by the testimony of those who had also been witnesses of the events in question. We can hardly blame them for a lack of critical judgment: they did not set out to discuss deep problems of a philosophical or social or economic nature. They described concrete events which happened in public, and spoke in the form of proverbs, allegories and parables of the clear dogmas of the Church. Even though the facts might in themselves be remarkable, and the dogmas might appear an impenetrable mystery, they did not offer any justification for them, but contented themselves with simply recording what they had seen or heard. The wonderful miracle of the loaves and the fishes, for instance, is told without any excited additions of astonishment or enthusiasm. This *quiet, unprejudiced method of registering facts* is the best possible guarantee we can have of their truth.

Their Gospels are objective rather than mystical; they are profoundly human and keep close to the reality of daily events. They are intimately related to a particular social milieu, and a particular period of history, details of which we find also in the works of other contemporary historians. They deal with human institutions and social customs which answer to the descriptions of Jewish writers as a whole.

Their local colour is no matter of the imagination. Palestine, with its towns and villages, is the definite background of their story. The subtle atmosphere of the country, with its political and religious life, and the typically Jewish way of thinking and of acting which we find also in the writings of the Talmud, is unmistakable, and gives us the setting of an historically recognizable place and period. We are, as it were, standing in the presence of chroniclers who shrug their shoulders at all our modern, critical quibbles with the reply: "We cannot help it—that is how it happened."

The same claim of reliable accuracy can be made also for the Gospel of St. John. He himself testifies that in writing about the Word of Life, he is recording only what he actually saw, heard or felt. This is indeed evident from the exact chronological details which he supplies, from his references to particular places, and the conversations which he reports. In all matters of importance the Synoptics are in agreement with him.

Finally—how could the personality of Jesus be a creation

of the human mind? Pascal has put the whole thing in a nutshell: "Who taught the Evangelists all the qualities of a supremely heroic soul which they have so wonderfully depicted in Jesus Christ?" And by way of giving an example, he adds: "Why do they make Him appear almost humanly weak in His death-agony? Do they not know how to portray courageous contempt of death? Obviously they do: for Luke, who describes both, seems to draw the death of Stephen with stronger lines than that of Christ."

The fact is that everything which these Evangelists relate of the Divine Master only goes to prove that they are relating the truth and that they are describing strictly according to reality.

4. *The Authenticity of the Gospels*

There remains the question: Were these Gospels in fact written by the authors in whose names we find them? In the foregoing passages we have already put forward an intrinsic argument in favour of a reply in the affirmative. The character of the writings themselves points to Matthew, Mark, Luke and John: it points to the Jewish Publican who became an Apostle; to the interpreter of the preaching of Peter; to the companion of Paul; and to the beloved disciple of Christ.

Furthermore, what we ourselves are able to deduce or to presume from the writings is confirmed by the witness of the centuries. About the year 200 the conviction as to the authenticity of the Gospels became general in the Church. I refer to Tertullian in Africa about A.D. 160; to Origen, a member of the famous School of Alexandria, 185-253; to Clement of Alexandria, 140-215; to the fragment of Muratori of the second century; to a list of books in use in the Church which was compiled in the early years of the third century, and in which are mentioned the "Third Gospel according to Luke" and "Fourth Gospel according to John". About the year A.D. 180 Irenaeus, in his treatise dealing with the heresy of Gnosticism, wrote: "Matthew produced, when living among the Hebrews, the written Gospel in their own dialect, whilst Peter and Paul preached the Gospel and established the Church in Rome. After their death (or after their departure) Mark the disciple and companion of Peter, handed down to us his preaching in writing, while Luke, the companion of

Paul, also put into writing the Gospel preached by the latter. Later on, John, the disciple of the Lord who had rested upon His breast, worked also on the Gospel during his stay at Ephesus in Asia."

This Irenaeus was a disciple of Polycarp who, in turn, was a disciple of John.

Beyond all this there is also the evidence of St. Theophilus, Bishop of Antioch (about A.D. 150); of Tatian in his Diatesseron, a harmony of the four Gospels (about A.D. 170,); and of Justin (A.D. 160). In their writings we find all kinds of quotations from our four Gospels. Finally in Eusebius we meet quotations from the big work in five volumes of Papias, Bishop of Hierapolis in Phrygia, whom Irenaeus calls "a hearer of John and companion of Polycarp", and in these quotations we read about Mark and Matthew, who wrote the "sayings of the Lord". In manuscripts of a still earlier date, such as a letter of Polycarp, and the seven letters of St. Ignatius of Antioch, we find quotations from, and allusions to, the Gospels. Incidentally the headings of our Gospels go as far back as the first half of the second century.

Thus both the internal evidence derived from an analysis of the Gospels themselves, and the external evidence of independent documents of about the same period, points convincingly to Matthew, Mark, Luke and John as the authors of the four canonical Gospels.

5. *Integrity of the Gospels*

These four Gospels are now in our hands, although the original manuscripts have been lost. But the original text was transcribed over and over again in the earliest days; indeed the number of copies made amounts to 1500. The very earliest were the 50 *papyri*, handwritten documents, dating from the second to sixth centuries, and containing only small isolated portions of our books. One indeed from the third century comprises the whole four Gospels, but in nine others only one Gospel is transcribed. Of the *papyri* we will especially mention—because they were discovered a few years ago in Egypt—the so-called Chester Beatty-papyri, in which are to be found parts of the New Testament probably dating from the third century. These contain no variations of any importance. There are also the Egerton-papyri, which consist of two sheets and a small fragment of a third sheet, containing four or five fragments of a hitherto unknown life of

Our Lord. This is said to be a compilation, in which, in addition to apocryphal works, the four canonical Gospels are also made use of, especially that of St. John. These date from the middle of the second century. Finally there is a sheet of papyrus, deposited in 1920 with the John Rylands Library, on which is a portion of a literal copy of the Gospel of John. The sheet is thought to belong to a codex which contained the complete fourth Gospel—written about A.D. 130.

Besides the *papyri* we possess manuscripts, transcribed exclusively in capital letters, (the so-called *uncials* of the fourth to the eleventh centuries) of which 66 are of importance in relation to the Gospels: about a thousand manuscripts in small characters (the minuscule manuscripts): and some 300 books of the Gospels for Sundays and Feastdays.

Either by negligence on the part of the copyists, or by the introduction of personal views: by the use of innumerable abbreviations and the omission of punctuation marks: by comments written in the margins and later on embodied in the text: by slips made in taking down from dictation—and perhaps sometimes even by intentional alterations—different renderings of one single text have come into being. Most of the variations, however, amount to no more than insignificant differences in spelling, in the sequence of words, in the use of synonyms, and so on, while the sense of the passage remains unchanged. Out of the whole number, 200 at the most change the meaning of the words in any degree at all, and of these only fifteen change something of either historical or dogmatic importance, while it is noticeable that even these fifteen leave the doctrine of the Church entirely untouched. On the whole therefore we can genuinely claim that the integrity of the Gospels remains inviolate.

b. *The Remaining Christian Sources*

In addition to the four Gospels we also have the Acts of the Apostles and the Epistles. They are, generally speaking, of a didactic character, and not intended to convey an outline of the life of Christ. Their purpose is to spread revealed truth and to enlarge and deepen its meaning. The details of the life of Jesus are taken for granted, and even if one finds some of the principal events repeated, in most cases they only serve as a foundation for the explanation of moral truths or dogmas. We must not, however, forget that the authors of the Epistles were themselves actual witnesses of the events referred to.

In the Acts of the Apostles we find all kinds of allusions to facts related in the Gospels.

The Epistles of St. Paul are especially regarded as being sources of information as to the life of Christ. In his case the direct and indirect allusions to His earthly life are more frequent than in any other writings of the New Testament and they show a very exact knowledge of historical tradition of the period. Not that St. Paul took an historical interest in Jesus according to the modern sense of the word, for his attention was certainly not focused on a careful study of personal details. First and foremost he visualized the *Christ of Faith*. But because this Christ, Son of God, appeared on earth in the form of a servant, "He dispossessed Himself and took the nature of a slave",[19] his love and his attention were also turned on to the humanity of Jesus; on to the historical figure, the offspring of Abraham,[20] "from the line of David",[21] who "took birth from a woman".[22] We have to thank him also for the most reliable information which we have as to Our Lord's Resurrection, and in his Epistle to the Galatians, he pictures the Crucified Christ.[23] The Epistle to the Corinthians speaks of the Last Supper and of Our Lord's betrayal and death.[24] He quotes verbally the sayings of Our Lord, and indeed one can find in the Epistles of St. Paul the whole of the confession of faith of the Apostles: "The chief message I handed on to you, as it was handed on to me, was that Christ, as the Scriptures had foretold, died for our sins; that He was buried, and then, as the Scriptures had foretold, rose again on the third day."[25]

This man, who had persecuted the Christians because they worshipped a crucified Messiah, and for that reason had passionately resisted the testimony of the Apostles, now imparted what he had learned from God by spiritual communications, and the knowledge which those very men had shared with him. That which had formerly been hatred turned to love. And it is just this hatred and this love of his, which makes him such a credible witness as to the truth of Christ.

And so, in greater or lesser degree, the other books of the New Testament serve to give reliable confirmation of the narrative of the life of Christ as explicitly related in the four Gospels.

As we come to the end of this chapter we shall find ourselves

[19] Phil. 2, 7. [20] Gal. 3, 16. [21] Rom. 1, 3. [22] Gal. 4, 4.
[23] Gal. 3, 1. [24] Cor. 2, 23. [25] I Cor. 15, 3-4.

in a position to assume with certainty that Jesus did exist. Any other conclusion would be impossible. He existed and does exist, and for this reason the love of God has become a certainty for us also.

§ 2. *Jesus Christ*

Having proved that Jesus Christ did indeed live, and that His life has been recorded by reliable contemporaries, including eye-witnesses, there arises the great and vital question for us: Who was Jesus Christ? The present-day man, who has grown up largely outside the influence of religion, is alien to the Man of Nazareth. His name is familiar to him, and it is possible that the personality of this world-reformer inspires him with a certain feeling of respect and admiration. But, after all, during His actual lifetime He did not come to the fore as a man of overwhelming significance. From that point of view He stands more or less on an equality with the founders of other religions, such as Confucius, Buddha, and Mohammed, among whom He is perhaps the greatest, but, on the other hand, would not seem to possess the sole right to call Himself a Teacher. We live in Western Europe where Christianity is the prevailing religion, but if we had been born in Hongkong or Benares, we might now be looking up with admiration to Tao, or bathing in the sacred waters of the Ganges. So speaks the modern man.

The latter is not of course improbable, but it does not therefore follow that all religions are equally true. It is *possible* that God revealed Himself fully only to Jesus Christ, and that those others were merely preaching a human wisdom and piety which owed its success to a certain intelligent psychological adaptation to the particular race or nation for which it was intended. In any case we ought not to reach some such shallow conclusion in advance as, "Oh, well, it all comes to the same thing in the end", but we should try honestly to obtain a deeper insight into this important matter.

If we listen to what Jesus Christ had to say when He first made His appearance in Palestine some two thousand years ago, it will become obvious that He Himself was absolutely convinced that He was the Son of God who had come to fulfil a mission entrusted to Him by His Father. Let us take His own unequivocal words:

"I am come, a light into the world, that whosoever believeth in Me may not remain in darkness. For I have not spoken of Myself; but the Father who sent Me, He gave Me commandment what I should say. The things therefore that I speak, even as the Father said unto Me, so do I speak. For God so loved the world as to give His only begotten Son, that whosoever believeth in Him may not perish, but may have life everlasting. For God sent not His Son into the world to judge the world, but that the world may be saved by Him. Amen, Amen, I say unto you that he who heareth My word and believeth Him that sent Me, hath life everlasting. I am the resurrection and the life; he that believeth in Me, although he be dead, shall live; and everyone that liveth and believeth in Me, shall not die for ever. I am the way and the truth and the life. No man cometh to the Father but by Me."

No one has ever spoken like this. The founders of other religious sects have indeed preached a message, but not one of them has ever dared to call himself the Only Begotten Son of God; not one of them has ever claimed for himself, as did Christ, "The Father and I are one". And did anyone ever pray like this before leaving the world? "Now, Father, do Thou exalt me at Thy own side, in that glory which I had with Thee before the world began."

Only of Christ has it ever been testified by a disciple and eye-witness (John) that He was the Wisdom as well as the Word of God, and this disciple places Him for ever above all other religious teachers known to history, by the opening words of his Gospel: "At the beginning of time the Word already was: and God had the Word abiding with Him, *and the Word was God.*"

No other spiritual leader, except Christ, can claim an age-long introduction by means of prophecies, so that a chosen section of mankind was watching for His coming, generation after generation, and was able to recognize Him immediately at His advent. Jesus of Nazareth does all this. We have already shown how in a long series of prophetic utterances, narratives and canticles, the leaders of the Jews proclaimed their expectation and their hope, their loving admiration for the Lord's Anointed, who was one day to leave eternal light in order to descend on Earth and there establish His Kingdom.

Although Christ never found it necessary to prove His doctrine, but was content to explain it as one with absolute authority, He nevertheless continually pointed out that that authority was above question. He specifically referred to the prophecies which were fulfilled in Him, and to the miracles which He worked as proof.

I. JESUS CHRIST, THE FULFILMENT OF THE PROPHECIES

To the believing Jew it was absolutely clear that "once the seal was affixed to vision and prophecy"—which means that once the Messiah had appeared in their midst as had been foretold by the prophets—then whereas "In old days, God spoke to our fathers in many ways and many means, through the prophets; now at last in these times He has spoken to us with a Son to speak for Him." His voice had reached them through Him who had accomplished their cleansing from sin and, after the atonement, had taken "His place on high, at the right hand of God's majesty".[26]

We shall therefore now endeavour to prove that the Messianic prophecies were indeed realized in the Person and life of Jesus Christ.

When, in reading the Gospels, we try to follow the life of this Jesus closely, there undoubtedly rises before our eyes a picture which immediately recalls to us the prophesied Messiah and the Servant of Jahve, as He was described and heralded by so many prophets of old.

To a simple and unknown young maiden called Mary, an angel of God appeared bringing this message:

> "Hail, thou art full of grace; the Lord is with thee; blessed art thou among women. . . . Mary, do not be afraid; thou hast found favour in the sight of God. And behold, thou shalt conceive in thy womb, and shalt bear a son, and shalt call him Jesus. He shall be great, and men will know him for the son of the Most High; the Lord God will give him the throne of his father David, and he shall reign over the house of Jacob eternally; his kingdom shall never have an end. But Mary said to the angel, 'How can that be,

[26] Heb. 1, 1-3.

since I have no knowledge of man?' And the angel answered her, the Holy Spirit will come upon thee, and the power of the Most High will overshadow thee. Thus this holy offspring of thine shall be known for the Son of God."[27]

In these words, spoken in the name of God to the one who was chosen to be the Mother of God, we hear the echo of the prophetic voices of the Old Testament. We then come to the wonderful happening of the virginal birth of Mary's child. His name already indicates His purpose in coming to earth, for Jesus means Redeemer or Saviour. His origin is veiled in divine mystery; He is the Son of the Most High and will be called Son of God; David is His father, and the kingship of David will again be assumed by Him and restored to all its former glory; and finally, this kingship is to have no end, and His kingdom shall never be overcome.

The story of the life of Christ, as it has been handed down to us by the Evangelists, may be considered as already sufficiently familiar to our readers. Matthew especially, who wrote for the Jews and therefore presupposes a knowledge of the prophecies, refers to them constantly. He repeatedly uses the somewhat stereotyped phrase, "that the Scriptures might be fulfilled" before quoting the appropriate prediction.

If we now compare the points noted in the last paragraph but one, with the life of Christ, we shall make the following striking discoveries:[28]

1. In His life Jesus had not only to contend with powers inimical to mankind, but He Himself considered this battle as His essential task and mission, while He was unshakably convinced of His ultimate victory. He applied the words of Isaias (Chap. 61, 1-2) to Himself. In his Gospel, Luke describes how Jesus entered the synagogue at Nazareth and, opening the scroll of the prophet Isaias, read the following passage to those present:

"The Lord has anointed me, on me His spirit has fallen; He has sent me to bring good news to men that are humbled, to heal broken hearts, promising the release of captives,

[27] Luke 1, 28-35.
[28] Compare the texts quoted in the chapter dealing with the Messianic prophecies.

the opening of prison doors, proclaiming the year of the Lord's pardon, the day when He, our God, will give us redress."

Then, in the tense atmosphere which followed on His words, He continued: "This Scripture which I have read in your hearing is to-day fulfilled." (Luke 4, 16-21.)

He not only showed Himself master of sickness and death, but also forgave sins and joined issue with what He called 'the world' of which the Scribes and Pharisees were the typical representatives. With fierce zeal and in stinging phrases He did battle against everything which was hypocritical, worldly-wise and self-seeking. Even when His own life was in danger He did not give way an inch. His fight with the consequences of Adam's sin was a life and death struggle and He knew that the victory lay with Him. "Take courage," he said to His faint-hearted and wavering disciples, "I have overcome the world."

Again, He quietly defied His enemies to destroy the temple of His Body, and declared that in three days He would raise it up again. It was sinners whom He had come to convert and to the poor that He brought the glad tidings of salvation. Again it was for the sake of the sick, who had need of Him, that He came to earth, and not for the healthy.

2. It might be the Jews who were first to profit by His battle and His victory against the powers of evil, nevertheless they were no longer exclusively regarded as the Chosen People. Jesus Himself, it is true, confined His public appearances to the circle of His own countrymen, but He made it abundantly clear that the Redemption which He had come to bring was destined for all. His apostles, to whom He gave detailed instructions for the continuation of His work after His death, were to go to all nations, teaching and baptizing them in the name of the Father and of the Son and of the Holy Ghost. On the occasion of the curing of the centurion's servant Jesus told His followers, "There are many who will come from the east and from the west, and will take their place in the kingdom of God."

The apostles were commanded to preach to "all nations", and they were to have the assistance of their Master "until the consummation of the world". So, in space as well as in time, the Kingdom of God continually grows. It never stands still but, in this sense, is always "coming" to mankind. That is why Christians so often repeat the prayer "Thy Kingdom Come".

3. When the people, full of enthusiasm after the miracle of the loaves and fishes, wished to take Jesus and proclaim Him King of Israel, He escaped from them and "went up by Himself on to the hillside, to pray there: twilight had come and He remained there alone". (Matt. 14, 24.) Yet, when the question was put to Him by Pilate as to whether He were a king, He answered simply: "It is thy own lips that have called me king:" from his subsequent words, however, it is clear that the Kingship of the Messiah to which He referred was essentially different from the kingship dreamed of by the Jews. "My kingdom does not belong to this world. If my kingdom were one which belonged to this world, my servants would be fighting to prevent my falling into the hands of the Jews; but no, my kingdom does not take its origin here." "Thou art a king then?" Pilate asked. And Jesus answered, "It is thy own lips that have called me a king. What I was born for, what I came into the world for, is to bear witness of the truth. Whoever belongs to the truth, listens to my voice."

Christ formally assumed His kingship by behaving explicitly as the 'Saviour of the people'. He came to save what was lost: it was the poor, the needy, the sick and the sinners who had His open sympathy and met with His royal help and support. He did not come to judge but to save the world. In the fight against evil His rôle was that of the intrepid commander, freeing man for ever from the grip of his own sinful nature by an act of full and efficacious redemption.

4. From the moment of the Annunciation of Jesus' birth it became evident that He was to be of royal blood. "He shall be great," the angel said, "and men will know Him for the Son of the Most High; the Lord God will give Him the throne of His father David, and He shall reign over the house of Jacob eternally; His kingdom shall never have an end."[29]

As they belonged to the House of David, Mary and Joseph went to Bethlehem, the City of David, for the registration ordered by the Emperor Augustus, and it was there that Jesus was born. It might seem at first sight that He was no more than the descendant of a no longer illustrious royal house, whilst in Israel nothing remained of the kingship of the great

[29] Luke 1, 32-34.

David, and Solomon his son. But the child of Bethlehem was to build on those ruins a new and glorious realm extending far beyond the frontiers of Palestine. So it was that the royal Saviour fulfilled the ancient prophecies and the deepest longings of the apparently exhausted and decadent Jewish people, which did but mourn over a great but vanished past, and dream of a future all too tardy in its coming.

The promised and long-expected "Son of David" was to bring back to Israel all its lost splendours once again. His aim was to achieve a new community of men, a reborn 'people of God', an independent royal nation, recaptured day by day from the domination of inimical forces, and brought anew under the leadership of one of David's lineage. And this time the sovereignty was to be everlasting, for the king Himself promised: "And behold I am with you all through the days that are coming, until the consummation of the world."

5. Jesus made no use of violence for the establishment of His kingdom. Even at the very bitterest moment, on the threshold of His supreme suffering, the too-hastily drawn sword was ordered back into its sheath. The battle for this kingdom of His was a purely spiritual combat. It is true that, for him, the world and evil had not ceased to exist, but the truth and the new faith which He had brought to earth was to work like leaven penetrating all things. Evil was to be conquered by good. The tares found among the corn were not to be rooted out, but both be left to grow together, and only at the time of final harvest was the good to be sifted from the bad. The disciples who desired to see the fires of vengeance raining down upon the Samaritan village which refused to receive Our Lord, were told sternly that they understood nothing of the spirit of the kingdom of God. "The Son of Man has come to save men's lives, not to destroy them."

It was only gradually that Christ revealed His divine origin. He did not suddenly take His hearers by surprise but prepared them for the knowledge beforehand. Once, however, the preparation had been thoroughly made, there was no further beating about the bush, and it became clear that He who IS "before Abraham was made" knew Himself for the Son of God. His language was unequivocal. He and the Father are one, and whosoever sees Him sees also the Father. In the original, divine message which He brought with Him, He addressed Himself primarily to His own people, but on the other hand He prophesies that many will come from the east and from the west to form part of His kingdom. The Gentiles also are to hear His teaching.

6. His passion and His death on the Cross were for Jesus the crown of life. The hour destined for His death He calls "My Hour". It seems as though the moment for His voluntary suffering is for Him the one supreme moment of existence. He has come to earth to suffer and to die: "Was it not to be expected that the Christ should undergo these sufferings, and enter so into His glory?" He says to His uncomprehending disciples.[30]

This Passion and this Death were freely *chosen* and not merely passively accepted by Christ. It was the will of His Father, and therefore His will also, that in this particular way, that is by the surpassing and all-sufficing sacrifice of His complete humanity, He should redeem the world. He displayed infinite patience when moved by grief; no protest escaped His lips; in the presence of His judges He offered no defence except when the divine nature of His mission expressly demanded it. Pilate could not rid himself of the guilt of the unjust sentence passed upon Christ, by a mere meaningless gesture of the washing of hands, for he had already openly stated that he could find no wrong in the man who stood before him.

The priesthood of Christ discovered in Christ Himself the victim for the sacrifice which was to be offered for all mankind, and in that sacred moment before the commencement of His passion, in the upper chamber where the Last Supper took place, He stripped this sacrifice of all its temporal and transitory qualities, in order that it might be continued everywhere and for all time, in memory of the Man whose Body was given and whose Blood was shed for the remission of our sins. According to the prophecy of Isaias, His hands and feet were to be pierced, and upon His vesture lots were to be cast. And so it was.

7. Christ never spoke of His passion and His death without referring at the same time also to His resurrection. "From that time onward," we read in the Gospel of St. Matthew, "Jesus began to make it known to His disciples that He must go up to Jerusalem, and there, with much ill usage from the

[30] Luke 24, 26.

chief priests and elders and scribes, must be put to death, and rise again on the third day."

And further on again: "While they were still together in Galilee, Jesus told them, The Son of Man is to be given up into the hands of men. They will put Him to death, and He will rise again on the third day. And they were overcome with sorrow."

And once more: "And now Jesus was going up to Jerusalem and He took His twelve disciples aside on the way, and warned them, 'Now we are going up to Jerusalem and there the Son of Man will be given up into the hands of the chief priests and scribes, who will condemn Him to death. And these will give Him up into the hands of the gentiles, to be mocked and scourged and crucified; but on the third day He will rise again'."

And indeed it is to be noticed that each of the four Evangelists, after telling the story of the Crucifixion, commences a new chapter in which is recorded for ever the glorious miracle of the Resurrection, in order that all might know that Jesus had finally overcome death, and continued in triumph the establishment and the spread of the eternal, and everlasting Kingdom of God.

In this way did Jesus Christ fulfil all the predictions of the prophets.

II. THE MIRACLES WORKED BY CHRIST

What is a Miracle?

Not everything, by any means, which cannot be explained is called a miracle. We live habitually amid inexplicable phenomena. Who can sound all the depths of the forces of Nature? Even when we have made a formula to explain their activities, we still have not fathomed them. What are Matter, Energy, Motion, Space and Time? What, if it comes to that, is existence itself? What is the difference between a possible Being, and the same Being when it becomes reality? These things are mysteries. Whoever looks round the world of Nature, cannot but be filled with a constant sense of wonder. Only the fool asks himself no questions.

But these inexplicable phenomena are not miracles, because in virtue of their nature and constitution they fit harmoniously into creation, such as it left the hands of God. The way in which the earth draws everything towards its centre is certainly inexplicable; but we must admit that it would be even more inexplicable if it ceased to do so.

Now the peculiarity of a miracle is that it cannot be explained by the existing laws of Nature, nor, for that matter, by those laws still unknown. This latter statement may sound strange, for it is always possible to assert that a miracle of to-day will be exposed later on as a perfectly natural happening. This has, in fact, repeatedly occurred in the course of history. The science of medicine, for instance, is nowadays so far advanced, that not everybody who manages to cure a patient of headache by the imposition of hands is to be venerated for life as a miracle-worker.

Still, there are limits to everything. When Christ stilled a raging storm with a single gesture, one can hardly plead as explanation a storm-stilling law of Nature—which moreover only becomes effective at a gesture from Christ and not of anyone else who might happily try it. In the same way the multiplication of the loaves and fishes, the raising of the dead, and especially the resurrection of Christ Himself, can in no wise be attributed to laws the discovery of which still lies in the future. It is always a reasonable principle not to try to explain a difficult thing by one still more difficult (*explicare obscura per obscurius*).

Consequently a miracle can be defined as a perceptible fact which cannot be explained by the laws of Nature, and which is therefore to be attributed to a direct intervention of God.

This divine intervention is usually the more apparent owing to the religious setting in which the miracle takes place (in places of devotion, for instance; through the intermediary of outstandingly pious persons; by the exercise of prayer and faith, etc.). This does not mean that the miracle is an actual infringement of an existing law of nature. The law continues to exist but, in some marvellous way, God who is, after all, the creator and supreme master of all the laws of nature, arranges that these do not operate on this particular occasion, nor have their customary effect. Normally, as an example, fire will by its composition consume any inflammable material, yet God may interpose some strong but impalpable screen which effectually neutralizes the consuming activity. Both the flame and the inflammable material retain their properties, but the anticipated effect does not follow. God is the free, almighty First Cause, on whom alone depends the *application* of the necessary laws of nature, while He Himself is not bound by any law of nature whatsoever.

Because the miracle can only take place by God's special intervention, it is a particularly suitable tool in His hand when considered as evidence in favour of a person or a doctrine. God cannot grant support through a miracle to either a cheat or an imposter, a deluded dreamer, or indeed to error in any form.

That is why strange phenomena are always a little suspect when occurring in a non-religious, occult, or in any way hysterical milieu. God is infinite truth and holiness, and He will not sanction anything which is not altogether true and altogether holy.

Let us now pass to the consideration of the miraculous powers of Jesus.

One has only to glance through the Gospels to realize that they attribute to Jesus Christ miraculous powers so efficacious, so vast, and so varied, that no other person in history is to be compared with Him. Usually these miracles contain in themselves striking evidence of His divine mission for the salvation of mankind. The blind, the paralysed, cripples, those suffering from fever, those possessed, are completely healed by the imposition of His hands, by a mere word or gesture. Nature also obeys His least command: the fig-tree withers, the storm abates, water is changed into wine, and beneath His hands raised in blessing a few loaves and fishes become enough to feed thousands. His power even penetrates into the unseen world of eternity: three times the Evangelists tell us that He raised the dead to life. And, further still, He worked the greatest miracle of all: after a terrible death upon the cross, after three long days in the sepulchre, He rose again from the dead by His own inherent power, and for forty days remained, with a glorified Body, among His disciples on earth.

These miracles should not be regarded merely as facts. They are far more than that. Taken in conjunction with the prophecies, with the inspired teaching of Christ Himself, and with the utterly spiritual character of His personality, they form a chain of indisputable evidence that here once more God intervened supernaturally in the history of mankind by sending His own Son as ambassador upon a divine mission. If one were to take one isolated miracle such as, for example, the curing of a sick person, it is true that the suspicion of suggestion, of hallucination of the onlookers, or of the agency of some then undiscovered law of nature might arise. But regarded as part of a great and consistent whole—the age-long prophecies about the Christ, His marvellous personality and enduring teaching, the kingdom which He founded and which has continued for two thousand years already—in such a setting a miracle gains *significance*: it becomes almost a matter of course and it would, one feels, be even strange if such a Person had not possessed a supernatural power placing Him altogether above Nature.

Moreover, according to the prophecies, the Messiah *was* to work miracles, and they were needed to furnish corroboratory evidence of His teaching. The miracles, therefore, were usually worked as a reward for the faith of a sick person, or to demonstrate to the onlookers that Jesus was indeed the Messiah. So He raised Lazarus from the dead "for the sake of the multitude that is standing round, that they may learn to believe that it is Thou who hast sent me".[31] Nicodemus, the Pharisee, said to Him: "Master, we know that Thou hast come from God to teach us; no one, unless God were with Him, could do the miracles which Thou doest".[32] And after the miracle of the loaves, the spectators exclaimed: "Beyond doubt, this is the prophet who is to come into the world."[33]

The miracles of Christ are entirely different from the demonstrations of witchcraft, the inexplicable apparitions associated with spiritualistic mediums, or the illusions which a skilful *fakir* can so easily produce. The miracles of Christ are *intelligent*. They are done, as we pointed out before, with a reasonable and normal aim in view, such as the proof of a divine mission, the healing of the sick, or the fulfilment of a prophecy. There is no question of sensational surroundings, ghostly appearances, materializations in a semi-dark room and an astral spirit who, for a consideration, will undertake to disclose the future.

We do not deny that some people may possess faculties such as clairvoyance or telepathy, but if one separates the actual phenomenon from the air of mystery with which it is usually surrounded, one will find that nothing remains but a natural gift—still largely unexplained at the present time. This gift of clairvoyance is not, however, as in the case of Jesus Christ, the outcome of a divine and supernatural personality, nor of a world-mission of redemption and faith.

With Christ the miracle was always incidental. Had His life and His teaching not been just as wonderful as His deeds, these latter would never have convinced. But the phenomena of His miracles, the sudden cures, the returns from death, the commands obeyed by nature, were the work of one whose ethics were unimpeachable. With the miraculous powers at

[31] John 2, 42. [32] John 3, 2. [33] John 6, 14.

His disposal He could have built Himself a palace of unexampled luxury, but He preferred to be poor: "Foxes have holes, and the birds of the air their resting-place, but the Son of Man has nowhere to lay His head."[34]

Christ always acted with a sympathetic, transparent sincerity. There was no playing to the gallery for Him, neither was there any trace of the typical fanatic, swept along by the force of his own ideas. Christ was never caught into the current of any stream: always He dominated. He dominated Himself; He dominated the crowd held under the spell of His words; He even dominated by His acute reasoning, the Scribes who tried to catch Him in the net of His own words. He stood up for right with uncompromising honesty. He called King Herod a sly fox, and His indictment of the Scribes and Pharisees, who laid heavy burdens upon the backs of the people and would not so much stir a finger to lift them again, is magnificent in its form: "Woe upon you, scribes and pharisees, you hypocrites that are like whitened sepulchres, fair in outward show, when they are full of dead men's bones and all manner of corruption within."

He is not a man who worked fraudulent miracles to obtain renown, or gain some high position, money or popularity. When commanding a *natural* power to obey His orders, we always find that the ultimate purpose is of an infinitely higher character: to demonstrate to man some entirely *supernatural* faculty or force.

It would be obviously superfluous, and even a little impertinent, to remind ourselves that Christ had a strong personality, were it not that so many representations of Him portray only the other side of His character. Everyone is familiar with the tasteless plaster casts, the insipid engravings, in which He is represented as a kind but mild figure. On the contrary, Christ knew no weakness. His whole life spoke of an enormous and essential strength, a spiritual equilibrium never shaken even amidst the greatest enterprises and dangers. He did not only bless little children but also drove the buyers and sellers from the temple and overturned the tables of the pigeon-vendors. To the curiosity of Herod, who held, humanly speaking, His life in his hands, He returned no word; and to the high priest who condemned Him He only addressed a calm warning of the retribution of God. How

[34] Matt. 8, 20.

often He took the part of the oppressed, and those outcast, against hypocrisy and violence!

Christ suffered from neither self-deception nor hallucination. He never for a moment lost sight of reality. In order to grasp this, one has only to read the magnificent parables with which the story of the Gospel is interwoven.

For these parables He chose the setting of everyday life with its quiet poetry. He painted word-pictures of birds and flowers, of ripening corn, of fishing boats on the lake, of flowing water, and the peasant as he sowed his fields. Striking pictures, easily understood by simple souls and bringing into view the tender love of the creator: the wealth, and the grace and the beauty of the Kingdom of God.

Here spoke the man who was mindful of reality even when reality was hidden from the eyes of other men. He could not talk in the language of the earthly realist, who is content to spend his life among visible, tangible things. His was the enormous task of bringing home to men, for the first time, unrevealed mysteries, deep hidden in the infinite nature of God. Yet this made Him no idle dreamer. There is an essential difference between the man who looks into the unseen, and the dreamer who merely drowns in the fantasies of his own imagination. Both may be difficult for the ordinary man to follow, but while the fantast becomes confused in the end by his own conceptions, the man of God held fast to the truth of which He was unceasingly aware. The dreamer inevitably fails, while the Man of God succeeded in spite of the opposition of the whole world. There is a Church two thousand years old to bear witness to that.

The fantast is non-social; he places himself outside the community. Christ is for ever the unsurpassed example of social charity which even Marxist atheists admire. His charity was not tainted by either the fanaticism of the democratic revolutionary nor the weakness of the emotional man. He was not the conventional "benefactor" to whom the poor were merely so many names on a relief-list and who had His alms distributed by servants at the door. It was the actual *person* of the poor, of the sick and of the sinner, which claimed His compassion. He did not put His love into the hand but into the heart of man.

When therefore a personality so wise, so sincere, so altogether harmonious and gracious, displays an unprecedented miraculous power, and when moreover this power is only used in a reasonable way, as confirmation of a divine mission; then, taken in conjunction with the age-long prophecies which preceded Him, and the two-thousand-year-old Church which still proclaims the reign of His Kingdom upon earth, we may safely assume that in Him we have a man whose teaching is believable beyond all doubt. This Man assured us that He is the Son of God and that He has come to earth to establish a kingdom. What follows? Surely that we repeat, with complete and humble confidence, those words once spoken by the child Samuel: "Speak on, Lord, thy servant is listening."

CHAPTER III

THE KINGDOM OF THE MESSIAH

SYNOPSIS

I. God has created us and is Lord of all mankind, therefore we are obliged to serve Him.
Now it should be sufficient to live according to the natural law which God has put into our hearts.
Instead of this, however, He has revealed that He desires to be served in a particular way, as we shall now endeavour to prove.

II. There exists a book, the Bible, the text of which is over two thousand years old, and this text has been authentically handed down to us. From this book it is clear that the Jewish people themselves were convinced that they had been chosen by God to prepare the way for the future Messiah. Many actual prophecies concerning the Messiah are contained in this same book.

III. Undoubtedly a Man has been born in whom all these prophecies have been fulfilled and who confirmed His divine mission by miracles: that is Jesus of Nazareth.
That He actually existed clearly follows from the testimony of pagan, Jewish and Christian authors. The Gospels, which tell the story of His life, unquestionably appear to be authentic books written either by apostles, disciples or actual eye-witnesses.

IV. We shall now set out to prove that the prophecies as to the *Kingdom of the Messiah* are equally true.

JESUS HAS SPOKEN. During three memorable years He climbed the hills of Palestine, turned downwards again and threaded His way in and out of the valleys, passed through towns and hamlets, and made occasional appearances in village synagogues and in the forecourt of the temple at Jerusalem. For three years, in the cool of the Eastern mornings, in sweltering midday heats, and sometimes till late into the night, He spoke to the people of His Kingdom.

His language was at once lofty and yet simple; He did not enter into details, nor indulge in speculation, as later His apostles and their followers were to do. It was for Him to lay the foundations only: He was the founder.

§ 1. *The Preaching of the Kingdom*

When Christ spoke of His Kingdom, or of God's Kingdom (both expressions are used), He meant the great family of which God Himself is the only Source, and into which men may be born as children of God. "A man cannot see the Kingdom of God without being born anew."[1] Let us listen to Our Lord's own words: "This Son of Man must be lifted up (on the cross) so that those who believe in Him may not perish, but have eternal life. God so loved the world, that He gave up his only begotten Son, so that those who believe in Him may not perish, but have eternal life. When God sent His Son into the world, it was not to reject the world, but so that the world might find salvation through Him."[2]

This was the great adventure of Christ: the founding of the Kingdom of God on earth, and the plan of its ultimate expansion, so that men might find their salvation, even here below, through participation in the eternal life of God. An adventure, because this Kingdom was to take root in the soil of our earth, and yet not to be of this earth nor of the world: an adventure because it had to be planted and to grow among weak and fallible men, amongst corruption and weeds, whilst slowly lifting its branches and its flowers towards the blue of Heaven above. "Here is an image of the Kingdom of Heaven. There was a man who sowed his field with clean seed; but while all the world was asleep, an enemy of his came and scattered tares among the wheat, and was gone."[3]

Christ did not come to earth to present us with the Kingdom of God already complete and in its entirety. In Him it had its beginning, but it had slowly to grow to proportions which could include the whole of mankind. Through all the ages which have followed, the prayer of the Christian has always been, and will always be: "Thy Kingdom Come." This Kingdom of God is "like a grain of mustard seed, that a man has taken and sown in his ground; of all seeds, none is so little, but when it grows up it is greater than any garden herb; it grows into a tree, so that all the birds come and settle in its branches. And He told them still another parable, The Kingdom of Heaven is like leaven, that a woman has taken and buried away in three measures of meal, enough to leaven the whole batch."[4]

[1] John 3, 3. [2] John 3, 15-17. [3] Matt. 13, 24-25. [4] Matt. 13, 31-35.

Christ spoke with the deepest love of His Kingdom. We learn from Him that to obtain it is worth every endeavour, for it is precious, "like a treasure hidden in a field; a man has found it and hidden it again, and now, for the joy it gives him, is going home to sell all that he has and buy that field. Again, the Kingdom of Heaven is as if a trader were looking for rare pearls: and now he has found one pearl of great cost, and has sold all that he had and bought it".[5]

This Kingdom appears to be worth more than anything else in the world. That is to say, our association with God, and with each other in Christ, surpasses in value everything which the world itself can offer. It rises far above it. "My Kingdom does not belong to this world," said Jesus.[6] It is a spiritual and not a political world, in the same way that the sovereignty of Christ is a spiritual sovereignty. As the papal Encyclical *Quas primas* tells us: "The Gospels present this Kingdom as one which men prepare to enter by penance, and cannot actually enter except by faith and by baptism, which, though an external rite, signifies and produces an interior regeneration. This Kingdom is opposed to none other than to that of Satan and to the power of darkness. It demands of its subjects a spirit of detachment from riches and earthly things, and a spirit of gentleness. They must hunger and thirst after justice, and, more than this, they must deny themselves and carry the cross."

In order to understand still more clearly the entirely spiritual character of the Kingdom of God, we have only to turn to the fifth chapter of the Gospel of St. Matthew, in which are recorded the words of Our Lord as, sitting upon the mountain-side, He first outlined to His followers the main principles of its essentially supernatural structure.

In this Christendom, we have inherited a living community: a spiritual as well as a visible community. It is perforce visible since it is made up of men, and since it is ruled by men in the name of Christ, and uses visible means by which to accomplish its work.

At the very commencement of Christ's mission upon earth we see that He was consistently moving towards *the formation of a community*. He did not remain aloof, but from the beginning gathered around Him a little group of men, later to be called His apostles. They journeyed with Him along

[5] Matt. 13, 44-46. [6] John 18, 36.

the roads of Palestine, and during His sermons formed the nucleus of an unfailing audience; they stayed with Him, listening still, when, after having preached far into the evening, He continued with further explanations, the unriddling of many parables, and the advice which was so very necessary for the practice of this new perfection. In reality He was giving them a particular and most careful training, and it became more and more obvious that He had special intentions regarding these twelve men. They received, as it were, mandates. If they followed Christ they were to become "fishers of men". They were to be the salt of the earth and their light was to shine before men. They were to become labourers in the field of Christ's great harvest, and He "gave them authority to cast out unclean spirits, and to heal every kind of disease and infirmity".[7] He Himself chose them and specifically mentioned them. "These are the names of the twelve apostles: first, Simon, also called Peter, then his brother Andrew, James the son of Zebedee and his brother John, Philip and Bartholomew, Thomas and Matthew the publican, James the son of Alphaeus, and Thaddaeus, Simon the Cananean, and Judas Iscariot, the traitor."[8]

These twelve were sent out by Christ with the words: "And preach as you go, telling them, The Kingdom of Heaven is at hand . . . and wherever they will not receive you or listen to your words, shake off the dust from your feet as you leave that city or that house; I promise you it shall go less hard with the land of Sodom and Gomorrha at the day of judgment than with that city. . . . And you will be brought before governors and kings on My account, so that you can bear witness before them, and before the Gentiles. Only, when they hand you over thus, do not consider anxiously what you are to say or how you are to say it; words will be given you when the time comes; it is not you who speak, it is the spirit of your Father that speaks in you."[9] The apostles therefore understood that they were to carry on the work of Christ in His own name and by His own power.

§ 2. *The Foundation of the Kingdom*

As we read the Gospels we shall see clearly that Christ did not intend His spiritual Kingdom to be altogether invisible.

[7] Matt. 10, 1. [8] Matt. 10, 2-4. [9] Matt. 10, 7-21.

The most beautiful element in it certainly was to remain the inner relationship between God and man, the attitude of the child—accepted both by faith and baptism—to his Father in Heaven. But in order to preserve this relationship for all future generations, and to safeguard the very means by which it was established and strengthened, He appointed dignitaries with particular and visible authority. The first of these were the twelve apostles (eleven after the death of Judas). But Christ knew that sooner or later these apostles would have to die, while His Kingdom was to continue to exist until His last coming, and meanwhile to expand and spread all over the world. How, then, was this Kingdom, which He also called *ecclesia* (i.e. community, Church), to continue both to preserve and to teach the truth which was enshrined within it? The answer was: Under the leadership of a permanent teaching Authority, as we shall now further explain.

It was an important moment when, just before the Ascension of Our Lord, He unfolded in detail the scheme for the future of His Church, which we shall henceforth call His Kingdom. The core of this last conversation which He had with "the eleven" has been recorded by Matthew, who was present at it, in the following words: "All authority, in heaven and on earth, has been given to Me; you, therefore, must go out, making disciples of all nations, and baptizing them in the name of the Father, and of the Son, and of the Holy Ghost, teaching them to observe all the commandments which I have given you. And behold I am with you all through the days that are coming, until the consummation of the world."[10]

It is obvious that on this occasion Christ was not speaking to all His followers indiscriminately, but to an élite, *the* eleven, whom He had gradually trained with the tenderest love and care during the three years of His ministry to become, in due time, the leaders and dignitaries of the new Church. We see, as it were, standing there before Him as He spoke, the *living authority* of that future Church, whom He solemnly installed in office now that He, the Founder, was about to return to His Father.

If we consider these words attentively, we shall inevitably be led to the conclusion that Jesus was here speaking over the heads, as it were, of the apostles actually present, to all the

[10] Matt. 28, 18-20.

future generations of ecclesiastical administrators who were to succeed them. For how else could it be possible for these eleven men, who would certainly be dead within a century, to teach all nations? Large portions of the world had not even been discovered at that time, and were not to be discovered until some thousand years later. Was it indeed, then, these particular men who were to bring the faith to the Mongols, the Sioux-Indians of America, and the natives of New Guinea, or was it to their successors that Christ was speaking? In the same way when He promised to be with them until the consummation of the world, the word "you" must necessarily refer equally to a teaching authority of any century—the second, twentieth, or the last century of human history.

We must admit that this is precisely the type of instruction given to the members of any administrative or governing body in a newly established society. The rules laid down and suggestions made, are intended to ensure that the first officials shall give a correct lead to all the administrators of the future.

We can therefore only draw the following conclusions from the parting words of Christ: He appointed the apostles to form the nucleus of a recognized teaching authority in the Church, and He intended that this authority should continue for the instruction of *all nations at all times.*

"And behold I am with you all through the days that are coming, until the consummation of the world." This single sentence explained the miracle which was about to take place. Eleven men, most of them with the education of no more than peasants or fishermen, whose natural capabilities would scarcely have sufficed to organize a village-community, commenced to lay the foundations of a world-empire. They brought to the task a Truth of which, up to now, even the most brilliant theologian has not succeeded in fathoming the full depth, and after two thousand years, the only hope of the world, if it is to be saved from ruin and destruction, lies in the doctrine which they first taught.

After Christ's Ascension they possessed indeed the power, but not as yet the opportunity, to commence their great mission. For, immediately preceding the Ascension, we are told: "And now He (Christ) gave them orders, as He shared a meal with them, not to leave Jerusalem, but to wait there for the fulfilment of the Father's promise. You have heard it, He said, from My own lips; John's baptism, I told you, was with water, but there is a baptism with the Holy Spirit which you are to receive, not many days from this. . . . Enough for you, that the Holy Spirit will come upon you, and you will receive strength from Him; you are to be My witnesses in Jerusalem and throughout Judea, in Samaria, yea, and to the ends of the earth."[11] (Once more we seem to become aware of that rapid glance into the future!)

So they went back to Jerusalem to await the coming of the Holy Ghost. They were gathered together as usual, with Mary the Mother of Jesus and about a hundred others, in the great upper room which they occupied in the city, when Peter performed the first act which denoted his authority: he drew attention to the necessity of filling the vacant place left by Judas Iscariot. A disciple named Matthias was accordingly chosen as the twelfth apostle.[12]

The next week must have been one of extraordinary tension for these followers of Christ. Their belief in the coming of the promised "Helper" had now become invincible. Their burning conviction as to the mission which had been entrusted to them, combined with their southern temperament, must have filled them with a longing desire for activity; yet how could they hope to succeed in their preaching to a people which so far had not been willing to acknowledge either the intellect or the authority of their Master? First, something fresh had obviously to happen, and Holy Scripture tells us the story of that happening.

"When the days of Pentecost came round, while they were all gathered together in unity of purpose, all at once a sound came from heaven like that of a strong wind blowing, which filled the whole house where they were sitting. Then appeared to them what seemed to be tongues of fire, which parted and came to rest on each of them; and they were all filled with the Holy Spirit, and began to speak in strange languages, as the Spirit gave utterance to each."[13]

One need not be a poet or a visionary in order to see in this first Whitsun-Fire a symbol of the light which was never again to leave the Church. It was at this moment that the Spirit of God assumed the guidance of the whole structure of the newly born Christian community: it was thus that the tiny kernel of faith which formed its centre was to increase and grow into an immense supernatural power, so that the

[11] Acts 1, 4-8. [12] Acts 1, 14-26. [13] Acts 2, 1-4.

parables of the mustard seed and the leaven should in truth be realized.

It would seem that this coming of the Holy Ghost caused some sort of a stir in the neighbouring streets, so that a great crowd collected, and once more it was Peter, with the eleven standing beside him, who addressed his first formal instruction to the people of Jerusalem. This speech evidently became famous among the early Christians, for thirty years later Luke was still able to collect enough details of its wording to give an extensive report of it.[14] It was delivered in fiery sentences, spoken at a distance of only a quarter of an hour's walk from Golgotha and seven weeks after the Crucifixion and the Resurrection, by a man in whose soul the light of the Holy Ghost had just for the first time shone. It is not to be wondered at that on this first Whit-Sunday about three thousand souls were baptized.[15]

Every year the Church celebrates the remembrance of this day which, together with Easter, ranks as the greatest feast; and in the liturgy of the Mass one still feels the stir of the Holy Ghost which, ever since, has continued to reach us as "a sound from heaven like that of a strong wind blowing".

From then on, Peter and the other apostles began to preach the doctrine of Christ, and to organize and extend *the visible Christian community*. From their conduct it would appear that they were fully conscious of their authority to teach and of the mission to *found* with which they had been entrusted. One need only read through the Acts and the Epistles of the Apostles to become convinced of this. Let us consider one single fact a little more closely.

Paul of Tarsus, who began by persecuting the newly born Church, became later on, by the grace of God, an apostle himself, and strongly resisted the demands of some of the Jewish Christians at Antioch, that converted Gentiles should also be circumcised. Paul decided to go to Jerusalem with his companion Barnabas and a few others, in order to consult the apostles and the ancients (presbuteroi, or presbyters, from which is derived our word priest). At this first formal Church-Council, as one might perhaps call it, Peter stood up and began: "Brethren, you know well enough how from early days it has been God's choice that the Gentiles should hear the message of the Gospel from my lips, and so learn to

[14] Acts 2, 14-37. [15] Acts 2, 41.

believe."[16] (He referred to a vision which he had had from God, see Acts 2.) He then went on to announce his decision that circumcision was not a matter of necessity, after which we have the very remarkable and significant comment: "Then the whole company kept silence."[17]

We have already repeatedly seen that Peter took the lead even in the presence of other apostles. In this connection countless other passages of Scripture become significant, as for instance those in which the apostles are enumerated: Peter is always mentioned first. (Matt. 10, 2; Mark 3, 16; Luke 16, 14; Acts 1, 13.) Matthew even uses this opening: "These are the names of the twelve apostles; first, Simon also called Peter." When a particular group of people is enumerated in a purely arbitrary way, it is not usual to begin with the word "first". Why, then, should it be done in this case? The answer is surely simple enough: because Christ Himself had appointed Peter as head of the future Church. It is now our task to prove this even more conclusively.

At His very first meeting with this apostle, Jesus, we are told, "looked at him closely, and said, Thou art Simon the son of Jona; thou shalt be called Cephas" (which means the same as Peter) i.e. rock.[18] At that time this name may have sounded strange, but later the meaning became obvious to all.

One day, when Jesus was alone with His apostles, He asked them (it would seem with some little anxiety): "What do men say of the Son of Man? Who do they think He is?" From their reply it was evident that the Jews had only the vaguest idea that Jesus was indeed an actual person at all. "Some say John the Baptist, they told Him, others Elias, others again Jeremias or one of the prophets." No doubt Jesus shook His head at each of these strange guesses, but apparently they were of no great interest to Him. His question had only been a prelude to one far more important: "And what of you? Who do you say that I am?"[19]

It must have been a memorable moment: the apostles were seemingly struck dumb for a time at this question, while Jesus scanned their faces, waiting for the reply. Then there stepped forward the man whose impulsive temperament was ever the readiest to respond to his Master—Simon, the son of Jona. And, for the first time, Jesus heard Himself fully recognized

[16] Acts 15, 7.
[17] Acts 15, 12.
[18] John 1, 42.
[19] Matt. 16, 13-15.

and acknowledged: "Thou art the Christ, the Son of the Living God."[20]

To this formal declaration of His divine mission—although Simon Peter had not had it revealed to him by ordinary means but by the Father in heaven—Jesus wished to return an equally solemn reply, with which was perhaps mingled a certain gratitude: "And I tell thee this in My turn, that thou art Peter (rock) and it is upon this rock that I will build my Church."[21]

He then continued: "The gates of hell shall not prevail against it; and I will give to thee the keys of the kingdom of heaven; and whatever thou shalt bind on earth shall be bound in heaven, and whatever thou shalt loose on earth shall be loosed in heaven."[22]

This phrase, mentioned in all manuscripts, is in itself a sure rock. Whoever reads it honestly and without prejudice, must surely admit that it confers a very particular dignity upon Peter, and furthermore that, by these words, a special function is granted and promised to him, which is decisive for the future government of the Church. This Church is to rest upon a single foundation; it is not a democracy but, among—yet above—all other ecclesiastical dignitaries there is finally to be one in whom the highest governing power is vested. We will now go even further into those important words which we have just quoted.

Christ was a supreme master of figurative language, and He knew the sensitive appreciation of the Jewish people for this type of phrasing. Where the matter-of-fact theologian would have expressed himself in a reasoned definition, He searched for an illustration from actual surroundings, and so made a picture of His meaning to place, as it were, before the eyes of his audience. In this particular case He called Peter a rock, and every Jew knew by experience that there was no more solid foundation. Christ employed this figure of speech purposely and with a special meaning.

We may recall that in a former parable He had made use of the expression: "and the rain fell and the floods came and the winds blew and beat upon that house, but it did not fall; it was founded upon rock".[23] It is obvious, therefore, that "rock", in such figurative language, symbolizes an unshakable, lasting foundation.

[20] Matt. 16, 16. [21] Matt. 16, 18. [22] Matt. 16, 19. [23] Matt. 7, 25.

1. *Unshakable.* It is remarkable that Christ did not point to Himself as the base of the new community or Church, but to the man, Peter. This is only comprehensible so long as we are speaking on the human level and are concerned with the actual Christian community itself and its organization. Of the revelation of the Christian Faith, He Himself remained the only rock, as Paul was to teach later on. But Peter, the man, was meanwhile given a function by which he was raised above all the other apostles, and above the ordinary members of the Church. He became the head, the leader, who was never to waver. When dangers threatened, when the rain fell in torrents and a storm sprang up, the Christian community was to have complete confidence in him. In moments of dissension or discord, in any doubt or uncertainty, one, unshakable as the rocks of Judea, was destined to be the support of the whole Church: Peter. The later words of the Master to this apostle fit equally well into the same pattern: "Simon, Simon, behold, Satan has claimed power over you all, so that he can sift you like wheat" (this means try your faith). Then, to Peter alone, and in the singular: "But I have prayed for thee, that thy faith may not fail; when, after a while, thou hast come back to Me, it is for thee to be the support of thy brethren."[24]

And, once again, when Peter had indeed come back, and Christ had asked him three times for a declaration of his love, He added: "Feed My lambs; tend My shearlings; feed My sheep."[25] So he became the shepherd of the whole flock.

Would it not indeed be unthinkable that this man should be allowed to lead the entire Church into error? Is it not reasonable to suppose that, in matters of Faith, when he is speaking for the whole Church, he cannot possibly err, and that consequently he is *infallible*? If this were not so, then the rock would lose all its strength and the house built upon it inevitably collapse. Were it not so, he would lead the flock forward to irretrievable ruin and destruction.

If we are in doubt, we have only to ask Christ Himself upon whom the Church is resting? He will answer us thus: "Did I not tell you clearly that My Church is founded upon Peter? As the temple at Jerusalem rose upwards upon Mount Sion, so the Church of Christ rises upwards on Mount Peter: unshakable. And it is more possible for Mount Sion to sink

[24] Luke 22, 31-32. [25] John 21, 15-17.

below the level of the ground than for the foundation of Christ's building to be removed. 'The gates of hell shall not prevail against it.'"

2. The latter words illustrate vividly the *everlasting* property of rock: so long as the gates of hell shall last, the rock shall resist them. Of what use would it be to the Church to have a rock, and a shepherd and a leader, if they were all to disappear after a few decades? Does Christ desire to abandon His Church to hell? Surely if this were the case, He would not have pointed to the indestructible rocks which bestrewed the mountain-side, but would have used a simile suggesting a more temporary support.

Do not let anyone make the objection that, after Peter, it was the Holy Ghost who was to guide the Church. At Pentecost the Holy Ghost was already guiding the Church, and guiding Peter, and Peter passed his whole life under the very special protection of the Holy Spirit. The point at issue is the visible organization of the Christian Church under one head, and no reason whatever can be found to suggest that that organization was meant to disappear after the death of Peter. There is no more reason to suppose such a thing than there is to suppose that material rocks will disappear suddenly from the face of the earth. As we said before, Christ spoke to Peter as one speaks to the president of any association; a particular name may be mentioned, but in reality one is speaking to all the successors of the person addressed. This is not so much a question of a man as a question of an *office*. So, just as Christ spoke, as it were, over the heads of the apostles to all the missionaries of future ages when He told them to go and preach to all nations until the consummation of time, so He spoke over the head of Peter, to all his successors, the Popes: "You are the rock upon which My Church has been built: the gates of hell shall not prevail against it."

The contention that Christ did not speak anywhere of a transfer of Peter's power is wholly untenable. This is not a case of the dead letter of the Law but of the living spirit behind Christ's thought. In the concrete image "rock" the abstract "everlasting" is included, and since Peter was bound to die eventually, and nobody could suppose that he would not, his power could not but be transferred if it were to endure. Christ, it is true, did not say this in so many words, but He said it over and over again by inferences and by the use of similes. To the Eastern mind such similes and illustrations were far more telling and comprehensible than any number of dry formulæ.

History, at all events, confirms the Catholic thesis, for what, in effect, has happened? In his later years, Peter set out for Rome. For a long time the stay of Peter at Rome was disputed, but gradually the historical evidence became so convincing that many modern protestants, among them von Harnack, found it necessary to revise their opinion.

It is now universally accepted that this apostle suffered martyrdom at Rome under the Emperor Nero in the year either A.D. 64 or 67. It is not to be expected that a college of cardinals was immediately found to nominate a successor. As is usually the case during the infancy of any new society or community, the actual administrative details have to be worked out bit by bit; Peter's primacy had not as yet been fully defined theologically, and it is probable that, when he foresaw his own death, he merely indicated his successor without further formalities. What is quite clear is that the names of his successors have all been preserved, and that the first two were Linus and Cletus. The list of the Popes is of great antiquity, for there are many traces of it even before the year A.D. 200.

No actual writings of these first two successors, or popes, have been preserved, and therefore there are no authentic witnesses to the exercise, in practice, of their supreme power. But we possess a remarkable letter of the successor of Cletus, that is of Clement, from which it is clearly obvious that this Bishop of Rome was conscious of a definite right of decision over the other bishops. The letter is universally agreed to be of about the year A.D. 96, or thirty years after the death of Peter. It was addressed to the community of Corinth, and is accepted as authentic by modern protestants such as von Harnack.

Now at Corinth a serious irregularity had arisen. Some of the younger members of the Christian community had dismissed the older dignitaries and taken their places, giving great scandal. The remarkable thing, however, was that neither the apostle John, who was living at Ephesus, nor the head of any other Greek community, raised his voice in official protest, but it was left to the successor of Peter to call the

Corinthian community to order with authoritative, if affectionate words: "If, indeed, there are some who will not listen to what He (Jesus Christ) has said through us, let them bear in mind that they will come to sin and great danger."

This letter was read out to the Corinthian community for many years, as one of their later bishops, Dionysius, A.D. 170, has told us, and the resemblance to a present-day papal decree cannot but be apparent.

There are many more instances which could be quoted from the early Christian days serving to demonstrate the undoubted special place accorded to Rome and its Bishop. There is the strikingly respectful beginning of a letter written by Bishop Ignatius to Rome about the year A.D. 110; again, the voyage, undertaken by Polycarp of Smyrna, a disciple of St. John, to Rome in order to ask for a settlement of the dispute which had arisen as to the date of Easter; once more, the appeal of Irenaeus, a disciple of this same Polycarp, to Rome regarding heretics: "On account of its more authoritative and prominent position, it is essential that, with this Church, all other Churches should agree."

Such facts as these are very simply explained if one accepts the major fact that the successors of Peter in Rome fulfilled the task of leading the Church, and on the other hand, they are quite inexplicable if with the death of Peter the whole foundation of that Church was intended to fall to the ground.

3. Not only the infallible guidance of the Holy Ghost was promised to Peter, but also the power of supreme government in the Church, which meant that he was not only to be the first and chief teacher, but was actually to wield final authority. Here once more Christ spoke by means of a parable.

In ancient days the *key* was of even more importance than it is now with us. It was a kind of hook, with which one could draw back the bolt, and it is obvious that the possession of the key thus represented a certain power. For example, with the surrender of a town, the keys of all the gates were ceremoniously handed over, and the head steward was the man who alone was allowed to open all doors and cupboards in the house.

From this one can gather exactly what Christ meant, when, on that solemn occasion, He said to Peter: "I will give thee the keys of the Kingdom of Heaven; and whatever thou shalt bind on earth shall be bound in heaven, and whatever thou shalt loose on earth shalt be loosed in heaven."

The Kingdom of Heaven is the kingdom with which we are dealing in the whole of this chapter: the Kingdom of God, the Church. It was over this Church that Peter received the supremacy. "Bind and loose" was a customary expression with the rabbis for "allow and forbid", and those apostles who were present on the occasion consequently heard, and were made aware, that the power of administering justice and government in general was placed in the hands of Peter. Is it to be wondered at, therefore, that his name is always mentioned first, and inevitably heads any list of the apostles; that, at the first formal meeting of the infant Church, it was Peter who spoke the decisive word, and that the See, or community, of Christians, in which he died (Rome) became the chief See and community in the Church?

Christ did not actually define it at this stage (or if He did, it is not noted down anywhere) but He granted the potential power, and as the years and centuries passed by, that power would inevitably develop according to the circumstances and the needs of the Church. In a following chapter we shall see how infallibility and supremacy came to be more precisely formulated. What was already established as a fact at this point was that Peter and his successors were to be the visible heads of the Church, and the substitute for that invisible Head, Jesus Christ.

Let us now turn once more to the apostles who, after receiving the tongues of Whitsun fire, spread out over the world to preach the Gospel, and by so doing, to lay enduring foundations for the everlasting Kingdom.

We have already seen that they felt themselves to be endowed with special authority, but what is of far greater importance is that they proceeded to appoint others to share that authority with them and to bear it after them.

It is not altogether easy to reconstruct from the Acts of the Apostles and from the Epistles, a distinct picture of the form of government in the earliest Christian communities. The Acts concentrate mainly upon the doings of Peter and Paul. The Epistles deal with subjects relevant at the time, but do not attempt to give a complete exposition of either doctrine or organization. Yet casual observations point in a certain direction as straws show which way the wind is blowing.

The Acts of the Apostles indicate a threefold structure in the government of the various Christian communities.

a. The highest dignitaries: the apostles, together with Paul and Barnabas.

b. We then read that Paul and Barnabas appointed elders by the laying on of hands,[26] and that Paul addressed the elders of Ephesus and Miletus with the following words: "Keep watch, then, over yourselves, and over God's Church, in which the Holy Spirit has made you bishops (over-seers); you are to be the shepherds of that flock which He won for Himself at the price of His own Blood."[27] From this it is evident that there existed a second group of lower dignitaries, the presbyters and the bishops, who were appointed by the apostles to rule the various communities.

c. Finally the Acts mention deacons, "men who are well spoken of, full of the Holy Spirit and of wisdom",[28] and who attended to the daily administration of charitable relief. Upon these the apostles also laid their hands, and among them were those who were to preach and baptize, such as Philip and Stephen.

The Epistles of Paul link up with all this information. In his epistle to the Thessalonians he begs them to "pay deference to those who work among you, those who have charge of you in the Lord, and give you directions; make it a rule of charity to hold them in special esteem, in honour of the duty they perform, and maintain unity with them".[29] In his epistle to the Philippians he greets the faithful with their "pastors and deacons".[30]

A clearer picture of the organization of the early Church may be derived from his epistles to Timothy and Titus. These two were his specially beloved children, to whom he frequently imparted the experience gained in his own ministry. He entrusted them—temporarily—with the highest offices in the government of the churches of Ephesus and Crete. Timothy was not elected, but appointed by him to live at Ephesus as governor of the College of Presbyters. Specially designated by prophecy, Timothy had received the grace of the priesthood by the imposition of hands, and later St. Paul also imposed his hands upon him.[31] Under the jurisdiction of the former, as well as that of Titus, were grouped

[26] Acts 14, 22. [27] Acts 20, 28. [28] Acts 6, 8 and 8, 5 and 38.
[29] I Thess. 5, 12-13. [30] Phil. 1, 1. [31] II Tim. 1, 6.

presbyters, bishops and deacons, of whom he had special charge. The bishops in particular were to be honoured, and should any of these be "living amiss" he was to reprove them openly.[32] Titus and Timothy were alone to be entrusted with the imposition of hands, but even so, they were not to bestow this grace rashly or without due consideration.[33]

St. Paul was the only shepherd of the immense diocese which he had won to faith in Christ. Titus, Timothy and others were his subordinates and governed the College of Presbyters. His churches were ruled by groups of clergy (presbyters and bishops) and ministered to by deacons under the immediate orders of his representatives.

From the letters of Ignatius it would appear that about 30 years after the death of St. Paul the expression "episcopos" (from which is derived our word bishop) had gained the day; it is from him also that we get the first clear definition of the three ascending degrees of the priesthood under the recognized designations of deacon, priest and bishop.

What is of great importance is the fact that the apostles definitely introduced and established functions within the Church, and there is no indication anywhere that these were to be abolished after their death. They were functions which necessitated the imposition of hands and which made great demands upon the recipients of them. "A special grace has been entrusted to thee," wrote Paul to Timothy, "prophecy awarded it, and the imposition of the presbyter's hands went with it; do not let it suffer from neglect."[34] The importance of their function is apparent from the fact that Peter put himself on a level with them (although there is, of course, a unique difference!). "And now I have a charge to give to the presbyters in your company; I who am a presbyter like themselves, I, who bear witness of Christ's sufferings, I, who have my part in that glory which will one day by revealed. Be shepherds to the flock God has given you."[35]

From the first days of the apostles, these functions have been handed down to successive generations. It is a wonderful thought for the young priest of to-day that the bishop who has just laid his hands upon him, ordaining him as a servant of the Church, in his turn received this imposition of hands from another bishop; and that the rite of ordination goes back two

[32] I Tim. 5, 17-21.
[33] I Tim. 5, 22.
[34] I Tim. 4, 14.
[35] I Pet. 5, 1-2.

thousand years, without interruption, to one of the apostles himself. This is the symbolical and unbroken chain which links our present ecclesiastical dignitaries and theologians with the eleven who received the command: "You, therefore, must go out, making disciples of all nations . . . and behold I am with you all through the days that are coming, until the consummation of the world."

§ 3. *The Final Conclusion*

We have now reached the end of the first part of our thesis. We have led the reader through the Messianic prophecies to the fulfilment of them in the person of Jesus Christ; then on to the completion of the foundation of the Church until, finally, we have reached the period in which the apostles appointed their successors, and not only preached their belief but sealed it with the blood of martyrdom. A young and burning Christianity had been born into history—one in its faith and its love.

But we shall find that throughout the following account of that Christianity, the treasure of its first faith has always had to be defended against aggressors, already beginning to make their presence felt even in the apostolic times. During the earlier centuries, the weed was only to be found growing occasionally amidst the wheat, but since the tenth century—and even more noticeably after the sixteenth—almost alarmingly big portions of Christianity have split off from the Mother Church. Perhaps more than ever at the present moment, the question is forced upon the modern man: "Where, in the midst of this torn Christendom, shall I find the Church that Christ intended?"

It is a matter of the greatest importance to grasp, first, the two following points:

1. That Church, which Christ intended, does still and in fact exist somewhere upon earth. Its Founder ascended to Heaven filled with the divine assurance that His Church would endure for ever. Men were never again to be without it, and it would rise among the nations as an everlasting trophy won for them by the crucified Saviour. Once again, has not Christ promised, "I am with you all through the days that are coming, until the consummation of the world"?

2. On the other hand, we are obliged to accept the fact

that there can be only one true Church, one sheepfold and one shepherd. That Shepherd Himself prayed, on the eve of his death: "That they too may be one in Us, as Thou, Father, art in Me, and I in Thee" (John 17, 21). He consequently willed that there should be no dissension in His Church, no collections of schools of thought, so that each one possessed indeed something good, but no one of them possessed the entire truth. That which He intended was clearly one single Church which should teach all those things which He had commanded, and which should be ruled by the administration which He Himself had unmistakably indicated and appointed "until the consummation of the world". In the foregoing chapter we have tried to show our reader this.

Where, then, amid all the dissensions, is that one true Church intended by Christ, to be found?

The conclusion is surely as simple as decisive:

The one true Church meant by Christ is the one which has ranged itself for ever under the banners of the successors of Peter and the Apostles: that is to say, under the Pope and the Bishops in union with Him.

It is the Church which stands upon that everlasting, unshakable rock.

IT IS THE CATHOLIC CHURCH.

§ 4. *Credo*

The foregoing pages undoubtedly point to one irrefutable conclusion. But does this therefore mean that anyone who has understood this first part of the book will, as a matter of course, bow his head in a thankful Credo? That, following the path of pure logic, one necessarily ends as a believing Catholic?

Not in the least. The foregoing chapters have merely been meant to serve as what is called the *apology*. We have tried to prove that commonsense can find no reasonable objection to the final conclusion towards which we are tending; but *belief* in the Catholic Church as the one desired by God, established by Christ, and through which *I* personally am to be sanctified, is something far above any logical conclusion; it is the complete acceptance of a world which is, humanly speaking, far above my comprehension, and which has only been very vaguely outlined to me by Revelation.

As long as serious intellectual difficulties continue to exist in my mind, there is of course no question of any such acceptance. But is is quite possible, in fact it even frequently happens, that the intellect accepts the triptych of Prophets-Messiah-Kingdom of God, and yet the heart remains unsatisfied. It "tells us nothing as yet". One has seen the *truth,* but cannot understand the *reality* which lies behind it, and it is only that rich, living reality which can fill the heart. Especially in the case of thoughtful, logical minds there exists the danger that they may be Catholic more intellectually than in feeling, and that they may thus fall into the error of thinking that Catholicism is a kind of abstraction which will never really grip them. Such people must learn to wait patiently until the whole interior process is complete. It frequently happens that, even after some months of instruction, one is still intellectually not ready for final conclusions. The arguments, it is true, have made an impression; many prejudices have disappeared; Catholicism appears to be deeper and more reasoned than one had imagined . . . but . . . somehow, one cannot yet altogether believe and accept.

This simply means that, as in the case of the former type of character referred to, one is afraid to surrender to this new, spiritual world, in which everything is so strangely different from all that one is accustomed to. It is not so much a matter of exterior difficulties: that is to say, human respect, fear of a rupture with one's family, dislike of the confessional, or of Catholic matrimonial laws. The psychological objection is much more vague than any of these: at times one cannot even understand oneself. On the one side one is undoubtedly attracted to Catholicism: on the other, one shrinks back as from some hidden danger. "What will become of me?" Conversion is like a leap in the dark, a giving up of one's deepest self to something unknown, to something—someone—who grips one powerfully and will not let one go.

It is a period of great unrest, sometimes of real emotional upset; it is the preparation for the final breach.

This last stage can only be passed by the help of God. In this process He is the invisible leader, who enlightens the spirit and strengthens the will. It is He who makes truth at last crystal clear and irresistibly attractive; who says things to the soul in inexpressible language—things which are not of

[36] This is more especially intended for non-Catholic readers.

this world. Perhaps you have not as yet perceived His action. But if, at the end of this first part of the book, you find that your position towards Catholicism has shifted, no matter how slightly; if certain feelings of dislike and contempt have disappeared; if you are becoming aware of a secret desire to accept this faith—then, in spite of many remaining obstacles, you owe this to the mysterious force of God's grace working in your soul.

This force we call *grace,* because without it the real conversion will never follow. Unaided personal effort can never lead you to a supernatural Credo. No amount of logical reasoning, no accumulation of convincing argument, can bring you to take this step. Between intellectual consideration and the surrender of faith, lies an unbridgeable gulf across which neither man nor angel can lead. Grace alone is efficacious, and this grace is obtained by prayer: humble, faithful, constant prayer made by yourself and others.

We will now pass on to the discussion of the actual doctrine and internal life of the Church. Theoretically we have established the conclusion that the Catholic Church is the true Church, and that it is guided by the Holy Ghost. It is evident that from now onwards the believing reader will approach the subject in a different frame of mind. Where it is a matter of God's revelation, one no longer asks for human arguments. It is sufficient to know that it is God who speaks in order to accept humbly even the most impenetrable mysteries. Once again let us echo the words of Samuel: "Speak on, Lord, Thy servant is listening."

What we wish to point out in the remaining part of this book is that the Source of all the doctrine of the Catholic Church is to be found in divine revelation, and it may well happen that the coherence, combined with the loftiness, of this doctrine will enable the reader, who has not so far reached any overriding conclusion one way or the other, to accept all the more readily the final deductions of this first part of the book in a genuinely believing spirit: *Credo in unam sanctam Catholicam et apostolicam ecclesiam.*

I believe in the one holy, Catholic and apostolic Church.

PART II

THE TEACHING OF THE CHURCH

CHAPTER IV

THE STRUCTURE OF THE CHURCH

SYNOPSIS

I. God has created us and is Lord of all Mankind, therefore we are obliged to serve Him.
Now it should be sufficient to live according to the natural law which God has put into our hearts.
Instead of this, however, He has revealed that He desires to be served in a particular way, as we shall now endeavour to prove.

II. There exists a book, the Bible, the text of which is over two thousand years old, and this text has been authentically handed down to us. From this book it is clear that the Jewish people themselves were convinced that they had been chosen by God to prepare the way for the future Messiah. Many actual prophecies concerning the Messiah are contained in this same book.

III. Undoubtedly a Man has been born in whom all these prophecies have been fulfilled, and who confirmed His divine mission by miracles: that is Jesus of Nazareth.
That he actually existed clearly follows from the testimony of pagan, Jewish and Christian authors. The Gospels, which tell the story of His life, unquestionably appear to be authentic books written either by the apostles, disciples, or actual eye-witnesses.

IV. The prophecies about the Kingdom of the Messiah have also been fulfilled. Jesus Christ preached, and founded a community, or Church, the government of which He handed over to His apostles before His Ascension with the intention that they should, in turn, hand it down to their successors.
Among the apostles, the first place was reserved for Peter. He is the unshakable rock upon which the Church is founded for all time. His power has been handed down uninterruptedly to his successors who, like himself, have supremacy in the Church. Where both the Pope and bishops go back historically as far as Peter and the apostles, we can be confidently certain that we shall find the true Church. This true Church is the Catholic Church.
In this second part of the book Catholic teaching is explained, and we will first show how the government of the Church has developed during the course of the ages.

THE GOVERNMENT OF THE CHURCH

THE FORM OF GOVERNMENT which is in use in the Catholic Church was not fixed by the Catholic people themselves but was introduced by Christ and the apostles, at all events in so far as its actual functions are concerned: that is to say, the papacy and episcopacy. Christ is the King of His realm, and therefore the visible Church takes on the form more of a monarchy than of a republic. Yet the Church differs from an ordinary monarchy in that, while its visible government receives its authority from God just as in the case of a king, it remains at the same time under the immediate guidance of the Holy Ghost.

On the eve of His death, and afterwards during the forty days which followed His resurrection, Jesus spoke in great detail to His apostles upon this very subject: "I will ask the Father, and He will give you another to befriend you, one who is to dwell continually with you for ever. It is the truth-giving Spirit. . . . He will be continually at your side, nay, He will be in you."[1] "He who is to befriend you, the Holy Spirit, whom the Father will send on my account, will in His turn make everything plain, and recall to your mind everything I have said to you."[2] "Enough for you that the Holy Spirit will come upon you, and you will receive strength from Him; you are to be My witnesses in Jerusalem and throughout Judaea, in Samaria, yes, and to the ends of the earth."[3]

How closely Christ Himself and this Spirit are connected is shown by His words immediately preceding the Ascension: "And behold *I* am with you all through the days that are coming, until the consummation of the world."[4]

Once more let us particularly draw attention to the fact that Christ had in view a world-wide Church which was still to remain long after the death of the apostles. (All through the days that are coming, until the consummation of the world.) The promised Holy Ghost, therefore, was not to leave the Church at the death of Christ's immediate disciples but, when they were no longer on earth, to remain for ever in the centre of the Church. This Spirit was to be the guiding principle and the very soul of that organization, for otherwise it would have been no more than a purely human enterprise which would certainly have disintegrated under the weight of the passing centuries. Since the miracle of Pentecost, this Spirit continually permeates the world, warming the hearts and enlightening the minds of men and, acting as a divine soul,

[1] John 14, 16-18. [2] John 14, 26. [3] Acts 1, 8. [4] Matt. 18, 20.

still dwells within and conserves the frail body of the Church until the second coming of Christ.

At the same time it is quite clear that Christ was not referring to the individual guidance of every faithful Christian only. It is true that the Holy Ghost speaks silently in every heart during the time of prayer, of the study of Holy Scripture, or of the reception of the Sacraments. But we are now speaking of the guidance of the Church as a whole and of those who govern it so that the truth may be preached.

So long as the apostles remained in the world, the assistance of the Holy Ghost never failed them, and they were thus inspired in their detailed explanation and completion of Revelation. It is evident from their writings that they studied and added the last touches to the final presentation of the doctrine of Christ. At the time of their death, the divine message had been put into its permanent form, and the task of the Church thereafter consisted mainly in faithfully keeping and handing on the treasure of its Faith. The Church, however, was not intended to do this purely mechanically, as a herald might announce news by means of his bugle, or a printer repeat himself on his press. The Church has never ceased to pray and meditate over Revelation, and to continue its study with an ever deepening intensity. In the course of the centuries the meaning of correlated texts has become clearer, individual truths have stood out more sharply one from the other, until finally it became possible to draw up a complete summary of the whole, which threw into relief more clearly than ever, the wonderful depths of Christ's truth.

Even so, all that the most brilliant intellects have discovered during twenty centuries, appears to be only a beginning, for at each fresh discovery new vistas open before us in this world of mysteries.

Was there no need, then, of guidance? Can anyone imagine that Christ, as a teacher and—in modern language—a psychologist, could allow his followers to sink, rudderless, in these fathomless depths? "He will give you another to befriend you . . . it is the truth-giving Spirit."

This is the Spirit who unceasingly, to-day as in the past, and in the centuries yet to come, is the great keeper of the holy mysteries of Faith, and who will see to it that no fragment, even the smallest, of the truth be lost.

We must not, however, try to explain this supernatural

assistance as a new and further revelation, or as a fresh inspiration by means of which the Bible is, as it were, continually being added to. The mission of the Holy Ghost is so to guide the leaders of the Church that they do not fall into error, and with them the whole Church of Christ. They are not, however, thereby in the smallest degree released from their duty to think, and a General Council (at which is presented the teaching of the Church as a whole) does not make its decisions at random, as might some Delphic oracle, nor work in a sort of trance. The preparations for such a Council follow a perfectly businesslike and matter-of-fact course.

Bishops from all over the world, accompanied by their theologians, meet together, and only after much prayer, and study, and discussion, do they come, under the guidance of the Pope, to some final conclusion: that is to say to a considered judgment of the Church as a whole.

On such an occasion one may be infallibly assured of the presence of the Holy Ghost, since otherwise it would be possible for the entire Church to fall into error. When reached, such a final conclusion, which is usually expressed in a short, clear formula, is called a dogma.

A declaration of this kind is never a matter of surprise to the Faithful for, as has already been said, the germ of every dogma of the Church is already contained in divine Revelation. Thus a newly formulated dogma has necessarily already been a matter of general belief within the Church. It is however possible, of course, that some people still had an open mind upon the subject; but, after a solemn pronouncement of this kind by the Pope, either alone or in conclave with the bishops, every doubt is removed. Should anyone, after such a formal statement, still obstinately and against his better judgment, continue to deny the truth of that dogma, he would be called a heretic and place himself outside the communion of the Faithful.

Naturally every dogma is only expressed—and how could it be otherwise?—in human language, and will therefore always be best understood in the milieu in which it originated. It is really only a case of a new wording, a more precise explanation, of an already generally accepted doctrine. Words, after all, can never be more than the symbols of an idea; and a dogma can therefore never consist of a mere string of words which might even end by killing the living spirit. On the other hand, one must not regard the formula as a temporal truth only, which might, later on, become an untruth.

The dogma is eternal, as God's word is eternal, and as God Himself is eternal.

The language of the dogma is as enduring as granite. That is because the Church is always consistent in her belief in divine guidance. She expresses herself with the same unshakable conviction with which Christ Himself, and later on His apostles, preached the Evangelical Truths: there is never a shade of hesitation or doubt. The Church is not merely supposing, nor does she give a judgment with reservations, nor leave a loophole for other ways of thinking. Like Christ she speaks *tamquam potestatem habens,* as someone with authority.

Were she not the herald of God's Word down the length of the centuries; were she not filled with the very Spirit of God Himself; her voice might perhaps sound over-bold or pedantic. But it is the voice of the one, holy, Catholic and Apostolic Church. It is just this quiet assumption of authority which is so often misunderstood by those outside the Church, and therefore occasionally condemned as arrogant. The reader who has followed us thus far, however, will readily understand that this is no question of human pride or dictatorial behaviour. Whenever a purely personal opinion is expressed from within the Church, it is done so with extreme modesty; but when it is a case of the pronouncement of some final judgment of the Church as a whole, then it is a different matter, and any hesitation would only imply distrust in the guidance of the Holy Ghost.

The unchallengeable certainty of the Catholic Church is her greatest strength. Of what use would an opinion be to the millions of the Faithful, however reasonable it might appear, if it were merely advanced as an opinion upon which they were left in the end to form their own judgment? Such leadership could never hold a Church together: it could only end in crumbling and disintegration. There would be no rock upon which to build, but only quicksand; no such edifice could endure to the end of time, but would inevitably disappear, along with those who built it, and all those thousands of other leaders who met disaster by making concessions—who were forced, indeed, to make concessions because they were only men.

Christ who promised "I am with you . . . until the consummation of the world" had only one form of guidance in mind: the infallible.

We will now consider the organization of the Church in greater detail. We have said that Christ was not only a teacher but what is called nowadays a psychologist. He knew that, without some form of permanent guidance, later explanations of His teaching would inevitably lead to error and to mutual quarrelling, and that a community of millions of Christians would never agree without a visible authority upon which to rely. We have seen therefore how, from the very beginning, He arranged for a college of rulers, or administrators, with the final and supreme authority resting in the hands of one person. Until the end of time the Bishops and the Pope will act as the rulers of the Church, whereas the other functions were successively introduced by the ecclesiastical authorities as necessity arose, in such a way that they can be changed if desired, or even wholly suspended.

We will therefore deal in order with the papacy, the episcopacy, and the other forms of government within the Church.

§ 1. *The Papacy*

The visible Head of the Church, and the deputy of Jesus Christ, has had his residence in Rome ever since the time of St. Peter. He is called Papa (pope) which means Father. The city which was once the heart of the Roman Empire has gradually become the heart of the world-Empire of Christ, and 260 popes have succeeded each other in a dynasty which is unequalled in history. They have governed the Church in peace and in war; they have been both honoured and persecuted; they have shone in sanctity and shown human shortcoming.

The Pope is a man and no more. Like all other men he has to acknowledge *homo sum, nil humani a me alienum puto*: I am a man and nothing human is alien to me. In company with other men there is a limit to his capacity, and by virtue of his nature he is liable to both error and sin. The Pope has his advisers, his critics, his confessor. The Pope also must be on his guard and "when he thinks he stands firmly, beware of a fall". Daily he begins his holy Mass, in common with every priest, with a confession of guilt: I confess to

Almighty God that I have sinned through my fault, through my most grievous fault. The title "Holy Father" is only an official title, which has no connection with the Pope's personal life but only with his ecclesiastical office.

On the other hand we must by no means assume from all this that the Pope is an example of human mediocrity. It is obvious that to be elected Pope, out of the very large number of eligible candidates, presupposes an outstanding and capable personality. After all, we can hardly suppose that, by some strange mischance, all the geniuses have been born outside the Catholic Church; and, if not, then it is certain that at any papal election, there will be present some candidate who, either as theologian, philosopher, scientist, or administrator, belongs to the ranks of the greatest minds of his time.

All candidates for the papacy are, by virtue of their humanity, sinful men, yet the choice will surely fall on one who, by his noble character and sanctity of life, is able worthily to fulfil his high office. The Pope is indeed not only the administrator of a visible organization or society. The whole Christian world must be able to look to him as to a man who, by his evangelical mode of life, shows himself a true follower of his Master. In those very rare cases where a Pope was called "Holy Father" by reason of his office only, we shall always find that a worldly spirit had managed to invade the Church, bringing terrible consequences in its train. But these very men, even more perhaps than the greatest occupants of the papal throne, only served to prove that another Power, not of this world, has the supreme and ultimate guidance of the Church's destiny. "I will be with you . . . until the consummation of the world."

The Pope holds the primacy, that is to say the highest governing and teaching function in the Church. This power is not delegated to him by the Faithful (democratic) but by divine institution, because he is (not the successor but) the visible representative of Christ.

As Primate he is therefore not just an honorary president among other bishops (*Primus inter pares*), but he wields very real power which in spiritual matters (that is faith and morals) all have to obey.

The distinguishing marks of papal authority are:

1. The highest teaching authority.

2. The supreme governing power or jurisdiction, in which are included both the highest legislative and ecclesiastical jurisdiction.

The general laws governing the Church are set out in the Code of Canon Law (Codex Juris Canonici) which comprises 2414 articles or canons (canones) sub-divided into paragraphs. The Church also has its tribunals where disputes may be settled and even penalties (spiritual) imposed. The most important ecclesiastical tribunals are the holy Rota (for civil and criminal law) and the Penitentiary (for matters concerning conscience).

It must be understood that the Pope does not attend to all these affairs personally, but usually delegates representatives to deal with them. Only in the most important cases does he himself pass judgment; yet, even so, the cases are so numerous that his office is one of the heaviest and most responsible on earth.

Papal Infallibility

A clear distinction must be drawn between papal authority and infallibility, which is not actually a prerogative of that authority, but is a charism, or free gift of the grace of the Holy Ghost by which, under certain circumstances, he is prevented from all possibility of error.

Although in practice the infallibility of the Pope has always been acknowledged from the earliest times, the Vatican Council thought it necessary to confirm this point formally, and to define it as a dogma, in the year 1870. At this Session, 535 members of the Council were present, and only two votes were cast against it, so that we may accurately speak of general agreement. The Holy Spirit was clearly present in the midst of His Church.

We thus see that it is entirely misleading to say that the infallibility of the Pope has only been acknowledged since 1870. Infallibility was always a point of faith, but since it has been formally defined as a dogma of the Church, it can no longer be denied without falling into actual heresy. At the same time the Council clearly stated how this infallibility was to be understood. There is great misconception as to this matter among other denominations, and it is therefore, we think, worth while to go into it more fully.

The word 'fallible' (from *fallere* to deceive) may indicate a moral as well as a mental fault. This has led to the erroneous idea that the infallibility of the Pope also includes impeccability. What must be grasped is that, while the Pope can, in common with all other human beings, commit sin, in certain cases and under certain circumstances *he cannot make a mistake,* simply for the reason that it is the mission of the Holy Ghost to prevent any such error.

Once again, however, we must draw a distinction: the Pope is only infallible *on subjects of faith and morals.* As soon as he is on ordinary ground, and dealing with such subjects as, for instance, art, science or politics, his judgment has only a relative value. Even then, of course, one cannot deny a certain degree of guidance by the Holy Spirit, if such judgments form the basis of future infallible pronouncements. It would, however, be possible in such cases for His Holiness to make a mistake.

Further, even when it comes to matters of faith and morals, infallibility is only assured when the Pope is speaking *Ex Cathedra* (from his papal chair) i.e. when he is speaking officially as the Head of the Church, and has the definite intention of making a statement which shall be accepted by the Church as infallible. In short, the Pope is infallible only when he gives a formal ruling upon a subject of faith or morals which is binding upon the whole Church.

We would now like to refute an accusation which is often levelled at the Pope: "Jesus lived simply and in the greatest poverty, whereas the ruler of the Vatican is one of the richest men on earth." This reproach is not only to be met with in anti-Popish pamphlets. Many people who sympathize with Catholicism would still be happy to see the treasures of Vatican City sold at auction for the benefit of the poor all over the world.

Let us begin with this concession. A Pope who did adapt his own way of living to such luxury would not be worthy of his office, that I agree. But then we must remember that, for the Head of the Church, the Vatican is no more than an official residence in which he works, and works hard, for his people. From early morning until late at night he sacrifices himself unceasingly among a thousand cares: audiences, addresses, encyclicals, decisions of world-wide importance. A lonely figure, he stands at once above and outside his own surroundings. He has to conserve every atom of his strength for a task which, at the average age of a Pope, only a most mortified man could possibly perform.

Those of our readers who are older will agree that, for a septuagenarian, life is not transformed into a paradise by the mere act of looking at a fresco or at some beautiful marble floor. Any man who accepts the Papacy knows that by that act he is bidding farewell to any rest or legitimate relaxation such as he could enjoy as a private individual.

The words uttered by Christ to Peter, in a sense apply to the Holy Father also: "And carry thee where thou goest, not of thy own will." What, then, is the motive hidden behind the artistically beautiful and seemingly luxurious surroundings of papal Rome?

First we must remember that the Pope is not only a spiritual but an earthly monarch. By bequest of Pepin in the year 754 he received as a sovereign possession the territory over which he had, in effect, reigned since the invasion of the Barbarians. This territory, which in time was further extended by later bequests, was taken away from the Pope in 1870 when Rome became the capital of *Italia Una*. The Popes declined to acquiesce in this theft of the Church's property, and in consequence somewhat strained relations developed between the new kingdom and the Vatican (the Roman question), which were not restored to normal until the year 1929. In that year was signed a Treaty between Italy and the Holy See, as between two sovereign powers, and called the Lateran Treaty whereby, among other concessions, the Pope received back a small portion of his former territory, over which he was to rule once more as sovereign. This territory, known as Vatican City, is a little less than the size of Hyde Park in extent, but it is sufficient to guarantee the sovereignty of the Head of the Church. The Pope, therefore, is not a subject of any other Power. He has his own postal and telegraph services, his own radio station, etc., and is thus assured of his essential rights.

But such monarchy entails certain obligations. It is not possible to receive the ambassadors, ministers, and representatives of other nations under unsuitable conditions. If the Pope is to be regarded as a sovereign—and it is essential that he should be—then his exterior surroundings must, to a certain extent, be in keeping with the state of a sovereign.

There is moreover a further reason which justifies retention of the Vatican treasures. Rome is one of the few remaining centres of culture whose history is entwined with the history of Mankind. There is no need, surely, to enlarge upon the value of such a centre for civilization in general. The Church has always been the defender of all those spiritual, ethical and educational values which serve to establish men as Lords of Creation. She it is who has consistently preached charity and justice: who has fought slavery of every kind: who has striven to give women their rights; and who has founded schools and universities and taken philosophy under her wing.

Non-Catholic readers may perhaps not altogether appreciate such insistence upon the close relationship between Christianity and human culture. But principles should never be glossed over: Catholicism both acknowledges and admires the gifts of God to men, gifts which, even in our fallen state, have not altogether been lost. (We shall have occasion to refer to this again later.) But for the encouragement and practical appreciation of the Popes, many of the greatest artists of the Middle Ages might never have had the opportunity which they needed in order to reach fame. Thus the Church has enriched mankind with wonders of plastic art and beautiful architecture, symbolizing Revelation in all the delicacy of exquisite line and colour. The Gospels are necessarily silent as to all this, but many people must have found it infinitely easier to visualize Christ in His preaching while looking at, say, Michelangelo's *Last Judgment* or that marvellous picture of the usurers being turned out of St. Peter's: *"This is the House of God."*

One questions if future generations would really be grateful to a Pope who exchanged all these wonders of art for banknotes, leaving such treasures to drift here and there and anywhere, all over the world. Rome herself has had too bitter and too personal an experience of the Barbarians to wish to fall into a similar vandalism. It is true that such a transaction might bring in money, but its distribution could only end by making Europe the poorer for ever.

One can honour and adore God in any surroundings, however artistically beautiful, as Christ himself prayed in the temple at Jerusalem. Such things depend upon an interior and not upon an exterior disposition. A saint can be spiritually free even in some great centre of culture and civilization, just as a materialist can sell his soul for cheap and transitory amusements wherever he may be.

The Pope has to be an example of just such sanctity: a pattern of evangelical detachment surrounded by regal pomp. He must be a man deeply conscious, in spite of great power, that his evangelical title is *servus servorum,* the servant of the servants. It is precisely in this way that he approaches most closely to His Master: "So it is that the Son of Man did not come to have service done Him; He came to serve others."[5]

If we limit our consideration to the Popes of this present century, we shall see that they both have been, and are, outstanding men who, if they were not actually set free from their human characteristics and failings by the reception of the Tiara, or papal crown, neither were they in any way deprived of their individual virtues and nobility of soul.

One has to be a Catholic oneself in order to realize the devotion felt by the Faithful to the person of the Holy Father. In this revered and grey-haired figure each sees in fact a father: wise, full of loving solicitude: to whom he may turn with the confidence of a son. One would touch a very tender spot indeed in any Catholic if one were to try to represent this loved ruler as a despot, thirsting for power. Those Zouaves who died at Porta Pia while defending the Vatican State were typical of the deep affection felt by the Catholic people for their Pope, and every generation will, if necessary, supply fresh Zouaves.

It is possible that the non-Catholic reader has followed the above with mixed feelings: has the average Catholic, then, to give up thinking for himself in order slavishly to follow the Pope's lead? Of course not. The Catholic remains a person, an individual; he is not in the least absorbed into anybody else. He obeys from his own personal conviction, and he takes the view that, by doing so, he is ultimately bowing to the authority of Christ Himself, who said to His apostles, and to their successors, "Whosoever hears you, hears Me." The Catholic who obeys the Pope realizes that he does not bow to this authority as man to man, but bows to the (delegated) authority of Christ, just as the civilian does not actually obey the Government, but God from whom all authority is derived.

[5] Matt. 20, 28.

Every Catholic, when all is said and done, stands alone before his Creator and has to render an account to Him of his deeds. But he also respects every representative of God, recognizing that it is God Himself who is speaking through the human person. Unless he is clearly aware that the Ecclesiastical Authorities are acting unlawfully (a thing which rarely occurs) he is obliged to accept their authority as coming direct from God.

It is in this loyal, conscious obedience to the Pope that is to be found the secret of the miraculous unity of the Catholic Church as a whole, and of the spiritual tranquillity of individual Catholics. Neither lawlessness, nor on the other hand, dictatorship, survive the centuries: only a confident recognition and acceptance of acknowledged authority will weather all storms.

§ 2. *The Episcopacy*

The Bishops are the actual associates of the Pope in the government of the Church, just as Christ ordered. They are the successors of the apostles, but with this difference: whereas the apostles could carry out their office wherever they were, the bishops are limited to their own dioceses.

A bishop, therefore, is not the Pope's deputy, but he wields an individual authority which is conferred on him by the Pope at his appointment. Apart from missionary territory, the world is divided up into dioceses, and in each diocese the bishop has the power to govern. He is the head of it; he has the responsibility of seeing that the laws of the Church are kept and that no abuses creep in. Above all he must make sure, by word and example, by initiative and organization, that the Sacraments are both administered and received, the word of God preached, and last but by no means least, that Catholic children receive at least a Christian education.

By joining several dioceses together, a Province or Archdiocese is formed, of which one of the bishops becomes the Archbishop or Metropolitan. Thus the Archdiocese of Liverpool, for instance, comprises the Suffragan Sees of Hexham and Newcastle, Lancaster, Leeds, Middlesbrough and Salford. Each bishop, however, retains supreme authority in his own diocese.

In the missionary territory, to which the greater part of

Asia and Africa, and a small portion of Europe, America and Australia belong, one finds instead of a bishop a Vicar Apostolic or (in more pagan territories) a Prefect-Apostolic, who is an ordained priest but who is not always consecrated bishop. These keep in closer touch with the central office in Rome than ordinary bishops. As soon as the Vicariate or Prefecture comprises a sufficient number of Christians, it is raised to the status of a diocese.

§ 3. *Other Functions*

A bishop is not able to govern his diocese, which consists sometimes of more than a million Catholics, unaided. The district is therefore divided up into parishes, the smallest local units in the Church, each of which is under the charge of a parish priest, usually assisted by younger priests or curates. The direct care of souls rest on these parochial clergy: that is to say, the offering of Holy Mass, administration of the Sacraments (Baptism, Penance, the Holy Eucharist, Matrimony, the Last Sacraments) preaching, instruction in the Catechism, visiting the poor and the sick, organizing and taking the lead in Catholic social life, at all events as regards its spiritual aspect.

Several parishes may be combined into a Deanery, which usually consists of a large city, or some smaller city with its environs. Among other duties the Dean presides at meetings of Parish Priests at which inter-parochial matters are discussed, and generally speaking represents the Church in his Deanery. He does not however possess any direct authority as regards the government of the dependent parishes, except the parish over which he himself rules.

Thus every Catholic is domiciled within some particular parish. He is not strictly bound to attend his own parish church, but it is obvious that, normally speaking, the parish church should be the centre of the spiritual life of its parishioners.

Direct pastoral care within the Church is therefore mainly exercised by the parish priests and their curates, under the direction of the Bishop, and finally of the Pope.

In addition to these essential functions, there are many others which were not actually instituted by Christ or His apostles, but which only came into being later and have developed with the passage of time. We will here only mention a few of the most important of them.

Originally the Pope—as did all bishops—had advisers and assistants. Already Pope Everistus (99-107) had seven deacons in his immediate service. The duties of the episcopal assistants were limited to the boundaries of the various dioceses, whereas gradually the sphere of the Papal Council began to extend to the whole Church. This Council developed, in the course of centuries, into the present *College of Cardinals.*

Although the bishops are the direct successors of the apostles, the cardinals, by reason of their more universal ecclesiastical function, are above them in rank. In addition to being Cardinals they have also, in nearly every case, received episcopal consecration. The work which they are given to do by the Pope is exceedingly varied. Many of them are occupied in Rome as heads of Sacred Congregations, Tribunals or Curias, and act as would Ministers in a secular government. There are, for instance, the Congregation of the Holy Office which (after the Pope) has the greatest authority as regards the protection of faith and morals; the Congregation of the Sacraments which deals with all legislation as to the administration and reception of the Sacraments; the Congregation for the Affairs of Religious, for the Affairs of Seminaries and Universities, or for the Propagation of the Faith—and many more. The papal Foreign Minister bears the title of Secretary of State.

One very important duty of the College of Cardinals is the *election of the Pope.* For this purpose they meet in solemn conclave, although in mutual isolation, in order to vote for their chosen candidate: this candidate, in order to be elected, must have a majority of two-thirds of the votes, plus one extra vote.

The Pope maintains diplomatic relations with different governments by means of his ambassadors who—according to the importance of the particular embassy—bear the title *Nuncio* or *inter-Nuncio.*

CHAPTER V

THE TRADITIONAL TEACHING AND ITS SOURCES

WHEN SOMEONE asks where the Catholic finds the substance of his belief, the answer is: from the living teaching Authority. This Authority consists of the Pope and the Bishops of the time, whose duty it is to promote the knowledge of revealed Truth.

The Catholic is thus freed from the necessity of personal investigation into doctrinal questions, and can live in a quiet certainty that the doctrine of the Church is the doctrine of Christ himself. "Whosoever heareth you, heareth Me." We shall here find the principal reason why the Catholic has so few theological problems in comparison with his protestant brother. The most vital truths are placed before him in clear formulae by an infallible Authority. The fact of obedience to this Authority, however, never exempts him from his moral duty of retaining his individuality and remaining a free person who obeys from conviction. The more the Catholic reflects upon the connection between Ecclesiastical Authority and Christ, the more he realizes all the truth and wealth of his Faith, the more convinced will he be of his beliefs. History is there to prove how many original thinkers the Church has produced in every generation.

But, for the Catholic, the living Authority of his own era remains the real source of truth and of his rule of Faith. One can perhaps liken the contemporary Catholic to a man who is standing on the bank of a river. The water which glides past him rose from a distant spring nearly two thousand years ago. The *tradition* of the Church can be compared to some such stream, whose waters flow straight from the source, by way of the Ecclesiastical Authorities, down to each generation in turn.

The Catholic Church attaches very great value to tradition, even in the profane sense, that is to say the tradition which grew up amid Jewish, Greek and Roman culture. She has always tried to preserve the spiritual value of all tradition, and if possible to absorb rather than to discard it. Where, during the passage of the centuries, she has encountered new peoples and new cultures, her aim has invariably been not to destroy these latter, but so to permeate them with the Christian spirit as to be able to return them, reborn as it were in God, to mankind.

That strong communal sense which is deep-rooted in the Church compels her to reverence all that is ancient, all that has grown and been shaped by Time. A world-community necessarily has its roots deep in the past and, so far from seeking to make progress with giant strides, slowly assimilates new values and adds them to those which she already possesses. She is conscious of the worth of ideas which have already been accepted and thought out over long periods and by the greatest minds. She is sceptical of the latest fashion: of the "has never been thought of before"; when they are used to attack long-matured verities. She is in a state of eternal evolution, but does not easily discard her hard-won possessions.

What we are here discussing, however, is not this sort of tradition for, although a purely human tradition is never without its significance, yet it will never serve as a sufficiently sure foundation for Faith. The development of the Church during her history has been two-fold: her development as a society or community, and her development as the channel of Revelation.

The Popes and the Bishops are never exonerated from their duty of study and research. Assisted by theologians their task is to trace back to the original sources the tenets of the Faith; to watch how these truths have developed and expanded throughout the whole Church during the course of ages; and to consider the underlying explanation of such developments. In this work they can always depend upon the promise of Christ to be with them through all future days, and so count upon the help of the Holy Ghost. This, however, as we have already seen, does not remove from them their responsibility as human leaders of men, but only ennobles it.

Research for them, in brief, consists in examining Truth on the basis of the Revelation which has been imparted to mankind. As by far the most important part of that Revelation was written down under the guidance of the Holy Spirit, two easily discovered sources are usually to be found for it: the inspired Scriptures and the infallible oral teaching. (The latter is also, of course, although in a different sense, called tradition.)

We will now deal separately with each of these.

§ 1. *The Bible*

Up to now we have considered the Bible merely as an historically reliable book and nothing more. The great value attached to the text of it we attributed to the authority of Christ who, again *on historical grounds alone, we have accepted as the Son of God*. Our readers, however, are aware that for Christians the Bible has a far deeper significance than this. The Bible is the Word of God, and no greater praise or assurance of credence could be given to any book.

If one asks upon what this Christian conviction is based, then Catholics and those Christians outside the Church (i.e. Protestants) may differ. Luther never clearly defined his views upon this subject, but Calvin unmistakably gave his opinion in several places. He said, for instance, that the same spirit which spoke by the mouth of the prophets must penetrate unto our hearts to be a witness to us that they (the prophets) have truthfully interpreted that which was commanded them by God. He wants no argument, but a submission of the intellect as to a matter entirely beyond discussion. Calvin, however, goes on to try to prove his opinion by texts from the Bible.

According to him, when reading the Bible God's spirit is present in order to testify that He speaks to His chosen ones (the certainty of salvation is also closely linked up with this witnessing by the spirit). We could perhaps describe it by saying that the Bible itself, when being read, gives evidence of its inspiration: it is said to be *autopistos*. The reader himself knows, by an interior light, which books do authentically, and which do not, belong to the Bible.

This Calvinistic view is no longer shared by many of those outside the Church and we will not delay by going into further details.

In opposition to this view, Catholic teaching maintains that, while it is possible to become extremely sensitive, through the grace of faith in the soul, to the voice of God in the Bible, and while such holy reading prepares the way for the work of the Holy Ghost, yet the final pronouncement as to the actual fact of inspiration, and the preparation of the Canon or list of the books composing the Bible, *belongs to the Church under the guidance of the Holy Ghost.*

Both Catholics and Protestants refer to the Holy Ghost, but the latter take the view that each one individually may speak from subjective experience (and relying on that experience may even place themselves in opposition to the Church!) whereas Catholics consistently rely upon the authority of the Church Herself over her members. "Go and teach." It is the Church who teaches and the Faithful who listen.

Although Calvin does not deny that the general opinion of the visible Church has its value, yet this value is only relative. The Church can never impose her judgment with infallible certainty.

The Reformers have thus moved the centre of gravity from the *one* Church to the subjective conviction of *various* people. History has proved that, from this, differing opinions can result, not only in regard to minor points, but also in the case of matters of great importance (for instance, the list of sacred books composing the Bible; the meaning of crucial texts, etc.). The possibility of appeal to an objective, universally accepted Authority is lacking; no Church Council, no Synod, no Oecumenical Congress, possesses the power to issue a final judgment.

We have seen that, within the Catholic Church, this final judgment belongs alone to the living teaching authority. What, then, has it to teach about the Bible?

1. The books which together make up the Bible are, both as a whole and each separately, *inspired.* Exactly what does that mean?

It means that God is the author of these books, although He did not use a pen as His instrument but a man. He inspired each one to write what He wished, and guided him to do this without error. Such a man, on the other hand, was not a mere automaton which mechanically registered the words uttered by God. God did not cause him to write while in a state of trance, as might some spiritualistic medium, but once again He showed His reverence for our nature, and even for personal disposition. Just as the same hand can form finer, clearer and more beautiful letters with one pen than another, even although it uses the two pens in exactly the same way, so, acting under the inspiration of God, one writer of the Scriptures has interpreted God more vividly than another, or more dryly: in a more lucid or more obscure style.

One must, of course, not for a moment imagine that God as it were dictated His communications to the scribe word for word (in that case the difference in styles and composition would be inexplicable). He inspired each one with His own thoughts, and His influence was predominant as to the mode of expression; nevertheless, He allowed the various authors to write down the thoughts, each according to his own character and circumstances, and according to his own cultural and historical background. If the Bible had been composed in our West-European Society of the twentieth century, we should find precisely the same contents but in a completely different form. Because this form is not entirely separate from that mysterious influence called inspiration, it is said that the Bible is inspired from beginning to end. One must not attempt to separate form and content in such a way that it becomes a kind of—psychologically impossible—vivisection. The influence of the personality of the writer has to be acknowledged and allowed for.

Although the entire Bible is inspired that again does not mean that each line has been *revealed*. Only something which is as yet unknown can be revealed and—particularly in a biblical sense—something which, without divine co-operation, never would have been known to mankind.

The prime intention of God in regard to the Bible was to reveal truths of Religion by which the relationship between Himself and men became clearer and more intimate. We must not expect to find scientific revelations in Holy Scripture. God did not wish to forestall science by revealing historical, geological and biological truths. No scientist will find that quoting Bible texts will do away with the necessity for his own independent research work, nor need he deny scientific facts on account of them either. One can quite clearly formulate the answer to all such questions thus: the Church is always willing, when explaining the Bible, to take into consideration all *irrefutably* proved scientific discoveries, for the very simple reason that God Himself is the only Truth, and simultaneously the Creator of both science and the Bible. But we must add the warning, all the same, that the hypothesis that Man as regards his body is evolved from an animal, or that Man did not originate from one human couple, does not belong to the number of these *irrefutably* proved discoveries.

To sum up, it may be said:

a. Both form and content of the Bible are entirely the result of divine inspiration; but not the whole of the Bible was revealed.

b. Only those portions of the Bible which the author had the intention of communicating as *certain*, have to be accepted as certain.

c. Each part-author of the Bible has transmitted his divinely inspired communications according to his own character and style, both of which were obviously in conformity with the ideas and education of his contemporaries. It remains an open question whether the revealed truths as to the creation of Man were directly made known to the author, or were a primeval revelation to Adam handed down from generation to generation, and finally fixed by the author of that portion of the Bible under inspiration.

It will by now be clear to the reader that in Bible exegesis there is a possibility of a subjective and an abritrary explanation. Where is the boundary-line between God's revealed truths and the author's literary imagination? How much did God intend to communicate and how much is merely the contemporary style of the author? Must one accept, for example, that woman was made from Adam's rib, that the serpent spoke, and that our first parents made themselves aprons out of fig-leaves? Or is it permissible to regard these merely as the mode of expression which was adapted to the writer's world of thought? Must one imagine God to oneself as He is represented in Paradise, or may one make a comparison between the latter and the artistic present-day representations of God in such countries as China and Japan, which answer to their conception of Deity?

The average Bible-reader will certainly not be able to solve these questions for himself. Even the professional interpreter will not always accept his learned colleague's explanations just as they stand. Such a situation, continued during the course of ages, could cause a positive welter of contradiction and confusion, so that God's Word would end by appearing to belong to a most obscure Book. But this is just where the Church steps in. According to the Catholic conception, the second and most important part of the Bible (the New Testament) is born *from the heart of the Church.* It did not exist during the first twenty years of Christianity, and from then onwards the various Books and Epistles were written for special occasions. These writings were originally intended for various parts of the Church—for example, for the community at Rome, at Corinth, or for Christians converted from Judaism. The primary purpose of most of these writings was not edification but instruction and, as is usual in such cases, it was intended that an oral instruction for less educated persons should be given from the matter of the written instruction.

In connection with the Old Testament, there is a remarkable passage in the Acts of the Apostles, Chapter 8, verses 26-40. One of the Couriers of the Queen of the Ethiopians was driving along in his chariot and reading the prophet Isaias. The apostle Philip, who was returning from a missionary journey, overheard him and asked, "Cans't thou understand what thou art reading?" "How could I?" replied the Ethiopian, "without someone to guide me?" Then Philip began speaking and preached to him about Jesus.

Although these writings were inspired, yet their supernatural contents were often above the readers' comprehension. It was not possible to leave to new converts, among whom were artisans and slaves of those days, the explanation of the evangelical allegories, St. Paul's Epistles, or the visions described in the Apocalypse, so that St. Peter, in his own Epistle, felt it wise to add: "Our beloved brother Paul, with the wisdom God has granted him, has written you a letter in which . . . he talks of this. (Though indeed there are passages in them difficult to understand, and these, like the rest of Scripture, are twisted into a wrong sense by ignorant and restless minds, to their own undoing."[1])

It follows from this that the Church, from whose heart these books were born, has the further task laid upon her of explaining them more in detail. Originally this work was undertaken by the pastors of the various communities—later on, by St. Paul himself, another method was found in the form of single government by the Bishops, who received the grace of holy orders by the imposition of the hands of the

[1] II Pet. 3, 16.

apostles. Later again, the Apostolic Successors, that is to say the Pope and the Bishops together, were the leaders designated to continue the work.

Usually the Church allows her theologians and interpreters great liberty in their explanation and commentaries on the Bible. Should, however, any serious difference of opinion arise, it is then left to the Church herself to solve the question by an infallible pronouncement. Such a necessity is quite exceptional, and many Popes have never had any occasion to make such a pronouncement during the whole course of their reign. Usually a question of this kind is settled by the formulation of directives, by which one has to abide in practice, until such time as a thorough study of the matter has clarified the doubtful point. Let us illustrate this with a concrete example.

In the First Epistle of St. John (5, 7) we find the well-known text: "Thus we have a three-fold warrant in heaven, the Father, the Word, and the Holy Ghost, three who are yet one." Some Catholic scholars rejected this text as unauthentic because according to their view, it was an interpolation of a later date than the Epistle. The Holy Office in Rome thereupon issued a decree which laid down that it was neither safe to deny nor to doubt the authenticity of these words. There immediately followed, however, a further explanation of the decree: "It (the decree) definitely does not wish to prevent Catholic writers from going more deeply into the question and, after having prudently and carefully weighed the arguments for and against—as the gravity of the matter requires—leaning towards the opinion which denies the authenticity of the passage, on condition that at the same time they make it clear that they are prepared to abide by the judgment of the Church to whom is entrusted the mandate not only to explain Holy Scripture but to keep it unchanged." (Denz. 2198).

The general direction of such matters has, since 1902, been placed in the hands of the Biblical Commission which consists of Cardinals assisted by some forty prominent scholars. The decisions of the Commission are published in the official Papal journal, the *Acta Apostolicae Sedis*.

One has to discriminate between such official interpretation of the Scriptures and the personal reading of them. The Bible holds for us the contents of our Faith, but from the earliest days of the existence of the Church, the Bible has been read with deep devotion, and the Religious, the monks and nuns as well as the pious laity, have meditated upon the sacred text in order to become filled with the love of God. On this particular point there is great similarity between Catholic and protestant reading of the Bible. There is, however, one very definite point of difference: the personal perusal of the Bible has not for the Catholic the enormous value attached to it by the Reformers, as being the sole means of sanctification. The Catholic reads the Gospels and Epistles as they were read by the early Christians to whom they were addressed: that is to say, as an instruction given by the Church, the profundity and devotion of which (and how could it be otherwise in the case of the word of God?) make it the most suitable literature to nourish the soul. The fact of St. Paul's Epistles did not make his instructions superfluous for his various communities, and for the same reason, this authority of the Church as an organ of explanation and clarification, in addition to the actual text of the Bible, is indispensable.

Many Protestants still have an idea that the Bible is a forbidden book for Catholics. This is obviously absurd in view of the fact that there is even a choice of Catholic translations and editions, and that English-speaking Christians—Catholic and Protestants alike—have had the recent delight of the new rendering in Modern English by Monsignor Ronald Knox.

Added to this, all those who have read the Encyclical of Pope Pius XII on the study of the Bible—which ends with the earnestly expressed wish that all the Faithful, especially professors, ecclesiastics, and preachers, may, by continuous meditation upon the word of God, experience how wholesome and salutary is the spirit of the Lord—cannot but realize that such an idea is entirely without foundation.

And yet there must be a reason for such a general impression. How did it first arise?

It is a fact that Pope Pius IV forbade in 1564, not the reading of the original text of the Bible, but of the translations into the vernacular, for fear of Protestant interpretations and annotations. By way of further safeguard, he increased the restrictions which already existed locally, and in a modified form, as a result of the rise of the Waldensian and Albigensian heresies in the thirteenth century. This last and strictest regulation, by which it became in practice impossible for most Catholics to read the Bible, was rescinded by Pope Benedict XIV in 1757. From then on every lay person has been allowed to read the Scriptures in the vernacular again, on condition that the translation has ecclesiastical approval and is edited with notes.

The explanation of the great importance which the Church attaches to the correct translation of the Bible is simply—and no intellectual reader will deny this—that a bad translation may completely alter and spoil the original meaning. An entirely different atmosphere can, as it were, be created by the choice of words, even though all of them are grammatically correct. Anyone, for instance, who translates the Greek word *episcopos* by minister, or *presbyteros* by elder, will receive a warmer welcome in the Reformed Churches than the translator who, with just as much grammatical correctness, uses the expressions bishop and priest in the authorized version of the Bible.

2. When St. John ended the Apocalypse with his final Amen, the Bible was complete; but we must not suppose that from then on the Bible appeared in its present form. The books of the New Testament in particular, which were composed by different apostles and disciples without any mutual or previous arrangement, had still to be acknowledged by the Christian Community in general. This must certainly have taken time. Some theologians assume that the apostles themselves handed these writings to the Church as being inspired; others suggest that, acting under the guidance of the Holy Ghost, the Church herself acknowledged their inspiration, and added them to the existing books of the Old Testament. Certain it is that, in either case, supernatural help was essential, for it was, humanly speaking, impossible for anyone to decide whether these writings did or did not contain the Word of God.

Without considering their precise number, we can be assured that there existed a *definite collection of books* which *had been inspired by God.* This conviction was strongly established among the Jews, and was later confirmed by Christ, the Son of God. "Believe me, heaven and earth must disappear sooner than one jot, one flourish disappear from the law; it must all be accomplished."[2] "All that was written of me in the Law of Moses, and in the prophets, and in the psalms, must be fulfilled. Then He enlightened their minds to make them understand the Scriptures."[3]

So far, however, this does not specify *which* books go to make up the Canon of Holy Scripture. Here once more the Catholic differs fundamentally from Calvin, who claimed that the Holy Ghost inspires each one individually when reading

[2] Matt. 5, 18.

[3] Luke 24, 44-45.

the Bible. The Catholic, who is consistent, looks to the living, teaching authority of the Church to determine the extent of the Canon for him.

This Canon, which from the end of the fifth century was completely accepted by the Church in general, was solemnly confirmed by the Council of Trent in the sixteenth century, and comprises the following books:

OLD TESTAMENT

a. *Historical Books.* The five books of Moses, viz., Genesis, Exodus, Leviticus, Numbers, Deuteronomy (usually called the Pentateuch). Josue; Judges; Ruth; 4 books of Kings (including two books of Samuel); 2 books of Paralipomena; 2 books of Esdras, of which the second book is also called Nehemias; Tobias; Judith; Esther; and the 2 books of the Machabees.

b. *Didactical or instructional books.* Job; The Psalms; Proverbs; Ecclesiastes; The Song of Songs; Wisdom; Ecclesiasticus.

c. Prophetic Books. The 4 Major Prophets, viz., Isaias; Jeremias with Baruch (Lamentations of Jeremias); Ezechiel; Daniel. The 12 Minor Prophets, viz., Osee; Joel; Amos; Abdias; Jonas; Micheas; Nahum; Habacuc; Sophonias; Aggaeus; Zacharias; Malachias.

NEW TESTAMENT

a. *Historical Books.* The 4 Gospels according to Matthew, Mark, Luke and John. The Acts of the Apostles.

b. *Didactical Books.* The 14 Epistles of Paul, viz., To the Romans; To the Corinthians; To the Galatians; To the Ephesians; To the Philippians; To the Colossians; 2 To the Thessalonians; 2 To Timothy; To Titus; To Philemon; and To the Hebrews. 2 Epistles of St. Peter; 3 Epistles of St. John; 1 of St. James and 1 of St. Jude.

c. *A Prophetical Book.* The book of Revelation or the Apocalypse.

In the authorized version of the Protestant Bible the following are completely missing:

Of the historical books; Tobias, Judith and 2 books of the Machabees.

Of the didactical books: Wisdom and Ecclesiasticus.

The reason for this difference between the Catholic and Protestant Bibles is due to the fact that the 'Reformers' did not accept the so-called deuterocanonical books (which they call the apocryphal books). Originally there was a difference of opinion among the Jews about these books; they were rejected by some while others considered them as inspired. The Catholic Church supported the latter opinion; the Protestants the former. They therefore changed from a Bible which had been in use for more than a thousand years to one which had fallen into disuse.

§ 2. *Infallible Preaching*

Christ and His apostles preached over a period covering many years. What remains in writing of these discourses only fills a small book which can be read in a few days. What has become of all the rest? Has it been lost for ever? Is there no possibility of recapturing anything whatsoever of it?

The question is important. "There is much else besides that Jesus did," St. John admits at the end of his Gospel. "If all of it were put in writing, I do not think the world itself would contain the books which would have to be written."[4]

The Reformation denies the possibility. The Catholic approaches the matter more optimistically: retracing history in a purely historical sense, one finds innumerable records and monuments (in the broad meaning of the word) of what was once preached. They point the way back to a general conviction which evidently existed among the early Christians, who of course included actual disciples of the Apostles. This conviction *goes a good deal further than can be proved from the Scriptures alone.*

It is indeed only human, a research liable to error, and brings us no further than to a more or less historical certainty. We cannot therefore accept it as a source of actual doctrine. But here we come face to face with the enormous importance of Tradition under the guidance of the Holy Ghost.

We have seen that the Church as a whole cannot err. That is indeed, to put it simply, the minimum which could be expected from the guidance of God. If, therefore, history can show us that in former ages there existed complete agreement in matters of Faith, then one is obliged to assume also that the Holy Ghost has removed all error. The Catholic Church has collected in the course of centuries, the inspired Scriptures, and also (at all events in part) the divine and apostolic preaching. She explains them, gives a clearer understanding of the truths—sometimes incompletely understood—contained

[4] John 21, 25.

in them, and thus, under the guidance of God, continually unfolds the meaning and the wealth of Revelation. The reader will readily grasp the close relationship between infallible preaching and tradition. Whereas the Bible is always a plainly perceptible source of knowledge (although, even in that case, the guidance of the Church is indispensable) on the other hand, inspired preaching is a source which (to keep up our imagery) one can only come to know by investigating the water of the river.

Let us make sure that we understand this very clearly. Tradition hands down to us both the Bible and the oral teaching, and these two together form one (double) source; but that which was not originally written down by those who preached, is still to be discerned by a close scrutiny of Holy Scripture. It requires a particular and separate treatment, and is of course totally dependent upon Divine Tradition. This second source is sometimes itself called Tradition, although naturally in quite a different sense (that is, the actual truths which have been handed down).

The oral teaching was certainly put into writing very soon, possibly even by those who listened to it. In this matter the writings of the so-called Apostolic Fathers are of great importance: Clement of Rome, Ignatius of Antioch, Polycarp of Smyrna, and others who were actual disciples of the Apostles, and the treatises of some of them were composed even before the Apocalypse of St. John. They did not write under the inspiration of the Holy Ghost, but their testimony is of great importance with regard to the general conceptions existing in the early Church. The concurrence of the later Fathers of the Church (as the saintly and learned writers of the first century are called) carries equal weight because from it may be gauged the general teaching which prevailed in the Church of their day.

Important evidence as to the original teaching of the Church is given by the definitions determined upon by the Church Councils, especially the general or Oecumenical Councils, at which all the Bishops were assembled under the presidency of the Pope. The earliest Councils (to which Protestants also attach great importance) were those of Nicea (325) and Constantinople (381), at which the Confession of Faith was compiled, which is still said nowadays in the form of the Creed during Holy Mass.

As still further evidence we can also mention the much older Confession of Faith of the Apostles, which was divided into twelve articles, of which the outline was already known in the first century; the legal acts of the martyrs; the liturgical books; ancient titles, sarcophegi, frescoes, etc., the most imposing collection of which is to be found in the catacombs. These are the underground Christian cemeteries situated close to Rome, dating, some of them, from the first century A.D. They were usually excavated from soft sandstone, generally very deep down, which is the cause of their long and excellent preservation. Their immense significance consists mainly in the fact that they bear witness to points of doctrine which are not actually contained in Holy Scripture, and which yet formed part of the Treasury of the Faith of the early Christians, as they still do of ours: such, for instance, are Infant Baptism, the invocation of the Saints, purgatory, and many more.

A Catholic feels completely at home in these catacombs and finds nothing around him which is not familiar. A Protestant may possibly feel somewhat ill at ease, sandwiched between representations of Our Lady and St. Peter, traced invocations to the martyrs, and prayers for the deceased.

The whole Church, then, shares in the same Tradition: priests and Faithful, theologians, saints and painters. And they all equally find their guarantee as to the Truth, in the authoritative voice of the Church, which declares what is to be accepted, and what rejected, as part of that divine Tradition.

As the Catholic stands beside the flowing stream of Tradition, there stands beside him the living, teaching Authority of his era, the latest representative of the *successio continua,* that uninterrupted succession which has never failed since the days of Peter and of the Apostles. Just so, also, has that unbroken continuity of the imposition of hands been assured to priests at their consecration, and just so have these words of the Divine Master reached them in their turn: "Go out, making disciples of all nations . . . and behold I am with you all through the days that are coming, until the consummation of the world."

Sources of Faith—Tradition—living Teaching Authority: it is the same Spirit which binds them together. Until Christ shall come.

CHAPTER VI

THE MYSTERY OF THE BLESSED TRINITY

THE FACT OF GOD presses irresistibly upon us. He made us. Everything that is good in Man and in Nature is derived from him.

But still the question persists: "Who is God?" What actually do I love when I love Him?

In this infinitely great Being the mind discovers all kinds of different attributes which it finds difficult to combine. He is unchangeable, yet Creator: He is present everywhere and in everything, and yet we find disorder in the world and in nature, the seemingly cruel and ruthless issue of inevitable events: He is infinitely good, yet allows both sin and suffering. He is without limit, and yet creates, next to Himself, the finite in all its multiple forms. He leads, yet still we are able to choose whatever seems good to us.

And then there arises the danger that we begin to belittle God in our own mind, until He comes to seem scarcely more than some engineer whose calculations and computations ultimately disagree, or a policeman who directs world-traffic to final and complete wreckage. Definitely no. God is, and must be, a *living* God. But in what *way* is He a living God? We want to understand; we are not satisfied with the mere picture of the Almighty which we are able to construct for ourselves out of the elements of Creation. We find that our mind constantly circles round God; that we try to express Him in a roundabout way; that we seek for a description in which the humility of the creature and the Truth of God draw nearer to each other. We adorn Him with the most beautiful qualities; interpret Him with the profoundest thoughts of which we are capable. He is the treasure-house of life. He is, who is. But still we reach out for His most intimate, interior existence: in Him we seek for the Living Truth: that goodness which is unendingly fruitful. Our whole endeavour is to know who He is and from whence He draws His own thoughts and actions. And although Infinity shows itself to us outwardly as an impenetrable mystery, yet how happy we should be to catch, through the dark opening of that mystery, one glimpse of its eternal light which shines upon all who enter this world.

All these questions are answered by Revelation, for it tells us of *the mystery of the Blessed Trinity*. It gives us a fuller understanding of God by showing us that life which is perpetually unfolded in Him in all its infinite perfection. Still, it remains true that God has actually revealed very little about Himself to us.

The Old Testament

In the Old Testament we find in the first place everything which the average intellect could discover for itself with a little thought: *there is one God*: eternal, unchangeable in His decrees, omnipresent and majestic in His mighty actions.

This emphatic insistence upon His singleness was, at that time, a direct challenge to the world outside Israel, which clung to its ideas of gods, of fate and of nature. But Israel was to be the guardian for all nations of the realization of, and belief in, one personal God; and for this reason God set the Jews apart. He spoke to them continually, either personally or through His prophets; He struck them with disasters and spoiled them with miracles and favours. It was difficult to guide the primitive instincts of His Chosen People along the right paths, and to keep alive in their hearts and minds the first of the ten commandments: "Thou shalt not have strange gods in My sight." Even such signs as thunder and lightning, the trembling of Mount Sinai, and the Voice from the midst of fire which said: "Thou shalt not make to thyself a graven thing," were not always able to convince this nation of the great truth that the God of Abraham, of Isaac and of Jacob, who was indeed Jahve, the name which is written with the tetragrammaton j h v h, which means: *"He who is*: He who alone exists by Himself and is omnipotent, without limitation: who alone desires to be honoured for His greatness, power and majesty.

No wonder that God did not as yet reveal His Trinity: the

conception of three gods would inevitably have taken hold of the thoughts of this People who were surrounded on all sides by great pagan nations. He tried, therefore, first of all, to keep alive in their minds the idea of *one* God who is invisible, immaterial, and can yet make His action felt on earth and in Time.

Sometimes athwart the unity, appears a touch of plurality as, for instance, when the inspired author of the Book of Wisdom describes the birth of Wisdom and represents her as a person, thinking, acting and speaking. She it was who created the world, and who gave advice to God when He was planning the Cosmos: "She, the glow that radiates from eternal light; She, the untarnished mirror of God's Majesty; She, the faithful echo of His goodness. Alone, with none to aid Her, She is all-powerful; Herself ever unchanged, She makes all things new. Bold is Her sweep from world's end to world's end, and everywhere Her gracious ordering manifests itself." Here, in a sense, we are drawing nearer to the full Revelation of the New Testament which will teach that God's Wisdom is the Second Person of the Trinity, described by St. John as the Word of God.

But always we find ourselves being drawn back to the idea of One God, who sees everything, knows all, and fills man with the dread of His presence.

This God loves His people; He regards Israel as His bride. His fidelity is stronger than death, and He tells Sion, who is reproaching Him with having forsaken her: "What, can a woman forget her child that is still unweaned, pity no longer the son she bore in her womb. Let her forget; I will not be forgetful of thee. Why, I have cut thy image in the palms of my hands; those walls of thine dwell before my eyes continually."[1] No, in His sight no one is forgotten; He is the God who keeps faith for ever, who redresses wrong and gives food to the hungry; the Lord who brings release to the prisoner; The Lord, who gives sight to the blind; the Lord, who raises up the fallen; the Lord who befriends the innocent.[2]

And yet, in this Old Testament Revelation, we miss that touch of the *Father* given to us by Christ: one feels oneself too much a servant, not enough a son. God appears so remotely great. We hear Him thundering in the distance,

[1] Is. 49, 14-17. [2] Ps. 145, 7-9.

roaring like a lion, smoking as a volcano. He is indeed the Lord.

Later Jesus Christ will amplify the witness of the ancient prophets; He will reveal to us the mystery of the Blessed Trinity.

The New Testament

We know that there are three Persons in God because Jesus Himself has taught us so.

On *four* outstanding moments in the life of Christ, the Evangelists draw attention to the intimate and interior life of God; that is, to the Father, the Son, and the Holy Ghost. *Luke* announces in the first chapter of his Gospel that an angel was sent to Mary with the message that she was to bear a Son, who was to be great, and whom men would know for the Son of the Most High: "The Holy Spirit will come upon Thee, and the power of the Most High will overshadow thee."[3]

When Jesus was being baptized by John, the heavens were opened—so *Matthew* recounts—and "he saw the Spirit of God descending as a dove, and heard a voice from heaven saying: This is My beloved Son in whom I am well pleased."[4]

We shall find the clearest explanation of the Blessed Trinity in the fourteenth chapter of *St. John,* when Jesus described the mutual life of the Three Persons, and also their life in the souls of true Christians. Later he summarized all this teaching in one short sentence when, just before His Ascension, He bade His apostles go out into the world to make disciples, "baptizing them in the name of the Father, and of the Son, and of the Holy Ghost".[5]

There are three distinct Persons who are one God: this was the recurring theme of the preaching of Jesus.

He continually spoke of God as His Father; the discourse after the Last Supper rings with it.[6] His Father, who dwells in heaven as Lord and God, is also the Father of us all; nevertheless Christ took great pains not to place Himself on a level with us. *We* are to pray: "Our Father, who art in heaven".[7] But *He* thanked *His* Father. And, when at last

[3] Luke 1, 26-38. [4] Matt. 3, 13-17. [5] Matt. 28, 18-20.
[6] John 3, 14-17. [7] Matt. 6, 9-13.

He departed from His disciples, He said: "I am going up to Him who is My Father and your Father, who is My God and your God."[8]

This special relationship which exists between the Father and the Son finds its outward expression, as well as its inward purpose, in a complete mutual understanding: *only* the Son knows the full extent of the glory of the Father, and only the Father apprehends the full wealth of the divine Being in the Son: they know each other in complete perfection. "None knows the Son truly except the Father, and none knows the Father truly except the Son, and those to whom it is the Son's good pleasure to reveal Him."[9]

Therefore Father and Son are *one*: not only one in thought and will, but also in Being; a unity which, in St. John's Gospel, is so repeatedly and so decisively stressed in such phrases as: "I am in the Father and the Father in Me": [10] "In that love which Thou (the Father) didst bestow upon Me before the foundation of the world": [11] "And this word comes not from Me, but from My Father who sent Me";[12] "My Father has entrusted everything into My hands";[13] and finally, "Father, into Thy hands I commend My Spirit".[14]

God is the Father who begets a Son.

Christ called Himself the Son of God.

He did not reveal Himself abruptly, but gradually, adapting Himself to the slow unfolding of man's spiritual perception, and patiently overcoming his resistance. He prepared His disciples little by little, by personal contact and general teaching to recognize Him as the Son of God, until finally the point was reached where Peter, in answer to His question, "Whom do men say that I am?" was able to reply, speaking under the inspiration of the Father, "Thou art the Christ, the Son of the living God."[15] A little later, all His disciples freely acknowledged: "Now we can be sure that Thou knowest all things; this gives us faith that Thou wast sent by God".[16] When, however, one of His friends still would not understand, He reproved him with great gentleness: "What, Philip, here am I, who have been all this while in your company; hast thou not learned to

[8] John 20, 17. [9] Matt. 11, 27-28. [10] John 14, 10-11
[11] John 17, 24. [12] John 14, 24. [13] Matt. 11, 27.
[14] Luke 23, 46. [15] Matt. 16, 13-18. [16] John 16, 30.

recognize Me yet? Whoever has seen Me has seen the Father".[17] Then, as the culmination of His teaching, He made this same declaration in the presence of His enemies: "Believe Me, before ever Abraham came to be, I am."[18] "My Father and I are one. At this the Jews took up stones to stone Him with."[19]

He appealed to men on account of His divine prerogatives and attributes: He had power to work miracles and to forgive sins.[20] In the prologue to his Gospel, and in the account of the discourses after the Last Supper, where St. John was considering Jesus in His relationship to God, to the world, and to man, he particularly describes Our Lord's divine self-consciousness. He is the only begotten Son, and therefore one in Being with the Father, the Father in Him and He in the Father.[21] In the prologue, it is John the Baptist who bears witness: "One is coming after me who takes rank before me; He was, when I was not",[22] thus confirming the *eternal pre-existence* of the Lamb of God.

But He is *not* the Father: He is *sent* by the Father. "It was from God I took my origin, from Him I have come. I did not come on My own errand, it was He who sent me."[23] Although Christ continually emphasized the difference between Himself and His Father, yet He also repeatedly stressed their complete unity of thought and mind, based on unity of nature: He bore witness to what He knew, to what His own eyes had seen.[24] "The Son cannot do anything at His own pleasure, He can only do what He sees His Father doing; what the Father does is what the Son does in His turn."[25]

This teaching resulted in His death. When the representatives of the Old Law asked Him categorically whether He were the Christ, the Son of the Living God, Jesus replied: "Thy own lips have said it."[26] These words contained the fundamental truth: Father and Son, two Persons, but one God.

Particularly towards the end of His life, Christ *spoke about the Holy Ghost*. Another Paraclete (Helper), He called Him, the Comforter.[27] He is not the Father, neither

[17] John 14, 9. [18] John 8, 58. [19] John 10, 22-39.
[20] Mark 2, 10. [21] John 10, 28 and 14, 10-20. [22] John 1, 30.
[23] John 8, 42. [24] John 3, 11. [25] John 5, 19.
[26] Matt. 26, 64. [27] John 14, 16.

is He the Son, but He is being sent by the Father in Christ's Name.[28] He is also being sent by the Son.[29] He comes from the Father: the Spirit of Truth who proceeds from the Father.[30] Yet it is from the Son that He is to derive the message which He brings.[31] He is to complete Christ's work,[32] and He will dwell with the apostles for ever.[33]

All these descriptions point unmistakably to the fact that He is one Person, proceeding from the Father and the Son, and yet one with Him in substance: the Spirit is God, equal with the Father and the Son, and for this reason we are baptized in the Name of the Father and of the Son and of the Holy Ghost.

The Holy Ghost is the third Person of the Blessed Trinity: He proceeds from both the Father and the Son.

It is in this way that Jesus Christ has described to us the infinite interior life of God, His infinite fruitfulness. He spoke of the Father, of Himself as the Son, and of the Holy Ghost. But He always spoke of one God. God is never alone, three are one. This is the mystery which has come down to us out of eternity.

The Dogma of the Trinity

Basing Herself upon this Revelation, the Church teaches us therefore: in God there are three Persons; one Person of the Father, another of the Son, and another of the Holy Ghost; but the Godhead of the Father, and of the Son, and of the Holy Ghost, is but one, the glory equal and the majesty co-eternal. These three divine Persons are one God, because all three have one and the same divine Being. The Father is made of none, the Son is of the Father alone, not made, nor created, but begotten. The Holy Ghost proceeds both from the Father and the Son. But Father, Son and Holy Ghost are uncreated, eternal, almighty, God and Lord. One God and one Lord.

The Father is the Creator, who did not fully reveal Himself to us at once. Instead, the Son was sent to reveal God's love to Man and to repair what was defaced (Redemption). The Holy Ghost was infused in order to fill everyone with divine life and divine strength. In such terms the Church

[28] John 14, 26. [29] John 16, 14-15. [30] John 15, 26.
[31] John 16, 14. [32] John 16, 13-17. [33] John 14, 16.

tries to formulate a mystery which still evades complete understanding.

What do we actually profess by accepting this mystery? That the life of God is unfolded in one divine, triune Self; that this infinite life is intrinsically fruitful. In God is an unfailing source of life: the bosom of the Father. As a woman carries under her heart the child who is dear to her, with God it is the Father who generates life and communicates it to a Son who dwells in His bosom eternally.

God has a Son, but in what *way* does God have a Son?

Scripture shows us that way. John commences his Gospel with the phrase: "At the beginning of Time the Word already was." That Word is the Son, and we can more or less picture it to ourselves as follows. Our mind is fruitful. We cannot but come to that conclusion when we ponder, for instance, over this very mystery. It continually forms interior thoughts, and these thoughts reflect that which we know. Thoughts are, in effect, inwardly spoken words. I can express myself in a thought: form an idea of what I myself am. I can think of myself. The whole of this process of spiritual generation can enact itself in my mind.

The Spirit of God is infinitely fruitful, The Father knows Himself, He knows His own nature with all its infinite perfections. He is, as it were, eternally forming a concept of Himself, a concept which reflects all the wealth of His divine nature—He expresses Himself in that eternal thought: He speaks—interiorly —one Word which reflects Himself in complete perfection. That is the divine Word—the Son.

This Word is a Person, and in Him God recognizes Himself, because this other Person reflects Him perfectly. He sees in Him His own divine Being. This Word, the Son, *is* God.

The precise way in which, in God, this image of the invisible God, the Word Himself, is truly God; the precise way in which the thought of the Father is a real Person, a living Son; we shall never wholly grasp. That is a mystery.

But Christ has also revealed to us that Father and Son are completely one in the Holy Ghost. Who, then, is the Holy Ghost?

When the mind has created an ideal in which it finds all its highest aspirations fulfilled; in which it meets itself, and which expresses all that is highest and dearest in itself—then that mind is enraptured: then it seeks to capture and to express this all-embracing intuition of the ideal. The result is Love, and from this Love flows action—the spirit of sacrifice in order to realize the ideal. God expressed Himself in His Word, which was His Son, and in Him He encounters all the infinite goodness and beauty of His own divine Being. In Him he finds perfect complacency. The Son, in turn, beholds in the Father the immeasurable treasures of infinite wealth; He is enraptured with this divine abundance, and in it finds His happiness and His repose.

The fruit of this incommensurable bliss which unites Father and Son, the ever-blossoming flower of their mutual inclination, is the Holy Ghost. He proceeds from the pure Love of Father and Son; and this love of God, in God, must be infinitely perfect: God Himself.

But again, the precise way in which the Holy Ghost is God and Person, distinct from Father and Son from whom He proceeds, we shall never wholly grasp. This, too, is a mystery.

The Trinity in Unity and Unity in Trinity cannot be explained in human language; one day we shall see it—but here below we can only stammer out halting phrases in an effort to explain this eternal inward life of God.

No words are able to encompass it, although the simplest words may best be able to express it. In God there is no loneliness. There are Three Persons, known perfectly to each other, united in the same perfect mutual love, and in this consists infinite joy.

In such a conception of the Triune God there is no contradiction in terms, because the three and the one do not refer to the same noun: we speak of one *Being* and three *Persons.*

This mystery is the most precious revelation bequeathed to us by Jesus Christ. All other dogmas depend upon this mystery, and through it God is revealed to us as a living God in an endless and perfect fellowship.

It is not surprising that the Church knows no Sacrament, no prayer, which does not include the Father, the Son, and the Holy Ghost; everything which takes place in the Christian life is performed in Their Name. Christians continually honour the Blessed Trinity in the sign of the Cross; while in the Divine Office the monks bow their heads every time they say "Glory be to the Father, and to the Son, and to the Holy Ghost; as it was in the beginning, is now, and ever shall be. Amen."

St. Paul's blessing at the end of his second Epistle to the Corinthians echoes through the Church: "The grace of our Lord Jesus Christ, and the love of God, and the imparting of the Holy Spirit be with you all. Amen."

CHAPTER VII

CREATION

THE MYSTERY of the Blessed Trinity is the most precious revelation left to us by Jesus Christ because it is the mystery of the intimate and interior life of God: of His manner of thinking and loving. This love did not remain enclosed in the infinity of His divine Being but (and this is another incomprehensible mystery) urged Him to create other Beings destined to share in His happiness.

The origin of the world and of man will always be a fascinating problem to the enquiring mind. The thinker wants to discover just where we have to place the beginning of the universe: this universe which half frightens him and never really satisfies him, yet which he feels to be indispensable to his existence, and which affords him happiness and a sense of wonder. From the contemplation of the universe his thoughts rise to the existence of God, the Creator; but he immediately encounters, at this first step in his attempted explanation, a baffling mystery. How can God thus multiply Himself into innumerable Beings, who reflect Him and yet never adequately express Him? Why did he create? The secret which explains the origin and existence of our world could only be unveiled if our minds were able to comprehend the universe as well as God which, for us, is impossible.

Everything which exists has been thought into existence by God of His own free will. That which first existed in the mind of God as a possibility, received from Him the gift of actuality and reality: this we call *creation*.

To create is a divine activity: that is to say a completely indepent act. A sculptor chooses a block of either stone or wood and gives it an entirely new form. He chisels or carves already existing material from which it is possible to produce such a thing as a statue. Even so, he is largely dependent upon the suitability of his material. When he has given his mind long enough to the shaping and modelling of it, the finished statue finally stands before him: his own production, it is true, but no longer in any way dependent upon him for its continuation.

Now the activity of God is something totally different: He needs no material from which to fashion His creations: everything comes into being simply through a spiritual impulse of His will: this world, all the energy contained and effectively employed in it; all the possibilities which are capable of future realization.

It is certainly untrue to say that this creation of ours exhausts God's possibilities. He alone knows all its potentialities—but He does not turn every possibility into a reality. The reason why He chose especially to make heavenly bodies, minerals, plants, animals, and finally men and angels, is His own secret. Other beings and objects would have been equally possible; things which we ourselves cannot imagine, but which later on—or perhaps never—may come into existence.

Here lies a mystery of God's wisdom before which we can only humbly incline the intellect: we, who were once ourselves no more than possibilities in the thought of God, and to-day owe it to His inscrutable will that we exist. And, just as this world and everything in it is a reality, just so, we must try to realize, would it again become no more than a possibility, did not God continue to keep it in existence from moment to moment. We are in His hand just as surely as the bird in the air or the swan floating on the surface of the water. There is no more entire and intimate dependence imaginable than that of the creature; it owes everything, without exception, to its Creator.

This Creator created without effort—completely and freely of His own will. He spoke, and it was made, as the Bible concisely expresses it. In Him there is no irresistible urge for outward expression, and inwardly His infinite life-force is completely satisfied by the eternal life of the Three Divine Persons. In Him there is no lack of happiness or perfection, therefore He has nothing to gain from creation. But even though He was entirely free to create or not to create, that does not mean that there was not a *reason* for creation. Liberty always presupposes a motive, and chance is entirely excluded where God is concerned.

Our finite mind cannot grasp *why* God should, in the last resort, have created this universe. The Creation is not a necessary conclusion of God's Being; and so we come to realize that this question must be left unanswered. The actual motive is hidden deep in His wisdom and His love. We do, however, know for certain that he created everything for His honour and as a manifestation of His infinite perfections. The work must praise and glorify its Master, and in praising the Lord it will find both its fulfilment and its happiness.

§ 1. *Angel and Devil*

The first thing to be created by God was the world of pure spirits. We know from the Bible that there are incorporeal spirits endowed with personality, who are closer to God than we are, and who are called heroes, powers or messengers. Their nature is not disclosed and very little is said as to their activities. *These pure spirits* form a very natural transition-stage between the state of the highest spirits and the state of man—that is, of a spirit enclosed in matter. It would appear that God has arranged all creatures in order of degree: dead matter constitutes the lowest degree, after which life unfolds itself in a triple and ascending form: vegetable, animal and human—the intellectual Being. But in us the mind develops but slowly; for a comparatively short period of life it is active, although even then frequently held prisoner by the imagination or by unconsciousness, and at the best of times a prey to the passions of natural instinct. Even in its highest expression, and most perfect activities, the mind is still lamentably subject to error. It is not therefore surprising that God should create a pure spirit divorced from matter.

The Bible assures us that this suggestion is indeed a *fact*: in both the Old and New Testaments, angels are mentioned, and the existence of these powers is presupposed by the description of their triple mission.

1. The angels adore God; they praise His majesty, kneel before Him, crying: "Amen, blessing and glory and wisdom and thanksgiving and honour and power belong to our God through endless ages, Amen."[1] And they stand before God's throne, serving Him day and night in His temple. The

[1] Apoc. 7, 11-12.

Apocalypse of St. John describes how the six-winged seraphs and the four-winged cherubim, with the four-and-twenty elders clothed in white garments and wearing crowns of gold upon their heads, incessantly sing to the Lamb, "Holy, holy, holy is the Lord God, the Almighty." They always behold the Face of the Father.

2. The angels serve God and man. They are the bearers of divine messages: their very names denote the nature of their work. Gabriel stands for the power of God: Raphael for God's healing power.

After the fall of man, it was cherubim who guarded the way to the Tree of Life with a flaming sword. Again it was an angel from heaven who cried out to Abraham: "Do the lad no hurt, let him alone."[2] In a dream Jacob saw angels ascending and descending a ladder.[3] An angel of the Lord went down into the furnace with Sidrach, Misach and Abdenago, and caused a wind to blow in the very heart of it so that it drove away the flames.[4] It was the angel Raphael who protected Tobias on his long journey to the country of his kinsman, and who encouraged him with much valuable advice and practical help. (Book of Tobias.)

At the beginning of the Gospel-story, it is the angel Gabriel —the Power of God—who, we are told, stood before Mary and saluted her as he presented his heavenly message;[5] and later, when the Child whose birth he had foretold, lay in the manger, it was angels in the sky who sang of peace to men of goodwill.[6] Angels ministered to Our Lord after the forty-days' fast and the temptation in the desert,[7] and an angel from heaven strengthened Him in His agony in the Garden,[8] while it was an angel of the Lord who rolled away the stone from the sepulchre and said to Mary: "He is risen."[9]

After the Ascension, as the apostles were still gazing up into heaven, two angels in white garments stood beside them and spoke to them of Jesus.[10]

In the playgrounds of children there are many angels, and woe to those who scandalize or treat these little ones with disdain, for their angels in heaven continually see the face of the Father.[11]

[2] Gen. 22, 11-12. [3] Gen. 28, 12. [4] Dan. 3, 49.
[5] Luke 1, 26. [6] Luke 2, 8-14. [7] Matt. 4, 2.
[8] Luke 22, 43. [9] Matt. 28, 1-5. [10] Acts 1, 11-12.
[11] Matt 18, 5-12.

3. Finally, the angels will be present in great numbers at the Last Judgment. The revelation of St. John describes their mysterious activities. They it is who will eventually settle the time of it, and allow a delay; they who will measure the Temple and sign the Chosen Ones; who again will call upon the four winds and instruct the horsemen not to begin the work of destruction yet. And it is they who are destined suddenly to sound the trumpet which lets loose the vials of God's wrath, to raise the standard of the living God, and to cast down the dragon, the beast, and anti-Christ into the pool of everlasting fire.

Scripture mentions the angels and their ministrations in many places. From these various descriptions, the Church has drawn the conclusion that, although angels can on special occasions manifest themselves in human form, yet they are pure spirits created by God. In so far as they are spirit, they have a resemblance to the soul, yet they differ from the soul in perfection, in so far as they are never able to become one with matter. From all the above data we might perhaps describe the nature of the angels in the following way:

The Nature of the Angel

The answer to the question in the catechism, "What are angels?" is that angels are exalted, immortal beings.

The characteristic mark of a spirit, which of its nature is not destined to be in any way connected with a body, is its independence from anything material or from anything entangled with the material. In that sense the angels are independent of time, are completely free in their movements, never change, and soar—numerous as the stars—above this ever varying life of earth which is so familiar and often so dear to us.

This independence shows itself primarily in their knowledge and in the strength of their intelligence from which this knowledge flows, as a necessary consequence, direct into their *will.* Contrary to our own manner of knowing, theirs is *intuitive, inborn,* and completely *independent of things.*

a. The human mind has to attain to truth by reasoning—by deep thought; it moves slowly, and often wanders into side-tracks, so that, even when at last it believes it has reached reality in a flash of insight, it is still inclined to stammer more than to speak. The origin of this condition is to be found in the matter with which the spirit is necessarily compelled to co-operate.

The spirit of the angel, on the other hand, does not reason; it is not obliged to draw laborious conclusions from isolated facts which it connects together; it does not argue as we do: "Everything that changes, is changed because of something else. Either this 'something else' is also, in its turn, susceptible to change, in which case the same question repeats itself endlessly; or else this 'something' is unchangeable, and in that case I call it God." No. The angel sees at once that the universe was created by God; he cannot see it differently. It is a direct comprehension of the Source, the Creator, as perceived in the finite, or created. He does not find out, by thinking, that he is immortal, but is aware from the beginning of the intransitory nature of his existence, and of the fact of his fundamental dependence upon God. The *existence* of the Creator can never be a problem to him, but he perceives and experiences the interior life of God through grace and in the light of heaven. He knows our secret thoughts and desires only in so far as he is shown them by God—far more accurately and clearly than by the best psychologist—or to the degree to which he can discover them from our normal behaviour and reactions.

b. We draw our knowledge from our encounters with the material world; from the events which happen; from listening to the thoughts and opinions of others: a child wakes up intellectually through contact with its parents and its surroundings. Without eyes and ears our mind would remain almost empty. But the knowledge of the created world, of human beings and their affairs, has been infused into the angels by God Himself. Finite light can only affect mortal eyes, and the sounds of earth can only reach mortal ears; words demand senses for their comprehension; and, when all these mediums of perception are lacking, it follows that the idea of matter has no access to a mind unless the infinite light of God shines upon that mind and presents to it the created world in a series of pure images. God constantly reflects direct into the angelic understanding all that He has created outside His own Being.

c. But the most characteristic trait of the understanding and knowledge of the angels, is its entire independence of matter and of the material world. It is for this reason that their thoughts are so profound and fertile that they penetrate at once into the very essence of things; that they know instantly what is of value and what has no importance; that they solve problems without difficulty which we should have to study for years; and even have a sure knowledge of the inevitable consequences which flow out of every cause. The angel does not learn his wisdom in this material world but receives it direct from creative Wisdom Himself.

This independence is most wonderfully expressed in the *active* power of the angelic freewill, which is never hindered by passions, which never hesitates over a decision, but is directly set in action by the clear judgment of the intelligence. Nevertheless an angel cannot perform miracles by the exercise of his will, except by the express permission of God, although he can achieve, unaided, feats for which we should require our hands or tools of some kind. We remember that, in one second of time, an angel transported Habacuc to Babylon.

The angel is not omnipresent: but owing to his spiritual nature he is not tied to any particular place, and can exercise his influence wherever he acts whilst remaining in heaven. We find the following written by St. Paul: "What are they, all of them, but spirits apt for service, whom he sends out when the destined heirs of eternal salvation have need of them?"[12] In the angel we encounter the life of created spirit in its most perfect form: he is endowed for ever with wisdom, generosity and strength.

Apparitions of Angels

Finally we come to apparitions of angels recorded in the Old as well as New Testaments. They appeared to Abraham, and were also seen by his wife, by Lot and his family, and other inhabitants of Sodom.[13] Raphael accompanied Tobias on his journey and was seen by various other people on the road. At the Nativity shepherds saw angels in the sky, and the women who sought Our Lord at the Sepulchre spoke with an angel sitting on the rolled-back stone of the tomb. It would almost seem that the Bible supports the supposition that they can assume a human body, although their spirit never manifests itself in the ordinary actions of everyday life. The angel said to Tobias: "I was at your side, eating and drinking, but only in outward show; the food, the drink I live by, man's eyes cannot see."[14]

Whoever asks how many angels there are, may gather from the vision of Daniel that they number thousands upon thousands, while the figure given in the Apocalypse is even higher. And certainly they have the first right to existence,

[12] Heb. 1, 14. [13] Gen. 18 and 19. [14] Tobias 12, 19.

since they were the first work of God's Creation and are its most perfect representatives. We are told in the Bible of nine choirs of Blessed Spirits who differ in degree the one from the other: Cherubim (Genesis), Seraphim (Isaias), Thrones Dominations, Principalities, Virtues and Powers (St. Paul, especially to the Colossians and the Ephesians), Archangels (Thessalonians), and Angels.

The Fall of the Angels

Among this band of pure Spirits, however, a tragedy developed and grew from the very beginning. The Catechism asks us, as one of its questions, whether all the angels remained both good and happy, and the reply, as we know, is that many of the angels sinned and so lost heaven for all eternity.

We may be sure that original sin must have had an instigator; it originated in the ruses of a powerful seducer and an inciter to evil. The evil Powers already existed before ever Man fell. The Church emphatically declares that Man was good by nature but became prone to sin through his own fault. The Church has taken this truth from the Bible, which speaks of devils.

The Apocalypse describes what happened as follows: "Fierce war broke out in heaven, where Michael and his angels fought against the dragon. The devil and his angels fought on their part, but could not win the day, or stand their ground in heaven any longer; the great dragon, serpent of the primal age, was flung down to earth; he whom we call the devil, or Satan, the whole world's seducer, was flung down to earth, and his angels with him."[15]

Christ said that the devil, from the first, was a murderer, "and as for truth, he has never taken his stand upon that; there is no truth in him".[16] An eternal fire is prepared for him and his angels,[17] and St. Peter tells us that he goes about roaring like a lion to find his prey.[18]

We do not know precisely why he and his angels fell, we only know the fact of their fall and the mystery of their power, allowed by God for His own purposes which are as yet hidden from us. We can, however, meditate upon their fall and then deduce, from the fact that this was a case of the sin of a pure spirit, that there must have been some form of probation in

[15] Apoc. 12, 7-9. [16] John 8, 44. [17] Matt. 25, 41. [18] I Pet. 5, 8.

question, some test, which lasted for at least, what we should call, a full moment. In that one flash of eternity they had to choose: for or against God. Either they had to make their submission to Him and acknowledge that from His hands alone they had received everything which they possessed of wealth and grace; or, rejecting God, make an attempt to attain happiness by their own power, and in that sense feel themselves equal to Him. In any case it is certain that their disobedience was absolute and therefore their fall irrevocable. They chose with full knowledge and with a completely free will: and by so doing, instantaneously brought hell into existence.

Their punishment is their own unbelief, although the keenness of their natural intellect cannot be taken away from them. Being hardened in wickedness, it is their hatred of God which alone keeps them in existence and is the source of all their activity: they are incapable of conversion because they persist in their choice. That is why they—who are by nature quick, independent spirits—are held in bonds by a base creature, fire, which for ever surrounds them as they wander restlessly from place to place. For them there is no room any more in heaven.[19] They are eternally excluded from the Beatific Vision, and from that true happiness for which every creature longs and strives.

The Power of the Devils

Christ, who Himself cast out devils and said, as He did so, that the Prince of this world was cast out,[20] is certainly in a position to give us a realistic warning against their evil influence. He tells us to watch and pray, for the devil sows cockle in the field of wheat, which is the world,[21] and takes the seed, which is God's Word, out of the hearts of those who hear it, so that they shall not find faith and be saved.[22] He, too, it was who put it into the heart of Judas Iscariot to betray Our Lord,[23] and claimed power over all the apostles so that he might sift them as wheat.[24] Again, St. Paul does not warn the Ephesians for nothing: "You must wear all the weapons in God's armoury if you would find strength to resist the cunning of the devil. It is not against flesh and blood that

[19] Apic. 12, 8. [20] John 12, 31. [21] Matt. 13, 39
[22] Luke, 8, 12. [23] John 13, 2. [24] Luke, 22, 31

we enter the lists; we have to do with princedoms and powers, with those who have mastery of the world in these dark days, with malign influences in an order higher than ours."[25]

God does not prevent all evil. He does not entirely put a stop to it, lest perhaps in gathering up the tares, the wheat should also be rooted up.[26] The devil tempts man; he knows, with his genius for putting two and two together; with his penetrating knowledge of cause and effect; his age-long experience of the human race; the psychological moment at which it is better to leave us alone, or more profitable to play upon our human imagination and instincts. We can never tell precisely at what point his evil seduction will begin, nor the actual moment when his whispering insinuations will first make themselves heard.

Christ and His apostles knew that this being, fast anchored in evil, would even turn his own perfections into something depraved, and that he would never cease to take delight in ruining others. In that sense belief in the devil has never become out of date. It is not even necessary to believe in the devil in order to serve him: on the contrary, one perhaps never serves him better than when one does not believe in him. But we also know, along with all this, that his power is by no means unlimited.

Pitted against the Lamb of God, who for ever forgives His erring world, the devil is bound to be defeated in the end. "The Lord Jesus will destroy him with the breath of his mouth."[27]

We know that man has the power to resist every temptation of the devil. Whosoever, by God's grace, does not give in, and repeats Our Lord's own words: "Away with thee, Satan; it is written, thou shalt worship the Lord thy God, and serve none but him,"[28] effectually neutralizes all his power. Neither angel nor devil can penetrate into the recesses of our soul. No creature can separate us from the love of God—and certainly neither can the devil.[29]

Our Guardian Angel

We are assisted in our struggle against evil by our *guardian angel*. Just as Raphael accompanied Tobias on every step of

[25] Eph. 6, 11-12. [26] Matt 13, 29. [27] II Thess. 2, 8. [28] Matt. 4, 10.
[29] Rom. 8, 38.

his journey, so each of us has an angel who has particular charge of us throughout life.

This is a matter of general belief in the Church, and is supported by the teaching of Christ Himself. When He warned the Jews against giving scandal to little ones, He said: "I tell you, they have angels of their own in heaven, that behold the Face of My heavenly Father continually."[30] This angel of ours, who is called our guardian angel, protects us in both soul and body; he encourages us to live a purposeful and persevering life, guided by the will and law of God; he makes use of our instinct of self-preservation to warn us of danger, and he shares his wisdom with us when our own fails us. He is also a messenger between God and us, offering up our prayers and requests for us.

Our guardian angel knows that we are always seeking for that which we do not as yet possess, our eyes raised from earth to heaven. These beings, who are initiated into the highest secrets of the supernatural world, and are imbued with God's own loving-kindness, are always ready to share their treasures with us, and to guide poor earthly wanderers, and those who have strayed from the right path, into their heavenly Father's house.

Although it is impossible to tell precisely in what way and at what moment the action of our angel is making itself felt in our soul, yet, according to the most ancient tradition and the Bible, they are always present in our lives to protect us, and especially so at the hour of death.

Therefore, although we dwell here on earth, yet we are continually surrounded by pure, invisible spirits, and our life is encircled by heaven.

§ 2. *The World and Man*

Did God create this world as it is at present? The answer is definitely no. Science is always engaged in advancing new theories regarding the original aspect of the universe. Was the whole thing at first just one atom? One enormous atom with the dimensions of our solar system, which occupied space entirely, and which, at a given moment, exploded so that parts of it were hurled away at an immense speed and the universe began to expand?

[30] Matt. 18, 10.

Or did God create a primeval nebula in which the elements slowly developed by means of—equally created—energy, into vapour and solar systems, into suns and planets, among which was our glowing *earth,* which gradually cooled down into a hard crust? We cannot be certain: but this we do know: that it was our earth which was chosen by the Creator to be the seat of wonderful happenings. At all events, nowhere else in the universe can we find any trace of that which caused this earth to become, in a sense, the very centre of Creation. At one particular moment in the course of evolution, the atoms and molecules on the hard outer crust of earth joined themselves together into a complete whole, in which each atom and each molecule, without losing its characteristic properties, began to carry out a *social function.* They were, for the first time in the history of the world, held together by some principle which suddenly emerged, and which, at all events at the present stage of scientific knowledge, cannot be explained by the ordinary laws of evolution.

Who directed these dumb elements towards each other in such a way as to originate a system of mutual service, in which they began to function harmoniously together as they had never done before?

The believer easily sees in this a fresh intervention of God. New forces were created; an entirely different and original concept, owing nothing to evolution, came into existence: this was *the life principle.*

Perhaps it was originally one cell; perhaps there were millions of cells straight away. But, by some miraculous process, they split up and multiplied themselves: the result was first *growth* and then *organization.* Cells combined and germinated into plants; not just one specimen but in endless variety; over the earth there spread flowers, prairies and forests.

Once God had created the life principle, evolution continued according to natural laws. Then suddenly there appeared fresh phenomena which cannot be explained even by those laws: living creatures, more or less independent of external forces, began to *move themselves* and to show consciousness: thus the *animal* appeared, swam in the water, set foot on earth, rose into the sky.

So the possibilities in the infinite mind of God became realities; inorganic matter and living vegetation were already there at their disposal; they found food awaiting them, received new organs by which they could see, hear and touch; they could swim, creep, walk and fly; they were able to experience pleasure and displeasure, to become prolific and to multiply. The earth continued to turn round the sun, but became increasingly separated from both sun and sister planets. God had designs for the earth.

He knew that the day would dawn when the whole of creation would find its true significance and purpose. The day when it would no longer exist without apparent aim or cohesion, but would become that for which it was first created, that is, a source of admiration and happiness to, and the object of the intelligent and conscious perception of, the best and highest portion of itself: Man.

For man the world still remains a concrete reality, but it has also become a transcendent idea existing in the mind of God. Creation was finally crowned with a Being who consisted not only of matter, but was a mysterious combination or entity, composed of both matter and spirit—a body animated by a soul.

For this man the universe was created: sun, moon, stars, vegetation, animals, and all inorganic substances. Man, for his part, should see the world as an expression of the infinite power of God, and direct it to Him by glorifying Him as the Creator, and by His service and love.

This Being, who is capable of spiritual things, and who can rise above mere earthly matter, must necessarily contain some element which is not material and does not owe its origin in any way to matter. From this we grasp the fact that at the moment of impregnation of every human germ-cell, a soul is created by God.

This visible creation, therefore, is crowned by a being who, although it is bound to it by matter and by the body, yet by its spirit and its spiritual capacities—mind and freewill—is raised far above it as being made in the *Image and Likeness of God.*

We shall thus see that the theory of evolution is in no way opposed to the conception of God's creative activity: at its earliest beginning stands His omnipotent power. At every moment of existence, at every stage of the world's development, He is present, active, the Creator. The very existence and survival of the universe, its development in accordance with possibilities and laws which He has linked together, testify just as surely, and perhaps even more surely, to His supreme sovereignty than would a world without evolution.

The Bible and Creation

"God, at the beginning of time, created heaven and earth. Earth was still an empty waste, and darkness hung over the deep; but already, over its waters, brooded the Spirit of God."

So begins the first chapter of the Bible—the story of Creation. When the twentieth-century man reads this story for the first time and meditates upon it, he almost inevitably receives the impression that this is a case of a writer with an Eastern imagination and impossibly naïve ideas. With quite a number of people who, as children, listened with intense interest to these descriptions, the question arises later on, "Has one to take all this literally?" And many young people who, in their adolescence, have passed through a religious crisis without sufficient guidance, have turned away contemptuously from such fairy-tales, and even sometimes in consequence rejected both Bible and Christianity itself. The story brought them face to face with an insoluble puzzle: The Creation of light before the sun? In six days? And so on.

The answer to all such objections lies in the correct interpretation of the purpose and significance of the Bible regarded as the Word of God.

The Bible—as we have already seen—is not a textbook for students of cosmogeny or biology, and the author of the book of Genesis is not trying to give a scientific explanation of the existence of the world and Man. He is not trying to teach us about the process of their development. The intention of the Bible in general is obviously religious. That also was the intention of the writer of these chapters, but when it came to the study of nature, which is the very foundation of this story (in which the earth forms the centre of the solar system), he naturally expresses himself as a child of his own era. His artificial division of time into six days also serves to show this. Nevertheless he was regarding the work of creation from the religious point of view. His purpose was mainly to present important *religious* truths in an intelligible way. The whole of this portion of Genesis is inspired, and even the form of the revelation has surely not been without divine influence.

But God had no intention at this stage of revealing the chronological order of events in the process of creation, nor (in the second chapter) the manner in which man was created.

One may safely take the Hebrew word jom (day) as indicating *period*; one may even go further and surmise that the author had used his imaginative faculty to place this cosmic occurrence within the framework of the Jewish week: six working days crowned by one day of rest.

In the first chapter of the Bible God Himself answers all those who argue in favour of the theories of everlasting matter, Fate, and the Demiurge of the Gnostics, by declaring that He created everything at the dawn of time. He spoke, and it was done. He alone created, and ordered everything without any difficulty by one movement of His will. Everything which He created was good in its original state: this assurance is repeated seven times. In particular the dignity of Mankind, whom He created, male and female, after His own image and likeness, stands out. Man was made Lord over all other creatures, and was destined to watch over the development of the human race. In this creative act, God, as it were, visibly expressed His own wisdom, love and power.

In the second chapter God is represented to us under the figure of a man (anthropomorphical). He is shown us as planting a garden and making trees to grow, and—in order to ensure its being properly cultivated and looked after—forming Adam from the clay of the ground, breathing into his nostrils the breath of life, and giving him a living soul. He also gave him permission to eat from every tree in the garden, including the Tree of Life, the fruit of which carried with it, in the eating, the gift of perpetual existence; but from the Tree of the Knowledge of Good and Evil alone he must never eat, for the reward was death. Adam knew himself as Lord of Creation: he gave all the animals names: but he still felt himself to be lonely. God saw this, and He caused him therefore to fall into a deep sleep, and taking one of his ribs, fashioned from it a woman. Then He led her to Adam who, in his joy, cried aloud: "It shall be called Woman, this thing that was taken out of man." And that is why a man is destined to leave father and mother, and cling to his wife instead, so that they two become one flesh.

The whole narrative goes to show how graphically the facts of Revelation are presented to us: and this type of description was particularly adapted to the childlike yet vivid Eastern imagination of the Jewish people at that period.

In comparison with the value of the religious truths which are revealed to us in this chapter, the mode of expression is comparatively unimportant. We learn that Man was created by a particular and individual act of God: his soul was also the result of special and divine intervention: his relationship to God was essentially friendly—nevertheless he had to undergo a test. It was necessary that he should, personally and freely, accept all that he had received from his Creator by formally acknowledging His absolute sovereignty. God asked of him the offering of his complete obedience by means of this one limitation placed upon his dominion over the world of nature. In this prohibition he was to see and recognize nothing else but the free will of God. In spite of his keen intellect, it was impossible for him to grasp, unaided, exactly why to eat of the fruit of that particular tree, and to transgress God's order, should inevitably mean his death. Here was a demand for complete surrender of the intellect and, through that submission and its fulfilment, the acknowledgment that he belonged to God: utterly and in every way.

CHAPTER VIII

THE FALL AND REDEMPTION

SYNOPSIS

The mystery of the Blessed Trinity is the mystery of the intimate and interior life of God: divine knowledge and divine love. This love did not remain enclosed in the infinity of His divine Being, but urged Him to create angels, men, and a world in which mankind could live.

Man was created in a state of friendship with God, but it was his lot to obey. We shall now see how man sinned against this obedience, and so lost God's friendship, and how therefore, as a consequence of this, all his descendants were also born outside the friendship of God (original sin).

§ 1. *The Fall and Original Sin*

THE FACT of man's fall is told, briefly and psychologically, in the third chapter of Genesis.

There was external temptation: the devil inspired the commission of sin, and through him—according to Scripture—both spiritual and physical death came into the world. He beguiled Eve into eating the forbidden fruit and, after eating it, she offered some to Adam, who also ate of it. Then their eyes were opened: they felt all the bitterness and humiliation of the deed, all the disappointment: but most of all were they aware of a new spiritual disorder in their souls, of a disturbance of the original harmony. They perceived that they were naked.

The first man sinned, intentionally and of his own free will. He deliberately refused God that fundamental subjection which was His due, and he did not refuse it under the urge of either passion or weakness, but with full knowledge of what he was doing. By this sin he refused God the one thing which He had asked of him. It was a sin of pride: a fundamental refusal to accept man's essential supernatural dependence upon God. Adam should have continued to accept by faith, that which he could not understand with his mind.

And immediately God called Adam, who had hidden among the trees, to come and give an account of himself. From the ensuing conversation, we can already gauge the limited natural outlook of this man, fallen from his high original state. The first man and woman lost sanctifying grace through their revolt, that is to say they lost the friendship of God. This we express by the words, the loss of supernatural life, which means participation in the inward life of God.

The first woman was punished, both as woman and as mother. She was to suffer in child-birth, and to be subject to her husband. The first man was also punished; his lot was to be lifelong toil and labour until he returned to that earth from which he was taken. The immortality of the body was in abeyance for the time being. God cast them both out of the Garden and, subjected to the penalty of death, they lost, with their vanished soundness of soul and body, the happiness of that world of theirs.

For a time God's love had to leave them to themselves: but not all Man's future hopes and prospects were shattered. God spoke to the devil in veiled language of a continued feud to be established between him and the woman, between his offspring and hers; and of how one of her seed—as we know indeed happened later on—was to crush his head.[1] God did not leave Man entirely to his fate; on the contrary, He even provided garments, made out of skins, to clothe the two of them. His loving care in regard to such a small detail, shows that the plan of Providence was ready from all eternity; a plan of love and mercy.

Nevertheless, Man's first sin fixed the fate of the human race. We still lack that which he lost for us. He not only harmed himself but all mankind: he robbed both himself and us of the friendship of God, so that we are now, in the words of the Psalmist, born in sin; guilt is already with us when we are conceived.[2] This sin, called *original sin*, is our bitter heritage, and the inevitable condition of man from the hour when he first sees the light.

This idea of original sin is perhaps apt to raise in us a feeling of indignation and, inspired by a sense of justice, we are maybe inclined to retort: "What connection have I with the folly of the first man? How can God tolerate such

[1] Gen. 3, 15.
[2] Ps. 50, 7.

injustice, particularly in the case of a sin where so many and such terrible consequences were involved?"

And yet it is a fundamental tenet of our Faith that we all enter the world tainted with original sin. The Church bases this belief upon St. Paul's Epistle to the Romans: "It was through one man that guilt came into the world; and, since death came owing to guilt, death was handed on to all mankind by one man . . . all alike were guilty men . . . this one man's fault brought death on a whole multitude . . . the sentence which brought us condemnation arose out of one man's action . . . a multitude, through one man's disobedience, became guilty." We see then, that from the fact that death is common to all men, the apostle deduces that original sin is also common to us all. Not all men have sinned personally, and yet they have all died, contrary to God's original intention which had offered us immortality. This fact of communal death, demands a communal cause: and that cause is the communal sin which all have inherited from Adam. This is the gist of St. Paul's reasoning. But even more important for us is his unequivocal statement that all have sinned, and all are sinners through the disobedience of one.

Here we are faced with one of the mysteries of God's impenetrable decisions: it is a mystery which only faith knows how to accept. We cannot prove it by the intellect, although we may agree with Pascal's remark that man, without this mystery of our Faith, would be still less comprehensible! It explains at least some of the conflicting elements in his nature: both his grandeur and his misery: that misery which is the result of his high aspirations, that grandeur which loses itself in self-seeking, avarice, pride, and the pursuit of trivialities.

What is this Original Sin? It is sin which is already present in every human being from the first moment of existence. But how, then, is this possible? How, for instance, can a newly born child be in a state of sin? Even though we may not be able to give a full and complete answer to these questions, yet we are obliged to accept it on the Word of God.

This guilt or sin is, as it were, impersonal, yet present in all the children of Adam. It is not a willed and individual deviation from the law of God, but a condition which we inherit: all men come into the world with this inescapable taint. It is a result of the breach between God and the human race, which followed on the first sin of the first man, and from whom it has been passed down to all men.

In what, then, does this guilt consist? Not in disorderly passions and desires which lead to sin; not in punishment; not in death; not in the wretched state of affairs which followed on the Fall; but in the death of the soul, in the loss of that union with God which the first man enjoyed, and in consequent deprivation of sanctifying grace. From this condition of sin, which is ours by inheritance, virtually proceeds the interior disorder of our nature: struggle, suffering and death.

Personally we are not guilty, but we share the guilt of the one who was appointed by God to be the responsible head and founder of the human race, that is to say of Adam. This guilt remains a mystery.

Adam, after all, could only pass on human nature in the state in which he himself possessed it. After the Fall, it was bereft of its God-given privileges. He could only transmit it in its maimed condition: turned away from the Creator.

All that he lost, both for himself and for us, we can dimly estimate by what Christ returned to us in even greater degree (as we shall see later on): by what He restored to us, we can to a certain extent assess the original condition. It is quite certain—and for this we have the authority of St. Paul—that God did not wish man to die. Immortality was his special privilege: a gift which exalted him, who was by nature destined to mortality, above his normal, human existence. Thus death came into the world through sin. The Church, mindful of the course of events after the Fall, when our first parents were ashamed of their nakedness, believes that before the Fall they possessed a vigorous and continual inclination towards good. Their spirit was capable of avoiding all the bad results which would normally and naturally flow from the combination of spirit and flesh. The body peacefully obeyed the reasoning of the mind; instinct allowed the spirit to flow freely and easily towards both its origin and its goal; passions only moved man to good; the soul was subjected to God. In return God bestowed upon man complete interior harmony, in which the spirit could freely expand, and in which he could live the life of a child of God in all its perfection. His nature, still untarnished and intact, was continually open to the action and the grace of his Creator. Thus he shared in

God's own life and God honoured him with His friendship and love.

By sin he lost for us all the privilege of immortality and of that interior harmony. The latter, in particular, we feel intensely: the constant fight of spirit against instinct, our everyday experience of life, all go to show our simultaneous desire for good and attraction towards evil. Yet this is only the bitter consequence of the loss of man's best gift: friendship with God. Human nature was torn away from divine life itself: with these wounds still upon us we come into the world.

We inherit the wrongdoing of Adam, although, as a matter of experience, we never notice either the guilt or the responsibility. What we actually experience are the consequences.

We need not, however, exaggerate these. It is true that our mind is darkened, our will weakened; the possibility of aversion from God has been introduced into the world; passions drive us against our spirit and will; our body is forever moving towards death and is chastened by sickness, suffering and labour; human society, in both its communal and domestic aspects, destroys itself by egoism and self-love. Man's nature has once more descended to its own level: the tension between spirit and matter has become very evident, without our nature in any way suffering destruction. Inclination towards sin does not imply total corruption. There remains an inclination towards good, an unceasing search for our original harmony and, that seeming paradox, a restless striving for rest in God. There remains both liberty and responsibility: nature is wounded but is not dead.

When, however, we come to the question as to *why* God has linked man with his first ancestor, we come to a mystery of faith. The answer which we cannot give would, in any case, have to take into account two other factors: our Redemption, and a solidarity which, while we cannot understand it, is nevertheless a reality. For actually each soul is not only linked up with its own body, but with a number of other bodies; that is with all those of its own generation, and through its generation with the whole of its race. Has not God perhaps more regard for this bodily connection between us than we suspect? He created us in a natural and supernatural union of destiny with the first man. I fell because of Adam, so also, I rise again, not of myself but in Christ. Community of redemption presupposes community of guilt. Nevertheless, this hereditary guilt remains a mystery, although not a mystery which arraigns either God's justice or His love. There can be no question here of injustice, because there was no abrogation of rights. Where no rights exist, no injustice can be committed. Of what did God rob us? Of an acquired right? No. He only took away that which he had originally given as an added gift—but a gift with a condition attached to it. We retain all that as men we can demand. We can even see His love entwined with the sadness of the Fall.

We are inclined sometimes to speak as of a divine plan which failed; as if, when God saw that His original intention was not being carried out, He again intervened and provided a Redeemer. This version of the facts is very human but very inaccurate. A divine plan which failed would be an impossibility.

God created a *man* who was neither an angel nor an animal, but composed of spirit and matter, bound together in a close and intimate unity. Now spirit means reflective consciousness; consciousness taking up a position in regard to things in general; liberty, choice, decision and responsibility. God's greatest benefaction to mankind was freewill, yet it is precisely through freewill that we are able temporarily to oppose Him.

The Creator saw this possibility of danger and disaster unavoidably joined to His most precious gift. In His eternal *Now*, He saw (and sees) that man would abuse it. He saw (and sees) Adam's fall, but He never saw it as one isolated fact. That which happens to us successively, in our *before* and *after*, is always present to His sight in all its detail, as one complete whole. From all eternity, Fall and Sin are connected with Redemption. The divine plan culminates in *Jesus Christ*, Lamb of God, who taketh away the sins of the world.

In the end, this mystery remains a decree arising out of wisdom and love. The sin of our first parents was not willed by God, yet gave Him the opportunity and made it possible for Him to show His love for us to the uttermost limits. It enabled Him to send His own Son as our Example, Redeemer and Saviour. Through Him, God was able to approach more closely to Man in order to share with him His supernatural life. Through the very abuse which man made of God's best gift of liberty, He was able, in the end, to draw His greatest glory. Thus Creation and Fall are a preparation for Jesus Christ.

By leaving man, in a sense, alone; by giving him back his own nature, and by not immediately restoring to him that lost harmony, God continually stirs in him a realization of his own impotence, and from this realization is born the longing for the Omnipotent, for the pardon and mercy of the Redeemer.

By giving man death as an inevitable certainty, God shows him the relativity of all earthly things, and allows him to learn by experience that no absolute values are to be found on earth. By the disturbance of his interior tranquillity and the resultant tension between flesh and spirit, He gives—with the help of divine grace—its full value to the human will by virtue of strength and perseverance. But the perfect balance, the inner peace, can only, in the end, be realized through Christ Himself.

God's eternal decree—to us an enduring mystery—remains to the Faithful a mystery of His love. And in the Easter Vigil the Catholic is able with genuine conviction to join with the Church in singing: *"O, felix culpa,"* "Oh, happy fault that was worthy of so great a Redeemer."

§ 2. *Incarnation and Redemption*

SYNOPSIS

I. The mystery of the Blessed Trinity is the mystery of the intimate and interior life of God: divine knowledge and divine love. This love did not remain enclosed in the infinity of His divine Being, but urged Him to create angels, men, and a world in which mankind could live.
Man was created in a state of friendship with God, but it was his lot to obey. Man sinned against this obedience, and so lost God's friendship, and therefore, as a consequence of this, all his descendants were also born outside the friendship of God (original sin).

II. We shall now see how God has redeemed mankind through His Son.

1. *Necessity of Redemption*

Cast out of Paradise, man roamed the earth a prey to all the fears of his darkened spirit, to the fruitless efforts of his weakened will, sighing amidst the disorganization of his unruly nature. The heavy load of evil which he carried for ever weighed down his paralysed soul; suffering attacked his body; he found his surroundings a poignant limitation with no relief, and death as the only and inevitable end. Redemption was sorely needed.

But only God could redeem: He alone was able to save man, too mortally wounded ever to rise again by his own efforts.

Sin is indeed an offence against the majesty of God. Every offence is measured by the dignity of the person to whom it is offered. The dignity of God is part of His infinite worth and excellence: an offence offered to Him is therefore measureless, limitless, infinite in its outrage, even though it be only committed by finite, limited man.

How then can satisfaction be given for an infinite offence? Only by some mark of infinite homage. Man, however, was unable to offer this. Once again, honour only receives its value from the status of the person who offers it. Infinite satisfaction, therefore, was, and is, outside the power of man. He is dead. To raise oneself from the dead is beyond human capacity and requires divine intervention.

Only God could redeem and—He wanted to redeem. Had He so willed, He could have pardoned quite simply, without further ado. He decided, however, to use other and very special means. There is no question here of *obligation*, for what man lost, he lost by his own fault, and that which he so lost was a pure grace and free gift. He had no right to share in the life of God nor to possess an harmonious nature. St. Paul says: "How rich God is in mercy, with what an excess of love He loved us! Our sins had made dead men of us, and He, in giving life to Christ, gave life to us too."[3]

Redemption, which is a necessity for man, is no necessity for God. It was love and mercy alone which decided Him to save. But this love follows a divine path.

God's love, indeed, embraces all the perfections of His infinite Being: in that love there flowers at once His unchangeableness and endless activity: His eternity and solicitude for temporal affairs: His pity and His justice.

Justice. His love desires to embrace the whole of His justice and, in saving man, to give one clear token of both. *He wishes to express by one and the same sign* His infinite regard for order and *justice,* and His surpassing *love.*

[3] Eph. 2, 4.

He it was who decreed that amends should be made in proportion to the insult offered: He demanded an infinite propitiation, a divine merit which was sufficient to satisfy His undiluted justice. Now this propitiation had to come from Him who had sinned: human reparation had necessarily to have its share in it.

That which was demanded by justice, was to be provided by love: He decided on the incarnation of His Son and the revelation, through Him, of both love and justice. As Man He was to take upon Himself all our guilt, and as God make an infinitely sublime act of reparation.

Mankind, which had sinned in its entirety through one man, could only thus be redeemed in its entirety by one Man also. God showed His forgiveness by the Incarnation of the Word: for this indeed was the sole means by which satisfaction could be offered in proportion to the guilt.

2. *The Incarnation*

The very heart of the Christian confession of faith lies in the mystery of God's Incarnation, which has been summarized for us by St. John in the first chapter of his Gospel: "And the Word was made flesh, and came to dwell among us."[4]

This Word is the Son of God who, from all eternity, proceeds from the Father: the Light which shone amidst the darkness of our world, and through whom God revealed both His Truth and His Love. He did this with divine superabundance: the Word of God—the Son of God—become man, with a created nature such as ours, and dwelt among us here on earth.

Christianity stands or falls by this double fact, that Jesus Christ was really God as well as truly man. His humanity was not merely an appearance, but was a real existing nature and was the Way by which God was able to approach and to redeem us. This was no case of God revealing Himself through the humanity of Christ: this man *was God* just as much as this divine Person *was man*. Jesus Christ suggests His divine origin by His miracles and His preaching; He appropriates divine privileges such as the forgiveness of sin. *All* that belongs to the Father, He tells us, belongs to Him.[5] He dwells in heaven and He *alone* knows the Father,[6] with

[4] John 1, 14. [5] John 16, 15. [6] Matt. 11, 27.

whom He is One.[7] Always conscious of His eternal pre-existence, He remains united with the Father.[8] He is the way and the truth and the life, and it is through Him that we receive eternal salvation.[9] He requires from us both faith and the surrender of the heart and spirit. St. Paul depicts Him as the true likeness of the God whom we cannot see, as that first birth which precedes every act of creation,[10] through whom and for whom everything exists, and to whom everything will finally be subjected.[11]

This God would seem to be man as truly as we are ourselves: fashioned as we are, only sinless.[12] His whole life as described in the Gospels, continually emphasizes this point: He thought, He loved, He was full of pity: He was indignant: He worked hard, and, weary, He sat down beside a well to rest. He prayed to God, and lived according to the precepts of a clearly defined interior life, always obeying His Father. After a painful agony, He died and was buried.

He was at once God and man. The Church expresses this insoluble mystery as follows: One divine Person possesses both divine and human nature, two natures unmixed in one Person. This human nature is at the service of Christ's divinity and it therefore follows that the least human deed has a divine value. In His human nature He is submissive to the Father, conscious of having received everything from Him; yet He is united to the Father by the one undivided divine nature which constitutes His Being. *In what manner* this union of human nature and divine Person took place in the womb of Mary remains an impenetrable mystery; although we know that it was through the Holy Ghost that the miracle was performed.

St. Luke tells us about the Incarnation: "When the sixth month came, God sent the angel Gabriel to a city of Galilee called Nazareth, where a virgin dwelt, betrothed to a man of David's lineage; his name was Joseph and the virgin's name was Mary. Into her presence the angel came, and said, Hail, thou who art full of grace; the Lord is with thee; blessed art thou among women. She was much perplexed at hearing him speak so, and cast about in her mind, what she was to make of such a greeting. Then the angel said to her, Mary, do not be afraid; thou hast found favour in the sight of God.

[7] John 10, 30. [8] John 8, 16. [9] John 14, 6.
[10] Col. 1, 15. [11] I Cor. 15, 22-28. [12] Heb. 4, 15.

And, behold, thou shalt conceive in thy womb, and shalt bear a son, and shalt call Him Jesus. He shall be great, and men will know Him for the Son of the Most High; the Lord God will give Him the throne of his father David, and He shall reign over the House of Jacob eternally. His Kingdom shall never have an end. But Mary said to the angel, How can that be, since I have no knowledge of man? And the angel answered her, the Holy Spirit will come upon thee, and the power of the Most High will overshadow thee. Thus this holy offspring of thine shall be known for the Son of God. See, moreover, how it fares with thy cousin Elizabeth; she is old, yet she too has conceived a son; she who was reproached with barrenness is now in her sixth month, to prove that nothing can be impossible with God. And Mary said, Behold the handmaid of the Lord: let it be done unto me according to thy word. And with that the angel left her."

Through the Holy Grost—the mutual love of the Father and the Son—it came about that He took our nature.

Finally, St. Paul thus summarizes the fact of the Incarnation in his Epistle to the Philippians: "His nature is, from the first, divine, and yet He did not see, in the rank of Godhead, a prize to be coveted; He dispossessed Himself, and took the nature of a slave, fashioned in the likeness of men, and presenting Himself to us in human form; and then He lowered His own dignity, accepted an obedience which brought Him to death, death on a cross."[13]

In powerful language the apostle describes how God the Son became a member of the fallen human race. He emptied Himself of His divine glory, of His majesty and splendour, by appearing on earth in the form of a slave, of an ordinary human being. In His mundane life, His helpless childhood, His eating, drinking and sleeping: under the guise of His human work and suffering, in His shameful death on the cross, He hid His divinity. One of the last words He uttered expressed His profound, His abandoned loneliness. "My God, My God, why hast Thou forsaken Me?"

But, St. Paul goes on to say, that is why God has raised Him to such a height; given Him that name which is greater than any other name, so that everything in heaven and on earth, and under the earth, must bend the knee before the name of Jesus.[14]

[13] Phil. 2, 6-9. [14] Phil. 2, 9-12.

3. *The Reason for the Incarnation*

Why did God become man? The reason for the Incarnation lies at once in God and in ourselves.

God became man, not so much to reveal His divine attributes, which we could have discovered by the aid of ordinary reason; not even primarily to prove His divinity; *He came to reveal His love.* The God-man is the irrefutable sign of God's invisible, divine Love.

Enclosed in that love lay the ultimate aim of the Incarnation —the Redemption: Incarnation resulted in Redemption because love always takes into account the actual, concrete situation of the one to whom it gives itself. Man, indeed, as well as the torn world to which the Son of God came down, had need of salvation. A lost child, wounded by sin, conscious of guilt and the punishment of guilt, wandered forlornly upon the earth, which produced for him but thorns and thistles. Then the Father bent down from heaven to seek, as a shepherd seeks his lost sheep.

He loved the world so much that He gave His only begotten Son, that whosoever believed in Him might not perish, but have eternal life. He did not send His Son into the world to reject the world, but so that the world might find salvation through Him.[15]

Now God could have saved mankind by a single decree of His will. Instead He chose the Incarnation in order to attain still other purposes. His Son was to announce a new teaching, and to perpetuate that teaching by establishing a Kingdom in accordance with it. In the Person of Christ, the love and mercy, the sanctity and the power of God was to reach us in the most tangible form possible. And finally it was to give us, in this Incarnate Redeemer, an example for all time, and for the whole of mankind.

4. *The Redeemer and His Redemption*

As we said before, God planned from all eternity to raise men to the high estate of His friends and children, and to draw them into His own divine life. And because He foresaw sin, He included it also in His resolve, but in such a way that both love and justice should shine out in the final forgiveness;

[15] John 3, 16-19.

in the *complete* reparation for sin, so that the original position, such as it had existed in the time of our first parents, should again be restored. So it was that this act of reparation became in fact a radical redemption, a " new creation " St. Paul calls it; a grace out of all proportion to the fault: the gift greater than the sin.[16]

This reconciliation, this redemption which we possess in Jesus Christ, settles the account for sin in all its forms. Sin was, and still is, a transgression against the will of God: an I-will-not-serve-God: and therefore an offence against His infinite majesty. Christ repaired and atoned for this offence by leading a life oriented solely towards God. The will of the Father was His daily food. He carried out that will from the moment of His birth until the moment of His death, during every instant of His existence on earth. Love urged Him to a complete surrender of thought and deed, of aspiration and desire, to the God upon whom everyone and everything alone depends. Thus each act of His assumed a redemptive value, each moment of such a life was sufficient to make complete and entire reparation, since each moment held within it the entire submission of a Man—but of a Man who was also God, and therefore impressed on this obedience the seal of His Divine value and fruitfulness.

Through sin, through the original turning away from God, a disorderly human nature had come into being, in which the appetites, the world and the devil were confusedly intermingled, and tore the spirit away from that goal for which it was destined. Christ remedied this wounded condition of nature by His life of complete detachment, not only from self but from everything which could impede the ascent of the soul to God. By His example, and that interior peace which was the result of the fixed orientation of mind and heart towards one eternal aim, He earned for us the strength which makes it possible for us once more to restore that interior order of our being. From this fact it again follows that *everything* which He did during His life was of importance for our Redemption, although it was the final act of that life which was of absolutely conclusive importance.

His life alone did not complete the Redemption of the world. But just before His death, Jesus Himself twice declared that His task as Saviour was fulfilled. In His

[16] Rom. 5, 15.

discourse after the Last Supper He said to His Father: "I have exalted Thy glory on earth, by achieving the task which Thou gavest me to do," and this task referred to the preaching of the Gospel. In His greatest agony upon the cross, just as He was about to die, He cried aloud: "It is achieved." Death and suffering belonged to the work of redemption and were its crown. God the Son, who became man for us, died on the cross for our sins. Is this Crucifixion, then, to be regarded as something accidental? An incident which was no more than the beautiful end of a courageous life, but which had yet no vital connection with it? No.

By the death of Christ, the Bible tells us, the Redemption was completed. John the Baptist had already pointed Him out as the Pascal Lamb on his first beholding of Him: "Look, this is the Lamb of God: look, this is He who takes away the sin of the world."[17]

St. Paul, constrained by the Spirit of God, could not be silent as to the cross of Christ: "I had no thought," he pleaded, "of bringing you any other knowledge than that of Jesus Christ, and of Him as crucified."[18] In many different passages and in various beautiful phrases, he refers to the redemptive death: "Now, through the blood of Christ you have been brought close, you who were once so far away . . . Both sides He would reconcile to God through His cross."[19]

St. Peter, in his first Epistle, refers to us as redeemed by the Precious Blood of Christ.[20] Jesus Himself, at the Last Supper, spoke of His Body which was given for us and of His Blood which was to be shed for us.[21]

It was here, upon the cross, that the complete restoration of the original condition of Man was effected: here upon the cross that Our Lord's perfect obedience to His Father's commands was placed in the balance against the sin of Adam; here that He fulfilled the will of God by the sacrifice of His life and of His Body, in spite of the terrible dereliction of spirit which overshadowed Him.

That great popular Catholic devotion, the Way of the Cross, repeats after each meditation upon the Stations, those words inspired by faith: "We adore Thee, O Christ, and we praise Thee, because by Thy Holy Cross Thou hast redeemed the world."

[17] John 1, 29. [18] I Cor. 2, 2. [19] Eph. 2, 13-16.
[20] I Pet., 18-19. [21] Luke 22, 19-20.

Why did the Father exact this death from His Son?

The Christian conception of God does not allow of the explanation that only a bloody death could be accepted as atonement: first He must see blood, and only then would He be able to forgive: first payment, then reconciliation.

Jesus did not suffer against His will; but He knew that this complete self-immolation as man was part of His messianic mission. In loving obedience to this Divine insight, and for love of Man, He made the offering. He did not only undergo the suffering, He accepted it. It was His free and conscious act. By this very freedom we were saved, and in turn became free from sin. Christ Himself lived out in its entirety the truth which He once expressed in a parable: "A grain of wheat must fall into the ground and die, or else it remains nothing more than a grain of wheat; but if it dies, then it yields rich fruit."[22]

Christ's sacrifice upon the cross was a true sacrifice. When we in our turn offer this Sacrifice of His, we express symbolically our own surrender to God; we directly acknowledge Him as our Creator and as our Last End. The essence of all sacrifice lies in the inward surrender with which it is made. The offering—or its destruction—remains no more than the outward expression of our interior desire.

In the sacrifice of the cross Christ offered Himself, His life, His Body, to the heavenly Father. Even His crucified death was not so important as the burning desire to surrender to God's will, the interior conviction of being destined for God, and the unshakable resolution to live for Him alone. All this he revealed by the offering of His Body and Blood. Once more, the magnificent sacrificial gesture was a true sign of His voluntary surrender to the Father, and for that reason it paid the highest possible honour to God.

Jesus Himself became the sacrifice and for ever so remains. He died of His own free will, and before He died He offered His life to God. This moment was the supreme height of His great love. He was able to save us, and to reconcile us to God, by this voluntary obedience and love, which was symbolized by the offering of His human nature on the cross. Vicariously, for our sake, He in reality commenced this sacrifice from the very first moment of His life, and continued it without ceasing in every action of His, until finally He completed it,

[22] John 12, 24.

unmistakably and visibly, before the whole world on Calvary. Jesus therefore was at once the Giver and the Gift: the Priest and the Sacrifice.

This was the way which He chose in order to unite both, the human and the divine: to achieve a total reparation for sin by balancing His own subjection against our disobedience, by offering His own surrender against our refusal of love; and thus, while honouring God in the highest possible degree, simultaneously giving the greatest proof of His love for us.

Thus the Redemption remains rather a mystery of love than of justice.

Precisely *what* did His Redemption effect in Man?

The death of Christ freed us from the guilt of sin as well as from its punishment. He Himself became reparation for sin, and with this reparation the punishment was also done away with. But the actual forgiveness of sin was only a beginning: a complete restoration of the original state of grace was the goal.

Through *faith* and through baptism—sealed by love—His death lives on in unsurpassed fruitfulness. An interior cleansing is effected, and restoration of our personal, supernatural union with the Father. At the same time the shadow of His cross fell menacingly upon the devil and all the powers of evil, who can now only attack us when we ourselves allow it. Although the interior tension between spirit and flesh remains, and our restless passions still urge us in the direction of sin, yet His example is ever before us, and the grace which he won for us by His death on the cross, is always at our disposal. By His Resurrection He has conquered death, and one day we too shall rise with Him from the tomb. Body and soul, equally imperishable, await together an eternity of joy.

Thus, in the end, His Redemption restored to us everything which we had lost in Adam. St. Paul tells us: "As our fault was amplified, grace has been more amply bestowed than ever; that so, where guilt held its reign of death, justifying grace should reign instead, to bring us eternal life through Jesus Christ our Lord."[23]

All share in this redemptive power of the suffering and death of Christ. "He died for all, He has given Himself as a ransom for all," writes St. Paul again, who was the first to link together Creation, Fall, Redemption and eternal bliss, in

[23] Rom. 5, 20-21.

one descriptive synthesis. No one is excluded. He brought eternal happiness to the souls of those who died before His coming. He still communicates His redemptive power by faith and the Sacraments to those who live to-day. Through His life, His Passion and His Death, He is the cause of all our blessedness—the Saviour of Mankind.[24]

The Redeemer

Jesus Christ is the Redeemer of all mankind. Jesus means Saviour: Christ, the Anointed. He was, through the power of the Holy Ghost, anointed with the Godhead, His humanity having been taken up into the oneness of His divine Person.

In the God-made-man, we encounter our Mediator; the One who stands between God and ourselves in order to reconcile God with us and to unite us to God. He is our Mediator because He brought us the truth; He revealed to us the mysteries of the intimate, personal life of God, and of His eternal plan for men; and He brought the eternal viewpoint of God to some extent within the compass of limited human intelligence. He is our Mediator because He made it possible for us to share once more in eternal life;[25] made us once more the children of God;[26] and bestowed on us the gift of the Holy Ghost.[27]

In this once dying, now risen, Christ, we acknowledge our *Saviour and our Redeemer.*

And in this Christ, anointed by the Holy Spirit, we acknowledge our *Priest,* our *Teacher,* and our *King.*

a. As God-man He is *Priest*

This priesthood is described in the Epistle to the Hebrews: "He did not raise Himself to the dignity of the High Priesthood; it was God that raised Him to it, when He said, Thou art my Son, I have begotten Thee this day."[28]

At His conception in the womb of Mary, at the moment when the union of both natures in one Person took place, Christ was ordained Priest: it was then that He was appointed Mediator, in the words of St. Paul, "A representative of men

[24] I Tim. 4, 10. [25] John 5, 24-26. [26] John 3, 15.
[27] John 14, 16. [28] Heb. 5, 5.

in their dealings with God, to offer gifts and sacrifices in expiation of their sins."[29]

He, however, is far beyond all other priests in stature, for His is a Priesthood which never ends: "Of those other priests there was a succession, since death denied them permanence; whereas Jesus continues for ever and His priestly office is unchanging; that is why He can give salvation to those who through Him make their way to God, He lives on still to make intercession on our behalf."[30]

Man from among men, He is "the High Priest that suited our need, holy and guileless and undefiled, not reckoned among us sinners, lifted high above all the heavens".[31] "One who has no need to do as those other priests did, offering a two-fold sacrifice day by day, first for his own sins, then for those of the people. What He has done He has done once for all, and the offering was Himself."[32]

In heaven He remains the sacrificed Lamb before the throne of God: there He acts as our intercessor: "Whatever request you make of the Father in My Name, I will grant."[33]

Now we can enter the sanctuary with confidence through the Blood of Christ.[34] We have only to knock, and it shall be opened to us. Everything will be accomplished through Christ our Lord.

b. As God-man He is our *Teacher*

Christ emphatically pointed out that among those belonging to the Kingdom of God there should be no competition for the first place. The Scribes and Pharisees had established themselves in the Seat from which Moses had once taught, and from this height they imparted their knowledge; nevertheless, He told the Jews, they would find themselves excluded from the Kingdom of Heaven. The followers of Christ, on the contrary, were not to claim the title of Rabbi, for whosoever exalts himself shall be humbled. We have but one Master and are all brothers alike. Nor are we to call any man on earth our Father; we have but one Father and He is in heaven. Neither are we to be called teachers; we have but one Teacher, Christ.[35] He is the Light of the world, and he

[29] Heb. 5, 1-6. [30] Heb. 7, 24-25. [31] Heb. 7, 26.
[32] Heb. 7, 27. [33] John 14, 14. [34] Heb. 10, 19.
[35] Matt. 23, 1-13.

who follows Him can never walk in darkness; he will possess that light which is life.[36]

"The words spoken by Him whom God has sent are God's own words."[37] And He only speaks of what is known to Him and testifies of what His eyes have seen.[38] And whoever hears those Commandments of His and carries them out, is like a wise man who built his house upon rock; and the rain fell, and floods and wind beat upon that house, and it did not fall; it was founded upon rock.[39]

As Teacher He gave us the example, a new example: as St. Augustine so rightly puts it: "He did not say, learn from Me how to build a world and raise the dead, but learn from Me; I am gentle and humble of heart."[40] He pleaded for interior detachment: "If any man has a mind to come My way, let him renounce himself."[41] In the Sermon on the mount,[42] He explained the whole philosophy of His new Kingdom: the Kingdom of God.

Unlike the teachers who had preceded Him, He taught as one having authority,[43] and often in parables.

On one occasion He rejoiced: "Father, I give Thee praise that Thou hast hidden all this from the wise and the prudent, and revealed it to little children. Be it so, Father, since this finds favour in Thy sight."[44]

c. As God-man He is *King*

We have already seen that the Messianic prophecies described a ruler who was to establish a Kingdom in which, at last, the honour due to God was to be paid to Him in full.[45] Christ fulfilled this prophecy. But He asked for a different form of Kingship to that which His disciples, following the ancient texts, tried to force upon Him. It was no part of His plan to be crowned.

His Kingdom was not of this world, although at last, when lifted up from the earth, He would draw all men to Himself.

In Him all created things took their being; they were all created through Him and in Him; and in Him all subsist.[46]

Above all He is King and Head of His Church upon earth,

[36] John 8, 12. [37] John 3, 34. [38] John 3, 11.
[39] Matt. 7, 24. [40] Matt. 11, 29. [41] Mark 8, 34 and Matt. 6, 24.
[42] Matt. 5, 6, 7. [43] Matt. 7, 29. [44] Matt. 11, 25-26.
[45] Ps. 2, 2-9 and Ps. 109, 1-4. [46] Col. 1, 16-17.

and through that Church He claims the whole human race. He is the Lord, says St. Paul, and every man comes within the range of His election; He shed His Blood for all, and the Spirit of Truth speaks through Him to all men.

"Art Thou a King, then?" questioned Pilate, and Jesus replied: "It is thy own lips that have called me a King. What I was born for, what I came into the world for, is to bear witness of the truth. Whosoever belongs to the truth, listens to My voice."[47]

He rightly claimed this Kingdom: He had received it from no one; he was a born King. It belonged and belongs to Him by right because of the Personal Union of God the Son with our human nature. He is King because He has ransomed us. He gave His life for us; He redeemed us; He is our only Mediator with the Father. Under this kingly title we are entirely dependent upon His love. His Kingdom belongs mainly to the supernatural order, for it is the interior kingdom of souls; nevertheless the whole of nature and the natural order are also subject to Him. Not for Him, however, is the actual administration of the material affairs of earth; that He leaves to us.

He rules for the sake of love. His government is full of solicitude. He resembles a loving Shepherd, who gives His life for His sheep.[48]

He desires reparation. The bruised reed He will not break. He is the Way, but He compels no man. He only invites and encourages, giving the support of His strength. His love draws us.

One day, at the world's end, He will come again to judge the living and the dead.[49] Whoever will not listen to the voice of love will then hear the voice of truth. But for those who have faithfully sought for the truth, and lived by the light which was vouchsafed them, an eternal crown has been prepared; in the contemplation of the infinite perfections of God, they will find their own perfection and eternal happiness. Then they will be, in the full sense of the word, *redeemed.*

[47] John 18, 37. [48] John 10, 1. [49] John 5, 27 and Apoc. 19, 11.

CHAPTER IX

GRACE

SUMMARY

I. The mystery of the Blessed Trinity is the mystery of the intimate and interior life of God: divine knowledge and divine love. This love did not remain enclosed in the infinity of His divine Being, but urged Him to create angels, men and a world in which mankind could live.

Man was created in a state of friendship with God, but it was his lot to obey. We have seen how man sinned against this obedience, and so lost God's friendship, and how therefore, as a consequence of this, all his descendants were also born outside the friendship of God (original sin).

II. In His eternal mercy God redeemed mankind through His Son.

III. We shall now see how, by means of this Redemption, man was given new life, a life of grace, by which he is raised to the supernatural order.

WHY DID THE SON OF GOD BECOME MAN? In order to reveal God's love for man. God is love, and this love showed itself at its greatest when Christ, His Son, hung upon the cross to redeem us. God's mercy desired to save man through the medium of the Sacrifice of His own Son, become man. In the following expressive words, St. Paul describes the process of Redemption: "With us Christ's love is a compelling motive, and this is the conviction we have reached: if one man died on behalf of all, then all thereby became dead men. Christ died for us all, so that being alive should no longer mean living with our own life, but with His life who died for us and has risen again, and therefore, henceforward, we do not think of anybody in a merely human fashion . . . when a man becomes a new creature in Christ, his old life has disappeared, everything has become new about him. This, as always, is God's doing; it is He who, through Christ, has reconciled us to Himself, and allowed us to minister this reconciliation of His to others."[1]

[1] II Cor. 5, 14-18.

The Redemption has its origin in God—in His infinite love—and produces its effect through Christ. But once God's love works in man through Christ, then not only is evil washed away so that a real interior deliverance is achieved, but there is also brought about a *new life*. The love of God, which is full of grace, does not *presuppose* any good, it *produces* it. From the mysterious depths of the divine life, grace, which is communicated to us through Christ, begins to bear its fruit. We will now discuss this invisible, divine life.

The Conception of Grace

The word *grace* (Greek *charis,* Latin *gratia*) is a purely Biblical term: one finds several different meanings attached to it in the New Testament which, however, are interrelated.

a. God Himself is grace. His gracious goodness, His unbounded generosity, He extends towards men, desiring to be their Father. For if one man's fault brought death on a whole multitude, all the more lavish was God's grace, shewn to a whole multitude.[2]

b. Spontaneously a new interpretation grew up. God's love is always creative; is always sharing with others. His goodness overflows in blessings and gifts. He gives grace to sanctify us, to assure us personal happiness. St. Paul exhorts us not to receive the grace of God in vain,[3] and St. Peter says that it is our duty to grow in grace.[4] Finally, let us refer once more to St. Paul's own testimony, given in a letter to the Corinthians: "Only by God's grace I am what I am, and the grace He has shown me has not been without fruit; I have worked harder than all of them, or rather, it was not I, but the grace of God working with me."[5] This grace depicts the situation of man after the coming of Christ; in this sense it is the very opposite of the law of Moses, and self-sanctification becomes a necessity.[6]

c. This grace, given us according to the measure of the gift of Christ Himself, makes us pleasing to God.[7]

d. Finally, the Bible mentions grace among those benefits

[2] Rom. 5, 15. [3] II Cor. 6, 1. [4] II Pet. 3, 18.
[5] Cor. 15, 10. [6] Rom. 6, 15. [7] Eph. 4, 7 and I Pet. 2, 20.

and assistances for which we have to thank God.[8] In the word *grace* we find a wealth and a plenitude which fittingly describes God's *love itself* which thus loads us with presents, by which we become agreeable in His sight and gratefully disposed.

The most striking thing about this explanation is that the word grace is used to express the pure gift of God: a benefit given us through spontaneous love, without any question of either right or duty. Grace is a sheer gift, the outcome of the free and loving choice of God. Grace and election go together.[9]

Grace is therefore a gift to which we have no natural right; on the contrary, it exalts nature, and is therefore called a *super*natural gift. Here, then, is a short analysis of this conception of grace.

The word supernatural refers to a state and to acts which surpass the nature of created beings, and therefore of man. It points to realities which, of themselves, do not belong to man's own actual sphere of life.

In this sphere which we designate as *natural*, are included: thinking, desiring, aspiring, deciding, feeding and reproducing ourselves. Man's whole inner structure is directed towards these various operations. Even the search for the existence of God, the highest truth and excellence, is within man's natural powers. He can deduce His existence from the created world. He also sees in Him the infinitely perfect Spirit to whom He is subjected. Through his own perceptions he realizes that God's laws regulate his life, and that his final happiness is linked up with self-control and obedience. All this belongs to his natural sphere of life in which, in a sense, we may also speak of rights and duties.

But, beyond all this, there remained a further possibility. God could raise man to a higher level than he would be able to realize in his own natural sphere. The Almighty could direct man towards a happiness which is infinite; He could give him an insight which his own unaided and limited intellect would otherwise never be able to comprehend; and He could inspire him with a longing and an ambition which he could never achieve by his own natural powers. In this way God links up man's sphere of life with His own divine

[8] Rom. 7, 25. [9] Rom. 11, 5-6.

sphere, and an elevation of man's whole nature, with its capacities, takes place which is in no way included in his ordinary, natural development, growth or desires. This state, this transformation, when it occurs, we call *supernatural*; it surpasses all natural powers and claims, and the rights and capacities of any living creature. This fresh sphere of existence we express by the term *supernatural* order. Grace, which is the result of God's loving activity working in us, belongs to this supernatural order and bears all its characteristics: it is a gift which enriches, ennobles, raises and cures nature: a pure overflow of God's mercy, to which we have absolutely no claim, and which we can never gain by our own energy or endeavours.

Holy Church, remembering the teaching of the Bible, distinguishes in grace a twofold function: in the first place it consists of a participation in the divine existence; it is a *source* of supernatural life, and the origin of activities which lead us, even here on earth, towards heaven. Under this head it is called *sanctifying grace*.

In the second place it is also a *force* in man, a continuous influence and help from God enabling us to live on the level to which He has raised us by sanctifying grace. It is then called *actual grace*.

Actual grace leads man into the state of abiding friendship with God which we call sanctifying grace; confirms him in that state; and progressively promotes a closer participation in the divine life itself.

We will therefore first consider sanctifying grace and then actual grace.

§ 1. *Sanctifying Grace*

The state of grace—sanctifying grace as it is called—is, of all the graces which God has vouchsafed to us, the greatest; it does, indeed, place man upon an altogether higher level of existence, by means of which he partakes, in a permanent fashion, of the divine life of Jesus Christ Himself, and assumes his correct and proper relationship with God. Christ Himself spoke about sanctifying grace in St. John's Gospel. St. Paul mentions it in many places, and St. Peter also in one passage of deep significance, although they do not use the actual word explicitly.

A. The Teaching of Holy Scripture

1. *The Teaching of Jesus according to the Gospel of St. John*

a. In the Conversation with Nicodemus[10]

During the night, for fear of compromising his position as a teacher, Nicodemus came to ask Jesus for a further explanation of His doctrine. Jesus continually spoke of the Kingdom of God and eternal life, but His visitor's secret query was: "Yes, but who is going to enter there?" Reading his hidden thought, Our Lord immediately answered him: "A man cannot see the Kingdom of God without being born anew."

Rebirth is the necessary condition attached to eternal happiness. But this suggestion annoyed the ageing man. How could he, a teacher, whose hair had become grey, begin afresh, submitting himself to a total change? Jesus took no notice of his querulous reaction, but quietly continued: "No man can enter into the Kingdom of God unless birth comes to him from water, and from the Holy Spirit." This new birth is accomplished by the operation of the Holy Ghost in a symbolical act. Thus, the new birth becomes a purely spiritual act, following the general principle, "That which is born of the flesh, is flesh," i.e. natural life comes into being by a natural birth, but "that which is born of the spirit is spirit," i.e. by birth through the Holy Ghost, a new, spiritual and divine life enters into existence which, contrary to the natural life, is imperishable. The action of the Holy Ghost fructifies, fertilizes, makes the water itself fruitful. Yet still Nicodemus is incredulous. Can such an invisible, spiritual birth have any real value? But Jesus again answers him: the birth by means of the Holy Ghost, although it is an invisible birth, brings about a real change in both the life and substance of a man. "The wind breathes where it will, and thou canst hear the sound of it, but knowest nothing of the way it came or the way it goes; so it is when a man is born by the breath of the Spirit." So, also, is felt the influence of the Spirit of God: an invisible influence, but real and powerful. This is indeed a new life: in its origin it comes to us from God, in its completion it is the possession of God: a spiritual, divine life which profoundly influences and changes man by the power of the Eternal Spirit Himself. Whoever lives in it, and through it, shall gather its eternal fruits.

[10] John 3.

It is apparent from this midnight conversation that Christ invites men to submit themselves to the interior action of God which brings about rebirth and a new life.

b. In the Discourse after the Last Supper[11]

This new life is likened by Christ in the parable of the vine and the branches to a participation in divine life.[12] Christ is the vine; we are the branches. Through both vine and branches flows the same life. The vine is the source of life to the branches and by feeding them enables them to bear fruit. Without Him man can do nothing.

Thus we share also in the divine life of Christ. He is the source of this life and He allows it to overflow continually into us. Whoever remains united to Him experiences, without ceasing, this fructifying action. This union with Christ is, in effect, the rebirth of which he spoke to Nicodemus.

This union with Christ also includes love. To remain united to Christ means to remain in His love, and to remain in His love means to desire, to strive for, and to seek ardently to follow His will and His desires: it means to keep the commandments.

Whoever is united with Christ in love, finds that He keeps His promise, " then he will win my Father's love, and we will both come to him and make our continual abode with him ".[13]

We will come to him: not to leave again almost at once, but it will be a real dwelling of the Father and the Son and the Holy Ghost in his soul. Through grace God *dwells* in us: the whole of the Blessed Trinity.

In the Acts of the Apostles we find St. Paul's discourse at the Areopagus.[14] He spoke of God, of the Spirit who made the world and all that is in it; who is not far from any of us: " It is in Him that we live, and move, and have our being." This idea we express nowadays by saying that God is omnipresent, for He constantly maintains the life of His creatures, preserves and governs them. But in this particular instance Jesus is speaking of a very special presence of God, of a new and close union with Him which is constant. This union, this contact, is a pure gift of God's love and consists in a mysterious communication of His own intimate life, such as it is in Christ. This communication of spiritual life is a

[11] John 14, 18. [12] John 15, 1-8. [13] John 14, 23. [14] Acts 17, 22-32.

mystery, and cannot fittingly be expressed in either ideas or words. In some way or another it is a finite participation in the life of the Blessed Trinity, a participation in the infinite knowledge of the Father for the Son and of the Son for the Father; a participation in the inexpressible love which binds Father and Son to the Holy Ghost. The grace of God enables us to share this close, communal life with Him. For that purpose He dwells in us. Whoever is united with Christ meets also in his soul, by faith and love, the Blessed Trinity.

c. In the Prologue to St. John's Gospel[15]

In the Prologue to his Gospel, St. John draws, in one sentence, an important conclusion from this rebirth, from this participation in the life of God Himself. After he has contemplated the Son of God before the Incarnation and has told us how He, the Light, shone in darkness, a darkness which was not able to hide Him, he adds: "But all those who did welcome Him, He empowered to become the children of God." All men of goodwill, all men who in their own way believe in Him, are children of God. How does this happen? Precisely how is this adoption brought about? Not by instinctive passion or the will of man who desires children, but by a spiritual rebirth through God; through a spiritual begetting.

God Himself—Infinite Life Itself—is communicated to us although we remain men. And in this communication God also remains closely associated with us: He does not pour out His grace upon us and then leave us. He touches the soul. He transforms it; He pours His own life into it; and then He remains. Here one can speak with the Church of a supernatural adoption, so long as one understands the meaning of the term clearly. From the above it is evident that we do not mean an adoption on the human level. A legally adopted child receives a new father, but *within* the child itself nothing at all happens, no change takes place, whereas in this case, "adopted child" means that God really becomes our Father, that we are really His children; that a new birth has taken place and that henceforward there is a genuine participation in His divine life. But in order to make clear the difference between Christ, the only begotten Son of God, and ourselves,

[15] John I.

who remain creatures and only through Him are able to participate in divine life, the Church uses the expression *adoption.*

d. Again in Christ's Discourse after the Last Supper

In this discourse, which we have already mentioned, another conclusion is reached with regard to the fact that we are reborn in God; we are not only the children of God, but His friends. "I do not speak of you any more as my servants; a servant is one who does not understand what his Master is about, whereas I have made known to you all that my Father has told me; and so I have called you my friends." (John 15, 14.)

Friendship is the fruit of mutual love, which forgets itself and shares everything with the loved one. That which is deepest, most personal and dearest to us is expressed by it. Through friendship there result mutual aspirations and ideals. There is no longer any self-seeking, no mere material satisfaction on either side, but on the part of both a devotion which alone desires to benefit the other without question of reward. Love itself is its own happiness and reward.

This friendship which God offers us is a participation in His own personal divine life. He has no need of us but, by imparting Himself to us, by allowing us to share in His life, He desires our happiness and our growth in Him and towards Him. Thus He tells us His secrets: He helps us along our path towards Him. Finally, when we follow His wishes and obey His will, we shall find that an intimate mutual intercourse develops between us in thinking, willing and feeling. We shall come to live according to His perceptions and motives; more and more we shall find ourselves trusting in His power and goodness. In the end, we only will what He wills, and as He wills it.

e. Heirs of Heaven

God does not offer us a share in His life only for the time of our exile here on earth, in order that we may be happy here and now. On the contrary, the life which God offers us never ends, and will only find its full maturity in the beatific vision, in the love which flows from it, and in eternal happiness. The very life of God Himself becomes our endless possession. This is the inheritance which follows from divine adoption: "God so loved the world, that He gave up His only begotten Son, so that those who believe in Him may not perish, but have eternal life."[16] Therefore rejoice and be glad, for your reward in heaven is great.

This also supplies an answer to the first question of the Catechism: "Why did God make us?" "God made us to know Him, love Him and serve Him in this world, and to be happy with Him for ever in the next."

2. *The Teaching of St. Paul*

In expounding the reality of salvation, St. Paul particularly stresses the redemption of *fallen* men. In his view, sin is the dominating factor; it is the condition which determines the existence of man: man is guilty in regard to God, and he cannot do away with that guilt. Without Christ he is doomed to death; he lives according to the flesh, is a slave of sin, and is under the law which leads him to sin.

In contrast with this sombre reality and complete impotence, the love of God awaits him: "By sending us His own Son, in the fashion of our guilty nature, to make amends for our guilt,"[17] Jesus Christ, who "never knew sin, and God made Him into sin for us,"[18] so that He "accepted an obedience which brought Him to death".[19] For what purpose? To redeem us from sin. God has redeemed us in and through Christ, that was the eternal resolution of His mercy.[20] The result of this Redemption is forgiveness of sin, original sin,[21] and personal sins,[22] but especially the "new creation",[23] by the new birth and the restoration of our nature through the Holy Spirit.[24] This is the "new kind of existence"[25] in which "I am alive; or rather, not I; it is Christ that lives in me".[26] In what way, then, does Christ live in man? By the Spirit we have now received, the Spirit of Adoption, which makes us cry out Abba, Father. "The Spirit Himself thus assures our spirit, that we are children of God; and if we are His children then we are His heirs too."[27] Continually St. Paul uses the expression, when meaning the redeemed man, "to be in

[16] John 3, 16. [17] Rom. 8, 3. [18] II Cor. 5, 21. [19] Phil. 2, 7-8.
[20] Rom. 15, 8-9. [21] Rom. 5, 18-19. [22] I Cor. 6, 11. [23] Gal. 6, 15.
[24] Titus, 3, 5. [25] Rom. 6, 3-6. [26] Gal. 2, 20. [27] Rom 8, 14-19.

Christ". He is in Christ,[28] for Christ gives meaning to his life, and by love and faith he is united to Him. His Spirit establishes in us the condition by which we become children of God, that is to say, a limitless trust in the Father and a surpassing desire for the Father.

It is no wonder that St. Paul so frequently stresses the real and complete forgiveness of sin. God does not *pretend* that our sins are no longer there, but He forgives them: "Thanking God our Father for rescuing us from the power of darkness and transferring us to the Kingdom of His beloved Son. In the Son of God, in His Blood, we find the Redemption that sets us free from our sins."[29] "But now you have been washed clean, now you have been sanctified, now you have been justified in the Name of the Lord Jesus, by the Spirit of the God we serve."[30]

The expressions which St. Paul uses all contain the same truth: he describes in various ways our predestination as Children of God through Jesus Christ.[31] He refers again and again to the condition of grace, continually emphasizing, however, that it is only by God's love and mercy that we are given renewed life through the Holy Spirit.[32]

3. *The Words of St. Peter*

In the first chapter of his Second Epistle St. Peter speaks of the high and treasured promise of God, by which we "are to share the divine nature, with the world's corruption, the world's passions, left behind". The idea of a rebirth is here expressed in a new and different way. By ordinary birth a man is given a nature. By this rebirth we do not become God, but we are given a share in the divine life; thereafter man can perform actions which, properly speaking, belong only to God. By faith he accepts the views of God. By love he unites himself to the will of God. His life now becomes, by the operation of the Holy Spirit, the life of God lived in and through him.

B. The Wording of the Church

Holy Church calls this rebirth a lasting participation in the

[28] Gal. 2, 20.
[29] Col. 1, 13-14.
[30] I Cor. 6, 11.
[31] Eph. 5, 1.
[32] Titus 3, 4-6.

divine life of Christ: *sanctifying grace*. To the question what is grace? the Catechism replies: "Grace is a supernatural gift of God, freely bestowed upon us for our sanctification and salvation." This grace is a gift of God by which He sanctifies our souls in an enduring way and makes them pleasing in His sight. According to the teaching of the Church it is liberating and cleansing, as well as ennobling and elevating. This cleansing refers in the first place to original sin, but refers also to all personal sins. The ennobling and elevating consist in a radical transformation and perfecting of our nature, which lies entirely beyond the reach of our natural powers, our energy or our study. This transformation we call the supernatural life. By means of this grace the Blessed Trinity makes its abode in us; we become children of God and heirs of Heaven.

Sanctifying grace is the purest form of grace, that is to say, totally undeserved. In this case God does not reveal Himself by extraordinary or visible signs, as He did in the Creation, but He comes to us in direct self-surrender. His limitless love draws the soul into the divine life in such a way that, imbued with new, divine powers, it begins to partake of this new life of knowledge and love.

Such a participation is Christian living in the strict sense of the word; it is brought about *by* Christ and it consists in a sharing in the divine life which it generates in the soul through the Holy Ghost, causing it to grow and to increase so that one day it will reach its full development in Heaven.

C. Realistic Revelation

From the preceding it will be seen that both the Bible and the Church teach that God looks upon our Redemption by His Son as having this result, namely from being sinners, we again become children of God. Let us emphasize that this is a question of a *reality*: of something which raises man to a supernatural level in such a way that he participates in the divine nature: to a supernatural life which is expressed by the words: *infused grace*. There is a real and definite change in man as a consequence. It is not merely a change in God's attitude towards us, but it is a transformation of the sinner into the child of God. The position of man is changed; it is no longer one of loss, deprivation, ruin, and aversion from

God, but instead the soul receives, in and through Christ, by means of the Sacrament, a created reality of an altogether higher order; a new condition which permeates, changes, and at the same time elevates it.

In this conception we differ from many non-Catholics who give an altogether different interpretation (particularly those whose theology is based on Lutheranism and Calvinism), to this supernatural truth. According to them, man remains in the fallen state in which he was born, and in that state, with the help of the Holy Ghost, he is renewed and re-established.

The renewal of which they speak is accomplished by listening to the Word of God, which addresses itself to each man *personally*. But this Word of God does not convey either infused grace or the obliteration of man's sinful state and condition; on the contrary, it teaches him that his ordinary, natural life, his sinful nature, remain, but that he comes, as it were, to a new focus on God through faith.

Seen from the point of view of man, his relationship to God remains that of a sinner. Only from the point of view of God—on account of the suffering and death of Christ—a relationship of Father and child develops, without, however, in any way changing man's original condition. He is a sinner, and only becomes interiorly a child of God at the second coming of Christ.

The Catholic Church rejects all such teaching as being contrary to Holy Scripture.

§ 2. *Actual Grace*

It is sanctifying grace which enables our soul and its faculties to be in such a state that it can orientate itself towards God and our salvation. From sanctifying grace originates that union with the Father, the Son and the Holy Ghost, such as it was described by Christ in His discourse after the Last Supper. But this participation in the inner life of God is subject to the law which controls each life: it requires preparation. The life of grace itself is a continuous movement towards a definite goal, towards an ever-deepening realization of that which we are: children of God. Growth and effort are its characteristics. Any coming to rest entails inevitable loss: a shrivelling up of vitality and a diminution of our life-force. God's love continually presses us. This condition cries out for unceasing help from God; it is a special operation of grace which prepares us to become His child and develops the life of grace in the soul in ever-increasing perfection. The Church calls this supernatural influence *actual grace*; it is God's work which spurs us on to deeds, and accompanies them towards their fulfilment. This help is that "breathing of the Spirit" spoken of by St. John, by means of which the Father draws us closer and closer to His Son, Jesus Christ, and by which we are enabled to live increasingly according to the Spirit.

It consists in an *enlightenment of the mind and a strengthening of the will.* It can orientate and move everything towards its final goal, penetrate everywhere, enter into all man's relations with life, into the interior movements of his soul, his external words and deeds, the example which he gives, even into the evil of which he may be the cause.

To this grace is ascribed a double function: it stimulates, and it accompanies our actions. The Bible explains to us this twofold operation.

1. *Grace Stimulates*

All good works which lead to our justification or to our elevation in the supernatural life, receive their first impulse and initiative from the grace of God.

It is God who draws man, as Christ said: "No one can come to me without being attracted towards me by the Father who sent me."[33] In the same chapter Our Lord explained that the words "Come to me" mean to have *faith* in His words: for even among the disciples there were some who did not believe that He was the Living Bread, descended from Heaven. He continued: "That is what I meant when I told you that nobody can come to me unless he has received the gift from my Father."[34] It is therefore not sufficient just to listen to the preaching and explanation of the doctrine of Christ, nor to have sufficient intellectual knowledge of these matters, or at least the desire for it. Divine influence is necessary in order to believe deeply and firmly in Jesus Christ, with that belief which penetrates to the very core of a man's heart. It is God who shows us His light; we alone are totally incapable of perceiving it. Grace is the first and indispen-

[33] John 6, 44.

[34] John 6, 66.

sable point of contact. Only those who have received the grace enabling them to listen to and learn from the Father, come to Christ.[35]

In the Acts of the Apostles, St. Luke relates the story of the conversion of Lydia, a purple-seller from the city of Thyatira, which exactly illustrates the meaning of Christ: "And the Lord opened her heart so that she was attentive to Paul's preaching. She was baptized with all her household."[36]

Christ stands at the door, knocking;[37] His grace invites, encourages and draws the soul, but it never forces it; its gentle influence takes into account human nature. Man is free to respond to, or to resist, the interior movement of God.

2. *Grace accompanies Action*

The operation of God's grace is always present, and expresses itself continuously in every kind of action, both as to interior decisions and exterior deeds. This grace helps and supports us when, having responded to the divine invitation, we endeavour to lead a Christian life and to fulfil our daily duties.

St. Paul, who called himself the least of the Apostles because he had persecuted the Church of Christ, was aware, none the less, that he had worked uninterruptedly for Christ. "Only by God's grace I am what I am, and the grace He has shewn me has not been without fruit; I have worked harder than all of them, or rather, it was not I, but the grace of God working with me."[38]

In another passage he combines truth and realism, with his own inimitable touch, in the phrase: "Both the will to do it, and the accomplishment of that will, are something which God accomplishes in you, to carry out His loving purpose."

Nevertheless, this continuous activity of grace can be impeded and prevented by man. The parable of the seed, related in the Gospel of St. Matthew, shows that there are those who hear the word, and even accept it gladly, and yet it takes no root since both resolution and perseverance fail.[39] Thus we see that, even in the matter of grace, God, as ever, respects man's freewill.

[35] John 6, 45. [36] Acts 16, 14-16. [37] Apoc. 3, 20.
[38] I Cor. 15, 9-12. [39] Matt. 13, 3-9.

3. *The Necessity of Grace*

Holy Church explicitly states why grace is so necessary to us. Although the natural man can of himself accomplish good deeds, and not everything that even a sinner does is to be condemned, yet natural man cannot, without the help of grace, keep even the natural law in its entirety, nor avoid sin for any long period. This opinion is mainly based upon the teaching of St. Paul, who points out, in his Epistle to the Romans, that neither Jews nor pagans are capable of following God's law.[40] When man is in the flesh, the passions of sin often prove irresistible.[41] Finally he states explicitly that it is Jesus Christ who has " signed the death-warrant of sin in our nature, so that we should be fully quit of the law's claim, we, who follow the ways of the Spirit, not the ways of flesh and blood ".[42]

The Catholic Church, bearing in mind the parable of the Vine and the Branches, points out that it is the grace of our Lord Jesus Christ alone which makes life fruitful for our everlasting happiness. Every thought, every resolution, every action connected with our eternal salvation, comes to us from God's light and strength.

She maintains that no one can persevere to the end in the grace of God without His particular help. This view is maintained by the recurring emphasis laid by the Bible upon the difficulties to be encountered even by the just, and the necessity for constant readiness for combat in the spiritual life.[43]

Christ Himself has summed up the common experience of men in those words of his: " The Spirit is willing enough, but the flesh is weak."[44] But, by the grace of God, even the worst temptation can be overcome, for He never allows us to be tempted above our strength,[45] and His grace is sufficient for us.[46]

4. *Grace is always sufficient*

Accompanying our unceasing need for all the support and blessing of God's love, is the unquestionable fact that He gives every man sufficient grace. He gives those whom He calls His friends the strength to control themselves and to carry out His

[40] Rom. 1, 21-29. [41] Rom. 7, 7-23. [42] Rom. 8, 4. [43] I Cor. 9, 24-27.
[44] Matt 26, 41. [45] I Cor. 10, 13. [46] II Cor. 12, 7.

commandments; further, He invites all sinners, even those who are the most hardened, and draws them by His grace. Those who do not know the true Faith meet Him in their hearts, where His love deposits sufficient strength to follow the voice of conscience and so to attain to the happiness of God. *No one will be lost except through his own personal fault.* Until the last moment of each life upon earth, the love of God beckons and urges, His supernatural influence continues to assist us, and no hair of our head can be touched without His divine permission.

Everyone receives sufficient grace in order to reach Heaven, for the simple reason that Christ died for *all* men, and these assisting graces have been merited for *all* men. St. Paul expressly points this out in his first Epistle to Timothy: "It is His will that all men should be saved, and be led to recognize the truth; there is only one God, and only one Mediator between God and men, Jesus Christ, who is a man, like them, and gave Himself as a ransom for them all."[47]

Everything that comes to us is grace, and all live by the grace of God.

§ 3. *The Merit of Good Works*

1. The state of grace is not a condition of rest in God, an idle expectation of His interior assistance, or an unconcerned reliance upon His strength and His help; on the contrary, it is life itself—life based upon faith and love which express themselves continuously in decisions and actions. Real faith, which is an effect of grace, works continuously through love; and without works, as Our Lord said, faith is dead. Grace is the divine germ, the divine seed. When from this seed a living plant shoots up, then indeed it may be said truly to deserve the name of grace. But if, from this life and this love, there proceed no more than words: if, for instance, a man, having all the worldly goods he needs, steels his heart against his brother in want: how can we say that the love of God dwells in him?[48] It is upon his works, upon his own efforts, that a man is judged, and it is to the good servant, who has gained five more talents with the five which he already had, that the Master says: "Come and share the joy of thy Lord."[49]

[47] I Tim. 2, 4-6.
[48] I John, 3, 17.
[49] Matt. 25, 11-27.

And it is to those who have fed the hungry and given the thirsty to drink that the King will say: "Come, you that have received a blessing from my Father, take possession of the Kingdom which has been prepared for you since the foundation of the world. For that which you did to one of the least of my brethren here, you did to me."[50]

Good works are therefore the reason for which God gives the reward of eternal life. "But every tree which does not show good fruit will be hewn down and cast into the fire."[51]

Even the *measure* of eternal happiness is given according to the work which a man does, for each will receive his own wages in proportion to his own work.

The final aim which God places before us is a prize. Every athlete, who desires to win that prize, has to keep all his appetites under control. "Let us too then run for victory."[52]

St. James tells us the prize is that crown of life which God has promised to those who love Him;[53] and therefore we know that our labour in the Lord's service cannot be spent in vain.[54] Christ Himself invites us to be glad and light-hearted, for a rich reward awaits us in Heaven.[55] It would even seem that this reward is founded on some sort of claim, for "God is not an unjust God, that He should forget all you have done, all the charity you have shown in His name, you who have ministered, and still minister, to the needs of His saints".[56] "As for me," says St. Paul to Timothy, "my blood already flows in sacrifice; the time has nearly come when I can go free. I have fought the good fight; I have finished the race, I have redeemed my pledge; I look forward to the prize that is waiting for me, the prize I have earned. My Lord, the judge whose award never goes amiss, will grant it to me when that day comes; to me, yes, and to all those who have learned to welcome His appearing."[57]

We see, thus, that the Bible encourages us to think of reward as the fruit of work. It addresses itself, as it were, to our sense of personal responsibility; it asks for an individual decision and acceptance of God's grace. The state of grace is not only a sanctifying state, but it also demands that we should earn the wages of supernatural life by our own labours.

2. The inclusion of this idea in revealed Scripture shows

[50] Matt. 25, 31-46. [51] Matt. 3, 10. [52] I Cor. 9, 24.
[53] James 1, 12. [54] I Cor. 15, 58. [55] Matt. 5, 12.
[56] Heb. 6, 10. [57] II Tim. 4. 6-8.

once more how Christ adapted Himself to those realities which play such a large and important part in everyday life. Again and again we are confronted with this truth, that God does not destroy His primeval creation but, on the contrary, elevates nature, healing and ennobling it. In the supernatural order Nature has not been robbed of its importance, but its possibilities have been extended and its susceptibilities brought to a much higher state of development. In the natural order of things, for instance, it is a recognized fact that reward is the fruit of personal endeavour and activity; it is this, indeed, which, to a great extent, makes human society possible. Those who freely give their services may justly demand payment for their individual work. God respects this general human law and, recognizing man's responsibility, rewards his fidelity in His service; only He raises the conception of reward for such service on to an altogether higher level, and surrounds it with the all-pervading and supernatural atmosphere of God.

3. If, therefore, the man who believes is to be judged according to his works then, in a certain sense, salvation hangs upon our manner of life. Yet elsewhere the voice of God says to us through St. Paul: "God offers us eternal life as a free gift, through Christ Jesus Our Lord."[58] "We are children of God; and if we are His children then we are His heirs too; heirs of God sharing the inheritance of Christ."[59] That which is a pure gift, and is given spontaneously out of love, cannot simultaneously be a reward for personal conduct.

Saint Augustine has already given us the answer to this difficulty for he says that grace is not given as a reward, but that the reward is the result of grace.

We have seen earlier that God always meets us first. Everything which takes place, takes place on His initiative. He distributes His gifts and favours to whom He wishes. Everything originates in Him: He is the source of all expectation and desire. Faith, hope and charity are infused into our hearts by the Holy Ghost. To possess real love of God remains one of the fruits of God's communication of Himself to our soul. There is nothing in man personally which could compel God to give him a share in His divine life.

In this sphere of our own insufficiency and God's free election, we are obliged to speak of "merit".

[58] Rom. 6, 23. [59] Rom. 8, 17.

Why, then, do we call our life, our work, our endeavours, fruitful? The answer is that God Himself connected fruitfulness with them. He *promised* a reward for our good deeds. He *promised* Heaven as the inheritance of His obedient children. That is what He has ordained for us, and in return He accepts what we, as unprofitable servants, are able to accomplish. "Holiness is all-availing, since it promises well both for this life and for the next," says St. Paul.[60] God's promise is a real guarantee, and it can genuinely be so for the reason that our actions are the effect of a *supernatural* principle.

That fruitfulness which our life and works acquire in the matter of eternal salvation, is not so much the result of what we do, as of grace itself. Once our soul is justified by the love of God, and raised to that state which we describe by the words sanctifying grace", it inevitably expresses itself on this supernatural level, and the more so as it is God Himself who intervenes at this stage and works in the soul so that all our actions are accompanied by His power and His help. Since our Lord's Death and Resurrection, Christian life is enacted on an altogether higher and more divine plane: we are the branches of Christ's vine. His influence, the sap and life-blood, runs unceasingly down even to the smallest twig. The good on which we decide, and which we endeavour to accomplish, is just as much a result of His grace and influence as it is of our own free choice. Therefore everything which we desire, and everything which we do; everything for which we are personally responsible, and which is in accordance with the law of God, is directed towards His honour and glory. It is He who influences us, and faith, which is His gift, purifies our motives. The stronger and firmer is our will to serve Him, the more powerfully will the supernatural principle and His grace work in our soul. The merit is therefore the fruit of God's grace as well as of our efforts. Eternal life and happiness, which are the complete fruition of His grace and love, remain purely an outcome of His mercy: nevertheless, that very eternal life is the reward and crown which He promises us for all the acts which we have performed in a state of grace and with good intention.

4. From this it also follows that our meritorious acts in no way detract from the merits of Christ. On the contrary: that

[60] I Tim. 4, 8.

which is purely human will never be able to merit a heavenly reward. The sole origin of any fruitfulness or merit in our life lies in the merits of Christ. It is from Him alone that we receive that grace which stamps our work as meritorious. So far from stealing from His glory, this fact makes us realize even more clearly in what a real sense He has redeemed us, and how deeply His power permeates our life and spirit.

Most of the Christian sects, outside the Catholic Church, avoid speaking of the meritoriousness of good works. The principal reason for this is that, according to their view, sin permeates right down into the very depths of man's being. The points of contact for grace are only to be found in the promises of God, since Nature itself can never recover from its wounds. Man remains a sinner; and he is so designated by God in His judgment. But by virtue of the merits of Jesus Christ, the same man becomes a child of God, and in this way attains to spiritual union with the Deity through faith. In himself he remains the same old Adam, and for that reason he cannot co-operate with God in his sanctification nor by his good deeds. It is true, of course, that God asks him to lead a good life, and to perform good works, but such Christian acts, weighed down by all their imperfection, have no more significance than would be accorded to any demonstration of faith; they are merely to be regarded as a result of grace or a sign of election. Protestantism is very concerned that nothing should be allowed to detract from the influence of Christ; His grace alone can build up the life of man. It points out the great danger of any over-emphasis laid by a practical Christian life upon the meritoriousness of individual work and effort, since it is likely to deteriorate finally into mere selfish action for the sake of reward and personal happiness. The reward is a result of our obedience, but must never be the overriding motive.

The reply to all this has, of course, already been given; our merits are indeed no ground for self-congratulation, for it is always to the grace of the Holy Ghost that we owe them. And yet, none the less, they are *our* merit, for we have not abused, but co-operated with, grace. That does not mean for a moment that we think ourselves to be without sin; we always need the grace of God and His salutary purifications; we remain beggars.

An exaggerated emphasis upon meritoriousness could certainly degenerate into mere formalism, in which the mechanical carrying out of orders and the performance of duty, were thought to be sufficient to assure one of heaven and avert eternal damnation.

Needless to say it has never been the intention of the Church to advance self-seeking in any form as the highest motive for action, but in her teaching she tries harmoniously to combine the truths contained in the two sayings of our Lord: "Thou shalt love the Lord thy God with thy *whole* heart", and "Rejoice and be glad for thy reward in Heaven is great".

God has given man an indestructible urge towards his own perfection and happiness, and whoever loves God and fulfils His will, will find that he has satisfied that urge.

Christian living is founded upon two truths: one expressed by Christ Himself: "Separated from me you have no power to do anything";[61] and the other by St. Paul: "Nothing is beyond my powers, thanks to the strength God gives me."[62]

[61] John 15, 5.

[62] Phil. 4, 13.

CHAPTER X

THE COMMUNION OF SAINTS

SYNOPSIS

I. The mystery of the Blessed Trinity is the mystery of the intimate and interior life of God: divine knowledge and divine love. This love did not remain enclosed in the infinity of His divine Being, but urged Him to create angels, men, and a world in which mankind could live.
Man was created in a state of friendship with God, but it was his lot to obey. We saw how man sinned against this obedience, and so lost God's friendship, and how therefore, as a consequence of this, all his descendants were also born outside the friendship of God (original sin).

II. In His eternal mercy God redeemed mankind through His Son.

III. We have seen how by means of this Redemption, man was given new life, a life of grace, by which he is raised to the supernatural order.

IV. We shall now see that, through this life of grace, a bond is formed between Christ and all those who are joined to Him by Grace, as well as between the members of the Church mutually.

CHRIST'S KINGDOM HAS SPREAD all over the world in a visible form. Visible in its Authority and its Faithful, its Sacraments and Liturgy, its laws and organization. Nevertheless we must never forget that it is also a spiritual kingdom, a kingdom of grace and of the interior life, and that only the Spirit can be the channel of the great values which this Kingdom has to bestow: Redemption and Grace. The millions who have lived since the death of Christ, those millions who died in the loving arms of God before or since His coming, continue, invisibly, that Kingdom.

All these are a part of the Communion of Saints. This communion of saints is not merely an exterior bond, it is not merely some sort of record or register, it is a living contact in and through Christ.

In this communion are included first those who are still living on earth: and who are, visibly or invisibly, members of

Christ's Kingdom and in one way or another united to Him as their Head: these form the Mystical Body of Christ.

But this Communion is not confined to the Church Militant, for the suffering souls in purgatory and the Blessed in heaven, are also living members of it. The Blessed in heaven have not lost their interest in the Church on earth for which they suffered and fought; nor do they cease to pray for that Church, which is the mystical Body of Christ, and for all those souls who died in the love of God but who still have to be purified from their earthly stains. The Faithful beg for the prayers of the saints who stand so close to the throne of God, even more than they ask the prayers of their friends still living. We do not know in precisely what way the saints hear our prayers but, just as a prophet is able to describe events which have yet to happen, so the saints, who in God behold all truth, are able to understand, in some way what is as yet hidden from us, the request or entreaty of a soul on earth.

The Catholic enters easily into the life of the saints, into that supernatural world with which, although not tangibly, we can be so united in spirit. It is true that popular imagination, perhaps misled by the excesses of some pious artist, has formed a picture of heaven which is scarcely realistic. Such ideas, although full of piety, are apt to raise a laugh. To the simple mind such conceptions are perfectly suitable, provided that they are in no way connected with superstition or magic. We must be broad-minded enough not to try and impose our point of view on others. Education, temperament, nationality, all play their part, and there will certainly be a considerable difference between the way in which a matter-of-fact Englishman, a South Italian, or some Aboriginal pictures heaven to himself.

In spite of this, all Catholics accept exactly the same teaching upon the Communion of Saints, that supernatural bond which binds together the living and the dead in the unity of one great company under their Head, Jesus Christ.

In this community we speak of the Church Militant (that is to say on earth), the Church Suffering (that is to say in purgatory), and the Church Triumphant (that is to say in heaven).

First we will take the Church Militant, which has already been discussed in the earlier part of this book from the point of view of an organization, founded by Our Lord. We will now however consider it more as the *Mystical Body of Christ* —that is as a mystical association with Christ as its head. Next we will explain more fully the communion which exists between the Church Militant and the Church Triumphant, dealing with the veneration of the saints in general and the devotion to Our Lady in particular. The Suffering Church will be considered in the fourth part.

§ 1. *The Mystical Body of Christ*

After the Last Supper, Christ drew a picture of the union which bound Him to His disciples in the parable of *the vine and the branches.*[1] "I am the true vine and it is my Father who tends it." Christ is the same to His disciples as the vine is to its branches, but He cannot visualize His own activity without reference to His Father: it was His Father who sent Him into this world in order to bring us divine life, and by so doing, to form us into one community in faith and love.

The task of the Father is similar to that of the husbandman. He prunes the branches and cuts away everything which would prevent us from bearing fruit. Whoever absorbs the words of Christ is purified; whoever obeys this Light, enters into the life of grace.

"Live on in Me and I will live on in you." Without the grace of Our Lord no one can bring forth fruit; we can do nothing; but it depends upon ourselves and our personal goodwill whether we remain in Him or not. If we do not, and if we separate ourselves from the state of grace by mortal sin then, like dead branches, we shall be cast off by the Father and wither away.

"As long as you live on in Me, and My words live on in you, you will be able to make what request you will, and have it granted." The strength of our prayer is, in fact, derived solely from union with Christ: it becomes His prayer, and for this same reason our union with Him becomes fruitful and glorifies the Father in a high degree.

How then were the disciples to live on in Him? By abiding in His love. They were to do all they could in order to be worthy of it, and never to forfeit it, and the surest means to that end was, and is, to keep His commandments. This calls for both self control and self sacrifice, but if we succeed, the

[1] John 15, 1-11.

joy of Christ, the happiness which He knows in His union with the Father and the Holy Ghost will also flow into us. We can thus discern the Father in the imagery of the Vine and the Branches, that Father who sent His Son down to earth for love of us: that Son who, as God, is equal to the Father, and as Man is one with men. Christ is the source of our supernatural life; vine and branches share the same sap. From Him we receive all our grace because His life overflows continuously into the branches; our union with Him thus becomes living and fruitful. In Him we call ourselves *Christians*: people whose lives and activities flow out from His, who share His knowledge and carry out His will. That which Christ Himself expresses in the parable of the Vine and the Branches, St. Paul describes in his favourite allegory of the Head and the Body. In order to express that intimate relationship which binds us to Christ, and in Him to one another; and which also binds the whole Church to Him; St. Paul says: *"The Church is the Body of Christ."* He explains how we all, how the Church, form one Body, an indivisible community with both interior and exterior unity. He indignantly repudiates any idea of schism or the formation of parties.[2] "You are one Body, with a single spirit; each of you, when he was called, called in the same hope; with the same Lord, the same faith, the same baptism; with the same God, the same Father, who is above all things, pervades all things, and lives in all of us."[3] Unity is the convincing strength and force of Christianity. The disciple of Christ is recognizable by his love for all; but especially he fixes his attention on Him who is the *Head* of the Body, Christ Jesus.

Christ is the founder of it because by preaching the Gospel, He imparted to us the truth by which we have to live, while by His suffering and death He redeemed us and placed at our disposal His own divine efficacy.

Christ is the *Head* of this Body; it begins with Him since His was the first birth out of death. It was God's good pleasure to let all completeness dwell in Him.[4] He guides the Church; His care anticipates everything. The words He uttered will never pass away, and He gives us those means of grace which, if we use them rightly, will bring us to our desired goal. He pours His light and strength into the spirit and heart of man, and visibly and systematically, governs this Body, the Church,

[2] I Cor. 1, 10-13. [3] Eph. 4, 4-5. [4] Col. 1, 18-21.

through Popes and Bishops. Although His grace is sufficient, and His help indispensable, yet He asks for the co-operation of His members for the distribution of His graces; He asks for their prayers and their sufferings endured for love, because just so His own love is enabled to pierce more deeply into the hearts of those who do not as yet know Him. "Thus do we help to pay off the debt which the afflictions of Christ leave still to be paid, for the sake of His Body, the Church."[5]

Christ *maintains* that Body. "A man's body is all one, though it has a number of different organs, and all the organs go to make up one body; so it is with Christ", says St. Paul.[6] Because He continues to live in it through His apostles and their successors to whom He entrusted His own mission and work, He continues to baptize, teach, govern and sacrifice, through them. His Spirit is all-pervading. That Spirit, the Holy Ghost, is the *soul* of the Body. This Spirit, and the love which binds the Father and the Son, binds also the Head and the Body, and forms, out of that multitude of members, one harmonious whole. "All this is the work of one and the same Spirit, who distributes His gifts as He will to each severally."[7] No wonder that St. Paul weaves together innumerable different words in the attempts to describe the mystery of our unity in Christ; We are planted together with Him; grafted in Him; growing up with Him; incorporated with Him; we are in Him, and He in us, in a hidden though very real manner. Therefore, that which we do to the least of His brethren we do to Him. Therefore when the Son of Man comes in His glory He will effect the separation of the just from the damned; He will call for an account of the glass of water that was offered Him, and judge us according to that standard of His "For I was hungry and you gave me food" or "For I was hungry and you never gave me food." . . . "Believe Me, when you did it to one of the least of my brethren here, you did it to me . . . when you refused it to one of the least of my Brethren here, you refused it to me."[8]

Our union with Christ is a *reality*, just as grace is a reality. We must live His life, and that means living it according to His standards, appreciations, values, and adopting a supernatural estimate of values: thus, through faith, He will live in us. His love must inspire us, and this occurs whenever we

[5] Col. 1, 24. [6] I Cor. 12, 12. [7] I Cor. 12, 4 and 11.
[8] Matt. 25, 31-46.

perform His will for the motive which He has put into our heart. It is then that the Body of Christ may be said truly to exist: that is, His *Mystical Body*. This term mystical, however, is not to be interpreted as something unreal. It is only used to distinguish Christ's Mystical Body from His Natural Body, which lives glorified in heaven.

Our union with Christ through faith and grace is called a mystical union because it is a mystery of divine love and divine operation. It is the grace of God which unites us all, and forms us into one Society. This Society is the Church, the Body of Christ. "Wishest thou to live of Christ's Spirit?" says St. Augustine. "Then be in Christ's Body."

§ 2. *Veneration of the Saints*

Catholic veneration of the saints has always aroused, if not the appreciation at least the interest, of non-Catholics. One of the very first things to strike them is the number of statues of Our Lady and the saints which enrich Churches, houses, and in Catholic countries, the Wayside Shrines. One sometimes finds real works of art among these statues, although others may be ugly and in bad taste: the latter are the very ones which seem to enjoy a devotion which the non-Catholic readily associates with superstition, black magic or idolatry. Even among those who are, on the whole, sympathetically inclined towards Catholicism, there often exists a feeling that they personally could never kneel down and pray before such images, and that all the usages connected with this cult are strange and bizarre. It is therefore rather important to have a right view of Catholic veneration of the saints, regarding which there must be a clear distinction between that which is obligatory and that which is voluntary, between approved and disapproved practices. . . . Not everything which Catholics do is necessarily justified theologically, and on the other hand not everything which those outside the Church say about the veneration of the saints, is necessarily Catholic teaching.

The veneration of the saints, as it has come to be practised nowadays, is nowhere described in the Bible. The reader will, however, we hope, have grasped by now that this is not essential. Besides written Revelation, the Catholic Church accepts a purely oral teaching, handed down to us intact under the guidance of the Holy Ghost. The *basis* of veneration of the saints is clearly expressed in Holy Scripture as we will now demonstrate.

It is clear from the Old as well as the New Testament that prominent religious personages were from the first venerated by the people; Abraham, Isaac and Jacob; Moses and the prophets; John the Baptist, Peter and Paul: all were considered as holy men of God who deserved and received particular attention and regard. From a good many Bible texts it is also evident that their intercession with God was regarded as having special power. "He (Abraham) is a prophet and will intercede for thy life."[9] "Job will pray for thee and because of him I shall not punish thee." "He (Samuel) prayed for Israel to Jaweh, and Jaweh heard him." There is even a text in Daniel (which however is not included in the Protestant Bible) where the virtue of the dead patriarchs is used as a plea: "Think of Abraham that was Thy friend, of Thy servant Isaac, of Jacob whom Thou didst set apart for Thyself."[10]

In the Apocalypse a very close bond is shown as existing between angels, saints and men on earth. The martyrs, above all, are exalted, and it is only natural that these heroes should have been regarded by the Faithful as their particular intercessors during the first centuries of persecution. St. Paul speaks several times in detail regarding the fundamental principle of the veneration of the saints, that is of the Mystical Body of Christ. He writes in his Epistle to the Hebrews:[11] "The scene of your approach now is the heavenly Jerusalem, city of the living God; here are gathered thousands upon thousands of angels, here is the assembly of those first-born sons whose names are written in heaven; here is God sitting in judgment on all men; here are the spirits of just men, now made perfect; here is Jesus, the spokesman of the new Covenant." Here we have the Communion of Saints described according to the teaching of the Catholic Church.

It will be clear from the foregoing that the veneration of the saints has evolved from the teaching of the Bible, and cannot in any way be ascribed to purely pagan influences. There is also very primitive evidence that the first Christians, that is the generation which followed the Apostles, venerated the martyrs and their relics. Polycarp was a disciple of the apostles who suffered martyrdom in the year 155. His death

[9] Gen. 20, 7. [10] Dan. 3, 35. [11] Heb. 12, 22-24.

is described in a document A.D. 156. "After Polycarp had been burnt by a centurion, we took away the bones, which are more valuable than any costly precious stones, purer than gold, and placed them in a suitable spot. Gathered together there, in joyousness, the Lord will permit us to celebrate the anniversary of his martyrdom . . . to prepare those who are awaiting martyrdom." It is only necessary to pay a visit to the Catacombs in order to realize that veneration of the saints is no invention of a later, more decadent period, but has been the custom since the foundation of the Church.

Following on the cult of the saints there arose a so-called *relative* cult, that is to say a veneration of articles having some connection with the saints. It is a characteristic of human nature to wish to have pictures of those who are dear to us, and to keep and treasure the things which have belonged to them with a certain reverence. After all, one does not casually throw away the picture of one's mother; and it is a custom to commemorate the anniversary of the death of some great man by laying floral tributes at the feet of his statue. It seems scarcely reasonable that one should be allowed to place a wreath at the Cenotaph, and yet not be permitted to put flowers before the statue of the Mother of Christ. Why should the former be called homage and the latter idolatry?

Expressions of homage, such as burning incense, lighting candles, kneeling down and so on, were originally no more than marks of respect normally accorded to earthly monarchs, who were in no way being acclaimed as gods but only as illustrious personages. There is surely more justification for rendering such homage to real saints than to the false gods to whom it has so often been applied?

The Church has not even feared to keep many of these customs in their original Southern form for she could scarcely be expected to foresee that, later on, she would be joined by men of other nations who do not normally show their deepest feelings outwardly, nor with many gesticulations. But this, after all, is a matter of national character and not of idolatry.

It would be unwise to maintain that the veneration of the saints has always remained completely free from any taint of superstition. Simple folk fall easily into foolish and unsound practices which have nothing at all to do with the genuine veneration of the saints. It is for this reason that the Canon Law of the Church contains regulations which condemn such abuses. The Church particularly impresses upon bishops that they should remove from any place of public veneration, statues which give an inaccurate representation of the teaching of the Church: for example, a statue of Our Lady which in any way gives the impression of placing Mary above Christ. They must also be careful to see that no superstitious habits slip into the veneration of the saints. (Canon Law, Canons 1278 and 1261.)

One speaks of superstition, when either the statue itself, or some exterior actions of our own, are credited with a certain power, instead of this power being attributed to the intercession of the saint; as, for instance, if one were to attach too much importance to particular attitudes, numbers, or rites, which, after all, have no value whatsoever in themselves. One must never attribute a *compelling* influence to any practice, but the result of the prayer and intercession must be left to the wisdom and the love of God. It is not always easy to distinguish between a case of superstition and a case of genuine filial confidence.

The Catholic Church has always recommended the veneration of the saints as "a good and useful work". (Canon 1276.) It is not a strict obligation, although a great reverence for the saints in general, and a certain devotion to the Mother of God, must be recognized as the bare minimum in the life of a convinced Catholic. Nevertheless it is possible to embrace the Catholic Faith without having any predilection for the actual practices employed in the veneration of the saints, such as decorating their statues, exposing their relics, saying the rosary, etc. Usually, in the course of time, one comes to take a different view of these matters. One must, however, always accept it as a point of doctrine that it is *permissible* to venerate the saints and to ask for their intercession, if one does not wish to come into conflict with the old-established and generally accepted teaching of the Church.

The Catholic enters into contact with the saints in three distinct ways:

1. By the actual *cult* chosen in order to pay them honour. There are various methods: for instance, by means of prayers, hymns, adorning of statues, processions, pilgrimages, veneration of relics. But one must thoroughly understand that, by honouring the saints, it is Christ Himself whom one honours in the first place. It is by His grace that these saints have

become what they are; of themselves they were weak enough, and it is to them in particular that we can apply those words of St. Paul: "By the grace of God I am what I am." They have taken their rank among God's most beautiful creatures. They have fought the good fight and won the battle, and now they are held eternally safe in the Bosom of God, holy, without spot, as Christ's Church herself is holy.

The issue is sometimes raised, of course, that it is impossible for anyone to know which souls have entered heaven. It appertains, however, to the Church on earth to pronounce in matters of faith and morals, which pronouncements must be regarded in certain cases as infallible. To this type of pronouncement belong *canonizations,* solemnly performed by His Holiness the Pope. Lengthy legal proceedings, carried out with the greatest exactitude, in which the life of some person or other is carefully examined, precede such canonizations. When at last it is ascertained that the person in question has truly practised heroic virtue, and that, after his or her death, two miracles have occurred as the direct result of his or her intercession, the ceremony of beatification takes place. Before canonization four authenticated miracles are required. It is a well-known fact, of course, how critically these miracles are examined, medical as well as every other sort of testimony being taken into account so that the examination ends by leaving no reasonable doubt as to their genuineness.

During the first centuries of the history of the Church, martyrs and others were canonized by the Faithful or the Bishop. Such a pronouncement was, of course, not infallible, and the veneration usually remained restricted to the diocese to which the "saint" belonged. Some time during the twelfth century (the exact date is not recorded) this power was withdrawn; from then on only the Pope could grant permission for any such veneration.

Nevertheless the honour paid to the already existing saints was allowed to continue as before. Since the year 1634, however (that is to say during the reign of Pope Urban VIII) such veneration ceased to be permitted unless it had begun prior to 1534. It is, however, possible for a saint falling into this later category, after a renewed process and investigation, to be formally beatified or canonized.

After the official canonization, the entire Church may then

join in the veneration, and the saint may become the patron of a church and be represented surrounded by a halo. After a beatification only, the veneration remains limited to a particular district.

2. By asking for their intercession with God. One does not, of course, pray to the saints in the same way as one prays to God Himself; one goes to them as one would go to a friend and ask their prayers: as, for instance, St. Paul continually asked for the prayer of his fellow-Christians. The power of prayer can be greatly increased when a number pray simultaneously; especially if among those praying there are some particularly pleasing to God, such as the saints. Precisely in what manner the saints become aware of our requests to them we do not know. We only know, according to the teaching of the Church and our own personal experience, that they do.

3. By following their example. At this point the non-Catholic will probably remark: "But surely Christ is our example?" Indeed, yes. But who can better give us the example of how to follow Christ than a saint?" We live in quite different times, under different circumstances. It is not always easy for us ordinary people to apply His teaching to our own modern circumstances. As workman, mother, priest, for instance, how exactly are we to behave? What should be our attitude to modern society? How can we best apply that charity and justice preached by Christ to our present-day conditions? The ordinary person unconsciously looks for a human example of unselfishness, chastity, perseverance in temptation.

The saints are, as it were, the answers to our human questions. They are the heroes of Christendom; they are the words of the Gospel come to life. We see courage in the martyrs, faith in the fathers of the Church, the spirit of apostolate in St. Paul and all the other great missionaries. No one has expressed seraphic love more beautifully than St. Francis of Assisi; nor given a more heroic example to the social worker than St. Vincent de Paul.

What objection can there be to one's putting a painting or statue of such a great man in one's room as a constant reminder? Why should it not be permissible even to treasure a lock of hair or a portion of something he had worn? As long as people continue to wear lockets and other keepsakes, from which they would not be parted for the world because of the remembrances they carry, a Catholic should not be reproached because he expresses his reverence for the saints by honouring their relics. In any case, anyone who does not feel drawn to the practice can leave it on one side; there is nothing obligatory about it even for Catholics. One should be broad-minded enough to allow people to follow their own personal taste in the matter.

By venerating the saints, the Catholic enters into the life of the Church Triumphant in heaven, by means of prayer, and art and poetry, following the teaching of deep and great thinkers in whom piety was so happily united to æsthetical imagination and good taste. Especially in the ages of ardent faith, the works of art produced were marvellous, not only by their beauty but by the sense of the supernatural which they conveyed. Even more so, in those golden ages, the veneration of the saints fired the imagination of the Faithful and led others to follow in the footsteps of those whom they had learned to honour.

§ 3. *Our Lady*

Among the saints, Our Lady occupies the first place. There is no greater dignity than that of Mother of Christ, and thus in the history of the world there is no woman who is better known or more venerated, and who has more greatly inspired the genius of poets and painters than this humble Jewish maiden.

We know the part which Eve played in the fall of mankind. It was due to her that Adam lapsed from his high estate and became the father of an accursed race, their faces turned to earth.

In complete contrast stands her antitype, Mary. She it was who prepared the coming of the new or second Adam, infinitely more glorious than the first: He who alone could remove the curse laid upon earth and once more turn men in the direction of heaven.

This scriptural parallel drawn between the mother of the human race and the mother of the Son of God; between the woman seduced by the serpent and the virginal mother of Christ: between the enticer to sin and the co-redemptrice—this parallel is the foundation of the devotion to Our Lady.

This does not imply that she was essential to God's plan for redemption. Christ is the only mediator between God and men. Endowed as she is, however, with so many privileges, she can be the supreme mediator between men and Christ, and thus, through Him, between men and God. Just as Adam could have sinned without Eve, so Christ could have redeemed the world without the voluntary consent of Mary to the wonderful dignity of becoming His mother. The Church calls Mary the New Eve, for, just as Eve played her part in the fall of mankind, so Our Lady played her part in the Redemption. We read of it in the Gospel according to St Luke[12] that she would be the chosen woman.

To the Jews, *the chosen woman* meant the woman who was to become the mother of the Messiah. Many women, born of the House of David, probably hoped and dreamed of this honour. It is probable, however, that Our Lady, in her modest humility, had never even thought of it in connection with herself, for we read that she was "much perplexed at hearing him (the angel) speak so, and cast about in her mind, what she was to make of such a greeting". Gabriel, however, reassured her, and proceeded to disclose God's plan: "Behold, thou shalt bear a Son and shalt call Him Jesus. He shall be great and men will know Him for the Son of the Most High, the Lord will give Him the throne of His father David, and He shall reign over the House of Jacob eternally; His Kingdom shall never have an end."[13]

This is the language of the ancient prophets but it is now prophecy at the point of fulfilment. With these words a portion of the world's history was closed for ever, and a new era ushered in; the long-expected Messiah was about to come down to earth, and the angel of God awaited the reply of His chosen mother. For a moment she still seemed to hesitate: "How can that be, since I have no knowledge of man?" A strange reply, for she was engaged to Joseph and therefore, according to Jewish custom, already counted as his wife. There is no other explanation of her words than that Joseph had agreed to respect her virginity, and the announcement that she was to become the mother of the Messiah consequently perplexed her.

God, however, had foreseen such a contingency: "The Holy Spirit will come upon thee, and the power of the Most High will overshadow thee. Thus this holy offspring of thine

[12] Luke 1, 26-28. [13] Luke 1, 30-33.

(there being no earthly father) shall be known for the Son of God."[14]

Then followed the maiden's humble acceptance of her wonderful destiny: "Behold the handmaid of the Lord; let it be done unto me according to Thy word."[15]

Voluntarily she agreed to the divine motherhood and gave her co-operation towards the preparation for the coming of the Redeemer.

Our Lady remained a virgin after the birth of Christ. This teaching of the Catholic Church is in no way affected by the fact that the Gospels speak of the brothers and sisters of Jesus. The Greek word employed is a translation of the aramaic "*ach,*" which is used to express consanguinity in varying degrees. On the other hand, Jesus is habitually referred to as *the* (not *a*) son of Joseph and Mary,[16] and from the Cross He said to His Mother: "Woman, behold thy son" (John) which would have been entirely superfluous had she had other sons. In no case are these "brothers and sisters" of Jesus called the children of Joseph and Mary.

Finally, it is possible to establish, with reasonable accuracy, that two of the so-called brothers of Jesus were the children of her sister. We have only to compare Matthew 13, 55, regarding "Jesus' brethren James and Joseph", with Matthew 27, 58, mentioning "Mary the mother of James and Joseph", who, in the same chapter, verse 61, is again referred to as "the other Mary", and in John 19, 25, as Mary the wife of Cleophas. There is therefore no reason whatsoever to doubt that Mary remained true to her pledge of virginity.[17]

A little later she went to visit her cousin Elizabeth, and in spite of her humility could not restrain the expression of her joy, and burst into the canticle of the Magnificat: "Behold, from this day forward all generations will count me blessed."[18] This prediction was inspired by the Holy Spirit, but, although every Christian feels a deep reverence for the mother of God, it is primarily the Catholic Church which gives her a place of honour accorded to no other woman, and applies, as it were, to itself those words of Our Lord to John: "This is thy mother."[19]

It is not, perhaps, very easy for the non-Catholic to understand this devotion to Our Lady. For the Catholic who has

[14] Luke 1, 35. [15] Luke 1, 38. [16] Matt. 13, 55.
[17] Luke 1, 34. [18] Luke 1, 48. [19] John 19, 27.

said the "Hail Mary" before her statue from early childhood and has continually been inspired by her wonderful example of virtue, reverence for her follows naturally: she becomes a living person: someone to whom one instinctively turns, and by whom one feels oneself to be protected.

To the non-Catholic she is perhaps more a Biblical figure out of the past: someone who has been dead for centuries, and is at the same inaccessible distance from our time as, say, Sara, Rebecca or the mother of the sons of Zebedee. Protestants do indeed regard her as the mother of God, but that is as far as they go, and that is the point at which the Catholic Church *commences*. Her dignity as mother of God is the starting-point for a very special devotion, and for all the prerogatives with which the Church endows her.

The greatest privilege enjoyed by Our Lady is, of course, that of her *Immaculate Conception* or complete immunity from original sin. The expression the Immaculate Conception is sometimes understood by non-Catholics as referring to the virginal conception of Christ. But this is not the case: it relates to Our Lady's own conception.

Such a privilege does not mean that the Virgin Mary was not in need of Redemption through Christ; but that this redemption was applied to her in a higher degree than to other men. Even before her birth, God planned to safeguard the mother of His Son, by virtue of His merits, from any taint of original sin.

This point of doctrine is not expressly dealt with anywhere in the Bible, nor was it preached by the apostles, and for many centuries it was not mentioned at all by the Church. Gradually, however, as the idea of the future dogma began to develop among the Faithful, theologians submitted the point to the closest examination, and finally, the view then generally prevailing was formally pronounced as a dogma of the Church by His Holiness Pope Pius IX in 1854. As far as Protestant theology is concerned, such a thing would, of course, be impossible, since no doctrinal point is conceded which is not contained within the written Word of God; thus those who consider the question from the non-Catholic point of view may well find it astonishing and even scandalizing. One must, however, to be consistent, explain a Catholic dogma according to Catholic principles, and one of these reads: "The Holy Ghost assists the Church in the development of the dogma in such a manner that a doctrinal point which has been accepted by the entire Church or (still clearer) proclaimed by the Pope as a dogma, is safeguarded from error."

However, just as in the case of every other theological doctrine, it was necessary that the idea of the Immaculate Conception should be contained in embryo, or *implicitly*, somewhere among the sources of Revelation. And here the theologian turns once more to the parallel between Eve and Mary.

"And the Lord said to the serpent, For this work of thine . . . I will establish a feud between thee and the woman, between thy offspring and hers; she is to crush thy head."[20]

From the earliest days the Fathers of the Church read into these words a messianic prophecy: a foretelling of the spiritual battle between the devil and the Redeemer, between the devil and the woman Mary. Such a battle must presuppose that this woman has never been within the power or under the influence of her opponent.

From the fact that the Virgin Mary had been physically constituted in a special and miraculous way to become the mother of Christ, it is permissible to conclude that God also created her spiritually pure, so that the Son of the infinitely holy Father should be born of an immaculately pure mother. This teaching as to the Immaculate Conception fits in harmoniously with all the Biblical facts, and is not in conflict with any of them, provided that one never forgets that the Virgin Mary was redeemed by Christ in common with all men.

It is a very generally held opinion in the Church (although not a point of doctrine) that God miraculously confirmed this dogma by the events which took place at Lourdes some little while after the formal pronouncement. We will here only give the historical facts. In 1858 a fourteen-years-old shepherdess, Bernadette Soubirous, had, according to her own statement, several visions of a Lady of heavenly beauty who, after some time, said slowly these words: "I am the Immaculate Conception." (The definition of the dogma took place in 1854.) A spring of water suddenly welled up where there had been none before, and in or close to this spring, sick persons began suddenly and inexplicably to be cured of their complaints. According to Bernadette, this had been

[20] Gen. 3, 14-15.

prophesied to her at the time of the apparition. A church was built by the local clergy, and Lourdes gradually developed into one of the largest shrines for pilgrimages in the world.

Many doctors, both religious and non-religious, offer their services annually to the Medical Consultation Bureau in order to observe and examine miraculous cures. In 1936, for example, 705 doctors did so, among whom were eleven professors. They never give any opinion as to the actual miracles, but upon the medical facts, and place on record in certain cases that the cure is scientifically inexplicable. Only actual organic diseases (and therefore no neurotic disorders) are considered, and even then are subject to the following conditions:

1. No remedies must have been used or applied in Lourdes.

2. The cure must be instantaneous, at least as to the origin of the disease: the dying off of bacteria, the sterilizing of toxins, the disappearance of cancerous or tubercular growths, etc. As far as the disease is concerned there is no period of recovery: the time factor in a cure is entirely eliminated, although, of course, the final results may come more slowly. A curious fact which has been noticed in some cases is that organs have begun to function long before they were cured. For instance, a peasant woman from the Vendée was able to see suddenly, although the optical nerves were still completely atrophied and were only cured a month later.

After the cure the patient remains for another year under the supervision of the doctors; if the cure persists it is then formally acknowledged as authentic. If, however, even one doctor can explain, and of course prove, the cure to be the result of suggestion, it is not acknowledged as miraculous. It is always possible to label such cures as cases of "suggestion" if one does not understand medical matters, but that is not to treat them scientifically as these are treated. Even quite small children have been cured. There is a report in 1928 by Dr. Geuillon of Fismes (Marne) who maintained that a little three-year-old patient of his, who was dying of bronchitis, was cured suddenly; and as late as 1949, a three-year-old child, paralysed from birth, completely recovered. Again, it is possible to raise objections in each individual case. These miraculous events should, however, be regarded as a whole. The following facts are incontestable. Shortly after the formal declaration of the dogma of the Immaculate Conception, an apparition of Our Lady was seen near Lourdes.

This apparition, which announced: "I am the Immaculate Conception," also told the child Bernadette that a spring would rise at the spot where she was standing, the waters of which would heal many sick persons. These events *did* in fact happen, and thousands have since been cured at the shrine which marks the place where the miraculous vision appeared. Surely no one can deny that such facts have a special significance in relation to the dogma of the Immaculate Conception!

Once again, however, one must point out that miracles at Lourdes are not an essential part of the Catholic Faith: the Church never formally expresses an opinion as to private apparitions, although she may allow their authenticity to be generally accepted by the Faithful. One thing, however, is certain and no one can deny it: at Lourdes "the blind see, the lame walk" and not even the most sceptical can dismiss such occurrences as pure fairy-tales, bearing in mind that the Gospels relate similar and even more wonderful events.

Arising out of the teaching on the Immaculate Conception and the Catholic view of the mission of the New Eve, between whom and the devil there has always existed a state of implacable enmity, there also developed a belief in the Assumption of Our Lady, soul and body, into heaven. This dogma was later formally defined by His Holiness Pope Pius XII in the year 1950.

At all events, it goes without saying that Our Lady's intercession must carry greater weight with her Son than that of any other saint. The faithful have always turned to her with unlimited confidence, and the best known form of prayer is, of course, the "Hail Mary", part of which is derived from St. Luke's Gospel:

> "Hail Mary, full of grace, the Lord is with thee. Blessed art thou among women and blessed is the fruit of thy womb Jesus. Holy Mary, Mother of God, pray for us sinners now and at the hour of our death. Amen."

Mary is called by Catholic writers the Mediatrix of all graces, and one must not perhaps blame the non-Catholic who expresses surprise at such a title, for without further explanation there may be a danger of misunderstanding.

The idea underlying the appellation is that since Mary has, by voluntarily accepting the divine motherhood, co-operated with the Redemption, it is to be expected that she should also play a part when the fruits of the Redemption are applied to men.

We would point out that the expression Mediatrix of all graces is used metaphorically, meaning that her power of intercession is so great, that her Son has graciously included her in His plan of salvation as a dispenser of graces to her fellow-men.

All Our Lady's merits must, after all, be completely dependent upon the merits of Jesus and thus, while special honour is given to her, nothing is taken away from the honour of our sole Redeemer, Christ.

In any case there is no suggestion that one is obliged to pray to Mary for every grace. It is always Christ who bestows the graces through the hands of His Mother.

The Catholic enters into a very close relationship with the mother of God which gives, as it were, a special hallmark to his spirituality. He will see her as closely associated with the actual application of the Redemption.

In the public Liturgy of the Church, Mary takes, as is only fitting, a humble place in comparison with her Son. She is, for instance, mentioned several times in the prayers of the Mass, but Christ, both Priest and Victim, so dominates the foreground, that His mother and all the other saints are present, so to speak, merely as witnesses.

In the actual lives of the Faithful, on the contrary, one hardly ever meets Christ without His mother. Just because Catholics are so infinitely more aware than are other Christians of the *humanity* of Christ, which is ever present in the Sacrament of the altar, and continually reproduced in sculpture and painting, so also are they more aware of the greatness of the woman of whom He was born. Meditations on the Nativity, the finding of Jesus in the temple, the wedding at Cana where, at His mother's request, He performed His first miracle, all these human events which bring Our dear Lord so close to us, inevitably throw into sharp relief His human relationship with her.

There is, after all, no more intimate relationship in the world than that between Mother and child. It is little wonder that Catholics see in this the highest expression of the union between Jesus and His mother, and that no other theme has so inspired painters and sculptors as the figure of the Madonna with the Holy Child. Catholic artists have indeed done much to fulfil the prophecy of the young Virgin of Nazareth: "And behold all generations shall call me blessed."

What has so nourished the devotion to Mary is her special affinity to mankind in general at all the varying stages of earthly life.

For the young boy, Mary is the symbol of the wise, perfect woman, and in the confused emotional feelings of adolescence he instinctively turns to her gracious serenity for consolation and strength. She is at once a saint of dazzling virtue and a loving mother, and the example of her pure chastity has helped many a boy and girl.

A little later the young man's attitude becomes more that of the chivalrous knight—an attitude which is reflected in his dealings with all other women. The fact that womanhood is accorded such an honourable place in Christian teaching, is mainly due to the devotion to our Lady.

The mother sees in the Madonna the ideal of all motherhood: Mary with the Child in her arms. She understands better than anyone to what almost unattainable heights this ideal has been raised; and, should suffering come to her through death and loss, there is always the Pieta, and Our Blessed Lady with her dead Son in her lap. Seeing some woman kneeling in the side-aisle of a church before such a statue, one would be a superficial judge indeed were one to attribute her ardour to mere superstitious piety.

A true devotion to Mary springs from love of Our Lord: it is at once deeply human and deeply religious. Such devotion must needs be expressed in visible form—no matter whether it takes the form of the wonderful æsthetical inspiration of the old Masters or the childlike and slightly pathetic clumsiness of a more primitive belief. Faith surrounds everything by that supernatural atmosphere which is the home of the saints of God. Our home too if we will. Catholics will always turn wistful eyes towards that other world, just out of reach, but never out of sight, waiting hopefully for the stray sunbeams which sometimes fall on us from it unawares.

CHAPTER XI

THE SACRAMENTS

SYNOPSIS

I. The mystery of the Blessed Trinity is the mystery of the intimate and interior life of God: divine knowledge and divine love. This love did not remain enclosed in the infinity of His divine Being, but urged Him to create angels, men, and a world in which mankind could live.

Man was created in a state of friendship with God, but it was his lot to obey. Man, however, sinned against this obedience and so lost God's friendship and, as a consequence, all his descendants were born outside the friendship of God.

II. God, in His infinite mercy, has redeemed mankind through His Son, Jesus Christ.

III. Through sanctifying grace, God gives man both constant help in order to follow good and avoid evil, and the possibility of a new interior life. By means of this interior union with God, his good works are rendered meritorious for heaven.

IV. By means of this life of grace a new bond is formed between Christ and the Faithful (the Mystical Body); and between the members of the Church individually (Communion of Saints). It thus becomes possible for us to invoke the saints and for the saints to pray for us. In this connection it is obvious that the Mother of the Redeemer will occupy an unique position.

V. We shall now see how this grace, which has been merited for us by Christ, and which reaches us through various channels, is above all conveyed by means of the *Sacraments*.

§ 1. *The Sacraments*

MAN SEARCHES FOR HAPPINESS in every direction. He asks himself where it is to be found. He is for ever discovering in his own consciousness a strange urge for it. If he sets himself to analyse his own activities, he will almost invariably find this motive lying at their root.

This happiness is to be found in God: in absorption in His everlasting glory, in the contemplation of His Infinite Being, and—here on earth—in union with Him by grace and love.

Once upon a time Man was happy upon earth, but this happiness was forfeited and left behind it no more than the memory of a lost paradise. Later, it was rediscovered and remerited for us, and now it is to be found in our Lord Jesus Christ. He it was who saved us from sin and shone for us as a light in the darkness. In this Light we can see and find the Truth which sanctifies us, and by participating in His divine life be again united with God, that is with the Father, the Son, and the Holy Ghost.

How then was this effected? It was through Christ's sacrifice upon the Cross that man became reconciled to God and thus was saved. His Cross is the sole cause of salvation. (Gal. 6. 14). It was from the Cross that He opened the way to Redemption, and it was His suffering upon the Cross that again flung wide the gates to happiness. On Good Friday Satan was vanquished, a complete propitiation for sin offered, and satisfaction made for the punishment due to man. The death of Christ is the one comprehensive cause of life and happiness. But how precisely does Christ become *my* Redeemer? How can I personally get into contact with the efficacy of His suffering and death? When He died, I myself did not exist: neither my soul, nor my sin, nor my strange craving for felicity. How then are His merits to be applied to me individually? How is the very depth of His humiliation to become for me personally the starting point of my ascent? How do I reach my own happiness? The answer is that by means of Faith and the Sacraments, the efficacy of Christ's redemptive suffering is conveyed to me: through these realities a bond is forged between myself and Christ in God.

Faith is a real contact with Christ. Without faith He is of little importance in our lives: He is, as it were dead, and we are dead to Him. The stream of His existence flows alongside of us, but without reaching or touching us interiorly. Possibly I may come to regard him as an attractive and congenial man; possibly He will exercise a good influence upon my life and my ideas—but I shall not truly meet Him in His Essence, nor be conscious of His real presence. This discovery is only made and confirmed by Faith, which establishes a living, spiritual contact which normally ends in loving and trustful attachment. Through Faith His Redemption is applied to me and I am thus already in step with His Church.

The Sacraments are so interiorly and spiritually bound up with Faith that this world of symbols and symbolical actions is apt to remain a mystery to the unbeliever. The Sacraments can only be given to believers, and it is through the Sacraments that Faith grows to full maturity.

If we turn to the Catechism we shall find the Sacraments described as sanctified words and actions, instituted by Jesus Christ in order to convey the grace which they symbolize. These sanctified words and actions, are signs which denote and effect grace. Again, a Sacrament is a symbol full of spiritual power by virtue of its divine institution.

What is important in the structure of the Sacrament is primarily the value that is attached to the sign or the symbol. Signs and symbols are very important in human life. They are continually to be met with in all our mutual relationships. Our language is only a complicated system of signs in order to ensure human contacts. If we wish to reach a man's mind and innermost being we are obliged to make use of a sign. This is the open sesame to the closed world of another human heart, another human spirit. A letter will reveal to us the workings of a friend's mind: a handshake expresses affection: a kiss deep love. A wave of the hand can overwhelm us with joy. From morning to night signs and symbols interpret for us the most precious content of our earthly possessions: acts, gestures, words, show what has grown and ripened in the living heart of a man.

Is it then to be wondered at that God, in the supernatural life, should also come to us by means of sacramental signs and tokens? That He gives a visible form to His love which shares with us its gifts? That in this way He makes His gift of graces intelligible to us?

The Sacrament is *a sign*. We can observe, describe, see, taste or hear a sign, but nevertheless we do not stop short at it. That which we have observed only points to something beyond. For instance, I see a signpost—a wooden or iron pole with letters and figures upon it: it points in a certain direction, it tells me how to reach the place I am looking for. I find somewhere the faint glimmer of dying embers: this tells me that a man has been working in this locality. I see the small forehead over which water is flowing, I hear words of deep significance: I believe that a child of God has been born. The Sacraments point to an invisible, interior effect. But

Christ has not just chosen signs at random as the marks of consecration or sanctification. He chose such actions, gestures, words and elements as had a definite affinity with the mysterious effect which they were to symbolize. He took simple things such as were in use in ordinary human life: bread, wine, oil, water, which by their very nature suggest to us nourishment, strength, healing and cleansing. By means of His word He attached a new meaning to them. The natural symbols become invested with a supernatural meaning and indicate to us grace and the supernatural life in all its forms and in every connection. Each Sacrament points out to us a special grace; taken together they light up for us all the possibilities of our deification, and the wonderful process of man's elevation to grace and glory.

The Sacraments illustrate the deepest truths contained in the Gospel, for the grace which each communicates has its origin in the suffering and death of Christ, and for its goal, Eternal Life. As a sign of grace, it brings us into contact with our Redemption, with the Cross of Christ, and as a sign it throws its light forward, foretelling future glory. Suffering is necessarily consummated in eternal joy: death and resurrection belong to each other.

"A sign," says Abbot Vonier, quoting St. Augustine, "is that which, besides the impression it makes on the senses, puts one in mind of something else." Then he continues: "When I see the baptismal water poured on the head of the catechumen, and when I hear the words of the priest who does the christening, if I am a man of faith, my mind, roused by these external rites and signs, travels a long way. I go back to the Jordan, where Christ is being baptized; I go back to Calvary, where blood and water issue from the side of Christ; my mind leaps forward to that people who stand before the throne of God in white robes which have been washed in the Blood of the Lamb; and, more audacious still, my mind gazes right into the innermost soul of the catechumen and distinguishes that soul from all other non-baptized souls, through that spiritual seal which makes it a member of Christ. The sacramental sign is pregnant with all that spiritual vision of my faith."[1]

The Sacrament is however *more than a sign.* It does not

[1] *A Key to the Doctrine of the Eucharist,* by Dom Anscar Vonier, O.S.B., p. 24.

only remind us of the sacrifice of Calvary, nor merely point to the interior and invisible action of Christ, but it does actually convey what it indicates. It brings to life the reality which it symbolizes. When the waters of baptism flow over us, and the appropriate words are spoken, a real cleansing from the stain of original sin and of the debt attached to it, takes place interiorly. These words and actions are merely tools in the hands of God, whose creative power works our salvation and sanctification by means of them.

But, we ask, exactly how does a Sacrament convey grace? The answer is that the Sacrament is a means of grace solely because it is the instrument of Jesus Christ: not because a good man performs the rite, or because a good man receives the Sacrament with a pure disposition. It is Christ alone who makes these symbols efficacious. The first and most essential element in our sanctification is not our own personal labour but our Lord's merciful purpose and intention regarding us: not the human element but the divine: not our merits but those of our Redeemer.

This view of the grace of the Sacraments effectually safeguards the bedrock of Christianity, which is the thought that *Christ is all* and His grace entirely unmerited. "The foundation which has been laid is the only one which anybody can lay; I mean Jesus Christ."[2] This foundation is protected by the Ecclesiastical teaching as to the Sacraments. Christ absolves us from sin through His Sacrament; at the same time man, too, plays his human part. The one who administers the Sacrament is required to act in the name of Christ.

Nevertheless any adult, who is able to decide and to judge for himself, and who wishes to receive the grace of the Sacrament, must prepare fittingly to receive it. He must believe; he must not be indifferent; nor must he have the intention of persisting in sin. Christ comes to meet us: but we have to make ourselves ready. No one can be sanctified in spite of himself. Grace and freewill go together.

It is the Sacrament itself which places us in contact with Christ, and applies His merits to us. Therefore it already acts upon a child held in the arms for baptism, and it helps a man by means of prayers and anointings, when he lies unconscious and in danger of death. That is why the personal state of the minister of the Sacrament can never affect its

[2] I Cor. 3, 11.

actual grace for the recipient. Christ has given these symbols to the Church, but the efficacy of them is solely dependent upon Him; it is He who gives life: it is He who delivers from sin.

It is clear from the above that the reproach levelled at Catholicism by Protestants is unfounded. The great difficulty they claim, is that the Catholic teaching as to the Sacraments is contrary to the general sense of Scripture. Grace is given to us through Faith, and not as something communicated to us in a natural way, outside our soul and personality. The result of the Roman interpretation, as also in other instances, it is argued, is the materialization of what should be sacred and spiritual. The material sign is no longer used in free and sovereign grace.

Let us first consider whether Scripture really so strongly disclaims our interpretation of a Sacrament: Is not the view taken by Protestants apt to be spiritually one-sided? And were the early Christians after all so greatly mistaken in the first centuries? The following will we hope provide an answer.

But apart from this, it is evident from what we have already said, that it is precisely the Catholic teaching regarding the Sacraments which throws into relief that it is the initiative, election and grace of Jesus Christ alone which is victorious. He communicates His life and spirit to us by means of symbols: there is no suggestion that the actions and the words used contain the grace in a material way, nor that they have some strange magical power. Such materialization is completely rejected. The sign is no more than an instrument which communicates to us the meaning of Christ, and which pours out over men His infinite redemptive power. The Sacraments bear witness to the greatness of God's mercy and the infinite love of the Sacred Heart of Jesus.

It remains true that Jesus is *in no way committed to them alone*: He can also reach and sanctify souls directly, and He does so in the case of many who are of goodwill and who have never met Him or His Church. He has remitted many sins without either Baptism or Confession.

But that does not alter the fact that He instituted seven Sacraments, and that through them He allows His divine life to flow into us. He has made them a source of grace: in this way He holds the central position between God and man. In the Sacraments it is His sanctifying influence which we receive.

Why did Christ institute the Sacraments? Why should He have chosen this way of initiating spiritual life in us and shedding light on our souls? Why has He thus combined the supernatural with things perceptible to the senses?

One will find the classic answer in the actual structure and condition of man who, as he now is, has need of Sacraments. For this there are three reasons.

1. We are composed of Spirit and Matter: a combination of soul and body. Matter is entirely proper to us, and yet we move continually in an immaterial world. Thoughts pass through the mind, aspirations are born in the soul, and turn towards an unchangeable ideal. Love is bound, yet creates for itself bonds which are eternal. Nevertheless our thoughts always carry with them traces of their origin; they are only able to arise with the assistance of sensory perception; they are accompanied by imagination and representation; they manifest themselves by words and gestures. Even a real conviction is only possible when it has been absorbed by the emotional life. Our entire spiritual existence develops in conjunction with instinctive, material existence, and translates itself necessarily into exterior signs.

All this holds good still more when we consider supernatural realities. What in fact do we know about them? What are we able to perceive of the process of divinisation and grace? Who is able to assure us that the communication of divine life to us is a reality? And yet we long for a sign that God is indeed working in us: we ask for some confirmation of our belief that in us that higher life has come to birth, or has again been offered us. The Sacraments fulfil these very human desires. They point explicitly to the inward grace which they convey; to the forgiveness of sin; the strength of Extreme Unction; the absolution from guilt; in other words in each case they bear witness to the grace of God.

2. We are sinful creatures. The first man fell because he allowed himself to become more attached to the creature than to the Creator. And still man allows himself to be enchained and enchanted by the impressions aroused by the material world and the flesh, and in his folly values the delights of the senses above the Author of them: the God who gave them to us in order to assist, and not to destroy, the spirit. In the very centre of our attention and our life there is always the Ego. The cause of sin is almost invariably to be found in attachment to matter where there should be dependence upon God. In His Wisdom He uses the material world as the symbol and the instrument of His almighty, creative power. Thus in the Sacraments He takes to represent that material world, which so often draws us away from Himself, the simplest, most universally used elements, and employs them to bring us His grace in spite of sin.

3. Man's nature expands normally in activity: the urge to action is an universal human urge. This action is not only the *result* of the interior purpose but also serves to fix and consolidate it. In a purely spiritual world man goes astray; he is then

apt to turn to rites and practices which only serve to further cloud his mind and obscure the issues.

But if he can express himself quite normally in a quiet gesture or an action directed to some specific purpose, then the flame of spiritual life continues to burn steadily in his soul. The folding of the hands, for instance, concentrates our attention upon God's presence within us, humility is increased by a genuflection. In each Sacrament God gives full scope to His loving heart; and he who receives the Sacrament will understand in each case the language of divine love. Man meets in the action, and hears in the words, the answer to all his interior longing for purification, and the assurance that Christ is truly with him.

Human nature demands symbols and visible means in divine worship. God respects his first creation and the characteristics of man's interior life. The Sacraments fulfil universal human needs; they offer us, in respect of the supernatural, guarantees which will contribute both to our peace of conscience and peace of mind. At the same time they throw into relief and strengthen the ties of our fellowship with one another.

Finally, the means chosen by God in the Incarnation of His Son, are still further developed in the Sacraments which He instituted.

The Word became Flesh. In Christ, the Divine Person was truly united with the human and with the visible, and in this way became a source of life and light. Christ's manhood sanctifies us, purifies us, strengthens us; it is the instrument of God's power; through His divine Person it gives us life. Christ as man spoke; went about doing good; worked miracles; He hung upon a cross, on the crest of a hill, visible to all. He offered Himself and all could perceive the offering. He died. But in dying He joined His Redemptive mission to the mission of a company left on earth to whom He gave the power and the authority to complete it.

The Church distributes its invisible graces—visibly—to the Faithful; it continues by means of symbols what He began in His Sacred Body. His gesture of forgiveness and blessing is, as it were, perpetuated in the sacramental action. It is His voice which we hear in the life-giving words. The Sacraments are the sacred relics of His Humanity, in which the vital essence of the God-Man and His suffering live on for ever—a perpetual multiplication in time and space of His Redemptive power.

So it is that the fruits of Christ's death are applied to us through the channel of the Sacraments; these latter rest upon the interior and spiritual purpose of the Incarnation, yet at the same time they have been instituted with a clear perception of man's needs and necessities.

The Church Possesses Seven Sacraments. These seven Sacraments each fulfil, most precisely, an individual function, and they include in their compass the whole of human existence. Physical life is born into the world: grows: falls ill: takes precautions against causes of infection and death; reproduces itself, and arranges its social order with a view to peace and tranquillity. All this finds its counterpart in the supernatural life lived in union with God, and from it one can infer the number of Sacraments required. In the spiritual order there is also birth, which is effected through Baptism: the life of grace is, like every other life, subject to growth, and for this Confirmation gives the necessary strength: it needs adequate nourishment, which is provided by Holy Eucharist, while Confession and Extreme Unction serve to heal and restore the broken link between God and the sinner. Children are born into the Kingdom of God through Holy Matrimony, and the Priesthood maintains and keeps in being the community of the Faithful. Each Sacrament has thus, as we have seen, its own function and character, and effects that which it expresses. The symbolism is the decisive factor in respect of the interior result in the soul. Taken altogether the Sacraments express the diversity of the operations of God's grace: rebirth, purification, strengthening, nourishment, pardon, healing, communion and union. They all effect in the soul one and the same thing, namely to make us—in Christ—the Children of God. They all bring us into contact with Him, but they all do it in a different way, adapted to man's need.

§ 2. *Baptism*

Baptism, like every other Sacrament, is as old as the Church Herself. In the New Testament, in the writings which date from the first centuries of Christianity, and later in the works of the Early Fathers, we read of Living Water, of Baptism in Jesus Christ, in the Holy Ghost and by Fire: we read of going down into the water and ascending out of it. As time went by, ceremonies began to develop: there was a definite preparation and initiation. Baptismal Churches appeared, not containing a font with still and motionless water, but with a great basin through which flowed running water into which one went down by steps—a gushing fountain with life at its source. The living water was the main point of the symbolism, cleansing from sin and effecting rebirth through water and the spirit: a birth from out of the heart of Mother Church. Immediately afterwards the newly baptized went from the Baptistry to the church, wearing their white christening robes and accompanied by the chanting of the Faithful, in order to participate for the first time at the Table of Our Lord. The ancient Church had a very clear idea as to the meaning of this Feast. She knew that each time the Faithful were commemorating a fresh encounter with the Blessed Trinity, a new spiritual birth, an entry into the Kingdom of God. Thus in Paschaltide she repeats the words of Ezechiel: "And behold waters issued out from under the threshold of the house towards the east . . . but the waters came down to the right side of the temple . . . and every living creature that creepeth whithersoever the torrent shall come, shall live."[3] Baptism, this age-old symbol, is now a Sacrament instituted by Christ to bring supernatural life to man and to make him a member of His Church.

I. BAPTISM IN THE NEW TESTAMENT

a. In the Gospels

Even heathens baptized, thus expressing their desire for interior purification. John baptized; he preached repentance to the Jews and for them Baptism became the sign of a firm purpose of amendment of life: to go down into the water signified contrition, the commencement of a new way of living. "In those same days Jesus came from Nazareth and was baptized by John in the Jordan."[4] Jesus, without sin, came to John. The latter was instantly aware of the fear of the Lord which dwelt in Him, and the sanctity of His interior life, and thus his first impulse was to refuse. Jesus, however, said to him "Let it be so for the present; it is well that we should thus fulfil all due observance. Then John gave way to Him."[5] In this act, was Jesus, as it were, merely obliging the Baptist? Surely the act had a far deeper significance. He permitted Himself to be baptized like everyone else: He willed to accept human existence in its entirety and to adopt this humble attitude in common with all. But as he was coming up out of the water, suddenly the heavens above Him

[3] Ez. 47, 1 to 9. [4] Luke 3, 21-22. [5] Matt. 3, 13-16.

were opened and a Voice said: "This is my Beloved Son in whom I am well pleased." This was the signal that the active Mission of Christ was about to begin. Nevertheless this Baptism performed by John was not that true Baptism which remits sin: he himself explicitly said so: "I have baptized you with water; He will baptize you with the Holy Ghost."[6]

This new Baptism we first truly meet with during the conversation of Jesus with Nicodemus, who visited Him by night. Nicodemus was an essentially good and honest man, rich and esteemed by the people, a teacher himself who thought deeply and was not likely to be caught by high-sounding but empty phrases. He examined all the issues carefully, and hesitated while he turned over the matter in his own mind. He was drawn to enquire more closely into the teaching of this Jesus of Nazareth, and being a prudent man, chose a quiet night for his purpose. Politely, and in the Oriental form of a compliment, he put the question as to whether Christ had indeed come to bring to earth the Kingdom of God? As we have already seen, Jesus then unfolded His teaching upon the rebirth which is necessary before it becomes possible to enter that Kingdom. He expounded the theory of the complete renewal of life represented by John's ideal: repentance and contrition. But the principle—the source—of that rebirth is the Holy Ghost, who accomplishes it by means of the waters of Baptism. This had already been foreshadowed by John as the work of the Messiah. "Believe me, no man can enter into the Kingdom of God unless birth comes to him from water, and from the Holy Spirit."[7] A certain spiritual death precedes this new birth, but as to that, Jesus remained silent. Later on, the subject was to be elaborated by St. Paul. Nicodemus also remained silent as he listened to the secret of rebirth through Baptism and the Holy Ghost. Whether he really visualized the Spirit, which once breathed over Chaos and formed an ordered world from out of it, now again moving over the water as it flowed across the forehead of man, is not clear. It is by means of *water* and the Holy Ghost that the new life is created, and it is from the latter that the water receives its creative power. This water also contains the property of fire, of which John spoke when he said, "One is to come after me . . . He will baptize you with the Holy Ghost and with fire,"[8] and so possesses that purifying quality

[6] Mark 1, 8. [7] John 3, 5. [8] Matt. 3, 11.

which was lacking in his Baptism. Whoever is not born afresh through it, misses the Kingdom of God, for this Baptism is indeed necessary for salvation.

A new birth, from which proceeds a new life, is the outcome of it.

As we have already seen in another context, after His Resurrection, Jesus called together His disciples upon the mountain-side. When they saw Him the eleven fell down to worship. Then it was that He said to them: "All authority in heaven and on earth has been given to Me; you, therefore, must go out making disciples of all nations, and baptizing them in the name of the Father, and of the Son, and of the Holy Ghost, teaching them to observe all the commandments which I have given you."[9]

A clear mission: to preach in order to spread the Faith and to baptize men of all nations.

Baptism is meant for all, and the meaning of this ceremony is a definite dedication to the Father, the Son and the Holy Ghost. John's prediction of a new Baptism was therefore thus fulfilled, and although we do not know precisely *when* Christ instituted it, it is obvious from what has already been said, that He connected together Baptism and Grace. It was He who gave the command to administer it. In the Acts of the Apostles we shall find frequent references to the remission of sins conveyed by Baptism in the Name of Jesus Christ; at Pentecost alone three thousand were baptized.[10]

b. St. Paul

St. Paul speaks of Baptism in precisely the same terms as it would be spoken of by any Christian in the present day. It was a ceremony known and used by the Faithful; it was administered in the Name of Christ; it consisted of an immersion in water, accompanied by the word[11] which, as St. Paul tells us, gives us new birth and restores our nature through the Holy Spirit.[12] At Ephesus he met disciples who had received the Baptism of John, but he Baptized them also in the name of Jesus, "and when Paul laid his hands upon them the Holy Spirit came down on them and they spoke with tongues, and prophesied."[13] He tried to explain to the

[9] Matt. 28, 19. [10] Acts 2, 37-41. [11] Eph. 5, 26.
[12] Tit. 3, 5. [13] Acts 19, 1-7.

Romans how, through Baptism, they must think of themselves as dead to sin and alive with a new life which looks towards God.[14] The ceremony of Baptism represents Redemption through Christ: His death and His Resurrection.

Once Baptized they were to belong wholly to Him; to be spiritually united to Him. The condition was death to sin, and it was Christ's death which annihilated sin. In the same way that Christ, through His death, laid down His earthly life and began a new and glorified existence, so Baptism meant for them the end of a sinful life and the beginning of a life of grace. The truth is that the whole life of man is connected with the life of Christ. With Him he is crucified, with Him he dies;[15] with Him he is buried; with Him he rises again[16] and his life is the life of Christ.[17] Magnificently Baptism symbolizes the universal cause of our salvation.

Death and Resurrection. The person receiving Baptism goes down into the font and is immersed in that living stream; He shares the death of Jesus, and the old man, full of sin, is buried with Christ. As he comes out of the water, he rises again with the Saviour; a new man comes into being, and a new life commences. Christ dies no more. His glorified life endures eternally, and he who has passed through death with Christ dies no more either. Life is never again completely extinguished; Baptism is not repeated. He may stray from the right path, but in his wanderings, far from his Father's home, he remains sealed with the seal of Christ through Baptism; his compass still, as it were, points towards the Father, the Son and the Holy Ghost.

Baptism has been compared by St. Paul to the Jewish Circumcision, but actually it far surpasses this latter in both meaning and power. It is a ceremony of initiation, introducing us to Christianity; it clothes us with Our Lord and incorporates us with Him. St. Paul lays great stress on the connection between faith and Baptism. Only through individual and convinced faith does the adult come to desire this Baptism, which incorporates him into Christ. The first real and logical consequence of belief in Our Lord is that one is ready to receive it. Through it one is effectually united with Jesus and the Church; through it one is drawn into that real fellowship of life and death in which the Christian life con-

[14] Rom. 6, 3-11.
[15] II Tim. 2, 11.
[16] Eph. 2, 5 and Col. 2, 13.
[17] II Tim. 2, 12.

sists. On the other hand, Baptism, in its turn, presupposes faith.

In this teaching of his, St. Paul closely follows Christ's revelation who, as St. Mark tells us, spoke of the need for faith as well as of the sacramental rite when He used the words: "He who believes and is baptized will be saved."[18]

II. THE TEACHING OF THE CHURCH

The Church calls Baptism the door or entrance to the spiritual life, through which we become members of Christ and of the Body of the Church. Drawing on the teaching of Christ, the customs adopted by the Apostles, and the practice of the early ages, She concludes that this Baptism which He instituted, is a Sacrament symbolizing a most important event in life and the soul. The flowing of the water over the forehead indicates purification, while the words are pronounced, "I baptize thee in the name of the Father and of the Son and of the Holy Ghost"; these words convey the true spiritual meaning of the purification: the cleansing of the soul, liberation from sin, and consequent dedication to the Blessed Trinity. In this manner water, which is present everywhere, is used to symbolize our entry into the Christian life; just as water washes the body, so the grace of God purifies the soul. The symbol represents grace; it indicates purification and dedication, interior sanctification through God.

To all those who have the will to receive it, and a true sorrow for sin, Baptism is the source of spiritual rebirth into supernatural life.

The implication is, in the first place, that even before the fruit has ripened, this ceremony gives a *right* to divine life. It is as though Christ laid His hand upon a person and said: "In future you belong to Me. I set My seal upon your soul and this seal gives you a permanent title to all those graces which are necessary to Salvation." It has been called an *indelible mark*. It is by nature spiritual; it makes us participants in the eternal priesthood of Christ; it consecrates us to Him in a special way.

Although in the Bible, and in the oldest ecclesiastical writings, this affixing of a seal is not clearly distinguished from the actual grace of Baptism, nevertheless it bears out the

[18] Mark 16, 16.

general conception given us by Revelation, namely that Christ takes irrevocable possession of the baptized person, who is thus eternally dedicated to Him. St. Paul told the Ephesians that those who believed in the Gospel had the seal set on their faith by the promised gift of the Holy Spirit.[19]

Two truths, already contained in the most ancient tradition, emerge clearly from this symbolism:

Baptism cannot be repeated; it binds man for ever to Christ and to His Church.

The effect of Baptism is to revive or bring back to life where this was hindered or prevented by our own fault. The exterior sign continues to call down graces from God. He who receives Baptism without contrition for sin, receives the token from God although not the grace: but should contrition arise later in the soul, then God bestows by means of the token, the grace proper to the Sacrament. Through this sign, this supernatural conformity with the Priesthood of Christ, a man is deputed to participate in public worship and to assist at Holy Mass. He is also enabled to receive other Sacraments, while by virtue of this Sign he is bound by all ecclesiastical laws and is obliged to bear witness to his faith as a Christian. Through Baptism he has, as it were, received the imprint of Christ's dignity and destiny, and become, first and foremost, *a member of the Church* and a citizen of the Kingdom of God.

As a member of the Church, conformed to Christ and united with Him, he has a share in the full application of Baptismal grace; this Sign finds its complete fulfilment in him. Plunged in the living stream, cleansed by that running water—which to us signifies purification, the original source of things, and, by its clear translucency, a certain receptivity to light—he is absolved from original sin, as well as his own sins and the punishment due to them. He receives no penance. Sanctifying grace is infused into him, and henceforth he participates in the life of grace of the incarnate Son of God, while the Father, the Son, and the Holy Ghost come to take up their abode in him. With St. Paul he exclaims: "I am alive; or rather, not I; it is Christ that lives in me. True I am living, here and now, this mortal life; but my real life is the faith I have in the Son of God, who loved me, and gave Himself for me."[20] The Primitive Church called this new life a light, and this rebirth an illumination. For Baptism, which has its

[19] Eph. 1, 13 and 4, 30 and II Cor. 1, 21.

[20] Gal. 2, 20.

origin in faith, gives us a fresh, inner perception, namely divine Faith, which inspires us to trust in the promises of God and to become active through love. It is by this Faith that the just man must learn to live.[21] The conflict between our instincts and the spirit may continue; death will come to us one day; but all this is but a passing shadow in comparison with the magnificence of the future glory to which this Sacrament destines us. And that life begins even now under the guidance of the Holy Ghost, who through His seven gifts, finds a solid foundation for His divine action: an open mind to receive His light, and a heart attentive to His gentle prompting.

The Church places this Sacrament first and, mindful of Our Lord's conversation with Nicodemus, designates it as *necessary* to salvation. Only those who are in a state of grace, spiritually united with Christ and consequently members of Christ's Mystical Body, can enter Heaven. This, however, does not depend on any specific external condition and therefore, in that sense, Baptism is not absolutely necessary: there may be exceptions. It is not the *only* means to reach the end. Nevertheless it is the means established by Christ under normal circumstances: it was He who gave his disciples the charge to go out: "Baptizing them in the Name of the Father and of the Son and of the Holy Ghost: teaching them to observe all the commandments which I have given you." That is why the Church is so solicitous that all her members should receive this Sacrament, to the point that, in case of necessity, anyone—believer or even unbeliever—may and must baptize.

Further she recognizes the symbol or mark of Baptism and its effect in the case of either *martyrdom* or the *Baptism of Desire*.

Self-Sacrifice—raised to the level of heroism—proves an over-ruling generosity and goodwill and thus, by means of his own death, or torture which would naturally result in death, the unbaptized martyr is plunged into the death of Christ, and by participation in it, participates also in His glory. The Church knows that Christ blesses those who suffer persecution in the cause of right,[22] and remembers that He said: "The man who loses his life for My sake will secure it."[23] And again: "This is the greatest love a man can show, that he

[21] Heb. 10, 22-26. [22] Matt. 5, 10. [23] Matt. 10, 39.

should lay down his life for his friends."[24] This is known as the *Baptism of blood*.

The expression Baptism of desire means literally that whoever longs for Baptism, but owing to circumstances cannot receive it, receives the grace by virtue of his goodwill. St. Augustine tells us that Baptism of desire is included in conversion of heart, if one does not know of Baptism, or, through no fault of one's own, fails to appreciate it. It consists in the will to do anything that God may ask, and consequently to use all the means which He has judged necessary for Salvation. It consists in the desire to fulfil God's will in everything. This faith and this love work out both forgiveness and supernatural life, for "if a man has any love for Me, he will be true to My word: and then he will win My Father's love, and we will both come to him and make our continual abode with him."[25]

Because these last two forms of Baptism are neither of them a Sacrament, the Church teaches that they do not imprint any mark upon the soul. Nevertheless we are brought by both, in some mysterious way, into conformity with Christ, and therefore, automatically, with the Church.

The teaching of the Church is equally clear as to the Minister and the recipient of Baptism.

The *Minister*, properly speaking, is *Christ*: Christ baptizes. From His glorified life there springs the life of grace within the Church. Therefore, it is He who baptizes, together with the Holy Ghost.[26] Our Lord has no successors on earth, but only instruments.

The Church further distinguishes between Baptism with ceremonies, which is administered under normal circumstances, and Baptism of necessity. In the first case the usual Minister is a Bishop, priest, or sometimes a deacon. This priest should be regarded as "Christ's servant and the steward of God's mysteries".[27] Such would appear to have been the practice during the early ages of the Church. Neither the unbelief of the minister, nor his erroneous ideas, or state of sin, invalidate the Sacrament, provided he truly desires to be the instrument of Christ's work and purpose. It is Christ who baptizes.

Let us repeat, for it always holds good: everyone *can* baptize and, in case of necessity such as danger of death, not

[24] John 15, 13. [25] John 14, 23. [26] John 1, 33. [27] I Cor. 4, 1.

only may but must baptize. He must pour the water over the forehead of the one to be baptized *while* he utters the words: "I baptize thee in the Name of the Father, and of the Son, and of the Holy Ghost."

The *recipient is man*. Every human being can be Baptized. Adults, however, must offer themselves, for God does not force His love and grace upon us. He invites, He asks, but also demands free assent. Consequently the intention of the will to receive from Christ and the Church that which is to be communicated in this Sacrament is required: namely, faith in God, who both recompenses and punishes; and sorrow for sin; after which follows the answer of God, His recompense for those who have thus sought Him. Normally, Baptism is preceded by a period of instruction and quiet reflection.

III. THE BAPTISM OF CHILDREN

The typical result of the sacramental action of Baptism is most clearly illustrated in the case of children. Neither faith nor goodwill can here bring any influence to bear; it is Christ alone who places the supernatural germ of life in the soul. The justification for such Baptism is contained in some of the fundamental principles expressed in Revelation. These children were born, in common with all men, in a state of death, for "death came owing to guilt, death was handed on to all mankind",[28] and yet "the Kingdom of Heaven belongs to such as these".[29] They therefore come under the conditions laid down by Christ for entrance into the Kingdom of God; Baptism by water and the Spirit; and should not then the Apostles have mercy on them also, in view of the universal command to baptize all nations?

In the Primitive Church no question was ever raised as to the validity of such Baptism although, even as late as the fourth century, the actual administration of it was by no means universal.

The fear that their subsequent life might not correspond with the promises—made in Baptism by godmother and godfather—frequently held back both priests and parents from conferring the Sacrament upon these little ones. In the Acts of the Apostles, however, we read that Lydia and her whole family, as well as St. Paul's gaoler and his household, were

[28] Rom. 5, 12-14. [29] Matt. 19, 14.

baptized. Origen also states that, in his day, the Baptism of infants was regarded as an apostolic institution.

After all, through this Sacrament the child receives forgiveness of original sin; further it is indelibly marked with the sign of Christ, and so continues to call down upon itself the grace of God which, because there can be no barrier, flows unimpeded into the soul. It thus becomes a temple of the Holy Ghost and the abode of the Blessed Trinity. In just the same way in which it is endowed with a natural ability to think and will, the action of Christ fills it with a supernatural ability for faith, hope and charity. Godfather and godmother are sponsors for its faith, and even more for the Christian integrity of the parents. It is for this reason that the Church is not normally willing to baptize a child unless there is assurance that it will have a Christian upbringing. Next to the godparents, that is the man and the woman who, as sponsors, make a declaration of faith and ask for Baptism on behalf of the infant, it is the Church which is responsible for the due observance of the baptismal vows.

Such a course of action does no injustice to the child, and is in no way connected with moral restraint. Christ has an absolute claim on every human soul. He wishes man to share His divine life, and that this life should penetrate as strongly and constantly as possible into each soul. The Church knows that fidelity to Baptismal grace is often imbibed with the mother's milk. Similarly a father registers the birth of his child with the Registrar, sends it to school in order that it may develop intellectually, and points out to it all kinds of dangers and some of the natural truths of life. Why, then, should it seem strange that this same father, himself a member of the Catholic Church, should introduce his child to that supernatural "way" which he believes leads to both truth and life. Later on, having come of age, the adult will have to acknowledge such Baptism and, able now to judge of the value of the gift which he has received, to confirm it by a free acceptance.

Although it is entirely false to contend that an unbaptized person is lost, yet Baptism is necessary to salvation. A child who dies without Baptism is certainly not damned; it does not suffer in the other life; it has no painful consciousness of a lack or a void; most probably it will find in God the happiness which belongs to it by nature—unless indeed God has decreed otherwise, which we cannot know. But in any case, injustice is out of the question: the supernatural life and the contemplation of the Blessed Trinity far exceed every claim and desire of our human nature.

The problem of the fate of the unbaptized child remains an open problem. God *can* sanctify the soul of a child without Baptism—that is clear. Whether He does so, and how, we cannot tell. He wishes to sanctify all men, and Christ died for all children. Nevertheless the Providence of God remains a secret: the secret of His love traces out its own ways, far above anything which we can piece together from any combination of texts drawn from Scripture.

IV. THE LITURGY OF BAPTISM

In the porch of the church the priest asks under what name the candidate for Baptism desires to become a member of Christ, and then proceeds to show the foundation of that membership, namely faith, which is the seed of the contemplation of God. This faith, both the child and the unbaptized adult ask of the Church and out of this same faith there flows the duty to keep the commandments, and to love God and our neighbour. First, however, it is necessary that the devil should be driven out of the candidate, stained with original sin, in order to make way for the presence of the Holy Ghost.

The priest signs the forehead and heart with the sign of the cross, and signs the forehead and the organs of sense with his thumb. Salt is put upon the tongue, the salt of wisdom, which symbolizes preservation of the taste for the divine, notwithstanding sin and corruption.

There then follows a threefold exorcism: the devil has to pay honour to Jesus Christ and to the Holy Ghost, and then to disappear for ever. At this point the candidate is led into the church and makes open confession of his faith reciting the Credo and the Lord's Prayer. Further questions follow, and once more he renounces the devil, and the Church anoints him with the oil of catechumens on the breast, and between the shoulders, in the form of a cross, so that from then onwards he will be able to bear the yoke of Christ.

When the priest has changed his purple vestments for white, the candidate solemnly makes his confession of faith in the Blessed Trinity and explicitly asks for Baptism. "Wilt thou be baptized?" "I will." The godparents hold him while the priest pours the water over his forehead, saying: "I baptize thee in the name of the Father and of the Son and of the Holy Ghost." As a member of the Church he is next anointed with chrism, and the priest then gives him a white garment, exhorting him to carry it without stain before the judgment seat of Jesus Christ, and bestows upon him a lighted candle, saying "Go in peace and the Lord be with you." The prayers used during all these ceremonies are extremely ancient, and illustrate in a most striking way the symbolism of each. The serious and subdued atmosphere in which the ceremony begins is soon transformed into a joyous welcome to grace and light.

§ 3. *Confirmation*

Through Baptism the life of Christ was born in us; it was a little germ which had to be carefully tended, confirmed and strengthened—a germ which was ultimately to grow into an adult Christian life. Therefore, by God's Wisdom and Providence, which surrounds this tender, divine life in man with watchful care, the Church joins to the Sacrament of spiritual rebirth (Baptism) a Sacrament suitable to spiritual manhood, to the formed adult, and calculated to produce fruitful work and valiant struggle. This supplement, as it were, to Baptism, which was formerly administered at one and the same time, is called Confirmation, and through it Christ communicates the Holy Ghost to us in a special way. It transforms us into self-reliant men of faith. Through it each of us becomes an official representative and defender of the Faith: a light set in a candlestick: a city upon a hill.

1. The teaching of the Church—which relies upon the promises of Christ—is that *Confirmation is a Sacrament.* The Church explains how Christ promised the assistance of the Holy Ghost to the Apostles, and to all the Faithful, and shows how that promise was performed in the early days of the Church.

In His conversation with the Samaritan woman Jesus tells her of the new life which transforms man inwardly.[30] "The man who drinks the water I give him will not know thirst any more. The water I give will be a spring of water within

[30] John 4, 14.

him, that flows continually to bring him everlasting life." The source of this water and this life is the Holy Ghost.[31] It is St. John himself who explains it as follows,[32] by telling us how Jesus stood in the temple and cried aloud: "If any man is thirsty let him come to me and drink; yes, if a man believes in Me, as the Scripture says, fountains of living water shall flow from his bosom." He was speaking of the spirit which was to be received by those who learned to believe in Him, the Spirit which had not yet been given to men, because Jesus had not yet been raised to glory.

The death of Christ, His Resurrection and Ascension preceded, according to the decree of God, the coming of the Holy Ghost; they were indeed the grounds for that coming. It is the Holy Ghost who inspires the Baptized Christian to bear witness to his faith; at Christ's request, the Father promised to give us another to befriend us, one who would dwell continually with us forever[33]—the truth-giving Spirit for whom the world could find no room. He, at His coming, was to bear witness to all that Christ had been:[34] He was in turn to make everything plain to us and to recall to our minds everything that Christ had said.[35] If we pray to the Father, He is ready to give from heaven, His gracious Spirit to those who ask Him.[36] Finally this promise is once more explicitly repeated at the Ascension: "The Holy Spirit will come upon you, and you will receive strength from Him; you are to be My witnesses . . . to the ends of the earth."[37] This promise to the Apostles was fulfilled at the first Pentecost.[38] Inspired and strengthened by this Spirit, they bestowed It also by means of the imposition of hands and prayers, upon the Faithful who were already baptized.[39] According to the narrative of St. Luke, in the very earliest days of the Church, St. Peter and St. John were sent by the Apostles to Samaria, to those who had received nothing further than Baptism in the Name of Jesus. These two came down and prayed for them, and then began to lay their hands upon them, and in that way the Holy Spirit was given them. Similarly, in Ephesus, St. Paul met catechumens who had been Baptized with the Baptism of John. Then "They received Baptism in the Name of the Lord Jesus; and when Paul laid his hands upon

[31] John 7, 37-39. [32] John 7, 37-39. [33] John 14, 15-18.
[34] John 15, 26. [35] John 14, 26. [36] Luke 11, 13.
[37] Acts 1, 8. [38] Acts 2, 1-4. [39] Acts 8, 14-20.

them, the Holy Spirit came down on them, and they spoke with tongues and prophesied."[40]

Anyone giving careful consideration to all this, will surely become aware of a definitely sacramental atmosphere. We find the symbolical gesture, the imposition of hands and prayer: a definite outward sign. This imposition of hands takes place after the ceremony of Baptism, by means of other ministers, at a different time, and is thus clearly distinguished from it. The procedure points to some interior effect which takes place. The Holy Ghost is invoked, and He descends upon those who offer themselves for this ceremony and fortifies them with both interior strength and sanctification. All this is handed down to us from the Apostles themselves, who by these ceremonies were interpreting and fulfilling the will of Christ. They could not impart the Holy Spirit by their own power, but only through the Hands of the glorified, risen Christ.

This is how Confirmation was understood by the Early Church. The newly baptized convert went from the Baptismal Font to the Bishop, who laid his hands upon him, anointed him with holy oil, and invoked the Holy Spirit in a short prayer. In the third century Tertullian wrote—and it comes to us as the echo of a custom—"The body is overshadowed by the imposition of hands, so that the soul may be illumined by the Holy Ghost." In the same century Cyprian also writes: "Two Sacraments co-operate towards a complete Christian rebirth; the one causes man to be reborn, namely Baptism; the other communicates the Holy Spirit." Originally this second was administered immediately after Baptism, but gradually the two became more distinctly separated: the inner meaning of the latter, which definitely pointed to a certain spiritual preparedness, automatically brought this about. At the present day children receive this Sacrament at any time after their first Communion.

2. The custom which we find described in Scripture, and in the records of the tradition of the first Christian era, is now set out in a more clearly defined form contained in the *Liturgy of the Church*.

Christ wished to mark by an outward sign the communication of the gift of the Holy Ghost to the Faithful. Both the Spirit and His gifts proceed from Him. By the symbols and

[40] Acts 19, 1-7.

the ceremonies He confers his interior strength, while the prayer calls down His grace.

He left the question of the precise way in which the outward symbol was to mark the interior grace, entirely to the discretion of Holy Church. This symbol has undergone some changes in the course of the centuries. It began with the *imposition of hands,* and prayer; this was the traditional manner of imparting the Holy Spirit: the gesture by which Christ Himself gained control of the man who was possessed, and cast out the devil: the sign by which He healed the sick and blessed the children who gathered round Him. From the third century onwards this imposition of hands was frequently followed by signing the forehead with a cross, first quite simply and later on with chrism. *Unction* is thus added to the gesture, and the meaning of this dates right back to the prophecies of both Old and New Testaments. In the Old Testament the Messiah is called the Anointed,[41] and Christ applies this text to Himself.[42] He was anointed—according to the text of the Hebrews—with the oil of gladness. The ancient Christian Church understood these Biblical references.[43] "It is God who gives both us and you our certainty in Christ. It is He who has anointed us, just as it is He who has put His seal upon us, and given us the foretaste of His Spirit in our hearts."[44]

Anointing with oil was a sign of the conferring of strength and encouragement, and a preparation for battle. Gradually more attention began to be paid to the meaning of the anointing than to the imposition of hands, although this custom was also preserved. Both the imposition of hands and the anointing are included in the present-day Ceremony of Confirmation. The candidate kneels before the Bishop, who lays his right hand upon his head, anoints his forehead with chrism in the form of a cross and says: "I sign thee with the sign of the cross and confirm thee with the chrism of salvation, in the Name of the Father, and of the Son, and of the Holy Ghost."

The imposition of the hands gives the strength to bear witness to the Faith; the sign of the cross with oil and chrism on the forehead gives the courage to confess Christ before all men; while the balsam within the chrism conveys the fragrance of virtue and the good odour of Christ. The cor-

[41] Is. 6, 1. [42] Luke 4, 18. [43] Acts 4, 27 and 10, 38.
[44] II Cor. 1, 21-22.

ruption of sin is thus remedied. The whole effect is of courage and pliable strength, of the honest defence of truth, without pettiness or narrow mindedness, and a steady witnessing to the Faith.

Finally the Bishop gives a slight blow on the cheek as a mark of enrolment in the army of Christ, and to warn us that there is much to be endured for the love of Our Lord.

This Sacrament confers all it symbolizes: namely, a greatly increased participation in the life of grace; the privilege of living by the Faith and openly confessing it so that there is no longer any contradiction between our way of life and our beliefs, the former becoming a constant witness to the latter. Through the grace of the Holy Ghost a truly Christian life begins in the soul, ready for action and, if need be, ready to bear reproach.

Through this Sacrament, as it were, the atmosphere of the Primitive Church is revived; it is a renewal of all the grace of Pentecost, when the Holy Ghost descended and gave to those present strength to live by the Faith interiorly and to bear witness to it exteriorly. It is through His grace that we fight the dangers of contemporary life, the destructive, undermining spirit of the world; and at the same time, guard against the dangers which threaten from within, that is to say weariness in well-doing, despondency, the indulgence of sense and instinct.

In this context, the Church speaks of the *indelible mark* of Confirmation. Apart from our increased participation in the life of Christ, His grace and power, there is also an increase in our conformity with Christ as High Priest, a conformity which we first received in Baptism. Through the rite of Confirmation we participate even more deeply in His Priesthood, we are more closely consecrated to Him. St. Paul says: "You had the seal set on your faith by the promised gift of the Holy Spirit."[45]

This indelible mark is a further extension of the mark of Baptism. The meaning of it may perhaps be explained in this way. Through Baptism we were admitted as simple citizens into the Kingdom of God; through Confirmation we are promoted into being soldiers of Christ. We are thus entrusted with a more important function in His Kingdom, because we have come to participate more fully in His King-

[45] Eph. 1, 13.

ship. We are called upon not only to fight, but also to suffer for Him and His Realm; no longer to regard this suffering as a humiliation, but to bear it as a sign of our election and conquest.

Finally, we are hall-marked by this Sign as "official bearers of God's Revelation"; the Apostolate in all its forms is the logical consequence, and it often brings with it an urge to Catholic Action. It follows that this Sacrament—although not necessary to salvation—is yet of inestimable value for Christian thought and behaviour. Only serious reasons should be allowed to prevent or to postpone its reception. Repetition is impossible: the mark impresses a lasting dedication to Christ on the soul.

Whoever receives this Sacrament does so in complete freedom, in a state of grace, conscious of the particular significance which it bears in the Christian life; conscious also of the grace and strength which, through the Holy Spirit, it will cause to fructify in the soul. After the imposition of hands and the anointing, as the Catechism expresses it: "We receive the Holy Ghost, in order to make us strong and perfect Christians and soldiers of Jesus Christ."

§ 4. *Confession*

Experience teaches us that some of the greatest objections raised against Catholicism are in connection with the Sacrament of Penance. The objections are not only theoretical, such as "How can a man forgive sins?" or "Is it not enough for God alone to see one's repentance?" but they are also concerned (above all!) with quite practical matters. It is not easy to confess one's sins to a priest, even if one is able to accept the teaching that he can absolve in the Name of God. Moreover, what should one say, and what not say? In what form should one express it, and with how much detail?

Usually a non-Catholic completely misrepresents all this to himself. Neither God nor the Priest desire a minutely detailed account of the faults committed. Contritely—the stress is on the contrition—one should confess one's faults under the generally accepted headings; I have grieved my parents deeply, I have committed impurity with myself. When, in addition to this, the number of occasions is mentioned, such a confession is usually sufficient. More details are only asked in unusual circumstances, and, especially in sexual matters, or in matters allied to it, the greatest reserve is recommended to both penitent and priest, so that no more is said than is strictly necessary.

Certainly, even then, such a confession can be a humiliation, but it need never become a psycho-analytical torture. Instead, quite often, it is followed by a wonderful sense of liberation and the rediscovery of peace between God and one's own soul.

This Sacrament has no connection with either vengeance or punishment, but is, on the contrary, an undiluted grace. It is the continuation of those words of Christ echoing down the Ages and bringing redemption to mankind: "Thy sins are forgiven—go in peace."

In this chapter we shall do our best to elucidate this.

By virtue of Baptism and Confirmation we already have a share in Our Lord's life of grace. Experience, however, teaches us how fragile is this divine life in us, and how easily it is affected by the vicissitudes, the unrest, and unceasing change of our existence. God leaves us our freedom; He does not take away all our temptations. He offers us His grace and His help, but does not forcibly obtrude Himself upon us. We know that Man sins. But even as far back as the Old Testament, we can hear the words of the prophet Ezechiel telling us that God does not desire the death of the sinner, but rather that he should be converted and live.

Christ, the incarnate revelation of God's love for us, came down to save sinners and to convert them; the Good Shepherd seeks for the lost sheep along the mountain paths and valleys, and every morning the father goes out to see if the prodigal son has yet returned. It was Jesus who defended Mary Magdalen from the scorn of the Pharisees, as she wept at His feet; and saved the woman taken in adultery from a purely human justice. We are told, and it is true, that in heaven there will be more joy over one sinner who repents, than over ninety-nine just men who are in no need of repentance. Christ knows what man is really worth; He values him at his just value. The high ideal which He puts before us, and the sanctity which He attaches to the hunger and thirst for such an ideal, do not make Him forget that nevertheless sin and man are in truth but one. He knows that man stands in constant need of Him as the great Physician. He does not desire to refuse forgiveness even after the rejection of a proffered grace, and so He has instituted a Sacrament which goes far beyond the mere remembrance of His mercy and is a token of His enduring solicitude that the smoking flax shall not be quenched nor the bruised reed broken, but repaired and healed.

I. RESTORATION OF THE LIFE OF GRACE ACCORDING TO THE BOOKS OF THE NEW TESTAMENT

A. *Gospels*

1. It was John the Baptist who announced the coming of the Kingdom of the Messiah and as a preparation for it, stirred people to contrition and penance. Neither Pharisees nor scribes, Jews nor pagans, thought much of conversion of the heart. Proud of their prerogatives, head bent and mind absorbed over the letter of the Law, the Pharisees carefully carried out all the exterior rites and precepts connected with purification; but purification of the heart no longer received any attention. They built up their own religious life: that was their whole work: the result of day-to-day achievements for the Lord God. They did not understand anything of that attitude of soul which was expressed to an angel from Heaven by a maiden chosen from their own race. "Behold the handmaid of the Lord; be it done unto me according to thy word." But John, who leaped in his mother's womb at his first meeting with that chosen woman, taught them otherwise. He did not hesitate to proclaim the truth fearlessly. Straight from the desert, still clothed in his wind-roughened camel's hair garment, he boldly preached his message of penance and humility.

The desert stirred; his words reached even to the towns of the uplands: "Repent, the kingdom of heaven is at hand." And to the Pharisees and the Sadducees, he cried: "Who was it that taught you, brood of vipers, to flee from the vengeance that draws near? Come, then, yield the acceptable fruit of repentance." He pointed out to them the venom of their lives; the pride by which they made themselves mediators between God and the simple people whom they despised. In the end crowds flocked to him from up and down the valley of Jordan; dwellers in the towns and at the foot of the hills. Throughout Judea they came asking for Baptism, which was the decisive step on the road to repentance: the sign of that contrite heart on account of which God forgave sin. Therefore at this Baptism, men confessed—which was something entirely new—the sins they had committed. The obedience to God who spoke to them through the voice of the prophet John: the exterior act of purification symbolized by Baptism: the confession and repentance for sin—all this called down God's mercy upon them: it was like a wide, general confession as a preparation for the coming of the Kingdom of God.

2. *That which John began, Christ fulfilled*

a. He forgave sins—by His own authority[46]—for which the Pharisees were never to forgive Him. It was in Capharnaum that they first saw Him do it, in a house where it chanced one day that He was teaching while some Pharisees and teachers of the law were sitting by. Suddenly an opening was made in the roof and a paralytic was let down, between the tiles, bed and all, into the clear space in front of Jesus. A silence followed, as all eyes were turned in the direction of the man, who remained quietly lying there, his very immobility showing his faith and desire. Then the miracle happened. Jesus said to him: "Thy sins are forgiven thee." In the heart of the paralytic what a transport of joy and happiness: in the hearts of the Pharisees only astonishment and anger at such presumption. "Who can this be, that he talks so blasphemously? Who can forgive sins but God, and God only?" And Jesus, knowing these secret thoughts of theirs, said to them openly: "Which command is more lightly given, to say, thy sins are forgiven thee, or to say, Rise up and walk?" Then, without waiting for any answer: "And now, to convince you that the Son of Man has power to forgive sins while He is on the earth, (here He spoke to the palsied man) I tell thee, rise up, take thy bed with thee and go home." And the man got up at once in full sight of them all, took up his bedding, walked past the Scribes and out of the door, and went home giving praise to God. The one miracle explains the other: the man's renewed physical life bears witness to the burning life of grace which flowed into his heart when Jesus washed away his sins.

Jesus forgives sins wherever He meets faith, contrition, and a desire often buried deeply in the soul, to draw near to Him. Tears of contrition affect Him profoundly: Simon never for-

[46] Luke 5, 17-26.

got the scene at that dinner to which he had invited Our Lord. Looking back, he saw again the Magdalen as she entered in all her beauty with her alabaster vase. He remembered the mingled horror and admiration with which the guests greeted her appearance. Before he could prevent her she had knelt before Jesus to anoint His feet, bursting into tears which rained down upon them. Suddenly, all in a moment, her love overflowed into a spontaneous expression of tenderness and contrition: she pulled her hair loose and dried and kissed those sacred feet. And Jesus uttered no word of rebuke: He seemed to feel Himself in no way compromised by the touch of a sinner. Was the Master mad? Looking back, Simon remembered the parable of the two debtors and their creditor, and heard once more his own answer to the question: "And now tell me, which of them loves Him the more, the one to whom He remitted five hundred pieces of silver, or fifty?" "I suppose" he had replied, for it seemed the only logical answer, "that it is the one who had the greater debt discharged." Then Jesus spoke the words which form the foundation of His teaching as to the forgiveness of sins: "And so I tell thee, if great sins have been forgiven her, she has also greatly loved." Further, to make it clear to all the guests that it was He who forgave the sins, He turned to the woman again: "Thy sins are forgiven;" and added in answer to their secret thoughts and amazement, "Thy faith has saved thee; go in peace."[47]

As an answer to faith and trust, as a return for love and surrender, He forgives sins. If, however, He meets only with obstinacy and self-sufficiency, hard-heartedness without any trace of desire or goodwill, then He refuses that forgiveness and says, as He said to the Jews "You will have to die with your sins upon you; you will die with your sins upon you unless you come to believe that it is Myself you look for."[48] He knows exactly our inward disposition, and condemns only where there is no other possibility open to Him. Sometimes He does no more than admonish the repentant sinner, who goes away strengthened and refreshed.[49]

b. It was this power to forgive sins which He promised to Peter, and afterwards to all the apostles. We shall find these promises in the sixteenth chapter of St. Matthew, (5, 13-20) following on Peter's confession of faith. Peter, as we have

[47] Luke 7, 36-50. [48] John 8, 21-26. [49] John 8, 11.

already seen, bore witness that Christ was the Messiah, the Son of God and, in His turn, Jesus replied: "Thou art Peter, and it is upon this rock that I will build my Church; and the gates of hell shall not prevail against it." He then gave him an universal power, and handed over to him the keys of his Kingdom, just as any master of a house might hand them over to a trustworthy steward in his absence. "And," He added, "whatever thou shalt bind on earth shall be bound in heaven, and whatever thou shalt loose on earth shall be loosed in heaven." Peter's judgment, therefore, is to hold good in Heaven. Everything he decides in connection with God's Kingdom on earth, with the salvation of souls, will be ratified later in the Kingdom of Heaven. God will so fill him with the divine spirit that he will be able to judge justly, to condemn and to release; to decide and to confirm.

According to the eighteenth chapter of the Gospel of St. Matthew, this promise was given in an even more concrete form to all the Apostles together when the Good Shepherd Himself was speaking to the future leaders and pastors of His flock. After having particularly stressed that they must have a special care for the lost sheep, Jesus made clear the connection between brotherly correction and the discipline of the Church. If a man has sinned, he should not immediately be regarded as an outcast and the sin be made known; it is sufficient to warn him privately. If he then remains obdurate, it is for the Church to intervene and, if necessary, have recourse even to excommunication. The Church is a Community, and thus can no longer assume responsibility for such a member, but that does not mean that he is entirely excluded from the love of Christ, nor that he may no longer hope for God's mercy. There is still, and always, a way of return. The Apostles, who guide the Church, have yet another power, namely the power to bind and to loose. God will ratify their judgment. What they condemn, the Father in Heaven will condemn. In this universal power is included the power to forgive sins.

c. This power, promised to the Church, Jesus *gave*, as an Easter gift, after His Resurrection. We shall find the account of it in the twentieth chapter of St. John's Gospel. The great day of the Resurrection had almost ended; the disciples were still together, and much moved by the story of Peter, to whom the Lord had appeared. For fear of the Jews they had locked the doors. Evening fell, and then—suddenly—He came, and stood there in their midst. They heard His voice: "Peace be upon you." So it was that the disciples saw the Lord and were glad. At first, however, they were filled with terror, thinking that they were beholding an apparition. Then Jesus, to reassure them, made them look at His hands and His side, which still showed an open wound, and He asked them if they had anything there for Him to eat. In their presence he ate a piece of roast fish and a honeycomb, so that they were at peace. Then there followed that mandate which laid the whole world at their feet. "I came upon an errand from my Father, and now I am sending you out in My turn." And with that, He breathed upon them, and said: "Receive the Holy Spirit; when you forgive men's sins, they are forgiven, when you hold them bound, they are held bound." From that time forward they received authority over souls. But that authority does not primarily consist in commanding and dictating, rebuking, becoming angry, and generally maintaining their prestige; rather it consists in reflecting the divine mercy by the forgiveness of sins. Only if there appears to be absolutely no hope, and their genuine charity can find no trace of contrition in the soul, will they refuse forgiveness.

Those who dispense grace in the Name of Christ, acting as His instruments, must necessarily also *judge*; they have to judge every concrete case on its own merits, and their verdict is recorded in heaven.

This is the way in which the Church received from Christ Himself the power to continue His task of forgiving sin, although He did not precisely define the exterior conditions under which the Sacrament was to be administered.

B. *The Epistles of the Apostles*

In the Epistles we find only a few indications. James speaks of the confession of sins one to the other. "Confess your sins to one another, and pray for one another, for the healing of your souls,"[50] the meaning of which is not perhaps altogether clear.

John writes in his first Epistle: "Sin is with us; if we deny that, we are cheating ourselves; it means that truth does not dwell in us. No, it is when we confess our sins that He

[50] James 5, 16.

forgives us our sins, ever true to His word, ever dealing right with us, and all our wrong-doing is purged away."[51]

II. TEACHING OF THE CHURCH

That which we find in the Bible as to the power to forgive sins which—under the guidance of the Holy Spirit—subsequently slowly developed, has been gathered up by the Church into its teaching on the *Sacrament of Penance.* Through this Sacrament, the life of Christ, the life of grace, is restored to our souls. There is no question here of a re-birth, but of healing. Confession presupposes that the life, which was begun by Baptism, has not been entirely extinguished; it counts on a strong faith and a firm trust in God. If this is absent, there is not sufficient ground in the indelible marks of Baptism and Confirmation for the grace of conversion, although the fact that one is an intrinsic member of the Church can never be effaced. The aspect of healing, which is expressed and worked out by this Sacrament, corresponds directly with Christ's Revelation, but the power of healing, of forgiving sin, was, according to the Gospels, bestowed under very special conditions. It was bound up by Our Lord with a definite *commission and faculty.* He told His disciples: "When you forgive men's sins, they are forgiven, when you hold them bound, they are held bound." This power to forgive, or not to forgive, therefore, presupposes a just *judgment.* Christ distinguished between bind and loose, and it is therefore evident that a decision is required, a pronouncement. How can a decision be made if there be no judgment? And this judgment must depend upon an enquiry which, in its turn, depends upon sin being made known, in other words upon confession. In short Christ has instituted this Sacrament as a judgment, and a loving administration of justice. He is both physician and judge. He will always forgive sin if there be both contrition and goodwill.

Therefore, as a matter of course, the Church requires for our reconciliation with Christ, our Head, not only absolution from sin, but contrition, confession and satisfaction. On the part of the one who has sinned the sign or token consists of contrition, confession and satisfaction: on the part of the Church it consists of absolution: that is to say remission of

[51] I John 1, 8-9.

sins. Taken all together these form the sacramental sign or token, through which the healing, in the form of a judgment, is effected.

This power of healing began with Christ, by virtue of His Passion and Resurrection. The benefit of His death was and is applied to us. Christ forgives, now as then, and says: "Go in peace and sin no more." Through this divine forgiveness the vistas of the future again open out before us: Eternal Happiness once more becomes the promised goal of the restored life of grace.

1. *Contrition*

The highlight of Confession is contrition. In this Sacrament, as in the Sacrament of Baptism, the principal thing that God asks, after faith, is contrition. We read in the Gospel of the stern answer given by Our Lord to those who related to Him the story of the Galileans whose blood Pilate had shed in the midst of their sacrifices: "I tell you . . . you will all perish as they did, if you do not repent."[52] There is no conversion, no sanctification, no forgiveness possible without contrition. It lies at the very core of conversion of the heart: it is the necessary condition for it. Confession and satisfaction remain a command, but contrition is indispensable, by the very nature of the case and, in emergency, suffices *alone*.

What exactly is contrition? A conversion, a return to God; a detestation of sin. It begins with a certain turning of the will towards God. "Never again will I will as I have willed; if the past could return, under no circumstances would I again follow my former will. The reason for this is that I realize that my will itself was evil."

Contrition is by no means the same thing as remorse. In remorse one feels oneself to be guilty, frequently even detestable, and discouraged. One stands ashamed and impotent; one's act fills one with pain and sorrow, horror and despair; the future appears to be full of secret yet threatening danger. The essence of remorse is sorrow, now dull and blunted by the will, which seeks to distract itself; now sharp and searching; one realizes that by one's wrongdoing one has suffered the greatest defeat which one could undergo. One agonizes

[52] Luke 13, 1-6.

beneath the reality of one's wickedness; one perceives one's guilt. Remorse reveals to one the failure of one's personality, for one sees oneself in one's freely willed action which one now condemns and rejects.

This emotion can become an *opportunity* for contrition which is, before all, a free act of the will. Remorse in itself is unprofitable, and checks a person's natural development, but contrition is a spiritual resurrection which bears much fruit. It makes a man free and open to joy.

Contrition, therefore, does not consist in sensible sorrow. That God cannot demand; there are all kinds of factors, quite independent of the will, which either decrease or stimulate the intensity of our feelings.

Contrition consists in the firm intention to return to God; a fixed purpose and a genuine decision, here and now, not to commit that sin again; an honest desire for amendment of life, in spite of the fear, even the foreboding, that later on one may fall again. This is accompanied by trust in the power of the Almighty, for it is a state of will which has its origin in grace, and is the answer to an invitation from God. No one can, of himself, rise from a state of mortal sin. It is God who makes the first move. He it is who listens for the first hesitating movements of the heart in the right direction: for a dawning fear which begins to show itself; a remorse which smarts; a certain resentment at the state in which the soul finds itself. He strengthens motives which arise in the subconscious self and reminds us of the mercy which never fails. He leads us towards that interior peace which gives strength to act; His grace works through our own consciousness of guilt. Sincere contrition, which goes deeper than any spoken formula, is always associated with sorrow for sin as an *offence against God.* He who only regrets his sin because it meant the loss of personal dignity, or affected his prestige, or merely because it transgressed the rules of a generally accepted code of behaviour, misses the very first elements of contrition, and knows nothing whatever of conversion.

For a contrite soul to offend God is, in the strict sense of the word, the very worst thing which can befall him. He can imagine no greater ill. It is most probable that the death of his wife, of his child, or his mother, will move him more deeply; that business worries will give him more sleepless nights than sin but, one must remember, this is not a matter of feeling but of supernatural perception, and of a *will* which moved by grace, turns away from the offence. When contrition is present, the question arises, in what particular form is contrition required?

Usually one discriminates between *perfect* and *imperfect* contrition according to the motive for which the sin is detested. The thought of the justice of God and His eternal punishments was advanced as one motive by Christ Himself when He said: "And I say this to you who are my friends, do not be afraid of those who can kill the body, and after that can do no more. I will tell you who it is you must fear; fear Him who has power not only to kill but to cast a man into hell; Him you must fear indeed."[53]

To deplore one's sins for this reason is very salutary, provided that it is not merely done through a sense of fear, while secretly uttering anathemas against the universal presence of God accompanied by a private wish that one could commit the sin without His knowledge. A righteous fear has its roots in the belief that God has been offended and that His punishment is just: a fear attended by the hope of forgiveness. Such contrition arises from a certain rather selfish love; nevertheless it contains enough hatred of sin to merit absolution. Fear of God as our Judge, shame before Him who we recognize as having always been good to us, is already a beginning of love. Although this contrition is, in itself, defective, yet it is sufficient to enable one to go to Confession.

Perfect contrition, on the other hand, proceeds from disinterested and selfless love. The first thought is God, and a desire for reconciliation with Him against whom the offence has been committed. The abyss of one's own unworthiness indeed divides one from Him, nevertheless this form of contrition looks beyond it to union with the One loved above all. It is not the thought of punishment which inspires the soul to the rejection of sin; neither is it fear which effects sorrow and regret. Only the desire to do God's will persists, irrespective of either reward or punishment. It seems to us very probable that a purely disposed heart, in which there is a continually growing determination to loosen the bonds of all which displeases God, plays a very large part in this contrition. For from the heart proceeds appreciation of God and the Divine, the recognition and consciousness of His unceasing love. The

[53] Luke 12, 4-6.

touchstone, however, of perfect contrition is always the strength of the purpose of amendment.

Perfect contrition, and the love which inspires it, ensure justification of the sin from the very first moment, and before confession. Even mortal sin is not proof against such love. Through love even great lapses are immediately and directly wiped out. It brings instant forgiveness, also, to those who have never heard of the Sacrament. St. John writes: "God is love; he who dwells in love dwells in God, and God in Him."[54] "If a man is without love, he holds fast by death."[55] For those who are members of the Catholic Church, this contrition includes, as a matter of course, *the intention of going to Confession,* since it is a complete surrender to God's will.

2. *Confession*

We read in the first Epistle of St. John: "Sin is with us; if we deny that, we are cheating ourselves, it means that truth does not dwell in us. No, it is when we confess our sins that He forgives us our sins, ever true to His word, ever dealing right with us, and all our wrong-doing is purged away." The power which Christ gave to His Church to forgive sins, necessitates both a judgment and a decision. In order to judge, a certain knowledge is necessary; and this knowledge is acquired through Confession. A man must be open with Christ and with the Church which is represented by the priest. Before the priest can become conscious of the sinner's contrition and be able to impose a penance, confession is obviously necessary. Such self-accusation is indeed a deep humiliation but, on the other hand, in no way a degradation. In this form it represents very clearly the constituent elements of sincere contrition. It presupposes a deep faith: to see Christ in a mere man who is simply a representative of the Church: to keep the human aspect in the background, and the sometimes unattractive personality before one, and, instead, to fix one's eyes only on Him who, through a man, forgives and judges: demands a profound understanding of God's will and a humility which must necessarily call down grace. On the other hand this disclosure of the self undoubtedly fulfils a deep-rooted need of the human heart. This however is not the main intention in Confession. To appreciate only the

[54] I John 4, 16.   [55] I John 3, 14.

psychological effect of this Sacrament is totally to misunderstand it; it means that the ideal of peace of conscience has not yet been placed at its proper supernatural level. Confession is not wonderful because it reconciles one with oneself but because it reconciles one with God.

The Church requires that all mortal sins committed after Baptism should be confessed in secret to a priest to the best of one's ability.

No question arises, of course, of public confession. The duty to confess mortal sin also exacts that the number and the kind of sins should be disclosed, as well as any circumstances which may affect the nature or type of sin. If the number cannot be remembered accurately at all events an approximate figure should be mentioned, while adding the words "about" or "more or less".

The type of sin need only be mentioned in so far as the penitent was aware of the sinfulness of the deed which he was committing. For instance, anyone who has committed a theft is bound to acknowledge it, if he knows that he has stolen; but if he only knows that he has committed a big sin, without knowing what kind of sin it was, it is then sufficient for him to say, "I have committed a great wrong." Circumstances can change the species of a sin. Anyone, for example, who steals a chalice, commits both a theft and a sacrilege. If a mortal sin is consciously suppressed, this suppression constitutes a new sin, and therefore the other sins cannot be remitted either. Should however anyone merely forget to confess a mortal sin, all other mortal sins are notwithstanding, forgiven, but he must confess the omitted sin at his next confession. Venial sins need not be mentioned: God forgives them through our own contrition, prayer, alms-giving and fasting. Nevertheless the Church advocates that they should be mentioned because the Sacrament acts as a preventative of sin, and calls down from God special strength to fight against the sins confessed. It is particularly profitable to confess those venial sins which occur frequently in our case, and which are due to a lack of self-control in some direction by which our life quite possibly misses the rest and harmony which it should enjoy.

3. *Satisfaction*

Through the contrite confession of sin, the guilt and the

eternal punishment are remitted. In His justice, however, God requires a complete equivalent reparation. From Scripture we learn how, although He does not retain the remembrance of our guilt after we are forgiven, He nevertheless punishes justly. We have only to think of the punishments meted out to Eve; to Moses who never entered the Promised Land: and to David who saw his child, the fruit of sin, die before his eyes. God the Father exacted from Christ also an equivalent satisfaction, and that was why He had to endure such bitter suffering for the one moment of pleasure which Adam had sought. John the Baptist speaks of the "acceptable fruit of repentence",[56] and St. Paul ascribes a lack of strength and health, and even death itself, to the unworthy reception of the Body and Blood of Christ.[57] All this points to the fact that punishment can still remain after the forgiveness of sin. These punishments must be wiped out before a complete recovery can set in and every vestige of the previous condition be eradicated. It is for this reason that the Church imposes a penance, or satisfaction, as expiation for those punishments.

Thus the penances which are imposed have a twofold purpose. First of all they restore the last traces of the ruin of sin, and in this way seek to balance punishment and penance. The question, however, always remains whether contrition has adequately counterbalanced the pleasure of sin, should attachment to it still remain in even the slightest degree. Adequate expiation therefore requires for both spirit and senses, which have given themselves up to earthly pleasure or advantage to an inordinate degree, a punishment which will repair that disorder and detach them from it. That is why the Confessor will, having regard to the spiritual state of the penitent, try to impose penances designed to draw him away from his weaknesses, and at the same time in this manner enable him to make good what was perhaps wanting in his contrition.

The means of making penance are extremely diversified. The Bible especially mentions prayer, fasting and almsgiving. Prayer induces the soul to return to God: mortification raises a man above the instinctive inclinations of the flesh, while almsgiving detaches him from possessions and wealth. These three forms of penance serve to renew him in Christ, and thus

[56] Luke 3, 8. [57] I Cor. 11, 30.

it is that in the second place, atonement acts as a preventative against future sin.

By virtue of the Absolution, the penances imposed acquire the power to work sacramentally, and thus, he who satisfactorily fulfils them, receives the remission of temporary punishments. In this way the penitent shares in the fruits of Christ's passion and death in the precise measure in which the performance of his penitential act has been painful to him. He must therefore always be prepared and willing to accept the imposed penance.

4. *Absolution*

When the Church has listened to the confession and imposed the penance, she next remits the sin by virtue of Absolution. The priest first of all calls down the mercy of God upon the sinner: "May the Almighty God have mercy on you, and forgiving your sins, bring you to life everlasting. Amen." Then, lifting his right hand towards the penitent as a sign of his power to forgive sins, the priest continues: "May the Almighty and merciful God grant you pardon, absolution, and remission of your sins. May Our Lord Jesus Christ absolve you, and I, by His authority, absolve you, from every bond of excommunication and interdict as far as I can and you may need." Then follows the actual absolution: "I absolve you from your sins in the name of the Father, and of the Son, and of the Holy Ghost, Amen." During this the priest makes the sign of the cross over the penitent, and then continues in a low tone of voice: "May the Passion of Our Lord Jesus Christ, the merits of the Blessed Virgin Mary and of all the Saints, what good you have done or what evil you have suffered, be to you for the remission of your sins, growth in grace and the reward of everlasting life. Amen."

The priest, authorized by the Bishop—since otherwise his ministration would be invalid and he could not absolve from sin—acts as a judge. He may if he thinks fit suspend his judgment and point out that in this particular case he cannot give absolution. But, once he is convinced of contrition—and he must accept the word of the penitent—he may not refuse to absolve him from his sins. Where there is danger of death he can forgive all sins and remit all punishments of the Church.

Every priest who hears Confessions is bound to keep secret all that he learns in the Confessional. He may not even speak or act in such a manner that others may guess anything in the smallest degree. There is *no exception* whatsoever to this secret of the Confessional. Neither to save his own life, nor to maintain or promote the well-being of the community or the State, may a priest violate such secrecy.

III. THE PRACTICE OF CONFESSION

FREQUENT CONFESSION

To go to Confession once a year, or when in danger of death, is prescribed by the Church for those who have committed mortal sin. Nevertheless her spirit and her recommendation is that the Faithful should go to Confession regularly. All kinds of dangers threaten us from within. The penitent who goes to Confession once a month, or once in two or three weeks, or even weekly, compels himself to review his immediate past. He has a better realization of the danger of falling into a mere mechanical routine, and he perceives more clearly where he fails on points which are important for the growth and progress of his interior life with God; he is more surrounded by the atmosphere of his Faith and his spiritual judgment remains clearer. He can be constantly on the alert for means to amend his life.

One sometimes hears the complaint: "I really do not know what to say in Confession each time." One of the causes for this attitude is that Confession is put off for too long: the facility for examination of conscience is thus lost; one has managed to slip out of the religious atmosphere, and one's lack of necessary self-knowledge makes one incapable of recalling and judging one's own past.

It is unpleasant to have to keep on confessing the same sin, but after all this shows up very clearly the necessity for confession. There are many failings, especially against charity, which we overlook too easily, although we point them out in others with extreme accuracy.

A regular Confessor is a very safe guide in such a case. We are, however, free to go to Confession to any priest, and in the church which we choose, and we may change our Confessor at will. Every priest appointed by the Church may be an instrument of Christ through whom God pours grace into a soul. A wise adviser, however, whom one has chosen oneself and who knows one, and who is interested in one's spiritual life and personal difficulties, may be a great support and help, and a guard against self-deception; he will show one how to form one's conscience on the right lines.

The great danger to be avoided is that of getting into a rut: of going to Confession as a mere habit. Sincere contrition, and a genuine desire for closer contact with Christ, accompanied by a firm intention of loving one's neighbour in reality, are the only things which give meaning to Confession and make it fruitful. The penitent who goes into the Confessional at Easter, because he cannot very well do anything else, or because it is the conventional thing to do, had far better stay at home. If, however, this Sacrament is accepted in the spirit in which Christ meant it to be, it gives peace and tranquillity of conscience, and while restoring the harmony of the soul is a source of eternal life. But for these effects to be enjoyed to the full, care and attention must be given to the whole matter.

§ 5. *Indulgences*

The expression indulgences has an unpleasant sound in the ears of non-Catholics. It gives them an idea of the barter of supernatural and temporal favours for money, of the forgiveness of sins without contrition but merely by means of the automatic repetition of certain prayers and actions. Such prejudices have their origin in the first beginnings of Protestantism. It was on the 31st October, 1517, that Luther affixed his famous ninety-five Latin theses on the subject of indulgences to the door of the castle church at Wittenberg, and soon his views spread throughout Germany. His protest was a reaction against the fiery preaching of the Dominican, Tetzel, whose sermons were certainly not altogether free from exaggeration. In general his teaching as to indulgences can be termed correct, but he undoubtedly laid too much stress upon what appeared to be a profitable transaction. A saying current in Germany at the time to the effect that as gold chinked in the coffers, souls leapt out of hell fire, was due to his preaching. Luther, however, attacked not only the abuses but the essence of the doctrine, and in his argument there was no place for either meritorious good works or indulgences for, to quote thesis 95: "The true Christian does not build upon the certainty which the trade in indulgences promises. He sees in afflictions the sure way to the Kingdom."

We will now endeavour to set out the teaching of the Church on the subject and try to trace the true meaning and significance of it.

1. An indulgence is a remission of the temporal punishment due to sin which has already been forgiven. Sin and punishment go together. The justice of God demands redress for the order which has been violated by the arbitrary action of man. God's love forgives sin when it meets with humble confession and contrition: thus eternal punishment is immediately remitted when mortal sin is dissolved by a sincere, honest and contrite acknowledgment of guilt. The child of God, born anew, now once more seeks his destiny in eternal happiness, and cannot therefore at the same time be weighed down by the threat of eternal damnation. Nevertheless, he is not freed by confession from all punishment. Venial sins and many other shortcomings remain to be purged away in order to satisfy God's justice, because of the transgression of that Order eternally fixed by Him. By means of contrition, confession, prayer and good works, He forgives many sins and forgoes their punishment; nevertheless any remaining temporal punishment still requires expiation. We find many examples in the Old Testament of those whom God forgave yet punished none the less.[58]

An indulgence serves to wipe out these temporal penalties; sin itself is never forgiven by it, but, by virtue of the Sacrifice of Christ and the co-operation and expiation of the penitent, a complete renewal and recovery are assured.

2. These indulgences are granted by the Church. In the name of God it is She who endows them with the power which they possess. Generally speaking, she takes some prayer or some good work, and enriches them with the faculty of remitting temporal punishment. Indulgences are therefore an Ecclesiastical Institution, which dates back many centuries and was originally founded upon the power which Christ gave to His Church. It was from Him that She received the ability to bind and to loose[59] and to remove all obstacles which might prevent Christians from entering Heaven. These obstacles include not only sin itself but the punishments due to sin. By virtue of this prescriptive right, therefore, given her by

[58] Num. 20; Deut. 34; II Kings 12. [59] Matt 16, 19.

Christ, the Church regards herself as competent to remit all temporal penalties by a "plenary indulgence" and a part of such penalties by a "partial indulgence".

3. Conscious of this power the Church draws upon her spiritual treasurers—that is to say upon the infinite satisfaction made by Christ, and the reparation offered by the saints—and lays these at the feet of God as a counter-balance for the punishment due to men.

The Church is Christ's Body, and it therefore follows that this Body continues to receive its health and its growth in perfection from the Head. Christ's Sacrifice upon the Cross, by which He expressed His perfect surrender to the Father, offered infinite and unending honour and atonement to God, and the Christian Community continues to exist through this very homage rendered to the Creator. Therefore she still has the power to call upon the merits of Christ's vicarious sacrifice, for she remains united to Him as are the branches to the vine.

The lives of the saints were immensely fruitful. By their constant attention to the interior voice of God, and by their obedience to His Will and to His Church, they became dear to Him: they knew that the best way to serve Him lay in their service to others, and thus they offered their lives as a supplication and a reparation for all those still laden with the burden of the punishment due to their sins. Through their good works they grew continuously in the love of God, but their expiation greatly exceeded that which was required for their own shortcomings. Recognizing their desire to share their spiritual wealth with others, the Church uses this overflow of the merits of her saints—joined to the infinite merits of Christ Himself—as an offering to God by which the balance of reparation due to His justice may be paid by their sacrificial love.

All this is based upon the conception of one community in Christ: upon this conception that each member can help the other, and that one may make good for the deficiencies of his brother. As St. Paul writes, if one member suffers, all suffer. The granting of Indulgences is thus an illustration of the strength and force of the Communion of Saints.

The principle upon which this teaching is based is to be found in Revelation itself: it exhorts us to remember the necessity for the complete expiation of sin: it speaks of

Christ's Mystical Body and the intercommunion between the living and the dead: it confers upon the Church authority over anything which could form any kind of obstacle to our salvation.

4. The teaching upon Indulgences reaches to the utmost limits of the Christian life of grace, and presupposes an intense interior life with God in the soul. The Indulgence only has value in so far as it is a matter of prayer, and the Church attaches to it various conditions. To experience its beneficial action a man must be a living member of Christ's Body; he must be in a state of grace and have the intention of receiving the remission of penalties due to sin. Confession, Communion, a visit to a church, and prayers for the intentions of the Pope are usually prescribed for the gaining of a plenary Indulgence. This complete remission of penalties and punishments due is only accomplished when true contrition has already obtained the forgiveness of all venial sin.

A partial Indulgence remits certain specific penalties when the prescribed task—not merely automatically but with both piety and attention—has been fulfilled. Such Indulgences usually have attached to them the recitation of prayers, although sometimes also the execution of some good work. In the case of these partial Indulgences we shall find certain numbers mentioned, such as "a hundred days' Indulgence". These numbers are used to give a general idea of the degree of remission granted, and are connected with the former practices of penance in the Church. For instance, an Indulgence of one hundred days means that one would obtain as much remission as was formerly associated with a hundred days of penance as then practised.

Indulgences are not an externalization of the Christian life but, on the contrary, a deepening of it. They pre-suppose forgiveness of sin, and it is common knowledge that detachment from sin calls for both discipline and sacrifice. They presuppose the firm will to conquer bad habits, and to regulate one's natural inclinations, and anyone who is not prepared to do at least that much obviously lacks the necessary contrition. They help to fulfil the great law of Christ, the law of continual charity, because Indulgences can be applied to the Holy Souls. In this last case the Church offers to God the prayers or good works performed for the relief of those who are still undergoing purification in purgatory. Finally they stimulate us to expiation and pity, and increase our consciousness that we never stand alone, but that in Christ, the lot of each member of the Church is bound up with the common good.

§ 6. *Holy Eucharist*

SYNOPSIS

I. The mystery of the Blessed Trinity is the mystery of the intimate and interior life of God: divine knowledge and divine love. This love did not remain enclosed in the infinity of His divine Being, but urged Him to create angels, men, and a world in which mankind could live.
Man was created in a state of friendship with God, but it was his lot to obey. Adam, however, sinned against this obedience and so lost God's friendship and, as a consequence, all his descendants were also born outside the friendship of God.

II. God, in His infinite mercy, has redeemed mankind through His Son, Jesus Christ.

III. Through sanctifying grace, God gives man both constant help in order to follow good and avoid evil, and the possibility of a new interior life. By means of this interior union with God, his good works are rendered meritorious for heaven.

IV. By means of this life of grace a new bond is formed between Christ and the Faithful (the Mystical Body); and between the members of the Church individually (Communion of Saints). It thus becomes possible for us to invoke the saints and for the saints to pray for us. In this connection it is obvious that the Mother of the Redeemer will occupy an unique position.

V. This grace, which has been merited for us by Christ, may reach us through various channels but is above all conveyed by means of the Sacraments.

VI. We shall now endeavour to show the supreme importance of the Holy Sacrament of the Altar, the Eucharist, because by means of it, the culminating point of our Redemption, that is the Sacrifice of the Cross, is mystically perpetuated day by day.

Baptism demonstrates the spiritual resurrection of the new man rising from the death of sin. Confirmation completes the Sacrament of Baptism by conferring faith and strengthening interior conviction. *Spiritual nourishment* is the purpose of Holy Communion. It changes us through Christ. The Sacrament is a memorial of Christ's Passion, a representation of His Sacrifice. It gives us a foretaste of heaven of which it is a pledge and a preparation. These mystical fruits we owe to Christ Himself: Christ who is present under the symbols of bread and wine. In this Sacrament we meet the mystery of God's love which can daily become a complete reality to us if we so desire. Thought alone cannot encompass it; feeling falls far short of its comprehension; only faith is able to grasp and accept this divine surrender of love by God to man. Surely the attitude of Mary, the Mother of Christ, is appropriate with regard to this marvel: her attitude as she bent over her folded hands with the words: "Behold the handmaid of the Lord, be it done unto me according to Thy word."

This Sacrament is the greatest of all Sacraments, because it alone has the Giver as gift. It will now be well to consult the Gospels themselves, and learn there of the wonders contained in those symbols of bread and wine—bequeathed to us as a memorial, a banquet, and a sacrifice.

I. THE GOSPELS AND THE EARLY CHURCH

A. *The Promises of Christ*

The sixth chapter of the Gospel of St. John begins with the story of the miracle of the loaves and the fishes. Jesus desired to withdraw into solitude, but the people insisted on following Him; they did not forget how He had cured their sick. When evening fell they were still listening, enraptured, to His words, when they should have been home again long since in their hamlets and villages getting ready for the evening meal. Now that they had at last come to look for the Kingdom of God, would Jesus be mindful of their need for daily bread also? He called to His disciples; between them they found a boy from whom they collected five barley loaves and two small fishes, and at the Lord's command, they divided the crowd of five thousand people into groups. Jesus then took the loaves and, giving thanks, broke and distributed them, and the same with the fishes. It turned into just a quiet picnic meal spread on the grass in the slowly fading light of day. The Host Himself presided and served the food, and all the guests were filled. This miracle, incomprehensible though it might be, was yet clear to everyone. The crowd saw before them Divine Power itself: they watched with fascinated astonishment the play of Our Lord's hands as He distributed the few small loaves to thousands. This, they decided among themselves, was beyond doubt the prophet whom the world awaited. Thus it was that Jesus prepared them for the big proof of their faith which He was about to ask of them: the miracle was but a preface to that reality of which He was soon to tell them, the Bread of Life and the Living Bread that had come down from heaven. This miracle was, psychologically, a culminating point in the teaching of Christ; it was a symbol of that Sacrament which we call the Eucharist. The following morning the multitude looked in vain for Jesus, and finally crossed to the western shore of the lake, where they at last found Him, not knowing how He had come there. Our Lord immediately plunged into one of His most remarkable discourses. Anyone reading the account attentively and with an unprejudiced mind, cannot fail to receive the impression that it is divided into two distinct parts which nevertheless lead one into the other. In the first, Christ is mainly talking of His own heavenly origin, and demands belief in Himself under the symbol of Bread to be eaten. Then, suddenly, in the second part, He breaks into: "He who eats my flesh and drinks my blood, lives continually in me and I in him."

"You should not work to earn food which perishes in the using. Work to earn food which affords eternal life unceasingly; such food as the Son of Man will give you." With these words Jesus linked up His discourse with the miracle of the day before, and declared His divine mission of bringing the Bread of Life to earth. What exactly did He mean by this Bread of Life? He Himself answers us: "Believe me, when I tell you this; the bread that comes from heaven is not what Moses gave you. The real bread from heaven is given only by my Father. God's gift of bread comes down from heaven and gives life to the whole world. Then, Lord, they said, give us this bread all the while. But Jesus told them: It is I who am the bread of life; he who comes to me will never be hungry, he who has faith in me will never know thirst." So we see that the bread of life is Christ Himself, our life-giving food. How can He be our food? Through His teaching. But His teaching begins and ends in belief in Himself, and he who believes in Jesus will be completely satisfied. "The Jews were by now complaining of his saying, I am Myself the bread which has come down from heaven. Is this not Jesus, they said, the son of Joseph, whose father and mother are well known to us? What does he mean by saying, I have come down from heaven? Jesus answered them, do not whisper thus to one another. Nobody can come to me without being attracted towards me by the Father who sent me, so that I can raise him up at the last day."

Faith in Jesus is therefore a gift of God: a present, as it were, from the Father. The powerful light of the Father enables us to believe, and in that belief we meet the man, Christ. This is to eat the Bread of Life. "Believe me, when I tell you this: the man who has faith in me enjoys eternal life. It is I who am the bread of life. Your fathers, who ate manna in the desert, died none the less; the bread which comes down from heaven is such that he who eats of it never dies."

The first part of this discourse lays great emphasis upon the necessity for faith in Christ, and so prepares us for the second part. What Jesus said in that, rises far beyond mere human conceptions, and requires a surrender which only faith can produce.

Almost automatically the question will arise: *How* does Jesus give eternal, everlasting life to men? How can bread give this life? And it is Christ Himself who answers: "I myself am the living bread that has come down from heaven. If anyone eats of this bread, he shall live for ever. And now, what is this bread which I am to give? It is my flesh, given for the life of the world." The Bread is His flesh of which we must eat, and with the eating is bound up eternal life for all mankind.

Let us see the reaction of the Jews. When Jesus called Himself the bread which was to come down from heaven, and asked them to believe Him, they shrugged their shoulders and made remarks about his parents whom they knew quite well. Almost dumbfounded, they looked from one to the other and fell to disputing: "How can this man give us his flesh to eat?" Although they took His words literally He does not seem to have found this a reason for offering them a further explanation. They took the words just as He said them, and found them ridiculous, fantastic: how could they eat His flesh? Jesus, however, calmly maintained His realism, if anything further emphasizing it: "Believe me when I tell you this: you can have no life in yourselves unless you eat the flesh of the Son of Man, and drink His blood. The man who eats my flesh and drinks my blood enjoys eternal life, and I will raise him up at the last day. My flesh is real food, my blood is real drink. He who eats my flesh and drinks my blood, lives continually in me, and I in him."

This eating, this partaking of His flesh and blood, was to be the necessary condition of living by Him, of remaining united to Him, of being raised up at the last day, and of having everlasting life. The Jews and Pharisees remained silent. If His flesh were really food and His blood really drink, then there was certainly nothing further for them to stay for. That ended every possibility of better relations; the limit of their religious credulity had been reached. The break with Christ was now complete.

But even some of His disciples shook their heads; "This is strange talk, who can be expected to listen to it?" They began to turn away, and just for a moment Jesus tried to hold them back: "Does this try your faith? What will you make of it, if you see the Son of Man ascending to the place where He was before? Only the spirit gives life; the flesh is of no avail; and the words I have been speaking to you are spirit, and life. But there are some, even among you, who do not believe." It was an appeal to their trust in Him. He asked them frankly to accept the sense of His words as they stood. Let them only be patient; when they saw Him ascend to the place where He was before, it would all become clear enough to them. Only the divine spirit gives life: the flesh—that which is changeable, mortal, human—is of no avail in the end. His words went far beyond the scope of human understanding but if accepted and believed they would bring with them the gift of eternal life. His flesh, which came down from heaven in order to impart life, had a share in His spiritual and divine nature. It was not flesh and blood alone which He gave, but divine flesh and blood. The contact between Himself and the Faithful is therefore not only a bodily contact but a bodily contact under the action of the Holy Spirit. His true Being is divine, although it is hidden beneath mortal flesh, and the life-giving power of which He spoke did not come from His mortal flesh but from the divine life which it veiled but which nevertheless spread out through it to men. In that sense it is, as He said, the Spirit which gives life and the flesh neither adds nor takes away.

Because Jesus insisted on the literal meaning of the expression flesh and blood "Many of His disciples went back to their old ways, and walked no more in His company."

It is evident from the reaction of the Jews, and some of the disciples, that they took Jesus' words literally—one might almost say materially. And now we come to an important question: had the Jews been scandalized because of a misunderstanding, and had the turning away of the disciples been simply the consequence of a misconception as to Christ's meaning, would not He have immediately pointed out that they had wrongly interpreted His thought? The smallest hint of some spiritual interpretation would have been sufficient to reassure them. He need only have said some such words: "To eat my flesh merely means to believe in Me." But he did not do so. On the contrary He reiterated His former assertion. Beyond that, since He had not come to earth in order to confuse the minds of the people, He entered into no explanations as to how He was to give His flesh to eat and His blood to drink: that He left as a part of the mystery of God's love.

Next He turned to the Twelve: "Would you, too, go away?" Even to them He did not retract His words; instead He claimed their faith and trust. It was then that Peter, speaking for them all, gave that wonderful answer which has come down to us through the ages: "Lord, to whom should we go? Thy words are the words of eternal life; we have learned to believe, and are assured that Thou art the Christ, the Son of God." He did not fully understand, but blindly accepted the statement of the Master. He was to eat and drink the flesh and blood of Christ, for upon that depended his whole spiritual life and happiness. How this was to be accomplished, he did not know: there remained the divine promise.

B. *The Institution of the Holy Eucharist*[60]

When evening fell, Jesus gathered together the Twelve in order that they might eat the Pasch together. And while they were still at table, He took bread, and blessed, and broke it, and gave it to His disciples, saying, Take, eat, this is My Body. Then He took a cup, and offered thanks, and gave it to them,

[60] Luke 22, 19-20. Mark 14, 22-27. Matt. 26, 26-28.

saying, Drink, all of you, of this; for this is My Blood, of the New Testament, shed for many, for the remission of sins.

Although the actual words in which the three Evangelists describe this Paschal ceremony are somewhat different, they are all agreed as to essentials. The accounts are short and temperate, but the disciples understood Our Lord's purpose, for He had already spoken of it. They remembered His expression that they were to eat His Flesh and drink His Blood. In the light of that explanation, recorded in the sixth chapter of St. John's Gospel, it is clear that the bread became Christ's Body and the wine changed into His Blood. And with this Blood the Saviour formally introduced the New Testament. These words were neither parable nor metaphor.

C. *The Practice of the Early Church*

In the Gospel of St. Luke we read: "This is My Body given for you; do this for a commemoration of Me." St. Paul testified that the practice of the Church carried out this command. In his first Epistle to the Corinthians (2, 17-34) he pointed out to them how much they lacked the true spirit of the Lord's Supper. In their case this Supper only gave rise to disunity, heresy and intemperance. They forgot that they kept it as a commemoration of the Passion and death of Christ, in a spirit of recollection and love for each other. According to the express command of Christ—twice repeated—it was their duty to do this and to repeat the ceremony instituted by Christ. St. Paul had already made all this quite clear to them by his personal preaching, but now once more he wanted to point out the dignity and loftiness of this holy Institution. "The tradition which I received from the Lord, and handed on to you," he wrote: "Is that the Lord Jesus on the night when He was betrayed, took bread and gave thanks, and broke it, and said, Take, eat; this is My Body, given up for you. Do this for a commemoration of Me. And so with the cup, when supper was ended. This cup, He said, is the New Testament, in My Blood. Do this, whenever you drink it, for a commemoration of Me."

So this command the Master gave explicitly. As often as the Corinthians ate this Bread and drank this Chalice, they heralded the Lord's death. No further words were necessary, since this Eucharistic Supper was itself a commemoration and a prefiguration of the death of Christ upon the Cross. And further, this commemoration was to continue for all time, until His coming. Anyone who through lack of charity, or other fault, profaned the Supper of the Lord, would be held to account for the Body and Blood of Christ, for it is Christ Himself who is present at this Sacramental Feast. A man must examine himself first, and he who does not recognize the Lord's Body for what it is, nor differentiates between it and ordinary food, eats and drinks damnation to himself.

It was the celebration of this most intimate Mystery of Faith which singled out the early Christians from all other men. They still prayed in the Temple, but the Bread they broke behind their own doors in every house.[61] In the early Church they spoke of the breaking of Bread and of the food which was called "the saving means of immortality". What remained of the Holy Sacrifice was kept either to be partaken of later, or to be given to the sick, or to be used as viaticum for the dying. The particles remaining could also be transferred to specially prepared repositories, near the Book of the Gospels in the sacristy. The earliest description of the celebration of the Eucharist is to be found in the *Didache* (probably the end of the first century) and in the first Apologia of Justin somewhere about the middle of the second century: a prayer, called *Eucharistia,* was said by the minister over the Bread and the Wine, after which the deacons communicated the Faithful. "No one," says Justin, "may partake of this but those who believe what we teach, and who are baptized with the Baptism unto the forgiveness of sins and rebirth, and who live as Christ has taught. For we do not receive this as ordinary bread and ordinary drink, but it is the Body and Blood of Jesus Incarnate as we have been taught."

We see from this that both the practice and the teaching of the early Church clearly indicate a belief in the real presence of Christ. As far as possible these early Christians kept the exact wording recorded in Scripture, and they understood that wording in its most obvious and direct sense.

D. *Protestant Christendom*

The strongest objection of Protestantism to the Catholic interpretation of the Last Supper is that it seems to be at variance with

[61] Acts 2, 42-46.

the general sense of Holy Scripture. Scripture is a preaching of faith and grace: grace which is given spiritually, on faith, and not as something, in a natural way, outside the soul and the personality. The sixth chapter of the Gospel of St. John must be read as a preaching of the Faith, no more, and that is the spirit in which the words of Institution, and the first chapter of the second Epistle to the Corinthians, must be interpreted.

What on the contrary did the Protestants do? They wanted to get back to the simplicity of the original Supper. This Lord's Supper ensures that we men remain in Christ and He in us. On the Communion Table are placed bread and wine because those were the tokens used by Christ. They bear witness to, and give us, His Body and Blood. We eat the Body and drink the Blood, however, not carnally but by faith, through the power of the Holy Ghost, never without, although always through the service of bread and wine. Nevertheless the bread only remains bread and the wine wine, and it is by faith alone that we partake of the Body and Blood of the Lord. In this Supper there is contained a promise for the future: the immortality of the flesh.

Present-day Protestantism may try to avoid both extremes—of Rome and of Zwingli—in their interpretation of the Last Supper. The teaching of Rome seems to them too materialistic, while the conception of Zwingli empties the rite of all meaning, it becomes merely symbolical. The Protestant Catechism mentions eating the crucified Body of Christ and drinking his Blood that was shed, with the intention of conveying that in the Last Supper the real Christ is indeed present in quite a different manner and degree than, for example, by the memory of mere words: more concrete, more intense, more real. Christ Himself does come to us, the whole of Christ, although bread remains bread, and wine remains wine. But the Last Supper is not *our* deed: it does not take place because we all assemble together and decide to think of Christ; it is the act or deed of Christ who comes to us—entirely and substantially—under the symbols of bread and wine. The human mind is unable to grasp in what manner Christ is present. The best way therefore is to pause at the mystery itself and to confess with the catechism—however paradoxical it may sound—that bread remains bread, and wine remains wine, and that yet Christ Himself is present, and we become (as one Protestant Catechism puts it) more and more united with His Body, flesh of His flesh, bone of His bone. We eat the real Body of Christ through *faith*: everyone present eats the bread and drinks the wine, but he who believes, eats Christ Himself.

I have here quoted one form of modern Protestant theology (the Heidelberg catechism), because, apart from the denial of an actual change of the *substance* of the bread and wine, the stress is very much upon the presence of Christ in the Catholic sense. It is a secret way of communion with Him. In practice some simple and straightforward Protestants already have the Catholic conception of the Sacrament without knowing it. This often becomes evident when they are converted to Catholicism.

The Catholic interpretation of the Gospels however adheres undeviatingly to the fact that Christ becomes present not only by faith, but in His totality and integrity, quite independently of anyone's personal belief or disbelief. When Christ is present there is no bread and wine, only the outward appearances of them. The proof of the truth of this interpretation, which is of course at the same time a rejection of the Protestant point of view, lies for us in the crucial root-meaning of the words of St. John, which throw light on the Last Supper itself, especially when taken in conjunction with the practice of the Early Church. St. Paul and all the other early Christians who committed themselves to paper, manifestly accepted the literal sense and interpretation of the words. If we look at it in the light of tradition, already beginning to be outlined in the Acts of the Apostles, then we must believe in the real presence of Christ, and explain His words to mean a genuine eating of His flesh and drinking of His Blood, upon which true life depends. With us, also, the actual manner in which this is accomplished remains a mystery.

II. THE TEACHING OF THE CHURCH

In this Sacrament the Church speaks of Transubstantiation. The Bread, that is, is changed into the Body of Christ, and the wine into His Blood. This transubstantiation, then, is not so much the sacrament, as the divinely revealed explanation of the truth of the Sacrament; transubstantiation is not the Eucharistic Sacrifice, but it is the hidden power that makes the sacrifice a reality, not a mere symbol.

The Church expresses the mystery itself in something of the following words: The Body and Blood of Christ have been given to us both as Sacrifice and Sacrament. In the Holy Eucharist, Christ Himself is present as Sacrifice, and at the same time as the Sacrificer. Our God and Lord, who was on the point of offering Himself on the Altar of the Cross to the Eternal Father through death, with a view to bringing about our eternal redemption, at the Last Supper on the night in which He was betrayed, offered up to God, the Father, His Body and His Blood under the appearances of bread and wine. This He did in order not to let His Priesthood come to an end through death, and thus He gave to His beloved Bride, the Church, a visible sacrifice in keeping with the exigencies of the nature of man. His object was this, that the bloody sacrifice which was on the point of being accomplished on the cross should be represented; that its memory should remain to the end of the world, and that its saving power should be applied (to us) unto remission of those sins which are committed by us daily; and in acting thus He declared Himself to be constituted a priest according to the order of Melchisedech for ever. Moreover He gave His Body and Blood under the symbols of the same things, to His apostles for their food, making them then priests of the same New Testament. Furthermore, He gave them a precept to offer up in sacrifice His Body and Blood, and in their name to their successors in the priesthood. This precept was conveyed in the following words: "Do this in memory of Me." Such has always been the understanding and the doctrine of the Catholic Church.

We have here quoted a rough translation of the words of the Church Herself as they were formulated by the Council of Trent. Four truths are embodied in this passage: there is only *one* sacrifice, namely the sacrifice of Christ upon the Cross. Christ instituted the new Pasch, that is Himself, to be immolated by the Church, through her priests under visible signs, in memory of His own passage from the world to the Father, that passage in which He redeemed us through the pouring out of His Blood.

In this divine sacrifice which is celebrated at Mass the very same Christ is contained and immolated in a bloodless fashion who had offered Himself up once on the Altar of the Cross in a bloody manner.

This Sacrifice (of the Mass) is truly the sacrifice of propitiation; for the Lord being appeased by the oblation of the sacrifice, giving grace and the gift of penance, remits the most heinous crimes and sins; for it is one and the same victim; the same is offering now through the ministry of the priests who then offered Himself upon the cross, the difference being only in the way of offering.

In the Eucharist we also find the sacramental symbol; under the appearance of bread and wine, the Body and Blood of Christ are really present as spiritual food for the soul. The total Christ is present under one single appearance, under the smallest part of that appearance: the risen Christ just as He now dwells in Heaven. We may therefore worship and adore Him in this Sacrament.

III. THE EUCHARISTIC SACRIFICE

The Eucharist as a Sacrifice is now indicated in the West by the word Mass, which means dismissal—a name which reminds us of the solemn Celebration of the Sacrifice in the Early Church, when the Catechumens (i.e. the candidates for Baptism) were dismissed after the reading of the Epistle and the Gospel, and the Baptized only at the end, just before the closing of the doors. In the Acts of the Apostles mention is also made of the breaking of bread; St. Paul uses the word "Eucharistia" in his Epistle to the Corinthians, and speaks of the thanksgiving, and this expression reminds us vividly of the main purpose of the Sacrifice. Such expressions as sacrifice, offering, victim, and sacred mysteries, are also frequently met with in religious literature during the course of the ages.

1. *The Sacrifice*

The Mass is a sacrifice. Christ's death upon the Cross is a sacrifice. In the Old Testament references to burnt-offerings, peace-offerings, expiatory-sacrifices, and the offering up of food, thanksgiving and incense constantly recur. In all religions we find, as well as certain purifications, holy ceremonies called sacrifices also mentioned. Whatever may have been the original sense of the sacrifice, at all events it points to a certain interior attitude which the outward ceremony symbolizes. The custom or ceremony which we can observe is closely bound up with the underlying religious life; it is its form. "Even before he had learned to speak, man was a ritualist," says G. K. Chesterton. In this action, in the sacrifice, the relation between God and man becomes apparent.

The source of all man's life is to be found in God. Through His strength and all-pervading power He maintains man's growth and development and, as his ultimate goal, He constitutes that happiness which man of necessity pursues. Creator and goal: starting point and divine inspirer: this points to total dependence and asks for total devotion in return. Such a relation of dependence and devotion is the fundamental relationship between God and man; man must acknowledge and express it, live by it inwardly and testify to it outwardly; for in this relationship is embodied his total human essence. He must completely surrender himself to God, and detach himself from everything which could impede that yielding. A return to God, and especially a reconstruction according to the plan of God, remains man's task; he goes to Him, not only by avoiding excesses and uprooting defects, but by working positively along certain lines, by his natural and supernatural development in every way.

The very act by which man tears himself away from sin and surrenders himself to God, is a sacrifice, a gift by which he completely realizes his union with the Creator. This inward sacrifice he makes concrete by means of a sacrificial gift—for instance, by withdrawing some precious article from all profane use and offering it to God, to express, as it were, his own total dedication. It follows from this that the Sacrifice belongs to the world of signs and symbols.

2. *The Sacrifice of Christ*

Our previous consideration of the Sacrifice in itself finds its highest example in that one sacrifice *par excellence*, of which all the early ritual of the Offering was only the prefigure: The Sacrifice of the Cross. The early Christian tradition holds Christ's death upon the Cross to be the perfect sacrifice. Analysing it, we find here the suffering and dying body of the victim, the shedding of blood. St. Augustine wonders meditatively, in the fourth chapter of his book on the Trinity: "Does anything more perfect exist which is to be eaten by man and sacrificed by man than human flesh? Does anything more suitable exist to be sacrificed than mortal flesh? Does anything so pure exist, and which possesses such a power to wipe away a man's sins, than that flesh which was born of a body without the least stain of fleshly desire, born in the womb of a Virgin? What can be sacrificed so full of love, and accepted so gratefully, as the flesh of our Sacrifice, which became the Body of our Priest?" I quote this passage to show how important the material element in the sacrifice is thought to be. Here the flesh has the rôle of sacrificial gift; the suffering and dying flesh. In suffering and dying the elements which constitute the sacrifice are contained, for this is the gift which Christ gave to His Father. He gave His life. He gave it freely and of His own accord. And the gift of His life is the same as the shedding of His Life's Blood. That is why St. Paul in his Epistle to the Hebrews says: "Meanwhile Christ has taken His place as our High Priest, to win us blessings that still lie in the future. He makes use of a greater, a more complete tabernacle, which human hands never fashioned; it does not belong to this order of creation at all. It is His own Blood, not the blood of goats and calves, that has enabled Him to enter, once and for all, into the sanctuary; the ransom He has won lasts for ever. The blood of bulls and goats, the ashes of a heifer sprinkled over men defiled, has power to hallow them for every purpose of outward purification; and shall not the Blood of Christ, who offered Himself, through the Holy Spirit, as a victim unblemished in God's sight, purify our consciences, and set them free from lifeless observances, to serve the living God? Thus, through His intervention, a new Covenant has been bequeathed to us; a death must follow, to atone for all our transgressions under the Old Covenant, and then the destined heirs were to obtain, for ever, their promised inheritance . . . Man's destiny is to die once for all; nothing remains after that but judgment; and Christ was offered once for all, to drain the cup of a world's sins; when we see Him again, sin will play its part no longer, He will be bringing salvation to those who await His coming."[62]

In these magnificent phrases one catches the deep theme of our Redemption. Christ's suffering, the shedding of His Blood, has a sacrificial quality. Christ offers Himself: accordingly He is, at the same time, both Priest and Sacrifice. He offered Himself unstained, without trace of sin, infinitely holy. And to whom? To God Himself. God was not able to refuse this token of dependence and devotion; He accepted the offering. It is for this reason that it is able to purify us interiorly; to dedicate us in spirit and in truth to the living God; to accomplish the expiation of our sins. As man dies once only, so Christ died once only, and this death was and is the determinative factor for all mankind. The Sacrifice can never be repeated. It is wholly perfect. One of the characteristics of perfection is simplicity: it does not need to be

[62] Heb. 9, 11-15, 27-28.

repeated or completed. Its results remain: the taking upon Himself, the bearing of the sins of mankind. His life and death had a substitutional intention and meaning; they expiated the debts and punishment of many.

In the sacrifice of the cross, in the offering of his suffering and dying Body, Christ expressed His perfect obedience and inward abandonment to the Father, joined to His fervent love. He chose death as the ultimate extreme of obedience. By this He gave the Father infinite honour, worship and glory. He sacrificed that highest and most precious possession, the only thing which really belongs to man, that is to say His own will. Self-emptying, St. Paul calls it, and it became visible in His obedience unto death. Therefore Christ our Redeemer said, as He came into the world: "No sacrifice, no offering was Thy demand; thou hast endowed me instead with a Body. Thou hast not found any pleasure in burnt sacrifices, in sacrifices for sin. See then, I said, I am coming to fulfil what is written of Me, where the book lies unrolled; to do Thy will, O my God."[63]

God accepted the sacrifice; this is proved by the Resurrection and Ascension of Our Lord. This sacrifice was the cause of the Redemption of mankind, of the union of mankind with God, because it gave satisfaction to God for all the sins of mankind. "Making peace with them through His Blood, shed on the cross."[64] Upon the cross He was, in the full sense of the words, "The Lamb of God; He who takes away the sin of the world."[65] For this reason, St. Paul tells us, he does not wish to make a display of anything at all except the cross of Our Lord Jesus Christ.[66] And again: "He would reconcile us to God through His Cross, inflicting death, in His own Person, upon the feud."[67] Through Christ God has been reconciled to the world.

Christ made this Sacrifice in place of Man. Man, left to himself, and alone, was not capable of making his way back to God. But God, in His infinite justice, first exacted an adequate satisfaction. The inward surrender of Christ upon the cross symbolized the will of mankind to turn once more to God and be united to Him. His Sacrifice was a token of the sacrifice which all men have to make, and it is the most wonderful token of all, for it merits grace. The sacrifice of

[63] Heb. 10, 5-7. [64] Col. 1, 20. [65] John 1, 29.
[66] Gal. 6, 14. [67] Eph. 2, 16.

the Cross is an expression of the personal surrender of Christ, and thus, as a sign of our will also to surrender and expiate, is already sacramental.

3. *Holy Mass*

a. Its Essence and Meaning

Christ wanted to make His Sacrifice of the Cross ever-present to us. He desired, in a certain sense, to renew it constantly. He desired to apply it to us in a sacramental form. It could not be a fresh sacrifice for, as the author of the Epistle to the Hebrews expresses it, through one sacrifice He brought those whom it sanctified to complete fulfilment. As far as the sacrifice is in question, everything is consummated: and yet He has perpetuated the Sacrifice in which He thus completed every sacrifice. In three of the Gospels, and in the first Epistle to the Corinthians we read, as it were, His final will and testament. He celebrated the Last Supper, and at it He already foreshadowed His victimization of the following day by the institution of a rite, by an offering, and a banquet. He took the Bread and the Chalice, just as now the priest takes the paten with the host saying: "Receive, O Holy Father, almighty and eternal God, this spotless host;" And after that, takes the chalice with the wine saying: "We offer unto Thee, O Lord, the chalice of salvation, beseeching Thy clemency that it may ascend as a sweet odour before Thy divine majesty, for our own salvation, and for that of the whole world. Amen."

Jesus gave thanks to His Father, He blessed the bread with the words: "This is My Body;" likewise He took the chalice with wine, saying: "This is My Blood, shed for many, to the remission of sins." Here we have the consecration of the Mass. There was at the Last Supper, and is now in the Mass, His crucified Body, under the appearance and symbol of broken bread: His shed Blood poured out in wine.

He broke the bread then, just as to-day the priest, after saying the Our Father, puts the host, broken into two parts, onto the paten. He gave it to His disciples: the communion of the Baptized.

The first Mass was offered by Christ Himself at the Last Supper. The first Holy Mass, together with all the others that have followed and will follow it to the end of Time, are for ever united with the supreme sacrifice of the Cross. The same gift: the Body and Blood of Christ. The same priest and offerer, Christ Himself. The same Sacrifice. Christ could only once make the sacrifice of His life. That one sacrificial act, with which He offered Himself to the Father, is still present even now. The offering of His Body and Blood, once more united in Heaven, brings life to us. That one comprehensive and final, unique and sacrificial death of Jesus Christ, takes place at Mass: not a new sacrificial death, but the same sacrificial death renewed. That which happens on the altar during the consecration, is in truth the same as the sacrifice of the Cross, and so it remains the very core and centre of our religion.

How precisely do we find in the Mass a real Sacrifice which makes the Sacrifice of the Cross still present with us even to-day?

The Mass is a Sacramental Sacrifice; simultaneously sacrament and sacrifice. That which happened on Calvary now happens by means of representative signification. A careful study of the consecration prayers will make it clear that the signs themselves here indicate a sacrifice. If they do this, then there *is* a sacrifice.

Here is bread which signifies the Body of Christ: for this is my Body which shall be sacrificed for you. According, then, to the promise and the institution of Christ His Sacrificed Body becomes present to us likewise now.

Here is the chalice with wine which signifies the Blood of Christ: for this is My Blood, shed for you. According then to the intention of Christ His Sacred Blood becomes present to us as an offering.

Body and Blood were the sacrifice of the Cross, the offering of the New Testament; at Mass a division is made of the appearances of bread and wine, and this division indicates the death of Christ—the separation of Body and Soul as it took place in the death on the Cross. The actual, natural separation of Body and Soul is renewed and made present under the symbols of bread and wine.

And yet there is a profound difference between the two sacrifices—the glorified Christ cannot die again. He can no longer suffer. He does not dwell in the Host wounded and emaciated as on that Friday mid-day of long ago. His humiliation is over. Now it is, as the Church expresses it, an unbloody Sacrifice. The separation of Body and Blood in the Mass takes shape in the form of representative signification: in the shape of bread, which symbolizes and makes present the Body, and in the shape of wine which symbolizes and makes present the Blood. In this sense there is a separation between flesh and blood, and thus a sacrifice: that is to say an expression of the will of Jesus to surrender Himself and to be sacrificed. In certain adventitious minor points the Mass and the Sacrifice of the Cross differ. The unsuffering, glorified, and everlastingly happy Christ still offers Himself under the representative signs of bread and wine, as a renewal of His will to be sacrificed. On the Cross itself, however, it is the Man of Sorrows whom we meet, with the crown of thorns and the wounds, and the flowing blood.

It thus becomes evident that the Mass is indissolubly bound up with the sacrifice of the Cross. This sacramental division of Body and Blood would be impossible had not first a real separation, a natural death upon the Cross, taken place.

The Mass is not a repetition of the Sacrifice of Calvary: Christ's dedication and complete surrender remain fixed: they have been accepted, once and for ever, by God. There is only one sacrifice, one sacrificial offering, one sacrificial gift, one combined Victim and Priest: once only has the obedient and loving surrender been made: upon the Cross and nowhere else. Mass is a representation, a relationship of symbols and signs, it is a relative sacrifice: all its meaning and power is founded upon the Sacrifice of the Cross. Without the Cross, there would be no Mass. On the Cross reconciliation was effected and grace was merited. The Mass brings us no new merits, no new atonement, no new reunion between God and men. Mass is only the means by which the fruits of Christ's suffering and death are applied to men in particular.

Unity is the essence of both Sacrifices: namely, the same Offerer and Priest, Christ—now however represented by the Church and Her priests—the same Sacrifice. In the Christian religion there is only one Sacrifice, the Sacrifice of the Cross—anticipated at the Last Supper, sacramentally made present in the Mass. Both honour and propitiation of His offended Majesty were offered to God on Calvary, and now again are offered in the Mass through the grace and the power of that one, unique, emptying-out unto death.

The Mass can only be understood and grasped in its relationship to the unique Sacrifice of the Cross from which it derives all its meaning and value.

b. Participation in the Sacrifice

The Sacrifice of the Cross is the sacrifice of Christ alone. He offered it vicariously for us, but without either our co-operation or consent. Now we believe in the love of Christ which moved Him to reveal to us the love of God in this way and so to save us. We are grateful to Him, and we continually trust in the power and efficacy of this Sacrifice; we place the hope of our salvation in this token of faith and love. So we live according to the cross in love and faith, but this Sacrifice offered in the form of the Mass, even anticipated our desires, by affording us the possibility of sharing in it.

The priest, as the instrument of Christ, and by virtue of the indelible sign of his priesthood, is empowered to make present to us Christ's sacrifice upon the Cross. That which he does, Christ does through him. As he speaks, Christ speaks. The priest himself is merely an instrument. But by the grace of Baptism, dedicated to Christ and sharing in His priesthood, the Faithful also are able to co-sacrifice. Through the priest—that is to say in reality through Christ—they give in this way the highest possible honour to God, and express their entire dependence upon Him and their surrender; in this way they unite themselves with the intention and obedience of Christ Himself. In this Sacrifice they offer thanksgiving to God, implore His help, and make propitiation for their sins. Thus Christ's Sacrifice becomes the Sacrifice of the whole Church, of all the members of the Mystical Body of Christ. This ability to co-sacrifice presupposes an interior intention to sacrifice which, at the same time, is itself the fruit of that Sacrifice.

The Sacrifice of the Body and Blood of Christ must be the genuine expression of our interior love and desire to sacrifice; otherwise we should lack the connection with Christ's surrender to the Father. Is it not true that by means of sacrifice one renounces oneself and gives oneself entirely to God? This state of participation in the Sacrifice is greatly increased by participation in the sacrificial repast. Although the repast does not belong to the essence of the sacrifice, yet it is not entirely disconnected. Sacrificed meats are usually eaten. St. Paul suggests: "Do not those who eat their sacrifices associate themselves with the altar of sacrifice?"[68] He who sits at the table partakes more intimately of the Sacrifice itself. Did not Christ at the Last Supper give His disciples bread saying: "Take, and eat," and did He not offer them the chalice saying: "Drink, all of you, of this."

I Cor. 10, 18.

He gave the Bread which is His Flesh for the life of the world. He gave His sacrificed Body. He bade them drink of the wine, of His Blood that was to be shed. This, for the apostles, was the only way in which they shared in Christ's sacrifice.

It was thus that the sacramental sacrifice was consummated in a sacrificial repast—in Communion: through this we still partake of Christ's Body and Blood which was sacrificed.

At the Consecration we acknowledge, with Christ, our entire dependence upon God, and offer ourselves, with His Body and Blood, to our Creator and Saviour. In Communion, God gives Christ's glorified Body to us as food, and we receive from Him an intimate union with His divine life. Our own life, which we offered as sacrifice, was accepted; our death to all forms of egoism reached the Heart of God. Through this death with Christ, we are allowed, in Communion, to share in His glorified life: He comes into our soul. From this it is evident that participation in the sacrificial repast is the most perfect form of participation in the Sacrifice itself. He who goes to Holy Communion during Mass, completes in himself the death and resurrection of Christ. It is, however, not obligatory. If we do not receive the actual fruit of the Sacrifice, we can always unite our heart and spirit with Christ in fervent prayer, inspired by love.

c. *The Fruits of the Sacrifice of the Mass*

The Church speaks of the Sacrifice of the Mass in the same way as she speaks of the Sacrifice of the Cross. In both the highest honour is paid, with Christ and through Christ, to the Blessed Trinity. God the Son became Man in order to *glorify* the Father; for that glory He died upon the Cross, offering His life as a Sacrifice.

The Church therefore sets forth Christ's foremost mission, and in the Mass perpetuates the highest act of the worship of God ever performed.

In this Sacrifice of the Mass, with Christ and through Christ, she thanks the Father for all His loving care of us and the richness of His gifts to Man.

But through the Sacrifice of the Cross Christ has redeemed mankind. Through His immeasurable self-sacrifice He reconciled us with God and expiated our sins. Now, again, in the Mass, the Church offers to God the same Victim, and gives the Faithful a share in the surrender of Christ, thus calling down the mercy of God upon our sins and His clemency over the punishment which we deserve. The Mass is a Sacrifice of Propitiation.

In the Sacrifice of the Cross *all graces were merited* and became available. To obtain these graces for us, the Church offers the Sacrifice of the Mass in the Name of Christ. Through the Sacraments, and along ways which only God knows, the Faithful receive all the necessary means to Salvation, and at the same time all the strength, help, light and consolation which they need. These graces descend upon us from the Cross; they reach us through Christ our Victim and are a direct fruit of the Sacrifice of the Mass. In that sacrifice the dedication to the Father, and the Redemption of Man, remain present for ever in the broken Body and the spilled Blood of Christ.

IV. HOLY COMMUNION

1. We have just been speaking of the great Sacrifice, and of Holy Mass. We believe that at the same time as the Sacrifice, the Sacrament is also present. We have seen how certain tokens, outward forms of bread and wine, symbolize the Body and Blood of Christ, divided as in His offering upon the Cross, and at the same time indicate the value of both as nourishment for the soul, as food and drink bringing us to eternal life.

Beneath these symbols we are offered that sign of love which is most natural and most comprehensive. Love seeks for the closest, most intimate contact. It remains unsatisfied when the longing for union ends in continued estrangement. He who loves desires to be absorbed in the Beloved; to sink his spirit deep in the thought of the other; to tune his will to the desires which he believes he has discovered in that other. This occurs mutually. One cannot adequately express and realize the closeness of that union.

These symbols of bread and wine, of the consuming of the bread and the drinking of the wine, strongly express our desire for union with God, for our oneness with Him in Christ. The nourishment is absorbed into ourselves. We also are absorbed into His life; He changes us into Himself. "Now I live no longer, but He in me." Just as, in a certain sense, my body becomes one with Christ's Flesh and Blood, so the union of my spirit and soul with God gradually grows more intimate. This token of nourishment accordingly symbolizes what is being operated in me by love. "He who eats My Flesh and drinks My Blood has eternal life," said Our Lord. Communion consists precisely in the reception and use of this Sacrament. By one infallible sign we can measure its effect: this Sacrament produces love. The chief fruit of this spiritual repast is a special union with Christ, with the eternal and glorified Sacrificial Lamb. "He who eats My Flesh and drinks My Blood, lives continually in Me and I in him."[69] This is pre-eminently the sacramental grace. So love finds its fulfilment in this closest of unions, which however should grow increasingly from day to day.

This union with Christ must also be a union with one another. The sacramental Body of Christ necessarily affects the mystical Body of Christ. He who loves Christ, loves its members: all those who fulfil His will or seek the truth.

St. Paul has spoken conclusively as to this: "Because it is one Bread, therefore we are, however numerous, one Body, for we all partake of the one Bread."

Consequences of a far-reaching nature are involved here. The thing which most impedes the action of this Sacrament is hatred and hard-heartedness, a lack of charity. Only the person however who is deeply conscious of this failing and mourns it, seeking in communion the strength to renounce himself generously, will receive charity itself as the fruit of the Sacrament.

The specific grace of the Eucharist is union with Christ and the whole Mystical Body. In Christ we meet the entire Church with all its interests and needs; we come into contact with all rightly intentioned men as well as with those whose errors we deplore or who offend and are unsympathetic to us.

And this union is the pledge of our Resurrection.[70] Through this sanctification in Christ we are protected from mortal sin, and our inevitable daily loss of strength is repaired. It has also the effect of wiping out venial sin as well as temporary punishments. It subdues our unbridled inclinations. It diverts us from purely human and physical joys, and assists our will in its continual struggle to keep our Baptismal vows. It tries to accomplish in us a complete

[69] John 6, 57. [70] John 6, 58.

restoration of inward, spiritual harmony, which penetrates through to the flesh and all its concupiscences. Peace and happiness in God should become our permanent state as a result of this conscious reception of the Body and Blood of the Lord. Most especially this Sacrament increases the fervour of our love, giving us a resolute will and desire to show it by deeds.

2. The Church has fixed, as the lowest obligatory minimum, once a year during Paschaltide, for the reception of Holy Communion, in order to fulfil the divine command to eat the Flesh and to drink the Blood of the Son of Man.[71] In danger of death this command is binding on all who have reached years of discretion. The wish of the Church, however, in harmony with the wish of Christ, is that actually we should go as often as we are able, provided that all the required conditions are fulfilled.

These conditions consist in: a state of grace, for "if anyone eats this bread or drinks this cup unworthily, he will be held to account for the Lord's Body and Blood".[72] A good Confession is therefore exacted from those who have lost the friendship of God.

The Church also requires abstinence from food and drink (water excepted) from midnight on, excepting in danger of death, or in any other circumstances which make fasting difficult. There are clearly defined regulations as to all these matters. The most outstandingly important requirement, however, is that of a good intention. There is great danger that lack of proper attention, or voluntary attachment to venial sins, may disturb the atmosphere in which this Sacrament should be received. He who approaches the altar rails from mere habit, or routine, had far better turn round again and go out. Habit and routine entirely destroy the fruits of this Sacrament. There is absolutely no grace in going daily, or several times a week to Holy Communion, simply because one has been accustomed to do so from childhood. Real preparation is necessary. Such a preparation might consist in a daily good intention of trying to love God, and of living in charity with others, but it must be completed by a personal, conscious advertence to the act which we are about to perform and a real desire to receive Christ and to unite ourselves to Him.

[71] John 6, 54.

[72] I Cor. 11, 27.

Receiving Holy Communion should never be allowed to become just a habit or daily business; it should be a highlight, a culminating point of interior concentration, of desire for the love of God, and of supplication for help and grace.

V. THE EUCHARIST

THE CENTRAL POINT OF ALL THE SACRAMENTS

On the Cross Christ merited for us every grace; from His one, unique Sacrifice proceeded the redemption of man and his reunion with God. That Sacrifice of the Cross, Christ Himself perpetuated in the Sacrifice of the Mass; there the Sacrificed and glorified Jesus is present and living, under the symbols of bread and wine.

The seven Sacraments bring man continually into contact with Christ, and serve to distribute His graces. These spring from the one Sacrifice of the life of Christ from which they draw all their strength and fruitfulness, His surrender on the Cross. His sacred Body and Blood—given and shed as a token of His interior obedience and love—thus offered as a Sacrifice achieving our Redemption, still lives among us in the daily sacrifice of the Mass, and this Mass is the foundation of His Church and its members; by this means He strengthens, nourishes and heals them, and leads them to eternal salvation. The Sacrifice and the Mass are one and the same reality; in it, by means of signs and symbols, we offer ourselves to the Father, with Christ and in Christ, and with Christ we are united with the Blessed Trinity. The Eucharist signifies just that—union with the life-giving Saviour. This is the first and greatest Sacrament originating from His Sacrifice. It contains Christ Himself, the source and the cause of all grace. It contains the Body and Blood of Christ under the appearances of bread and wine; that is to say Christ at the highest moment of His love and surrender; at the zenith of His redemptive mission; Christ now in His glorified state, risen, and in possession of all the joys of Heaven. Through this Sacrament He lives in us and we in Him; through it He continues His redemptive work.

It is round this Sacrament, which at the same time is a sacrifice, round this sacrifice which is also a Sacrament, that all the other Sacraments are grouped. They point to it and draw their efficacy from it.

Baptism, in its old form, and by the act of immersion, signified death, and burial with Christ; now as a sign it signifies a washing away of sin. Through this takes place our rebirth in Christ, and our dedication to Him, sealed by the indelible sign of Baptism. Both rebirth and dedication are the direct result of the Sacrifice of the Cross, now present in the Mass, and are a means of union with Christ, who still remains with us under the appearances of bread and wine.

Confirmation is a completion of the Rite of Baptism and its symbolism points to a strengthening and confirming of the life of Christ in the soul. Through this Sacrament, under the influence of the Holy Ghost, there arises in us an urge to live our faith and our contact with Christ interiorly, and to confess it exteriorly. But we owe this infusion of the Holy Spirit also to the Sacrifice upon the Cross, now present in the Mass. Confirmation presupposes our union with One who lives in this Sacrament.

The Sacrament of Penance restores the life of grace in the soul by removing any obstacles which might impede our union with love and with Christ. It is through the expiatory power of His Sacrifice, now present in the Mass, that we are cleansed. This Sacrament again points to the Eucharist as its goal, since it is at the Mass that union with Christ is most intimately and perfectly achieved.

Extreme Unction completes the Sacrament of Penance. Instituted to strengthen us against difficulties and temptations in the hour of death, and to heal us from our sins, it seeks to consummate our union with Christ in an eternal, blessed contemplation of Him. It is an initiation, and final introduction to eternal life, and it derives its power from the cry of Christ upon the Cross: "My God, my God, why hast Thou forsaken me?" It prepares us for the complete fruition of the grace which Christ communicates to us in the Sacrament of the Altar.

The Priesthood—that is participation in the mission and task and priesthood of Christ—gives the power to consecrate, to sacrifice and to offer His Blessed Body and Blood, and the charge of seeing that the faithful are properly prepared to receive the Eucharist. Priesthood consists entirely in the service of the Mass and Holy Communion; it derives all its meaning and efficacy from the sacrifice of the Cross.

The aim and ultimate goal of Matrimony is Christ, for it opens up the possibility of evoking fresh life, which will in turn share in the grace of God, and it is meant to sanctify both man and wife by mutual love and fidelity. It is the symbol of the relationship between Christ and His Church—a union already implied in the Eucharist. It is from the loving surrender on the Cross, realized in the Mass by means of signs, that this Sacrament receives its power to realize also this surrender in man and wife. The binding *yes* finds its deepest meaning and its realization in love expressed in sacrifice.

The Sacraments indicate that union with Christ which is given to us in the Eucharist. In this Sacrifice and Sacrament they achieve their purpose, namely surrender to God in Christ, and personal union with Christ and so, through Him, with the Blessed Trinity. In this link with Christ, the Head of mankind, we ourselves find each other in love and faith.

§ 7. *Priesthood*

Christ gave us five exterior signs intended to nourish and to complete the divine life in our souls. But who was to approach men with these signs? Who had either the capacity or the mission for such a task? Christ Himself left us. In the Sacraments He bequeathed to us the fruits of His Redemption, but someone must obviously be found to distribute these fruits of His Death, unless innumerable souls were to be deprived of His grace and to find themselves unable to come into contact with the Sources of life which He had opened up. Sacraments are for the service of man: they bring God and man together. In a certain sense they take over the task of Christ's Humanity. It was therefore clear that Christ's priestly mediation between God and ourselves, His own proper Redemption of sin, had still to be continued in a visible form. This could only be possible if someone else took His place: someone else who, in His Name and in His power, could administer those Sacraments and become steward of His mysteries.[73]

Christ instituted a Sacrament through which it became

[73] I Cor. 4, 1.

possible for the Christian community to experience lastingly all the grace and efficacy of His Redemption: namely the Sacrament of the Priesthood. Through this Sacrament He gathered together His divine gifts and bound them up in a form or system which would remind us vividly of Him, of Him as the *sole* mediator between God and the world. For the function of Mediator which He bestows upon certain men by means of this Sacrament has the effect of making them, as it were, disappear as men, so that they only speak in His Name; they only do what He did.

That which they hold in custody for others is nothing of their own; it is a pure gift of Christ, who only gives to men the power to *administer* those Sacraments. Without this ability received from Him, every priest would be powerless. Christ, the eternal High Priest, has conferred His priesthood upon His Church.

I. THE NEW TESTAMENT

In the New Testament writings, Christ is shown as the eternal High Priest and sole Mediator, who communicated His priesthood to His Church and to the Apostles. There is, and remains, only one High Priest, just as there is only one who, as Teacher and Shepherd, leads and teaches His Church. St. Paul states explicitly in his Epistle to the Hebrews: "Whereas Jesus continues for ever, and His priestly office is unchanging; that is why He can give eternal salvation to those who through Him make their way to God; He lives on still to make intercession on our behalf."[74] And elsewhere: "There is only one God, and only one Mediator between God and men, Jesus Christ, who is a man, like them, and gave Himself as a ransom for them all."[75]

From the very beginning of His public life, however, as we have seen, Christ assembled a group of disciples around Him. St. John, in His Gospel, tells us about their first meeting. "The next day after this, John was standing there again, with two of his disciples; and watching Jesus as He walked by, he said, Look, this is the Lamb of God. The two disciples heard him say it, and they followed Jesus. Turning and seeing them follow Him, Jesus asked, What would you have of me? Rabbi, they said, where dost thou live? He said to them,

[74] Heb. 7, 24-25.

[75] I Tim. 2, 5-6.

Come and see."[76] One of them was Andrew, the brother of Simon. He went to fetch him and said: "We have discovered the Messiah." These two, who lived on the shore of the lake, and were fishermen, Jesus bade follow Him. In the neighbourhood of Bethsaida He also found Philip, whom He called, and he, in turn, brought Nathanael. He chose his disciples from these men and their friends; in future, He told them, they were to become fishers of men.[77] Impelled by His conflict with the Pharisees, Jesus became increasingly open in His preaching, and declared that His teaching and His mission were not destined to end with Himself; He wished to choose men who would carry on His task. After many hours spent in prayer, and in a mystical relationship with the twelve tribes of Israel, He selected twelve successors whom He called Apostles. These He trained very carefully in their future work. He promised to give them power over the Kingdom of God and eternal life; they were to be able to bind and loose everything connected with the service of men's eternal destiny; they were to receive the Holy Ghost and the power to forgive sins or to retain them.[78] And when, at the Last Supper, He prefigured His Sacrifice of the Cross under the symbols of bread and wine, He said to them: "Do this for a commemoration of Me."[79] He gave them the injunction to baptize and to teach all nations. As His Father had sent Him, so He in turn sent them; He handed on to them His mission. From this it follows that "He who hears thee, hears Me."

II. THE SACRAMENT OF THE PRIESTHOOD

1. The exterior ceremony, by which Christ's power is conferred upon a human being and His grace in them is effected, points to a Sacrament. From the very commencement, it was widely held in the Church, that Ordination conferred both power and grace. St. Paul spoke of the gift of grace bestowed upon Timothy by the imposition of hands. This imposition of hands gave to him dignity, authority, and jurisdiction over the community, and also the faculties for the proper exercise of his function. Here, then, we have a Rite which confers grace. The imposition of hands is a symbol which both denotes and gives. To lay hands upon a

[76] John 1, 35-39. [77] Luke 5, 8-11. [78] John 20, 21-23.
[79] Luke 22, 19.

person means to accept him, to bestow upon him some higher power, to entrust something to him.

Even now, at Ordination, the Bishop lays both his hands upon the head of each candidate, and allows them to rest there for a moment. With this action the priestly power is transferred. Following after the Bishop, every priest present also imposes his hands in reverent silence. Then, both Bishop and priests hold their right hands extended over the heads of the newly ordained, and the Bishop beseeches God to confer upon these, His servants, the dignity of the Priesthood. The imposition of hands and the prayer of the Bishop communicates both power and grace. In this consists the Sacrament. What follows, serves to elaborate and explain the meaning and efficacy of Ordination. The anointing of the hands, and the handing over of the chalice and Host signify the duty of blessing and offering up the Sacrifice of the Mass; that is why, from that moment in the Ceremony, they all take part in the Bishop's Mass. At the end of Mass they make their Confession of Faith, the Bishop once more extending his hands over them and saying: "Receive ye the Holy Ghost; whose sins you shall forgive, they are forgiven them, whose sins you shall retain, they are retained." The newly ordained then promises respect and obedience to the Ecclesiastical Authorities. From henceforward he is enrolled in the service of the Mystical Body of Christ, His Church.

2. *Further Development of the Symbol*

The imposition of hands was the Symbol: the Holy Ghost descended upon this man, set him apart from ordinary people from among whom he was taken, and dedicated him specially to the service of Christ and the Church. The principal effect of this symbol is a permanent share in the Priesthood of Christ which the Church expresses by the words: indelible mark. This mark makes him, in the strict sense of the word, a priest. That which was begun in Baptism and Confirmation, is now completed: his permanent dedication to Christ has developed into a participation in His priestly power, in His power as Mediator between God and man, in His priestly task in general. Christ continues to exercise His Mediation visibly through him.

As an instrument of Christ, yet as a mediator always at the

side of the people, the priest offers up the Sacrifice of the Mass, carries out public acts of worship, and prays to God for the sins and the necessities of his flock. At the same time, as mediator from the side of God, he administers the Sacraments, preaches the Gospel and teaches the Faithful how to observe all that has been commanded them. He is the servant of Christ.[80] Through this indelible mark of the Priesthood[81] by which he belongs more intimately to Christ and is more conformed to Him as priest, shepherd and teacher, he is endowed with a certain power over the Body and Blood of Christ, over His Mystical Body, and over all the other Sacraments. In Baptism he has power over life and death; in Confirmation he confers strength by Faith; in Communion he communicates love; in Confession he judges and decides as to sins; and in Extreme Unction he opens the gates of heaven. But his principal task remains to offer up the Sacrifice of the Mass. His mission to preach the Word of God, to lead and to rule the Faithful, are all subordinate to this. With the help of the other Sacraments he has to try and prepare the Faithful for this greatest sacrament and sacrifice, for the service of God.

But he who receives authority, receives also the grace to fulfil his mission properly. This grace is bestowed upon him in the first place for the salvation of his own soul; he must be sanctified as a priest, more and more intimately united with Christ, more strongly concentrated upon God and the will of God. In this way he lives in accordance with the dignity and grace which he has received.

3. *Requirements for the Priesthood*

To be able to receive the Sacrament of Ordination the Church requires that a man should have been baptized; further, if he is personally to enjoy the fruits of his ordination, that he must be united in a living bond of grace with Christ, and satisfy certain regulations as to age, study, and formation. He is called in the same way as were the apostles: a certain leaning towards the vocation, strengthened by grace, and special spiritual, moral and physical aptitude are necessary. The real decision as to vocation, however, rests with the Bishop. Celibacy is required from priests in the Western Church because it gives more freedom in the service of God.[82]

[80] I Cor. 4, 1. [81] John 15, 15-16. [82] Matt. 19, 12.

The Eastern Ecclesiastics (apart from those educated in Western Seminaries or in Rome), are allowed to marry before the diaconate, and as deacon and priest to continue married life. Those, however, who are living in the married state may never become Bishops.

III. THE HIERARCHY OF THE CHURCH

The priestly state has diversified its *functions* in the course of centuries. These different functions nowadays constitute only steps to the Priesthood, properly speaking, and are awarded by successive stages. The Eastern Church has only four stages, but in the Western Church there are four Minor Orders and three Major Orders. The first of these spiritual functions begins after tonsure, with the office of *Ostiarius* or doorkeeper: this takes us back to the times when the door was carefully guarded lest unauthorized persons should obtain entry. Next comes the office of *Lector* or Reader, which in the early Christian Church carried with it the task of deciphering the difficult MSS of the Epistles and Gospels. After this there follows the office of *Exorcist*, which during the first centuries was intended for the casting out of devils from baptized or unbaptized persons. Finally there is the office of *acolyte* or light-bearer, the acolyte originally assisting the deacon in the breaking of Bread and the preparation of the Wine and water.

The Major Orders are called Subdiaconate, Diaconate and Priesthood. Formerly these first two were permanent offices; now they are only preparatory to the Priesthood itself. When receiving the subdiaconate, the candidate undertakes the obligations of celibacy, of the recitation of the Divine Office, and receives the right and the duty of singing the Epistle at Mass. The Deacon is even more intimately associated with this Sacrifice. He can administer Baptism and give Holy Communion.

The final step and completion of the Priesthood takes place at the Ordination by the Bishop. Usually the priest is then entrusted with the management of some section of the Diocese, and at the same time receives from the Bishop the mandate to preach the Word of God and to administer the Sacraments.

The priest is the dispenser of God's graces and mysteries:

never does the holder of any office recede more into the background than he who is engaged in the sacerdotal service. He is an instrument of Christ and, even were he to show himself unworthy or fall into sin, God would still give His grace through the Sacraments. The Spirit works where and as it wills, even by means of unworthy instruments. The priest is a representative of the Church; all that he does, he only does in Her name, according to Her instructions and using Her words. To ensure his full realization of his responsible task, and to safeguard his purity of intention and conduct in life, the Church removes him as much as possible from all mundane preoccupations and surrounds him with a wall of duties, insisting that he must set aside even the cure of souls for the recitation of the breviary. The great solicitude of the Church is to ensure that she has blameless and holy priests; they must be the salt of the earth, and if the salt loses its savour, wherewith shall it be salted? It is no longer of any use.

Prayer for good vocations to the Priesthood is indeed a pressing necessity.

§ 8. *Matrimony*

There are many varying points of view in regard to matrimony. Broadly speaking, and disregarding the finer nuances, one can perhaps divide people into two groups: those for whom the Revelation of God is either no criterion of conduct at all, because they stand completely outside it, or those who subordinate its teaching to their own opinions; and secondly, those who accept the Revelation of God as the only rule of conduct in life.

The former group raises questions as to marriage by which the whole institution is placed on a shifting basis, and becomes dependent upon the changing inclinations and circumstances of each individual. All the questions can really be reduced to one question: is personal happiness (and this happiness is often regarded in a very restricted sense) the *only* standard to be considered when it comes to the making and the continuing of this unbreakable bond between two people: of this normal way of living and expressing love, safeguarded by fixed laws and customs?

The second group is as keenly aware of the practical difficulties which beset married life as is the first group but, in the light of God's Revelation, it regards this mode of realizing individual love as a part also of the natural and supernatural well-being of mankind as a whole.

The right answer to the problems and practical difficulties is closely connected with the fundamental and very topical question: what is the purpose of marriage? A correct view of this matter makes the solution of questions as to divorce, etc., perfectly simple.

I. PURPOSE AND MEANING OF MARRIAGE

In order to discover the intention of God when He created Man—male and female—it is useful to consider the process of development of which marriage can be the result.

In the years of puberty when the adolescent is slowly fixing his position with regard to certain values, and is growing into a new relationship with himself, his neighbour, and above all God, his sexual life develops also—psychologically as well as physiologically. He has taken the first steps upon the path of the formation of his own personality, but there is still a great need for adequate completion of it. Interest in the outside world will then begin to arise. The two sexes, which hitherto have walked side by side through life more or less indifferently, now, as it were, meet each other instead. The boy and girl begin to look to each other instinctively for completion and perfection. They wish to share their growing knowledge and experience in every way; they find their happiness in the mutual experience of each other; in thinking together, and feeling together, and being together. This spiritual bond, this mutual love, is greatly enhanced, influenced and strengthened by sexual affinity. Combined with certain physical emotions there also develops in the adolescent finer psychical feelings and desires. Eventually the two young people wish for this mutual love to be confirmed and assured in a state in which they can remain together for life. The natural goal of this mutual affection is therefore the conjugal bond.

At the beginning of married life the wonderful possession of each other will fully satisfy their love, but later they will discover for themselves that their happiness will only be perfected when the wife has a child to care for. At the same time the husband becomes more conscious of his own importance and duty in life when he realizes that he will go on, as it were, living in his child. And so this urge to love, by which man and woman are driven to the mutual possession of each other, is fulfilled in the creation of a new life.

God has arranged for the propagation of the human species. Beginning from the general and natural human tendencies, absorbed by love, the whole process is designed to assist the duty of reproduction. There are clear instructions upon the subject in the Book of Genesis: God's intention is that man himself should see to the continuation of the human race.

At the same time we must not forget that, with the birth of a child, everything is by no means accomplished. Years of spiritual and physical training must follow, before this young life is brought to full development and educated into becoming an independent being. From this we may draw the following important conclusions.

A necessary condition for the birth, growth and development of a human life is the union of one man and one woman in a state, stable enough to enable them to devote themselves entirely to the welfare of their children, and at the same time increase their own mutual love. Such a union must necessarily be for life. Even a good all-round education is apt to fail without family life behind it. Only parents can give their children what they need in order to become in every sense of the word complete human beings. That is why marriage, in the last resort, is not regulated by purely personal and egoistical motives of happiness, but by the conditions which serve to secure a harmonious propagation and expansion of the human race.

But although the primary purpose of marriage may be concern for posterity, the personal happiness of the married couple is certainly very much included in this aim. Man happens to be an independent being with his own purposes, his own rights, his own individual existence. He is never a mere means to an end. He does not exist because of his species, but because of himself. That is why marriage is needed to develop him into a conscious personality, to complete him in every way. For this social, economical, psychological and moral completion, family life offers the most favourable conditions, provided, that is, that from the beginning there is the assurance that this union is going to be lasting. Then only can that desire, which is so strong in all of us, come to its harmonious maturity: the desire for companionship and home comfort; the desire for the consolation of family affection. Then indeed it becomes possible to have a fair division of labour and a sharing of opinions and ideals.

Such mutual completion and happiness can only be achieved with love as its basis. But, here again, love which is not backed by a steady and lifelong fidelity and union cannot fulfil its real task, and lacks the necessary strength for sacrifice and unselfishness. Love always improves relations, brings about greater mutual understanding, and increases unselfishness, if it can build upon an indissoluble bond.

At the same time married life is the safeguard of chastity. Natural inclinations are guided into their proper channels, where they serve the general welfare of mankind as well as the personal happiness of those concerned. Harmony and integration are the result, and a kind of pleasant but quiet activity which distinguishes many married people from the unmarried.

The aim therefore of marriage is the care and upbringing of the child and, closely connected with this, the general moral perfection and protection of the parents. In the service of the community, the individual will find his real happiness and his own self-development. As the necessary condition for all this, however, love is, and must remain, the animating principle. It is evident that marriage, both because of its twofold purpose and of its very nature, must be a life-union of one man and one woman. The value of marriage is for the most part centred in love brought to its full fruition by man's natural tendencies. Love, in its essence, is more however than just a developed instinct. It desires the highest happiness of the beloved; it gives itself totally, and forgets itself, and is a movement and an urge in the direction of a cherished ideal. Love discovers values completely hidden to others, and appreciates the spiritual qualities of the beloved. The measure of it is sacrifice. Instinct knows no sacrifice, unless it be the sacrifice of the other to its own satisfaction.

In married life sacrifice forms the steady background against which the home-life is lived, with its pleasant, sociable atmosphere notwithstanding, and many lighter touches. When husband and wife know each other well enough to understand without all those useless words which usually only give rise to misunderstandings, then we may be sure that true love is to be found.

For married love to come to fruition there should, nevertheless, be a certain physical attraction. Many marriages are unhappy because two people think that they are in love whereas in reality they only respect or amuse each other. This natural attraction is absorbed and elevated by love, and its expression actually translates the mutual love which is felt. The highest expression of love is the conjugal act to which, at the same time, it gives purpose and meaning. The most intense expression of love is at the same time an act of propagation. From this it is evident that married love is oriented towards reproduction as its purpose, and finds there its moral standard.

But if love is lacking, marriage does not cease to exist, although it may be checked in its legitimate aspirations. From this it follows that genuine married love keeps an open mind as regards children, although naturally influenced by practical considerations. Undue restraint in this matter can affect love; mere selfish motives can easily produce mutual estrangement. If there are serious reasons for denying to love this particular form of fruition, then it will know how to adapt itself to the situation and to make sacrifices for the general good of the family and the children. In its essence love contains the whole of marriage with all its consequences, and it is sufficient in itself even should there be no children.

II. MARRIAGE AS A SACRAMENT

Marriage has been raised by Christ into a Sacrament. On the strength of the Bible and tradition, this is the teaching of the Church. In Holy Scripture we meet with the following comparison made by St. Paul in his Epistle to the Ephesians, where he speaks of the duties of the married: "As you stand in awe of Christ, submit to each other's rights. Wives must obey their husbands as they would obey the Lord. The man is the head to which the woman's body is united, just as Christ is the Head of the Church, He, the Saviour, on whom the safety of His Body depends; and women must owe obedience at all points to their husbands as the Church does to Christ. You who are husbands must show love to your wives, as Christ showed love to the Church when He gave Himself up on its behalf. He would hallow it, purify it by bathing it in the water to which His word gave life. He would summon it into His own presence, the Church in all its beauty, no stain, no wrinkle, no such disfigurement; it was to be holy, it was to be spotless. And that is how husband ought to love wife, as if she were his own body; in loving his wife a man is but loving himself. It is unheard of that a man should bear ill-will to his own flesh and blood; on the contrary, he keeps it fed and warmed; and so it is with Christ and His Church; we are limbs of His Body; flesh and bone we belong to Him. That is why a man will leave his father and mother and cling to his wife, and the two will become one flesh. Yes, those words are a high mystery, and I am applying them here to Christ and His Church. Meanwhile each of you is to love his wife as he would love himself, and the wife is to pay reverence to her husband."[83]

This mystery of marriage is great for the very reason that it is connected with Christ's relationship to the Church. From the fact that Christian marriage has an analogy with Christ and His Church it draws its sanctity.

Even for the Jews and heathens, marriage had a religious meaning; they connected marriage closely with religion and called it a mystery, a sacred ceremony, a union with a deep, hidden and spiritual significance. To the Jews it represented the relationship between God and His people; with the Greeks it was honoured as a liturgical drama at which was commemorated the marriage of the gods, of earth and heaven, of Zeus and Hera. St. Paul disclosed, however, an even greater mystery.

Christian marriage is an image of the relationship between Christ and His Church. The relationship between husband and wife should therefore be like the relationship between Christ and His Church. That relationship involves: 1, docility. The Church is docile to Christ, and the wife should be likewise in regard to her husband. This obedience presupposes authority. 2, self-sacrificing love; again the example is Christ, who delivered Himself up for the Church. 3, solicitude. Christ feeds the Church, and the husband should care for the wife as for his own body. The relationship between Christ and the Church is of a supernatural character; it is a supernatural bond, of which marriage is the symbol.

[83] Eph. 5, 21-33.

The symbolism of marriage all points to the reality behind it, which is derived straight from God, and can only be called by the name of grace. Without this grace husband and wife cannot represent the relationship between Christ and His Church, and that is why marriage itself, just as in the case of that other wonderful relationship which it represents, cannot fail to be a source of grace and strength. Indirectly this is the foundation of the teaching of the Church upon Christian marriage, and the Council of Trent definitely points out that the Sacrament is indicated by it.

In Scripture the purpose of marriage is also mentioned. In the opening chapter of Genesis we read: "And God pronounced His blessing upon them. Increase and multiply and fill the earth, and make it yours; take command of the fishes of the sea, and all that flies through the air, and all the living creatures that move on the earth."[84] In the second chapter the writer presents, in a delightfully human way, how God sees man's solitude, and then takes counsel with Himself as to how to end it: "But the Lord God said, It is not well that man should be without companionship; I will give him a mate of his own kind."[85] Mutual perfection, and consolidation by means of love shine out through these words. While St. Paul, with his eyes fixed upon the actual surroundings in which he lived, came to this yet further conclusion: "But, to avoid the danger of fornication, let every man keep his own wife, and every woman her own husband . . . it is better to marry than to feel the heat of passion."[86] The protection and harmonious development of the personality, in which the spirit rules and knows how to use the instincts, is thus very practically presented to us.

This threefold intention forms one single purpose. Towards this the state of marriage is oriented; this is God's intention, and remains the intention of His creative wisdom even when marriage is actually unfruitful. Among these three purposes there is distinct order and interdependence; to forward and safeguard the propagation of the race is foremost; but for this, the inspiration of love is necessary, and self-restraint also has its part to play as a regulating factor.

Marriage—the union of two people for life for the good of the child—remains the most suitable environment in which to help and perfect each other also; and it assists the har-

[84] Gen. 1, 28. [85] Gen. 2, 18. [86] 1 Cor. 7, 2-8.

monious reconciliation of the mind and the senses, of the spirit and the passions, more naturally and more effectively than is possible anywhere outside that state.

Nevertheless if marriage is to be a Sacrament, it must bear a supernatural seal or mark. By mutual consent the married couple announce their intention of bringing up their child as a member of Christ and the Church of Christ, and in this way they help to forge that perpetual bond between Christ and the Church. Their love, expressed by increasing understanding of each other and mutual sympathy, is influenced by the grace of God and lifted up to a supernatural union of interests and of mind in their life together.

The husband tries to express in his love, the love of Christ for His Church; the model of the love of the woman, is the love of the Church for Her Bridegroom. In their personal lives they will gradually acquire poise and a certain interior integrity. The senses will come more and more under the sway of the will, and both will and senses be submitted to God. They will be an example to their children, who will instinctively lean on them and come to regard home as a haven of safety. That is how Christian marriage makes good the ravages of original sin with all its consequences, and works out the grace of Redemption by means of symbols.

What symbol did Christ choose for the Sacrament? He simply took what was already there; the loving and manifest consent of both husband and wife; the formal agreement to live together and to contract an alliance affecting the survival of both world and Church. The interior and invisible consent Christ also included in the symbol, and He fortifies it with His strength so that it becomes the instrument of that grace. This consent, quite unconsciously, is supernaturally oriented towards Christ and His Church. In this Sacrament the spoken "yes" is the sign of the free agreement of the will. By it husband and wife offer to each other, and mutually accept, their willingness to realize the purpose of marriage. Both offer and acceptance are publicly made, and by means of this free and open agreement Christ bestows His grace.

That Christ raised marriage to the state of a Sacrament is evident from the constant belief of the Church which has always seen in this life-union the symbol of something supernatural, that is to say of the union between Christ and His people. This is clearly expressed in the Liturgy, while in the works of the Mystics we frequently find contemplation, and absorption in God, described in the language of the Spouse and the Bride.

Were marriage to be absent from the list of the Sacraments there would be a strange void. All the six Sacraments are applied to the redemption of man as an individual. And the Priesthood ensures that the five other Sacraments are able to fulfil their function in regard to men. But at the end we come to this question: yes, but where do all these people come from? These people to whom the Sacraments are to be administered? How do the generations follow each other like this? What is the meaning of this unending succession? And the answer is, by means of the Sacrament of Marriage, which is the servant of Society and of the Church. This Sacrament completes the sequence.

III. THE EFFECTS OF THE SACRAMENT

1. *Man is sanctified by Matrimony*

The Sacrament of Matrimony carries with it all the graces which are necessary to enable people to lead their married life as Christians. Through Marriage two people are, as it were, appointed to be the co-operators of God. Through their mutual, spoken consent they have placed themselves in a particular state of life and are therefore obliged to fulfil its duties properly. This permanent tie, this special way of life, indicates appropriate graces and confers the right to them. The union of their two lives, the result of their spoken consent, pours out graces upon the couple because of the symbolism of the relation between Christ and His Church.

These graces are connected with the purpose for which marriage was instituted, that is for the good of the child, and to strengthen the conjugal tie: for the personal perfection of each and their complementary rôle in regard to each other. All these means effect a more intense life in Christ, an increase of sanctifying grace, and help to create an environment in which family life develops peacefully and happily. In such an environment the husband will grow in a wise discretion and the wife in quiet competence; both will learn an unselfish forbearance and an urge to help, and to back each other up, and they will even vie with each other as to who shall love the most and sacrifice the more cheerfully. To do this is to follow the example of Christ. Such grace harnesses all the natural instincts to the service of love and Society.

2. *Marriage is Indissoluble*

The Sacrament strengthens unity and increases the indissolubility of marriage.

a. Unity excludes polygamy. Neither party can have more than one wife or one husband. Polygamy is in opposition to the Christian purpose of marriage, namely the care of the child, while the position of the wife degenerates into that of a slave. The Old Testament does indeed record the polygamy of the Patriarchs, who were, notwithstanding, praised for their adherence to belief in one God whilst living among Pagans. But in this case God gave, as it were, a dispensation and adapted His decrees to the primitive conditions then ruling, which allowed, nevertheless, for the proper upbringing of the children. We must assume that the interests of the human race were at that time best served in this way.

Since then, however, the singleness of the marriage tie has been reinstated definitely and completely by Christ Himself. Divorce is forbidden. In his Epistle to the Romans St. Paul writes: "A married woman, for instance, is bound by law to her husband while he lives; if she is widowed, she is quit of her husband's claim on her; she will be held an adultress if she gives herself to another man during her husband's lifetime, but once he is dead, she is quit of his claim, and can give herself to another man without adultery."[87]

b. Indissolubility forbids Divorce

As a matter of fact, husband and wife can never validly break their marriage contract and marry afresh. This is in force for all marriages—baptized as well as unbaptized—although, of course, in the latter case the marriage is not a Sacrament. This intrinsic indissolubility arises from the very nature of marriage. Both husband and wife have consented to a lifelong alliance in fulfilment of a purpose set before them by God. This purpose is even more important than their personal happiness and is the purpose of the continua-

[87] Rom. 7, 2-3; comp. I Cor. 7, 2.

tion of the human race. It calls for the most propitious conditions possible, and demands a lasting and intimate union of husband and wife, which alone can create a genuine family atmosphere in the home, suitable for the upbringing of the child.

In general, to bring up children is a life's work, and even when the parents have ensured an independent position in society to their children, they themselves must continue to serve mankind by staying together and so working for the survival of the race as a whole. This strict law takes into account the happiness and well-being of everyone; it seeks to create a condition of things in which marriage itself is made unassailable for the sake of its lofty purpose. Whoever for one reason or another, however important, wishes to leave the decision as to the breaking off of a marriage to the actual husband and wife involved, immediately impairs the well-being of mankind as a whole: a situation is then created which no longer offers sufficient guarantees either for the safeguarding of the principal purpose of marriage, or for the mutual support and affection of husband and wife. The very conviction that marriage is a lasting state, and that two people begin together a definite vocation in life, gives love a safe and tranquil basis upon which to build. If the continuation of life together becomes a real impossibility, then a simple separation is the solution.

It is this intrinsic indissolubility which Christ explicitly re-established as a return to the original state of things. In Genesis God makes it quite clear that he created husband and wife for the increase of the human race.[88] In spite of the Pharisees, and the disciples, Christ reinstated the original institution of marriage, beginning from the basic principle: "What God then has joined, let not man put asunder."[89] St. Paul also takes this view in his Epistle to the Corinthians[90] and to the Romans.[91]

Such facts become even more conclusive when Marriage is regarded as a Sacrament, and as a symbol of Christ's fidelity to the Church—a fidelity enduring for all time. Two baptized persons are, of course, more closely united than the unbaptized can ever be, because their union is a symbol of the indissoluble tie between Christ and the Church, and from

[88] Gen. 1, 27.
[89] Matt. 19, 5-6. Mark 10, 1-12. Luke 16, 18.
[90] I Cor. 7, 10-12.
[91] Rom. 7, 2-3.

the very symbol they draw the grace which enables them to keep that tie loyally and lovingly.

Marriage can only be dissolved by God

God can dissolve marriage directly (Abraham-Agar);[92] He did it through Moses.[93] And, in the New Testament, He did it through Christ who gave this power to the Church. Christ entrusted to St. Peter and the Apostles the power to loose on earth whatever had need to be loosed.[94] All marriages over which the Church has no jurisdiction are, however, excluded; such, for instance, as the marriage of unbaptized persons. These can, in point of fact, never be dissolved. Furthermore, the Church declares that a marriage which has been sacramentally consecrated and consummated can never be dissolved. The Pope, however, has the power to dissolve a marriage between baptized persons which has never been consummated.

In his First Epistle to the Corinthians, St. Paul speaks of the case of unbaptized pagans who have contracted a valid marriage, and later one of the two is baptized. "If the unbelieving partner is for separating, let them separate in such a case the brother or the sister is under no compulsion. It is in a spirit of peace that God's call has come to us."[95] So here God gives what is known as the "Pauline Privilege", that is a privilege to the Christian partner for the good of his faith. If the unbaptized partner is willing, both are free. The purpose of this is to forward conversion to the Faith and to assist perseverance in it. For this privilege to be applicable, however, the following conditions must be fulfilled: there must exist a validly contracted marriage between two unbaptized persons; one of the two must then receive Baptism; the unbaptized partner must no longer wish to live with him or her. The Church can then give permission for the entering into of a new marriage, but only when the baptized partner actually marries again is the former marriage dissolved. Finally, for the same reasons, the Pope has the power to annul a validly contracted marriage between one who has been baptized outside the Catholic Church, and an unbaptized person. But when two people have been baptized outside the Catholic Church, and are validly married, the Church is

[92] Gen. 21. [93] Deut. 24, 1. [94] Matt. 16, 19. [95] I Cor. 7, 15.

powerless. In three cases only does the Church consider that She can, in the Name of God, dissolve a marriage for the sake of a higher spiritual good.

Outside these three, there is absolutely no case for dissolution: no Authority whatever with power to dissolve a marriage. A divorce granted by the Civil Authorities, for no matter what reason, can neither dissolve a marriage nor give any right whatsoever to contract a fresh one, even in the case of a Protestant marriage where the blessing of the Church was originally lacking. No purely human agreement, and no decision by any purely human Authority, can dissolve marriage: even a marriage between unbaptized persons, as already said, can never be dissolved.

As a matter of course, then, the Church condemns the following: free-love, any marriage-contract which ends automatically when the agreed time has passed; the trial-marriage; the platonic marriage, legally contracted, but with the right to obtain a divorce at any time by agreement; legal divorce in any form.

There may, however, be lawful reasons why a couple should cease to live together and ask for a separation. Such a reason would be the misconduct of one of the parties, or reasons such as a criminal and disgraceful life; great danger to the body or soul of one of the parties; cruelty, etc. But these only give the right to a temporary separation. In all these cases recourse must be had to the Parish Priest or to the Bishop. A married person may only abandon his or her home upon personal judgment, in a case where there is an urgently serious reason, or where delay would involve genuine danger. As soon as the reason for the separation has ceased, the normal way of life should be resumed immediately.

IV. HOW A CHRISTIAN MARRIAGE IS ENTERED INTO

1. *Free Will and Marriage*

Mankind has a general duty to see to the survival and continuation of the human race. The duty is clearly stated in the first chapter of Genesis, where God is shown as blessing both man and woman and saying to them: Increase and multiply. In point of fact, however, no one is individually bound by this duty, although in principle everyone should be ready to co-operate in the general aim. Since Christianity was first founded there has been an increasing realization of the meaning of virginity in connection with the general welfare of mankind.

In assuming the duties and the state of matrimony the human will has an important part to play. Once bound by the matrimonial state there is no freedom to behave precisely as one pleases: husband and wife bind themselves to enter into this union, bearing in mind the purpose for which it was originally instituted. But that does not alter the fact that everyone is free to decide whether he will marry or no, and whom he will marry. The Church, as well as the State and the actual individual, only benefit from happy marriages, in which the two partners get on well together and are mutually congenial. Generally speaking, the parties concerned know best what they have in common and whether they are likely to be happy. The young man and woman take upon themselves important duties for life: therefore free choice is theirs by right. Actually, the man and the woman administer this Sacrament to each other, for their spoken consent is the outward symbol of it. By saying "yes", the offer is accepted, and an equal offer made in return, which is accepted by the other party.

When two unbaptized people who are already married, are received into the Church, they receive at the same time the Sacrament of Matrimony; through the symbol of Baptism their former matrimonial consent stands for the union of Christ and His Church. No renewal of the marriage is required. But most probably the marriage of a baptized person with an unbaptized never ranks as a Sacrament, even should a dispensation have been obtained.

2. *Conditions for Marriage*

The Church has attached certain conditions to the solemnization of marriage.

a. It must be solemnized before the Parish Priest (or a priest authorized by him) and two witnesses. In the presence of the two witnesses, the Parish Priest, who must be present of his own free will, puts certain questions, to which the couple reply expressing their consent. This is necessary for the validity of the marriage. The usual form is as follows: "N, wilt thou take N here present, for thy lawful wife (husband) according to the Rite of our Holy Mother the Church?" The answer is, "I will". The bride is then given away to the bridegroom by her father or a friend. The man holds the woman's right hand in his right hand and plights his troth in the following words which he repeats after the priest: "I, N, take thee, N, to my wedded wife, to have and to hold from this day forward, for better, for worse, for richer, for poorer, in sickness and in health, till death do us part; and thereto I plight thee my troth." Then, loosing hands and joining them again, the bride repeats the same words, substituting husband for wife. They then take each other's right hand and the priest says, while making the sign of the cross: "I join you in holy matrimony, in the name of the Father and of the Son and of the Holy Ghost, Amen." With these words the Parish Priest testifies that the man and the woman have administered the Sacrament to each other. In danger of death, or if for some reason it is foreseen that neither the Parish Priest nor another priest authorized by him can be present within a month, a marriage contracted before two witnesses is valid.

b. None of the impediments to matrimony, which have been fixed by the Church, must exist. Not every man and woman are eligible to marry each other. There are certain relationships, and other matters, which are judged unfavourable for a lasting union, unlikely to produce healthy offspring or to ensure their satisfactory upbringing. The Church therefore has made certain regulations. Not all impediments debar to the same degree. Most of them render the marriage invalid: for instance, should a couple, between whom such an impediment exists, nevertheless contract the marriage, the whole ceremony is null and void. It might as well not have taken place.

Some impediments, on the contrary, merely forbid marriage. Should such a marriage nevertheless be contracted, then the marriage is valid, but the law of the Church has been infringed.

One cannot validly contract marriage with a non-baptized person; with a blood relation, and a relation-by-marriage within the forbidden degrees; with godparents, etc., etc. In some cases, however, the Church can dispense from these impediments.

c. Mixed marriages are forbidden by the Church. The danger of loss of faith, or of a cooling off in the faith, and the dangers for the Christian upbringing of the children, make the Church extremely strict and guarded in these matters, particularly as domestic happiness and the unity of the family frequently suffer severely under such circumstances. However, for serious reasons and to prevent a greater evil, or for the well-being of already existing children, She does usually grant a dispensation, when both parties are willing to give the necessary guarantee as to the Catholic upbringing of the children. Such a marriage is solemnized before the Parish Priest and two witnesses.

V. THE DUTIES OF MARRIED PEOPLE

In the encyclical of Pope Pius XI *Casti Connubii*, a triple blessing is assigned to marriage: the child, fidelity, and the Sacrament. At the same time, a triple error is denounced: birth-control, free-love and divorce. The Sacrament and divorce have already been dealt with.

1. Children are of inestimable value in relation to marriage; they are the natural outcome of it. The child unconsciously safeguards and increases the love of its parents. But the further question arises: how far is it the *duty* of married couples to bring as many children as possible into the world? Marriage is undoubtedly intended, among other things, to ensure the survival of the human race. On the other hand, there is no benefit to the child in the gift of life, if its parents cannot enable it to build up an adequate, independent existence in which it can serve God as it should and acquire its full spiritual and physical development. A good education is one of the principal means to this end.

Marriage, as we have already said, is intended to safeguard and perfect the mutual affection of husband and wife. A certain moderation in the married state is advisable to maintain the right balance of conjugal love. There may, for instance, on occasion arise a question of danger to the life of the wife. It is evident that the primary purpose of marriage itself, which is the family, may sometimes be frustrated by a too rapid increase in it; temporarily it has reached the limit of its expansion; for the normal growth and development of the existing children, no more are desirable for the moment.

Nevertheless it remains a difficult and delicate matter to judge rightly in such a case, and not, for purely selfish motives, to invent an emergency state of affairs which in reality is non-existent.

If such a situation has genuinely arisen, and there is no other solution, even so a couple are not free to make a frivolous appeal to the Providence of God and then proceed to act as they choose. God gave us reason precisely in order that His plan for Creation should be carried out in a responsible way. How then may a married couple, legitimately and for the moment only, avoid an increase of family? Continence is one way, but for this both grace and real love are necessary. It will not be found possible for everyone to embrace this method habitually and under all circumstances.

Any neomalthusian methods are unconditionally rejected by the Church. Since they are unnatural, She sees in them an attack on the essence of marriage itself. Periodical continence cannot, however, be called unnatural, and there is no direct offence against the laws of reproduction. This practice may or may not be justified: the justification depends upon the motive for which it is employed. If complete continence is either very difficult or impossible, and if there are not sufficient means to support any further additions to the family, then the exclusive use of the sterile periods may relieve the situation. Mere personal self-interest must never be taken as the criterion of conduct, but the welfare and happiness of the family itself. A Catholic should take the advice of his confessor.

There are dangers connected with this practice, and in such a delicate matter the motive is of the greatest importance. A mentality may easily arise which entirely excludes the idea of sacrifice, and turns married life into a mere calculated play of instinctive and wholly selfish satisfactions. Love itself is attacked, and the relationship gradually degenerates into something altogether unspiritual.

Anything approaching abortion the Church considers a grave crime, since She argues that God, who alone gives life, alone has the right to take it away. That is why man can under no circumstances renounce his own right to live, but on the contrary is even obliged to see that it is respected by others. It is for this reason also that the State has no right to kill any innocent human being. Self-defence may, of course, under certain circumstances lead to the killing of the attacker.

The unborn child is an innocent, living human being, and abortion is therefore direct murder. Even pity for the mother, who may be in serious danger of death, can not be shown in this way, since murder can never be justified. To try and safeguard the lives of both mother and child in every possible way, and with every known remedy, is of course the duty of the doctors. To perform some operation which is not direct abortion may also be allowed for really serious reasons. But, as St. Paul said, we should not do evil in order that good may come of it.[96] The much-vaunted case in which the murder of the child is necessary in order to save the life of the mother, does not in fact seem to occur according to the evidence of expert gynæcologists.

2. The fidelity which is promised by husband and wife before God has for its first object the unity of marriage, and therefore does not allow, in either thought or desire, any friendship to be entered into which could attack this essential union. The strict attitude which firmly rejects and condemns every sign or act of physical affection for another, is neither weakness nor jealousy, but is a direct result of this beautiful fidelity. Such virtue leads to a higher appreciation of real married love and is in itself the fruit of that love which is the basis of family life. It is that which makes family life in common possible, and gives the right positions to the husband and wife respectively.

If the husband is in a position of authority that is neither a privilege for him nor any slight to the wife. As to function, purpose, and spiritual dispositions, the two are absolutely equal; but every form of co-operation requires leadership of some sort, and, according to St. Paul anyway, this leadership belongs to the man. His leadership, however, only serves the interests of his wife and children, and takes its attitude and standard of behaviour from them. Usually the wife will know how to use her irresistible powers of persuasion, and her intuitive practical perception of a situation, in such a way that the husband will always say and order what is in the best interests of herself and the family.

That is why the Encyclical *Casti Connubii* is not in favour of the unlimited emancipation of woman, which would make her

[96] Rom. 3, 8.

free not only socio-economically but physiologically. A physiological emancipation which withdraws a woman from her duties as wife and mother, and in which she is free to act as she chooses, is entirely condemned. As regards economic emancipation, this gives her freedom in matters which then begin to take precedence of her care for husband and children, which is not good for the success of married life. She is tied to her family, and if she transfers all her interest to political or business affairs, the family is robbed to that extent of her help and guidance. Any overstressing of individual personality or dignity, and the rights which develop from them, are therefore also to be rejected. In marriage she is dependent upon her husband, and her own special and individual task has to be accomplished through that very dependency.

In the end it is only love, which is neither selfish nor seeks itself, which is able to build up life together into a genuinely happy Christian marriage.

§ 9. *Extreme Unction*

The Church, which by baptism brought into existence the child of God, and from then on has guided it through life, is also waiting to be present at the last hour of man. Helpless and, owing to his weakened condition, often incapable of bringing his mind to bear upon God, or to fix his will firmly upon his ultimate goal, maybe burdened with sin, the dying Catholic surrenders himself to the love and care of Mother Church. The Church succours him in his last decisive battle, and does all that is possible to ensure that he may awake—for ever—in the bright light of Heaven. It is at this moment that she offers him the Sacrament which initiates him into everlasting life. She tries to help him to enter into the agony and death of Christ, and finally to slip peacefully away from this life into the eternal grace and happiness of God.

I. EXTREME UNCTION AND DIVINE REVELATION

We read in the Epistle of St. James: "Is one of you sick? Let him send for the presbyters of the Church, and let them pray over him, anointing him with oil in the Lord's Name. Prayer offered in faith will restore the sick man, and the Lord will give him relief; if he is guilty of sins they will be pardoned. Confess your sins to one another, and pray for one another, for the healing of your souls."[97] The priests are to pray over the sick person and anoint him with oil in the Name of the Lord. This prayer and this anointing derive all their efficacy from Christ Himself. The healing of the invalid rests upon the basis of prayer, and Christ comforts him by means of the Unction, forgiving his sins. Thus encouragement and comfort and healing are all three brought about by prayers and unction. That which the "brother of the Lord" advised the Faithful to do, the Church now recognizes as a Sacrament.

There is no evidence in Holy Scripture that Christ Himself ever spoke of this desire to heal and comfort the sick, and to forgive men's sins by means of the anointing with holy oil. It is true that St. Mark tells us how Christ sent out His apostles, two by two, and gave them power over impure spirits; how they exorcised many devils, and anointed many sick people with oils, healing them. The whole emphasis, however, is upon the miraculous power of the healing: of any particular sign or token with which Christ connected this grace, there is no mention at all.

In the case of this Sacrament, apart from the Epistle of St. James, we depend upon the teaching of the Church which has received the mandate from Christ to preach and to expound the Gospel.

During the first four or five centuries of early Christianity, the anointing of the sick was undoubtedly spoken of; but the question arises whether we have to do in this case with an actual Sacrament? Most probably the sick were under the charge of people who had received the gift of healing direct from God, and in that case they would heal by means of that power. Sometimes they anointed the sick with holy oil, or gave it to them that they might anoint themselves. This quite common custom could scarcely, however, be reckoned as a Sacrament. In the more or less detailed descriptions of the illnesses and deaths of holy men and women, there is also no mention of any Sacramental anointing. So we are justified in coming to the conclusion that, so far as can be ascertained, the administration of this Sacrament during the first four centuries was by no means an universal practice; it is only occasionally mentioned here and there.

[97] James 5, 14-16.

The actual Epistle of St. James only became really known in the Church much later on, and possibly before that time, the explanation of the influential Origen as to the meaning of St. James' words still held good. He interpreted them in connection with the healing of the soul, that is the forgiveness of sins, and for this there was already a Sacrament. Further, the habit of being baptized upon one's deathbed was still very common.

The classical testimony to the tradition is contained in a letter as to Extreme Unction, written by Pope Innocent I (410-417) to Bishop Decentius. In this letter the Pope gives a detailed explanation of the text of St. James' Epistle. He states that the expressions used must undoubtedly be understood as referring to persons physically ill. He states that it is the custom in Rome to have this oil for the sick blessed by the Bishop; it may then be used by all the Faithful in physical need of it. But the liturgical imposition of hands accompanied by prayer and unction is reserved for the Bishop or the priest.

A public sinner, however, may not receive this unction since he is debarred from the Sacraments. From this testimony it would appear that the unction which we now call Extreme Unction was, after all, recognized as a Sacrament, although as yet the admonition of St. James "Is one of you sick? Let him send for the presbyters of the Church," had not been thoroughly absorbed by all the Faithful.

The concurrence of Greek Schismatics and the dissenting Eastern sects on this point is further evidence of the existence of such a Sacrament; they have all preserved the custom from the days when they still belonged to the one Apostolic Church. The Council of Trent also laid down formally the teaching of this early tradition. It gave an explanation of the precise terms of a Sacrament as defined in the Epistle of St. James: there is a symbol or outward sign, in this case prayer and the anointing with oil; both word and action indicating grace, strengthening-power, healing, and the forgiveness of sin.

The actual effects of grace are described by the apostle when he speaks of the healing and the comforting of the sick person and the forgiveness of sin. Grace proceeds from Christ, and it is He alone who has the power to join these gifts to external symbols and signs.

II. THE MODERN CONCEPTION AND PRACTICE OF THE CHURCH AS REGARDS EXTREME UNCTION

This Sacrament is intended to complete the Sacrament of Penance. It is for this reason that the Church requires that the sick person should be in a state of grace and have contrition for sin: should, however, the patient be incapable of making any confession, mortal sin is no bar to the reception of the Sacrament. This is the last anointing administered by the priest in the name of Christ, to bestow upon the dying man complete health of soul. It is in no case intended for those who are well and healthy. For them—even should they be called upon to face battle, the scaffold or martyrdom—the grace of Confirmation suffices.

1. *Extreme Unction effaces the consequences of sin which has been forgiven by the Sacrament of Penance*

Our expiation of sin, and of the punishments due to sin, sometimes means but little to us amidst all the distractions of the daily life which surround us. The penances imposed in the confessional are either carelessly performed or even altogether forgotten. Mortification, and the checking of natural impulses, is often omitted. The justice of God continues to demand atonement for sin but, at the end of life, His eternal mercy still offers us one final and wonderful opportunity for forgiveness. His love intervenes, as it were, for our welfare. He desires that the soul should enter Heaven at once. He wants to do away with all its hardness and rigidity, and where there is no resistance to the action of grace, the remission of all temporary punishments is achieved by means of this Sacrament. Even though the body has no strength left to perform for itself the purifications of prayer and fasting, yet the dying man may put his whole trust in this Sacramental Unction and prayer, which completes his own confession and contrition. And if he is no longer capable of making his confession, then, even so, it forgives his sins.

2. *Extreme Unction both consoles and strengthens the sick man*

This Sacrament conveys to those who are dying, an

unlimited trust in the mercy of God. Sometimes bodily weakness may cause a great despair and faint-heartedness in the soul; but this Unction serves to console, to keep hope alive, and to give the courage to repeat with the dying Christ: "Father, into Thy hands I commend my spirit." There arises resignation and patience to bear any sufferings, and peace in the disturbed heart. The temptations of the devil are nullified. Occasionally with this healing, strengthening and comforting of the soul there is also a noticeable corresponding revival of the physical powers.

3. *Extreme Unction is an immediate preparation for salvation*

By means of this Sacrament the sick person becomes like one who awaits the coming of His Lord so that he may open the door at once when he hears the expected knock.[98] For Extreme Unction reminds one strongly of the dying Christ, who through His death vanquished sin and entered into the glory of God. From that very death the Sacrament derives its power to overcome the devil, to remit sin and its consequences, and to confer the grace of salvation. This is the goal of our personal sanctification and of our personal redemption through Christ. Extreme Unction, as it were, rounds off all the other Sacraments and the effects produced by them, and completes the Christian life; it opens Heaven.

It is the outward sign of the following effects: The anointing of the senses, the sources of sin, with Holy Oil: feet, hands, eyes, nose and ears. From this the word Unction is derived. Oil heals wounds, soothes pain and strengthens physically. This unction is explicitly joined to forgiveness by the words of the priest: "By this holy anointing, and of His own most tender mercy, may the Lord forgive thee whatever thou hast committed by thy . . . (sight, hearing, etc.) Amen." Thus all the senses are once more orientated towards God. And so Christ has instituted this Sacrament for all who have reached the age of reason and who may be in danger of death either through sickness or old age. In order to gain the full effects of this spiritual healing one should not wait until the very last moment, or until immediate danger of death.

The priest administers this Sacrament once only in any

[98] Luke 12, 35.

illness which involves danger of death. Should there be recovery but the danger be renewed later, he can again be summoned.

III. THE LITURGY OF THE SACRAMENT OF EXTREME UNCTION

The priest who is called to a sick bed first hears the confession of the penitent if he is able to speak, and then gives him Holy Communion as Viaticum. As he enters the house, he says "Peace be to this house and to all who dwell in it."[99] He sprinkles the sick person and all present with Holy Water. The confiteor is then said, Absolution given, and after the words: "Behold the Lamb of God who takest away the sins of the world" he gives the patient Holy Eucharist saying: "Receive, Brother, the Viaticum of the Body of Our Lord Jesus Christ who will defend thee from the evil one and lead thee to eternal life, Amen." He gives him the crucifix to kiss and prays that the house may know the grace and the blessing of Christ. Another confiteor is then said and subsequently the priest anoints, one by one, the sick man's five senses, i.e. eyes, ears, nose, lips, hands and feet, while repeating, as quoted earlier: "By this holy anointing, and of His own most tender mercy, may the Lord forgive thee whatever thou hast committed by thy sight, hearing, smell, taste, speaking, touch."

Extreme Unction is followed by the Papal Blessing which confers a Plenary Indulgence at the moment of death.

Of anyone who has thus received these three Sacraments at the end of his life, people may well say "He is fully prepared: he is ready for heaven."

§ 10. *Sacramentals*

That which strikes one perhaps most about the Catholic Church is the great and varied use made of material things, to which are attached spiritual meanings or effects, and the attention which is given to exterior actions aiming at some supernatural result. To these things or actions which the Church uses in order to honour God and to obtain spiritual favours, has been given the name of Sacramentals. In this

[99] Matt. 10, 12.

word we easily recognize "Sacrament", which points at once to a similarity and a difference.

Sacramentals are exterior signs or symbols; they include Rites, Blessings, Ceremonies, Sacred Objects, etc., etc. They are tokens used in the service of some religious conception, which has grown out of a Christian tradition and has been accepted, either by the general approval or the formal institution of the appropriate ecclesiastical Authority. In this we recognize Our Lord's own way of procedure, for He so often spoke in parables and added to the effect of His action by picturesque symbols. He healed the man born blind with Unction, and in the case of the deaf-mute He put His fingers in his ears, then spat and touched his tongue. The Church is exceedingly mindful of Our Lord's words and behaviour, and seeks to copy His methods as far as possible in the worship of God, and in the sanctification and edification of others, and so strives, by means of blessings and consecrations of every kind, to make the grace of God all-pervading.

The power to bless belongs to God alone who, at the beginning of Time, blessed the whole of His Creation. As far back as the days of the Old Testament we see that He delegated this power to man: to begin with to the father of the family and to kings, and finally only to priests. In the New Testament we find Christ continually blessing both men and things: children, the Apostles, bread and fishes: and He handed on this same custom to His Apostles.[100] In our days, the Bishop still tells the newly ordained priest that he must bless, since everything which exists should be brought back to God and become obedient to the movement of His Holy Spirit. The Church has understood and grasped this teaching, and it is her desire that everything material should be subservient to the supernatural, so that nature and human culture are closely linked to the Kingdom of God. She therefore makes use of a book, which can be continually added to as necessary, called the Ritual, which contains formulas for many different Blessings and Consecrations. Although these do not convey grace to the soul by virtue of their own power, nevertheless they serve to produce certain spiritual effects. The difference between Sacraments and Sacramentals lies in the fact that Sacramentals do not convey any grace *of themselves*, but only through the suffrages and the merits of the

[100] Matt. 10, 12-13.

Church. It is the prayer of the Church which gives them their efficacy, and not the institution of the Rite by Christ as in the case of the Sacraments themselves. The Church prays, and God hears the prayer; the Church blesses, and God gives fruitfulness to the blessing. The Church consecrates, and God sanctifies the person or the objects which the Church has consecrated. This is not a case of sanctifying grace being conferred, but of spiritual benefits, which, however, presuppose union with God.

At the present time, two groups are to be distinguished among the Sacramentals: things and actions. These may again be divided into consecrations, blessings and exorcisms.

It is difficult to make a division which is at the same time complete and clear. Perhaps one may best consider the Sacramentals in connection with the actual Sacraments and in connection also with the daily occupations of the Faithful.

At Baptism there are many ceremonies which are elucidated and explained by the accompanying prayers: exorcism, imposition of hands, unction, signs of the cross, salt, a white garment, a burning candle, and again and again the blessing of God invoked. Holy water is also used; that water which has been consecrated through the exorcisms and prayers of the Church, and which has received the property of averting the influence of the devil and sanctifying and purifying the person upon whom it is sprinkled.

In connection with Holy Eucharist we find the consecration of all vessels and accessories which belong to the celebration of Mass: altar, vestments, chalice, paten, etc., etc. The Church building is solemnly consecrated by the Bishop to the service of God with many ceremonies and prayers, and the bells which are to call the Faithful to the worship of God are first sprinkled with Holy Water and anointed with oil and chrism. During Mass itself, Bread and Wine receive a blessing at the Offertory, while the Paschal Candle which is the image of Christ is surrounded with solemn benedictions and the singing of the Exultet. On Palm Sunday, the branches of palms, reminding us of Christ's triumphal entry into Jerusalem, are also sprinkled with Holy Water.

In connection with Confirmation, Ordination and Extreme Unction, both oil and chrism are used, first blessed by the Church, for the imparting of strength or the alleviation of suffering. During the wedding ceremony bride and bridegroom are blessed that they may persevere in mutual love and the fulfilment of God's will. At their invitation, the priest subsequently enters their new home with the words: "Peace be to this house and to all that dwell therein" and, sprinkling it with Holy Water, asks God to send His holy Angel to guard and keep its inhabitants. The wedding-ring is also blessed.

Everything connected with public worship, that is to say, fire, light, water, crucifixes, rosaries, scapulars and medals, receive a special blessing by means of prescribed prayers. It is possible in this way to sanctify the whole of daily life and to lift it completely on to the supernatural plane. For example there is the frequent sign of the cross with Holy Water, the ringing and recitation of the angelus three times a day, the blessing of children and of the sick, and the prayers for the departing soul.

In this Ritual, in which are set out the various blessings and formulas, we find that practically the whole sphere of human life is thus drawn into and included in the Kingdom of God. The Church formally blesses the fruits of the earth, as also fountains, ships, fields and sick animals; even bees are remembered. Modern life is also included by such blessings as those for railways, cars, aeroplanes, telephones and television. The desire of the Church is to sanctify everything, and to accept and use everything for the salvation of mankind. "Oh, God," She prays, "whose word sanctifies everything, extend Thy blessing over all creatures, through Christ Our Lord."

We have made use throughout this explanation of the terms blessing and consecration. There is a difference between them. A Blessing calls down God's help and power upon a person or a thing: for instance, upon a mother and child, or upon medicine and food. But Consecration elevates the person or thing to the level of a Sacramental: in other words, the person becomes dedicated to God and the thing permanently withdrawn from all profane use. Holy Water, for instance, must no longer be used as ordinary drinking water; a chalice has no part in a household meal; and a nun lives for the service of her Creator alone.

It is, however, of the greatest importance to bear in mind that these Rites, and the persons and things affected by them, do not of themselves possess any supernatural power, since their efficacy depends entirely upon the Church's suffrages offered to God for the intention that the persons using them may derive from them certain spiritual advantages. The Church is the Bride of Christ and her influence is at all times dependent upon His merits and upon His surrender to the Father. This influence can extend over both spiritual and temporal matters. In the spiritual sphere there is, for instance, the forgiveness of venial sin (provided contrition accompanies the Sacramental), the reception of various graces, the weakening of the power of the devil. God also grants temporal favours according to His holy will and the usefulness which they may possess for our eternal salvation.

Those who make use of Sacramentals, must be very careful to avoid all danger of mere superstition, of falling into a rut, of becoming automatic: The greatest safeguard is a strong sense of faith. The effect of Sacramentals is entirely dependent on our own personal attention and zeal in regard to them, on our belief in the efficacy of prayer, and our intention to grow more and more in the love of God by means of such symbols and dedication, also requires a personal appreciation phere which surrounds them, the atmosphere of holy rites, of symbols and dedication, also requires a personal appreciation on our part of its supernatural beauty, and at the same time a realization of the fact that by the use of these Sacramentals, which are only as it were situated at the edge of our faith, we hope to get to the very centre of Christianity, and to become more and more united to Christ.

PART III

LIFE IN THE CHURCH

CHAPTER XII

LITURGY AND THE LITURGICAL LIFE OF THE CHURCH

THE CHURCH IS A REAL COMMUNITY. It is not just a sum-total of all kinds of individual men, but an organic whole, living and growing; a reality composed of people working and praying together who, by the divine life of grace, have been born again in Baptism as new men into a supernatural unity. In a profound and complete sense the members of the Catholic Church belong to each other. They are even called collectively the Mystical *Body* of Christ, as we saw in the chapter upon the Communion of Saints.

This organic Community is oriented towards God, its final and only destiny. It lives and exists for the purpose of divine worship. There is no necessity to make any secret of such an aim, since it coincides with the true destiny of the whole of mankind. Whatever, therefore, the Church does or desires, she does and desires openly. She worships in public; anyone may be present, both to see and to hear. Divine worship has a certain definite form; the Church is visible to all, the community serves and worships its God with soul and body, faith and love, words and actions. It is in this way that we begin to speak of the *liturgy*, that is to say of the public service of God by the Church. (*Leitourgia* originally meant among the Greeks service under the State, which rich citizens were obliged to perform at their own expense.) In this public worship of God, the prayer and the activity of the separate members of the Church are combined into one living whole, just as the individuals themselves achieve a new uniformity within the living community of Christ.

The attention of His Church is especially concentrated upon the mystery of the Sacrament of the Altar. The most essential public act of worship is to be found in the Mass. It is in the atmosphere of the Eucharist that the prayer of the Church has always flourished the most, and it is in the Mass that She has attained to her richest splendour.

All that is most perfect and beautiful in human culture: dignity of word and gesture; delicacy of Ecclesiastical art; tasteful blending of colour; restrained but significant use of symbolism: all this was first introduced and applied to the public representation of this greatest gift of our religion. This definite form of worship, its particular style and the customs surrounding it, are called "liturgy". In the eighth and ninth centuries people began by understanding this word "liturgy" simply to mean the celebration of Holy Mass. As a general definition of liturgy, however, one might perhaps describe it as the public worship of God formally arranged by the Church.

The following pages will deal very particularly with the Sacrifice of the Mass, as the principal act of Christian worship. In doing so, we shall continually bear in mind that all these outer forms and symbols are only exterior trappings concealing the profound spiritual life hidden beneath them, and that our purpose is to discover that inner life, and to show in what rich and varied magnificence it finds its expression by means of what we shall hereafter call the *Liturgy of the Mass*. Liturgy presupposes liturgical life; this means that wherever the Church organizes public services and prayer, she has spiritual intentions and purposes, and that these are also aroused in those who join with her in her ceremonies and worship.

§ 1. *The Historical growth and development of the Liturgy of the Mass*

1. *The Last Supper*

At the Last Supper, when Jesus and the disciples were gathered together, He took bread, blessed it, broke it, and gave it to them, saying: "Take, eat, this is My Body." Then, taking the chalice, He offered thanks, and gave it to them, saying, "Drink, all of you, of this; for this is My Blood, of the New Testament, shed for many, to the remission of sins. And I tell you this, I shall not drink of this fruit of the vine again, until I drink it with you, new wine, in the Kingdom of my Father." And so they sang a hymn, and went out to Mount Olivet.

This is the Gospel account of the institution by Jesus Christ of the Sacrament of the Altar and the Sacrifice of the Mass. Here is the exterior setting in which the essential Sacrifice and Sacrament are enshrined. To begin with, Jesus placed the bread and the wine before Him, and then took them in His hand. This drew the attention of the apostles. By His prayer and His gesture He blessed the food and drink. He then proceeded to what we call the "consecration"; the bread and the wine were changed into His Body and His Blood by the words which He used. Immediately He gave this new bread and new wine to the apostles for them to consume.

In the previous chapter dealing with the Eucharist, we saw that by this short ceremony, Jesus, as it were, lifted His Sacrifice out of the rut of passing Time to preserve it for all future generations as a living memory, and indeed as an ever-recurring reality. The Sacrifice, and our union with Him who was sacrificed, is the deepest reality contained for us in Mass and Holy Communion. It is, however, a hidden reality which we cannot properly estimate except by faith. Our faith has to unearth the mystery, the hidden treasure, from beneath the exterior and perceptible symbols by which it is represented to us. But had we been present at the Last Supper, we should have found ourselves standing before the same exterior symbolism. That which Christ did could both be seen and heard; He too used external means by which to put His disciples in contact with spiritual reality. He used words and gestures in connection with the bread and the wine. There was the table; the platter upon which stood the bread; the cup; the blessing and the prayer of Christ; there was the reverent attitude of the apostles, the distribution of the food and drink, and the unforgettable peroration by which the ceremony was concluded. Referring to the eternal banquet in heaven, He said: "I shall not drink of this fruit of the vine again, until I drink it with you, new wine, in the Kingdom of My Father." And, when the hymn of praise had been sung, they left the chamber. The whole point of this event lies in the symbolism of the repast in connection with the coming Sacrifice of the Passion. The surroundings merely served to emphasize and illustrate these two things which together formed a living whole. Bread and wine were taken and set aside by Christ, and then offered to His Father accompanied by prayer. From material food and drink they were turned, by the power of His word, into something filled with spiritual and divine vitality; and at the same time became a timeless Sacrifice in the hands of the High Priest who, with His own Body and Blood, offered to God the whole human race mystically united to Himself. Finally, this bond between the Mass and the Christ-Sacrifice is wonderfully confirmed and strengthened by Holy Communion (a marvellous union such as exists between food and the body) and the distribution of this sublime offering to all who wish to participate as closely as possible in the Sacrifice. A prayer of thanksgiving here also closes the ceremony.

2. *Apostolic Days*

The Apostolic days were characterized by a gradual liberation of Christianity from the narrow bonds of Jewish sentiment. The Church had not yet been accepted as a part of general public life. Christians still had to be careful and to reckon with all kinds of spiritual and political obstructions from both the people and those in Authority. Worship could not as yet be performed openly as was its due: much still had to be relegated to the limited circle of living-rooms and inconspicuous parlours. The prayer, public as far as possible, took place in the Jewish temple or synagogue. As yet no Christian churches could be built and preaching for the most part took place in streets and city squares.

In the Acts of the Apostles in which St. Luke gives us a vivid picture of the early Christian community, we cannot fail to notice that Our Lord's: "Do this for a commemoration of Me" had been thoroughly understood by the Apostles. Men did *"it"* and evidently considered it as something very precious and intimate. They did not parade it before the inquisitive eyes of ill-disposed outsiders. "The breaking of bread"—the somewhat neutral term purposely employed in speaking of it—could not, needless to say, take place in the synagogue in the same way as the public prayer. Instead it took place in the home of any disciple who had accommodation for it. It was not spoken of abroad. It was done in silence, in an atmosphere of intimate communal solidarity. As regards the exterior ritual used, nothing has come down to us with any certainty, but we may take it for granted that it did not greatly differ from the procedure at the Last Supper.

Only after the Church had stretched far beyond the borders of Palestine do we come to hear more of it.

In an Epistle written by the Apostle Paul to the inhabitants of Corinth, he describes and condemns some excesses which had occurred at the "Lord's Supper". From this description we may infer that, in addition to strong belief in the actual Mystery, a development had occurred in the exterior form of the ceremony. "And when you assemble together, there is no opportunity to eat a supper of the Lord; each comer hastens to eat the supper he has brought for himself, so that one man goes hungry, while another has drunk deep. Have you no homes to eat and drink in, that you should show contempt to God's Church and shame the poor? Praise you? There is no room for praise here."

This is followed by an explanation of the meaning of the Last Supper, and how the secret of this Sacrament was imparted to Paul by the Lord. The conduct of the Corinthians is then censured in contrast with Its divine origin. "So, brethren," concludes the Apostle, "when you assemble to eat together, wait for one another; those who are hungry had best eat at home, for fear that your meeting should bring you condemnation. The other questions I will settle when I come."[1]

It is evident from this that the Lord's Supper—at least at Corinth—had become confused with the usual daily meal. Respect for it, even merely exterior respect, had suffered, and Paul refers them back to the origin of the mystery and its true significance in order to bring them to a realization of their lack of respect, and to persuade them to revert once more to a dignified and Christian performance of the Rite.

From all the evidence it is obvious that the feature of a repast had been preserved. Prayers no doubt were still offered as taught by the apostles, but the holy and mysterious atmosphere of the Last Supper had evidently been submerged in the noise and profanation of large and luxurious parties. Everyone was welcome and each brought his own food with him. Differences became noticeable between rich and poor, and more and more the borderline between communion with the Body and Blood of our Lord, and an ordinary profane supper-party was being overstepped. The religious form of the *liturgy* was increasingly threatened by the clamour and laxity of unrestrained feasting and sociability.

In the beginning the intention was evidently to associate the memory of the Last Supper with philanthropy towards the poor. There was an attempt to unite physical and spiritual food. The word "agapes" began to be used, i.e. the brotherly feasts of the early Christians which the poor were charitably allowed to join. At these they received from God and His Church not only the divine gift of the Eucharist, but also took part with their fellow-Christians in material gifts of food and drink. Those who were

[1] I Cor. 11, 20, 34.

able to share their good fortune with the less fortunate had thus an opportunity of genuinely associating themselves with the Sacrifice by pressing offerings from their own wealth into the service of Christian benevolence. The Sacramental Sacrifice and ordinary daily life were thus united in one common action. It was not to this that St. Paul was opposed, but to the lamentable lack of respect shown by the Corinthians in their behaviour during the Rite. Had their practice continued unchecked, the whole thing would have degenerated in the end into the mere enjoyment of an ordinary good meal with no spiritual significance whatever attached to it.

At what point of the ceremony did the charitable relief of the poor occur? It goes without saying that it was before the Consecration, at the moment when the bread and wine were made ready by the celebrant. In this way, the community could join with him by bringing in their gifts for the needy. The Mystery had so far not been celebrated. In apostolic days the supper, properly speaking, almost certainly began immediately after the faithful had joined with the priest in the "offertory"; this meal was of a perfectly normal description yet full of the atmosphere of brotherly love and of the symbolism of the spiritual repast which was to follow. At the Last Supper also the institution of the Eucharist was preceded by an ordinary meal.

Later on the two elements, sacred and profane, were again separated from each other, especially with a view to eliminating the excesses indicated by the Apostle Paul; thus the celebration of the Sacred Rite gradually regained its wholly mystic and symbolical character. Respect for it thus reflourished, and with this respect the exterior setting which surrounded it began to receive a renewed and greater attention.

3. *The First Centuries after the Apostles*

From the earliest Christian documents it would appear that only the general procedure and the prayers were fixed and that, as regards the rest, ample latitude was allowed for improvization. If one pauses to think for a moment of the frequency of the *Charismata* in those days, (that is to say of exceptional gifts and graces granted by God to certain individuals, among them the gift of prophecy), this latitude was not surprising. The prayers to be said before and after the meal, which we find set out in the book named the *Didache*, could be extended at will. In regard to the prayers of the Mass this was also the custom. Only when the *Charismata* began to be less frequently conferred, were certain precautionary measures adopted. The Faith had to remain both sound and pure, and when the Holy Ghost spoke less often by the mouth of His prophets, a certain formalization in writing became necessary. Recognized formulae, which often held rich memories of persons and events, were handed down from generation to generation; certain familiar expressions and turns of phrase recurred in every fresh rendering in an ever-growing variety.

At the commencement of the third century during the life of the great Ecclesiastical writer Origen who was responsible for committing many prayers to paper, we shall find also the oldest manuscript of the Liturgy of the Mass. In the *Apostolic Tradition* of Hippolytus of Rome, there is, in addition to the liturgy of several other Sacraments, an arrangement of the prayers for the Sacrifice of the Mass. It is a remarkable fact that the prayers which surrounded the actual Consecration, even then contained the same thoughts, and even the same words, as those to be found in our present-day prayers from the beginning of the Preface, up to and following the Paternoster. This appears to be the original core of the Liturgy of the Mass, round which all the other prayers and ceremonies have gradually been grouped.

Each Christian Community celebrated the Lord's Supper and the memory of His Passion, in its own way. One copied from the other; one extended the celebration on account of some fundamental necessity; fellow-Christians arrived from other cities and were entertained as guests; letters were exchanged; and all were animated by one and the same spirit. Thus there appeared different Liturgies of the Mass, which, however, breathed the same life and showed many features in common.

In the district surrounding important cities such as Rome, Antioch, Alexandria and Milan, there arose definite spheres of influence which gradually became responsible for the liturgy of their part of the country. In this sense, mention is sometimes made of liturgical Ecclesiastical provinces.

After the first excesses, a deep realization of the wonderfulness of the Mass began to develop. The hidden, and even sometimes underground, character of the actual ceremony undoubtedly contributed to this, but we must never underestimate the pervading consciousness of the early Christians of the treasure which they possessed in this divine mystery. Their admiration for it grew deeper, their respect increased, and they began to look round for means of expressing their religious emotions. However, they were obliged to keep all this secret from the gentiles, and others who might be ill-disposed. They had no intention of casting their pearls before swine. So they came to use cautious phrases with hidden meanings such as *eucharistia* (thanksgiving) and *mysterium fidei* (secret of the Faith), and in general they shrank from any distinct references to the Mass. Even to-day we find the words *mysterium fidei* coming very close to the actual words of consecration, as a sort of warning to the Faithful, full of meaning to the initiated: "Now," they seem to say, "we have come to the heart of the secret of our Belief: this is what we are really gathered together here for."

All that has remained to us of those first days in pictures or representations is only a vague and elusive symbolism. Bread and chalice were never depicted, but allusion was made to certain events of the Old Covenant which, according to the primitive Christian translation of the Bible, pointed to the Eucharist. In addition certain parables of Christ and certain miracles, such as the multiplication of the loaves, were depicted. More direct language was purposely avoided. Even in private circles careful wording was used, and *éclat* of any sort was scrupulously shunned. This continued until the Edict of Toleration of Constantine and Licinius (313) was agreed upon and published at Milan, and Christianity was at last able to flourish and expand, even exteriorly, in full freedom. Now there was plenty of space in which to house the precious Eucharistic possessions and treasures of the Church; richly ornamented shrines and tabernacles, in which beauty and art had full play, and in the surroundings of which the Church could at last use all the ingenuity of magnificent liturgical forms to express its deep love. The mutual influence of the various Christian communities continued to increase, in spite of the absence of any rigid liturgical regulations. Rome became more and more the Spiritual centre of the whole, and during the following centuries the Liturgy of Rome grew to be the prescribed form in many isolated districts by which the Rite of the Last Supper and the Sacrifice of Christ was brought to the people.

4. *The Roman Liturgy*

At the beginning, the Roman Liturgy was no more than one among many. Generally speaking, two groups of liturgies were to be distinguished: the Eastern and the Western. To the Eastern belonged the Greco-Alexandrine, the Coptic, the Syrian-Palestine or Antioch-Jerusalem, the Byzantine, the Armenian, the West-Syrian and the East-Syrian Rites. The Western group included: The Gallican, the Mozarabic, the Celtic, the Ambrosian and the Roman. From the fourth century onwards—that is to say from the century in which the Church was officially recognized—all these various liturgies developed along their own lines, and only gradually did the Liturgy of Rome and middle Italy, the Roman Liturgy properly so called, become predominant. For some time large districts in Western-Europe still followed the Gallican Rite, which certainly influenced the Roman. From the ninth to eleventh centuries the position in the East became more stabilized, and at the same time influenced by Rome, there was also a tendency in the West towards more unity in the liturgy. Between the eleventh and the sixteenth centuries there still remained local differences, but the Roman Rite steadily gained ground. This predominance continued, and in all the new missionary countries it was the Roman Liturgy which was introduced. Not only did it reach West and South Europe, but also Eastern Asia with its many groups of islands, Australia and the North and South-Americas.

§ 2. *The structure and meaning of the present-day Roman Liturgy of the Mass*

In the following pages we shall try to see in precisely what form the present Roman Liturgy, which has been adopted by the greater part of the Church including our own country, is presented, and what meaning it has for us. Our first consideration will be the actual place of its setting; and our second the priest, as liturgist, or minister of the liturgy. We will then consider the different Sacred Vessels used, and all the other altar requisites, each of which has its own particular significance; and finally we shall try to get some insight into the way in which this Sacrifice of the Mass is celebrated, and how best we ourselves may enter into the spirit of the Church.

A. Church Buildings

We have already drawn attention to the way in which, in apostolic days, the "breaking of bread" was celebrated by the Faithful in a place set apart, usually in the house of one of the disciples. The first publicly recognized churches to be built were called *Basilica*: large buildings which consisted of three parts: the courtyard, destined for the catechumens and the penitents; the nave, in which the Faithful were seated; and the sanctuary, for the priests and the servers. The sanctuary was usually partitioned off by a semi-circular apse behind the altar. Of these divisions only traces are to be found in our modern church buildings. The courtyard has shrunk to the size of a small porch or entrance hall, and the apse is in general far less noticeable than in former days.

The word *Church* is derived from the Greek word *kuriakon* which signifies the House of the Lord.

As in the case of Church-dignitaries, there is also a sort of hierarchical order in the different Catholic church-buildings. There is one church only named *papal,* the Basilica of St. John Lateran in Rome, which is regarded as the mother-church of Christians all over the world. That is why the anniversary of the consecration-day of that church (all churches are consecrated or blessed by a bishop before being used), the 9th of November, is celebrated in all Catholic churches. In the same way each diocese has its cathedral-church, usually called cathedral for short, the name being derived from the episcopal chair or *cathedra* which is found in such churches on the right-hand side of the altar. In England there are many beautiful pre-Reformation cathedrals, as well as the more modern examples such as Westminster, Liverpool, Birmingham, etc., etc.

Most of the churches in towns and villages are simple parish-churches, which means churches meant for the use of the Catholics of the districts, who form a small community under their *parochus* or priest. The parish-church is the church in which this community assists at the celebration of Mass, receives the Sacraments, and hears the preaching of the Word of God.

In addition there are also *rectorial* churches, which are under the direction of a rector, and often serve as a chapel-of-ease to some large parish; *public churches,* which have been established for a distinct group of persons, but are open to the public for all the principal divine services; *semi-public churches or chapels,* which have been built for some special community or congregation (for instance a monastic order) and are only open to the public by courtesy; and *private chapels* which have been established in a private house for the use of some particular family.

After this brief description, let us now suppose that we are entering a church. It has been built (if possible) with its frontage (that is to say the sanctuary-end for the use of the priests) facing towards the East so that, when facing the altar, one has the north on the left and the south on the right. When a church has been built according to this plan the symbolism, with which we shall deal later on, is appreciated at its best. Normally a church has at least three annexes: the sacristy, the room in which the priest vests for the divine service, and in which the vestments and furnishings of the altar are kept; the Baptistry, on the north side (that is at the back of the church) where the font is placed; the tower, which is a landmark for the countryside, indicating the presence of the House of God, and from which the bells call the Faithful to worship.

In the church itself the first thing which strikes the eye is the *altar*, which is always given the most prominent place. It is at this altar that Mass is celebrated. The high altar stands directly in the centre of the sanctuary end of the church, whilst on each side, and even sometimes down the aisle of the church, smaller altars are placed, in case several priests wish to celebrate Mass at the same time. The shape of the altar roughly resembles that of a table, in memory of the Last Supper. In the middle of the table-part of the altar, upon which Mass is celebrated, an altar stone has been slightly sunk into it; this contains the relic of some martyr, in remembrance of the days when Holy Mass was said upon their graves.

During the celebration of Holy Mass the priest frequently venerates this altar-stone. The top, or table part, of the altar, is covered with three linen cloths.

In general, the sanctuary is somewhat higher than the remainder of the church. One usually ascends three steps in order to stand before the altar itself. This is to symbolize the ascent to Mount Calvary, which again is more clearly indicated by the crucifix, which is placed directly above the altar. Beneath the crucifix, and resting upon the altar itself, we shall find the tabernacle. In this the Blessed Sacrament is reserved, and upon the top of the tabernacle there is what is called the throne, a ledge or shelf where the Blessed Sacrament may be exposed to the view of the people. The respect felt for this tabernacle and its Divine Inhabitant, finds its symbolical expression in the oil lamp, which burns continually before the altar day and night.

Turning away from the altar and walking down the church, we shall first come to the altar-rails, long narrow rails at which the Faithful receive Holy Communion during Mass. During this time the rails are covered with a white linen cloth. Towards the middle of the church, on one side of the rails, we shall next observe the pulpit, from which the Word of God is preached to the congregation. Usually in the aisles, or down the sides of the church, are placed several confessionals, to which people go for the Sacrament of Confession. As a rule, the various priests assigned to the church have each their own confessional outside which is placed the name, so that a penitent knows to whom he or she is going. The Stations of the Cross are often to be found either painted or carved upon the walls of churches: that is to say, fourteen representations of the Passion and Death of Our Lord. These representations are a constant reminder to the Faithful of the Crucifixion and an invitation to meditate upon it, and are most suitably placed in church-buildings in which it is daily commemorated in the Holy Sacrifice of the Mass. To "make" the Stations of the Cross one passes along the fourteen pictures or carvings, pausing to pray and meditate before each.

Even more highly ornamental statues and pictures are frequently to be found in Catholic churches. According to some people this practice may be regarded as exaggerated, but, apart from the actual good or bad taste of the art itself, there is no objection to the representation of saints being placed in churches. The saints are a part of the Church itself, and belong to our community. They too, like ourselves, are "of Christ", and indeed understood better than we during their lifetime and at the hour of their death, the meaning of Christ's Sacrifice.

B. *The part of the Priest in the Liturgy of the Mass*

In the chapter upon the Sacrament of Ordination we pointed out that the priest continues, as it were, Christ's own work, by preaching, by administering the Sacraments, and especially by the celebration of Holy Mass. That is his principal function. One might even say, with St. Thomas Aquinas, that the priest is only concerned with these two matters:

1. The oft-repeated realization of the Sacrament of the altar.

2. The preparation of the Faithful, by means of preaching, and the administration of the other Sacraments, for the par-

ticipation in the great Sacrament of the Altar. Just as, in the life of Christ, the Sacrifice upon the Cross was of predominant importance, so in the life of the Church of Christ, the Sacrifice of the Mass takes the first place. During the offering of the Holy Sacrifice we see a Catholic priest engaged in his principal task. At no moment does he enter more completely and truly into the priesthood of Christ; nowhere else shall we find him so identified with Christ Himself.

In order to help us as far as possible to forget his own personal individuality the priest appears during Mass in special vestments which symbolize his holy function.

These vestments are strongly reminiscent of the holiday attire of the ancient Romans. The Church has adopted this form of attire, supplementing and amplifying it, and at the same time attaching to it a symbolical significance.

The normal attire of the priest is the Soutane: for His Holiness the Pope this is white, for cardinals red, for bishops purple, and for ordinary priests black.

When the priest goes to vest for Mass in the Sacristy, he first washes his hands, then puts upon his shoulders an *amice*. The amice is a white linen cloth, and is a reminder of the bandage placed over the eyes of Christ, serving at the same time as a symbol of repentance and trust.

The *alb* next worn is a long linen garment, falling to the feet.

The *girdle* is a white cord securing the alb round the waist; it may also be worn of the same colour as the vestment of the day.

The *maniple*, in origin a handkerchief, is attached below the elbow of the left arm, the colour and material matching those of the chasuble.

The *stole* is also of the same colour and material. The priest wears the stole crossways over the shoulder as a sign of his duty and his dignity.

The *chasuble* is the top garment which is worn over all the rest. It is usually made of silk, having a column down the front, and a cross upon the back.

In order to distinguish the particular character of the feast or otherwise which is being celebrated at Mass, the Church makes use of various colours, which we have already mentioned as *liturgical colours*. These different colours are seen in the chasuble, stole and maniple, and also in the veil spread over the chalice. Six different colours are used: white, red, purple, green, black and rose-colour.

White is a token of joy and chastity, and is used on the days when the joyful mysteries of our Faith are celebrated, as also on the Feasts of the Blessed Trinity, Our Lady, Confessors, Saints (other than those who suffered martyrdom) and virgins.

Red, the colour of fire and blood, is employed as a symbol of love. It is used at the Feast of Whitsun, in Masses of the Holy Ghost, and on the Feasts of the Precious Blood, the Holy Cross, and of martyrs.

Purple may be regarded as a softer shade of red, and is therefore used for the more sorrowful seasons and feasts in a spirit of penance. During Advent, for instance, when we are preparing ourselves for Christmas, or in Lent as a preparation for Easter; and on the eves, or vigils, of great festivals, this colour is therefore worn.

Green is a quiet shade suggesting tranquillity and hope, and expresses the feeling of the Church at those seasons when no great Feasts are to be celebrated, such as from the Octave of the Epiphany up to Septuagesima Sunday, and again from the Octave of Whitsun (Trinity Sunday) until Advent.

Black is used as a symbol of mourning on Good Friday in memory of the Crucifixion, and in Masses for the deceased.

A colour only occasionally met with during the liturgical year is rose-pink, a happier and more festive tone of purple. This is employed on the Sundays half-way through Advent and Lent (that is Gaudete and Laetare Sundays) expressing a sober joy at the thought of the approaching Feasts of Christmas and Easter.

C. *Requisites for the celebration of Mass*

The priest, vested as already described, mounts to the altar in order to celebrate Holy Mass. He is usually preceded by two *acolytes,* who assist him during the celebration, and who answer the prayers in the name of the people.

Upon the altar, on either side of the tabernacle, are candlesticks with *candles,* of which two at least must be burning. Originally these candles were genuinely intended to light the priest as he read the prayers, but at the present time their value has become almost entirely symbolical. They burn to the very end in the service of God, thus typifying Christ the light of the world and the faithful Christian.

On the right-hand side of the altar is placed the missal or Mass book containing all the prayers to be used. In the middle of the altar, and to the right and left sides of it, standing upright against the back, are the altar cards, upon which are printed those prayers which are most commonly used during the Mass, the object being to aid the priest's memory, should it fail at any time during the celebration.

Usually speaking, the priest carries the *chalice* with him to the altar. In this chalice he consecrates the wine; it is made of gold or silver, gilded inside, and is consecrated by a bishop before being used. Over the top of the cup is spread the purificator, a small length of white linen, with which the chalice is wiped. The chalice is then covered with a paten, a small dish made of the same metal as the chalice, and gilded at least on the inner side. Upon this little paten the Host is placed, and over it the pall, a small square of white linen, slightly stiffened, with which the chalice is covered during the time when the paten is lying upon the altar. Finally, over the whole, is placed the chalice-veil of silk of the same colour as the chasuble of the priest. In the burse, a silk case again of the same colour, the corporal lies folded, a white linen square which, at the commencement of Mass, is spread upon the centre of the altar, and upon which the chalice and the Host then stand during the celebration.

Wine and water are put ready in glass cruets upon a small table, called a credence, standing at the Epistle side of the altar.

The Hosts which are left over after the communion of the Faithful are kept in the ciborium, which is put away in the tabernacle. Except during the hours of divine service, the tabernacle is always kept locked.

D. *The Liturgy of the prayers of the Mass*

No one will be surprised to find that, during the course of the ages, the Church has surrounded this central ceremony of the Sacrifice of the Mass with all its most beautiful prayers. The life of the Church indeed flows out to us here in the richest liturgy. In the structure of the Mass there is, as it were, a certain unaltering kernel or heart of prayer which is used every day; this is called the Common of the Mass. Round this Common are grouped those variable prayers which change according to the seasons of the ecclesiastical year and the feasts being celebrated, as to which a short explanation will be given in the following pages.

1. If we turn in the missal to the prayers of the Common of the Mass we shall observe that the Liturgy of the Mass is divided into different parts. The principal parts are the Offertory, the Consecration and the Communion. At the beginning of this chapter, when describing the last Supper of Christ and His disciples, we pointed out that in the first institution of the great Sacrifice of the Mass these three principal parts were also present.

The offertory is the preparation of the offerings, which are withdrawn from profane use and reserved for the service of God. In the accompanying prayers God's blessing is asked upon the offering or sacrifice. This offertory is still preceded by what is known as the Mass of the Catechumens, a collection of prayers and collects with which Mass commences, and which in some liturgies is ended by the Creed, while in other liturgies the Creed is not said, and this introduction to the Mass is ended by the reading of the portion of the Gospel for the particular day or feast.

The priest commences Mass by prayers said at the foot of the altar-steps in which he gives expression to his joy and at the same time to his consciousness of human guilt (the confiteor). After these the Introit is said at the right-hand side of the altar, and then a short prayer for mercy before the crucifix, which is again followed by the *Gloria in excelis Deo* or hymn of praise. These prayers are concluded by one or more of the variable prayers, after which the priest proceeds to the reading of the Epistle, and then, from the left-hand side of the altar, to the reading of the Gospel for the day or feast. This part of the Mass is concluded by the Creed.

With the *offertory* begins the Mass of the Faithful, a name which recalls historic memories of the early days of Christianity when the custom was for the Catechumens to be admitted only to the first part of the Mass. The meaning of the offertory has already been discussed. Bread and wine are offered to God, priest and Faithful are dedicated to Him; the priest washes his fingers (because, originally, at this point he accepted the gifts for the poor) and the low, whispered prayers end in an audible prayer of thanksgiving (the *preface*) and the *Sanctus*.

At this point the second, and at the same time most ancient part of the Mass has begun—the Canon. Before and after the consecration proper, some silent prayers are said, during which both living and dead are commemorated, and the great saints of the first Christian era invoked. Most likely on account of the length of the list of names of saints these prayers were summarized and named simply the *canon* (list) of the Mass. At the moment of consecration itself, the culminating point of the whole ceremony, the same words are used by the celebrant as those spoken by Our Lord at the Last Supper over the bread and the wine. By these words the offerings are changed into His Body and Blood. Elevated by the priest they are presented for the adoration of the people.

With the saying of the *Pater Noster* (Lord's Prayer) the third and most important part of the Mass is commenced: the *Communion*. The Host is broken over the chalice, and for the remission of sins Christ is invoked as the "Lamb of God, who takest away the sins of the world". Deeply inclining before the centre of the altar, the priest says a humble prayer for peace and happiness, then bows low over the sacred elements and himself communicates before administering Holy Communion to the Faithful. The Hosts left over are again locked away in the tabernacle, after which follow the prayers of the thanksgiving. With the final words: "Ite, missa est" "Depart the Mass is over" the priest draws the attention of the people to the fact that the ceremony is ended. He then reads (standing on the left-hand side of the altar) the prologue to the Gospel of St. John, and descends the altar-steps, accompanied by his acolytes.

2. The essential and deepest intention of the variable prayers of the Mass is to call before our mind the Person, the life and the doctrine of Christ. In the course of the Ecclesiastical year we see this life and this doctrine, slowly growing and taking shape before our eyes through the prayers, the Epistles and the Gospels of the liturgy of the Mass. Beginning with the first day of the Ecclesiastical year (the fourth Sunday before Christmas) and going on to its last day (Trinity Sunday) the sequence is complete.

During the period of Advent, that is the four weeks before the feast of Christmas, the Church enters, by all its varying prayers, into the expectations of the Jewish people, who waited so longingly for the coming of the Messiah. In company with this great people and its great prophets, she considers how mankind still looks for its Redeemer, who is to save and to raise it from its misery. Once more the voice of John the Baptist sounds through the wilderness of our world, bidding us "prepare the way of the Lord, straighten out His paths". By means of prayers and hymns the prophets inflame us with their ardent desires, and reveal to us their visions, in which the Redeemer appears among us, who still dwell "in darkness and the shadow of death", from out of the depths of the Wisdom and the Love of God. This is the Church in a quiet, almost austere mood, for He who is coming is not to reign as an earthly king, but only in the secret of our souls, whose very sins make His advent so vitally necessary. Purple, the colour of repentance, dominates; for only by repentance and penance can the way be prepared.

With joy mingled with awe, the Church commemorates in three successive Masses on Christmas Day the Incarnation of the Son of God. The first is in a tone of respectful gladness; the second of still slightly subdued joy; and the last filled with an unconcealed and jubilant happiness. By means of the liturgy we listen to the simple story of the shepherds, and then to the sublime language in which St. John the Evangelist interprets to us the mystery of this divine secret. The life of Christ upon earth has commenced for us and will, during the coming months, once more pass slowly before our eyes. At first, in the Sundays after Christmas and the Epiphany, we follow His childhood; then His public life and His preaching; finally His journeys and His miracles. Once more we listen to His words as He taught the people; they are stimulating, almost revolutionary, yet at the same time tranquil and full of authority. His gestures are mild; His hands are raised in blessing and in prayer; they are filled with graces both for souls and bodies; wine for a freely bestowed joy; healing for our wounds; forgiveness for our sins.

But after this there appear the forerunners of a slowly growing threat. A new period of the Ecclesiastical year is ushered in upon Septuagesima Sunday, the seventieth day before Easter. By His suffering and death the Redeemer is to give back to man his lost supernatural life and happiness. There are only two more Sundays, Sexagesima and Quinquagesima, and the solemn season of Lent will be upon us: a period of forty days during which we recall to mind, helped by the prayers of the Church, that it was our sins which were the cause of the Passion and Crucifixion of Christ.

On the first day of Lent, Ash Wednesday, the sign of the cross is made upon the foreheads of all the Faithful as a symbol of the insecurity of human life ("Remember, Man, that thou art dust, and unto dust thou shalt return") so that we may be stirred to free ourselves from the shackles of Time in the fight against sin, and to bring all our desire to bear upon heaven and the supernatural life. After this there follows a period of retreat and mortification. Adults, unless prevented by old age, sickness, or heavy manual labour, perform a fast, and even children are taught to deny themselves some pleasure or luxury during these days. When we assist at Mass during Lent, we learn from the Epistle (taken from the Old Testament or one of the Epistles or the Acts of the Apostles) of the worldliness and wickedness of the Chosen People who were awaiting their Redemption. The Gospels tell us how the enemies of Christ gradually drew the circle of their net closer and closer around Him. Christ was well aware of this, but He quietly chose His own hour. He did not evade the Passion, but when the appointed time for it came He was eager to encounter and challenge it. His purpose in coming to earth was to suffer and to die. In the last week before Easter, that is during Holy Week, we commemorate with the Church by means of the Liturgy of the Mass, the tragic, human and divine secret of this appalling Passion and lonely death. Especially in the last three days, the Church completely loses herself in this deeply loved and adorable mystery.

In sober and appropriate ceremonies, with infinite variety of prayers, hymns and colours, the Church desires to bring again before us the gripping drama which was once enacted in Jerusalem. In subdued accents she tells us of the terrible suffering which preceded her own birth, and of the Man of Sorrows, who Himself became the Seed, which, falling into the earth, died, in order that it might bear abundant fruit. For this death is no final passing away, there is nothing definite and conclusive about it. It rises above all our earthly folly through the absolute certainty that He who is losing His life, is finding life again for us. Even at the most tragic moment, the moment of deepest mourning, this certainty never fails. Hidden in the darkness, the light lies dormant. With the ceremonies of Holy Saturday, this certainty breaks triumphantly through the gloom, as the new fire is struck from out of the hard stone, and as the new light is carried into the church, and from there passed on to relight all the lamps of the Faithful. "Lumen Christi" sings the deacon triumphantly. "Thanks be to God" reply the people.

Easter morning is one sustained echo of joy because of this new life. Christ is risen from the dead. The apparent defeat has been followed by glorious victory, by the triumph which brings us to the culminating point of the ecclesiastical year. White as the colour of unshadowed happiness is once more in use. Christ is with us again, but now as a conqueror, bearing the glorified signs of His Passion. With the doubting apostle Thomas we are able to put our finger into his wounds and our hand into the opening of His pierced side. Yes, it is indeed He; He is speaking again now, uttering His last words, His last injunctions to the apostles. The Sundays after Easter are full of the story; and when, on Ascension Day, He returns to His Father, we, too, are able to enter into the joy of the apostles as they descended the mountain-side and took the road to Jerusalem.

The Holy Ghost, whom He had promised, descended upon the apostles on Whitsunday, and from then on all fear and diffidence left them. The newborn Church began its triumphant march through the world, and the teaching of Christ, into which we shall plunge during the Sundays after Whitsuntide, brought new life wherever it penetrated. Men could perceive for themselves that Christ still lived. Through the Holy Spirit, He will continue to inspire and direct His Church until the day when He returns to judge the living and the dead. That day, the Day of Judgment, we look forward to as the prize of eternal life.

At the close of the ecclesiastical year Christ speaks to us of the ending of Time; He turns our eyes towards the celestial Jerusalem which we shall inhabit when, of the ancient earthly Jerusalem, not one stone remains upon another. After this year lived in company with the liturgy of the Church we understand better the meaning of all that happened at the coming of Our Lord, and better what is the meaning of our own individual lives. The Church has known how to teach us many things through the richness of the Liturgy of her Mass throughout the cycle of the year; chief among them the unforgettable fact that, although our feet rest upon earth, we are nevertheless oriented towards heaven by faith, hope and charity; that the world, so marvellously created out of the void, but still more marvellously restored and redeemed by the Sacrifice of Christ, is for us no abiding city, but a temporary dwelling-place in which we live among all the things which in His goodness He bestows upon us while we yet share with Christ His attachment to the Cross.

Interwoven with the whole of the ecclesiastical year we constantly meet the thought of the saints, who are commemorated almost daily in the prayers of the Mass. This remembrance, and the cycle of the ecclesiastical year, only serves to give liturgical form and stature to the marvellously rich and varied personality of Christ, who dominates the whole life and prayer of the Church.

In this way, by the example which she sets in her Liturgy of the Mass, the Church forms in us a strong interior respect for the Blessed Sacrament: a respect filled with holy awe, deepest admiration and gratitude, and quiet appreciation. With all that is most costly: with silver and gold and richness of colour and vestment: with works of art of every description: and with the most beautiful which we either possess or are able to find, we surround these offerings of ours, this remembrance of the Passion and Death of Christ.

APPENDIX

In addition to the Mass, still further attention is paid to the Sacrament of the Altar by the Church in her liturgy and her ceremonies. In former days the monastic custom of the public celebration of Vespers was gradually superseded by the introduction of *Benediction*. Attention became focused upon the lasting character of the Sacrament of the Altar, by which it is distinguished from all other Sacraments. That which is realized during its celebration does not immediately pass away. Christ continues to dwell in the tabernacle, even when the Sacrifice of the Mass is long since over. The need was felt for some form of worship, and this form was found in a ceremony which, while it follows a certain general scheme, nevertheless allows sufficient latitude for the desired variation. Benediction at which the Faithful are able to assist in church on certain afternoons and evenings during the week, is no more than a rather loosely strung series of prayers and hymns before the Blessed Sacrament Exposed. At the beginning of the service the priest takes the Host from the tabernacle and places it in the monstrance (monstrare—to show) and then puts the monstrance containing the Host on a throne above the tabernacle. The ceremony is concluded by the priest once again taking down the monstrance and solemnly making the sign of the cross over the people with it.

The liturgical attention of the Church is also very much upon those other Sacraments which, at the most decisive moments of our lives, are both the source and the strength of the divine life within us. The Church surrounds us with her most loving care in these Sacraments, supplying appropriate prayers and ceremonies, which are calculated to arouse in us the right dispositions to make us appreciate the importance of these supernatural moments in life, while offering us food for further meditation when they have passed by.

If one is responsible for a family, and some member of it is privileged to receive one of these Sacraments, all the other members who are available should also assist at it. If, for instance, the priest visits the home, and brings with him Our Lord, in order to give Holy Communion to someone sick, as many as possible should be respectfully present. The liturgy of the Church does not stand outside ordinary daily domestic life. When necessary, she brings to her children all the strength and nourishment of which they may be in need.

There is a blessing for newly born infants and mothers, and we need never hesitate to ask the Church for these Sacraments and Blessings. We cannot exist without the Sacraments, and we should remember that when the Church blesses, she prays for us in the Name of Christ. "Peace be to this house" says her representative, the priest, when he visits our home, and the peace which he confers upon us is the same as that which Christ conferred upon His disciples when He came into their midst. The greatest desire of the Church is to bring Christ to us. He who blessed mothers and little children; who went among men doing good; who understood their needs and ministered to their pain; is still being brought by His Church to those who need Him. His statue has a place in every Catholic family. By what is called the ceremony of enthronement, which we may ask a priest to perform in our home, we are able to acknowledge Him openly as Master and Lord of the family. We can have our house blessed, and the priest will pray that there may dwell in it "health, purity, strength, modesty, goodness and mildness, devotion to duty, and gratitude towards God the Father, the Son, and the Holy Ghost".

To sum up we may call the liturgy a mode of expression for the whole inner community-sense of the Church. There is a very real and vital union, between interior and exterior acts. Interiorly the Church is exceedingly conscious of her existence as a living community, and it is therefore as a living community that she will represent herself in her exterior prayers and worship. Not merely as a gathering of those who assist at any given liturgical ceremony, but as the complete community of all the Faithful. In its prayers the liturgy of the Catholic Church does not say "I" but "We", and in this "We" are included not only those present, but all the Faithful. It might even be said that the Church in her prayers and ceremonies is aware of and purposely demonstrates her incorporation with those who already, in eternal life, are united with God. The prayer of the whole Church is thus brought together in the liturgy, and offered to God "through Jesus Christ Our Lord".

That which we have said about the spirit of the ecclesiastical year applies also to liturgy in general: it is always, in the deepest sense, some kind of representation of Christ. One might even say that the Church desires to be, before God, as much as possible Christ Himself, made in His likeness, and growing to His full human stature. This desire is to be detected throughout. The liturgy is what is known as Christo-centric, that is to say that He is the centre of it, both the beginning and the end: His Name is the most frequently mentioned: the Church prays in living communion with Him. The life, the words, and the actions of the Redeemer are always in the foreground. It is His ideals and His ideas which find new expression each time the priest acts as His representative; prayers and ceremonies used are in no way arbitrary, but are always used in His Name.

However, the whole of this liturgy, of which Christ is the

Alpha and Omega, the first and the last figure represented by it, is dedicated to the triune God. In this sense we may also call it Theo-centric: it is a way by which we associate ourselves with God; it is a living worship of Him "who liveth and reigneth with Thee in the unity of the Holy Ghost, one God, world without end. Amen." The spirit in which we thus approach the Deity is not a spirit of servitude or slavery, but a spirit of profound consciousness of our status as children of God whereby we address Him as Father. Filled with this consciousness, it is then indeed the Holy Ghost who works in us during these prayers and ceremonies. He is the constant inspiration of the Church, the very soul of her sublime liturgy.

Another conclusion which we may reach from these considerations is that the Church has no contempt for material and external adjuncts, but knows how to make suitable use of them to enhance even the most supernatural acts which she performs. Water and fire, candles and flowers, poetry and music, art and culture, all belong to this world, yet all are employed by her. The Church remembers that "God so loved the world that He gave His only begotten son". This only Son became man and learnt how to identify Himself with the world and mankind. As He sanctified mankind He sanctified also the world in which man lived. This earth became the base upon which is built the Kingdom of God, and all that is excellent upon this earth may be used for the worship of God. It is owing to these profound beliefs of the Church that she always exercises a civilizing influence wherever she holds sway. In the old days great artists were employed by her, and drew their inspiration from her faith and from the sources of her faith.

The Church in the choice of her own liturgical renderings has always remained grave and cultured. There is no exaggeration. The Roman liturgy of which we have been speaking is essentially controlled, and leaves no room for subjective moods and feelings. It expresses the feelings and moods of the Church, and these are always quiet, and filled with the perfection of a beautiful but restrained emotion.

Yet there is noticeable in the liturgy an unmistakable driving-force, a strong and secret striving after completion and the fulness of happiness. One might say that she is constantly on the alert for a time yet to come, a time when she knows that the exterior trappings of her liturgy will no longer be required. She prays, and she believes that the Kingdom of Christ is coming. And she believes too, that all who are in union with her are destined—and are entrusted to her that they may be made ready—for this final and perfected Kingdom. It is clear from the liturgy that the Church lives in the world only as one lives through a passing springtime. The exultant summer of eternity has yet to follow.

CHAPTER XIII

THE MORAL LAW

§ 1. *Principles*

EVERY MAN, including the most primitive bushman, and even the greatest villain, carries in his heart the law: Thou shalt do good, thou shalt not do evil. But at that the general moral law comes to an end, for as soon as the question is raised, "What is good and what is evil?" there is a difference of opinion. After all, the burning of witches, head-hunting and similar practices have been known to pass as virtue, and on the contrary, even in our own day, have we not sometimes felt that gentleness and mercy were merely looked upon as weaknesses?

The question is, ought we to regard such questions merely as matters of convention, custom, or tacit agreement, determined by the particular state of society and the spirit of the times, or are these problems open to argument? Do there exist, apart from the state of society and the passing centuries, certain fixed standards by which some actions, at any period and of themselves, will be acknowledged to be either moral or immoral?

Christianity answers this question in the affirmative: there exist certain incontestable, external moral laws, unassailable either by the individual or by society. When therefore as Christians, we ask ourselves the question: "How ought I to live?" we will leave aside the natural moral law (ethics) and answer the question with a direct: "We ought to live as Christ has taught us to live."

The answer would be very simple indeed if the Christian moral law had been set out in the Bible, but that is by no means the case. On the contrary, the Gospels and Epistles contain much good counsel and many injunctions, but there is no consistent connection between them, nor is their practical application to all circumstances, and particularly to modern conditions, formally dealt with. The theologian, therefore, has to approach these matters with a mind enlightened by faith. In this way he can discover those principles from which logical reasoning is able to determine their correct application. It follows that, in difficult cases, one is not dependent upon a vague intuition sometimes—incorrectly enough—called "conscience", but that there is a real possibility of arriving at well-considered and reasonable conclusions.

Christ gave the command that we should "pray always", but when we come to think about it, we realize that He did not command us to pray always in the strict sense of the word, since in that case all our other duties would run the risk of being neglected. The underlying meaning of such a commandment has to be seized and explained according to reason, enlightened by faith. This must not be taken to mean, however, that our reason stands higher than the commandments of God; but the Christian moral law is never in conflict with that other gift of God, common sense, and we must use common sense if we wish to arrive at any constructive system of Christian laws and the origins and causes upon which they depend. Such a system is called Moral Philosophy or Ethics.

It is possible that the above, although so simple, will be a revelation to the non-Catholic reader, particularly to the Protestant reader. He should, however, bear in mind that without such a scientifically applied Moral Philosophy it would be difficult to adapt the Gospel to every situation, and a definite interpretation, essential both for society as a whole and the individual in particular, would be lacking. For the rest, the Catholic believes that the Holy Ghost guides the Church morally as well as spiritually, and that in such matters papal pronouncements are entitled to claim infallibility.

It is not our intention to present to the reader a treatise on Moral Philosophy. There are many excellent works which can be consulted upon the subject; we only propose to consider more closely some of the main principles which it is necessary to understand in order to judge of the morality of any given action, and which we will try to combine in a chapter called: human action.

a. Human Action

Not every human action comes under the Moral Law.

When one breathes in one's sleep, for instance, no sensible bystander will raise the question as to whether this is allowed or forbidden. And why not? Because no typically human action is being performed; that is to say an action by which man is distinguished from any other being such as an animal or a plant.

An action becomes typically human (and that is what we understand by Human Action) when it is performed under the influence of those two human and spiritual faculties: reason and freewill. One must bear in mind that no action can be either good or bad in a case where freedom or knowledge are (inculpably) absent. The reason for this is simple: man is only responsible for typically human acts for which both knowledge and freewill are necessary.

1. *Knowledge of Moral Values*

One is, in conscience, only responsible for an action in so far as one knows that it is good or bad. If a person removes someone else's overcoat from the hall under the impression that it is his own, obviously he is not stealing so long as he remains convinced that it is his property. Again if someone commits perjury, thinking it to be only a slight fault, he will obviously be sinning less than someone who considers it a serious transgression (which it actually is).

We are presuming that this ignorance is not due to the fault of the person concerned as it would be, for example, were someone to be unaware of a law which had been promulgated either on account of sheer negligence or with the deliberate intention of keeping himself exempt from it. It therefore becomes a duty to take the necessary steps to obtain all reasonable information.

One is not only responsible for the human actions which one performs, but also for the consequences, *in so far, that is, as these can be foreseen*; or rather, in so far as *one should have foreseen them.* Culpable carelessness cannot do away with the responsibility. A motorist who drives at a reckless speed through a village, is responsible for all the damage he does, even though he did not know beforehand what was going to happen. If a man neglects the education of his children, he cannot wash his hands of the consequences if later on they are failures in life.

The moral guilt for the *unavoidable* consequences of any act, however, ceases as soon as sincere contrition for the fault is present. The natural sorrow remains, but God no longer holds the sinner accountable for those consequences. Otherwise, in certain circumstances, it would be impossible ever to regain the friendship of God.

2. *Freedom when performing an Action*

The normal man is interiorly free. Even though he may be exteriorly compelled to an action by brute force, yet interiorly he can continue to refuse his consent to it. A man can be tied on his knees before an idol, but no one can make him commit a free interior act of idolatry so long as he is determined not to do so. One is only responsible for those actions performed with interior liberty.

This interior liberty may be stronger or weaker, according to circumstances, or it may even disappear altogether. With the degree of consciousness, the moral, typically human value or responsibility for the deed also diminishes. One cannot, for instance, sin during sleep, and is only relatively, and not entirely, responsible for an action performed in a state between dreaming and waking. One of the most important influences diminishing consciousness is passion. Usually this word is given an unfavourable interpretation because the guilty consequences are included in one's judgment of it. And yet passion as such, as an urge of the senses, is not in itself evil. Those urges can be directed towards some morally good object; to a just cause, or the well-being of one's neighbour, or some scientific purpose. Passions are like wild horses, full of strength but blind; what they need is a leader; and it is just those men with strong, but well-controlled passions, who achieve the most in life.

We are here considering the passions only in so far as they act as violent emotions obscuring the mind. Love as well as hatred, fury as well as sensuality, can so diminish freedom of action that a man is no longer himself and does things which he would never have done in his sober senses, and wakes up later as from a state of intoxication. It is possible to knock a man down in a temper without being responsible for it, because freedom of action is absent. It does not, however, follow from this that one can never be guilty during a fit of passion. Usually sufficient consciousness remains to make the act sinful, and one is certainly responsible if one has anticipated the rousing of some passion and has voluntarily consented to it. If a person knows that he will commit immoral actions when drunk, and in spite of that gets drunk, he is naturally guilty for those actions.

There is another influence which tends to diminish consciousness and that is habit. By force of habit one gets into the way of repeating an action, and it requires more strength of character to break oneself of it. In this case, also, the foregoing modifications hold good; anyone who forms a habit is responsible for the consequences of it so long as he does not check it by sincere contrition; therefore one is guilty if one does not take the trouble to get rid of an acquired bad habit.

The precise degree in which passion or habit has either diminished or entirely done away with guilt, can only be decided separately in each case. Undoubtedly, wrong thoughts, feelings and desires, crop up in men's hearts without any freewill, and therefore without guilt. On the other hand, one must be careful not to take refuge in a supposed lack of *freewill* when all that was actually missing was the *desire to try*. In such a case a sensible Catholic asks the advice of an experienced confessor and follows it.

b. Conscience

Any man who is not completely degenerate, frequently faces the question as to whether some action which he intends to perform is good or bad; and, after reflection, he, as it were, passes judgment upon himself This judgment as to the moral value of any act to be performed is called *conscience*.

The term conscience is often used in a different sense, that is to say as indicating some kind of sensation of either peace or disturbance in the mind *after* an action. One speaks of a good or a pricking conscience but, in the technical sense as used in moral law it would be more correct to employ the expression: "My conscience tells me . . ."

The following is an example: One is about to make up one's mind as to whether one should retain or return to the owner, a stolen bicycle which one has bought. By applying the principle that a person remains the owner of a thing so long as he has not lost the proprietary right to it, one comes to this conclusion: when a person loses an object by reason of theft, he does not lose the proprietary right to it; this bicycle has been stolen from Mr. A, therefore Mr. A still has the proprietary right to it.

So far, one has only reached the general *moral* judgment. When one continues, and draws the practical conclusion, "I shall therefore have to return this bicycle to Mr. A", one has arrived at the judgment which is called conscience (or sometimes the verdict of conscience). One can define this verdict as the application of general moral laws to any particular action which one is about to perform.

It is, however, quite possible to be unable to make up one's mind as to whether an action is permissible or not. In that case what should one do?

As long as there is any doubt one should not act, since in that case one would be voluntarily running the risk of transgressing the law. It is, however, possible to arrive at a solution if (after serious reflection which is always *de rigeur*) the doubt persists. There is a clause in moral law which tells us that a doubtful law does not bind. From this it *conclusively* follows that the doubt which occupies one's mind at the present moment lays one under no obligation, so that in a sense one is no longer in uncertainty. When one is in doubt, one should first try to resolve the matter by serious reflection. If one still achieves no certainty, then it is permissible to reason in the following way: I am not sure whether a certain law obliges me in this case: but a doubtful law does not oblige, therefore in this instance I am not bound by the law.

One should, however, always be careful to remember the following conditions which are attached to this reasoning.

1. It must be a *serious doubt,* not a slight suspicion as to whether one is, or is not, exempted from the law. One must be able to defend one's uncertainty by argument.

2. It must concern the point as to whether an act be *permissible,* not whether it be *valid.* E.g., a priest, when administering the Sacraments, must always be on the safe side.

3. The definite rights of someone else may never be violated: for instance a doctor is obliged to prescribe the most effective remedies.

Once, however, these conditions have been fulfilled, one may, even when in doubt, act quite freely. Thus, someone who in the morning is uncertain as to whether he drank something (other than water) during the night, may go to Holy Communion. The same rule applies when one is uncertain as to whether one ate something before or after midnight. If anyone has a doubt as to whether a certain act which he committed were a mortal sin or not, then he is not obliged to confess it. As long as one is not sure whether or no one has to follow the Lenten laws of fasting and abstinence, then one need not do so. We may therefore say that conscience is a judgment of the mind; but it is not always the keenest wits which judge the best. It is remarkable that simple people often have a more sensitive appreciation of what should be done or not done, than those who shine by their cultural or scientific development. The reason for this is that conscience acts more correctly in proportion to the degree of relationship with virtue. A man who is charitable, pure of heart and just in mind, judges more rightly in such matters than one who is self-centred, sensual, or careless of the rights of others. The judgment is greatly influenced by the will, and it is easy to make oneself believe in some inclination which one then proceeds to call one's conscience. In the end it is the love of God which points the way to truth. Conscience will always be apt to misread God so long as that love is lacking. "None knows the Father truly except the Son, and those to whom it is the Son's good pleasure to reveal Him."[1]

c. Sin

Whoever thinks or speaks of conscience is bound, sooner or later, to encounter the question of sin. Although it is true that many people are almost deadened in the matter of right and wrong, and will produce only a tired smile or a shrug of the shoulders at the mention of the particular nature of sin, yet the reality of the Christian consciousness of it still holds its own. It is, after all, not possible to allow the question of the fundamental essence of good and evil to depend on the answer given as to whether a particular action be economically sound, or whether it runs counter to the ordinary rules of

[1] Matt. 11, 27.

etiquette and decency. Even the criterion of general social welfare is not, in the last resort, really decisive. At all periods of the world's history, and in nearly every country, the realization of moral guilt, of sinfulness, and of an almost ineradicable inclination towards the transgression of divine law has existed: this shows that an attitude of pretended superiority to all moral standards is a symptom of weakness and decadence. Whoever honestly examines his own actions will be obliged to admit that after many of them he finds his conscience accusing him, or even that he is assailed by remorse. At the moment when one becomes conscious of having violated a moral value, then one frequently feels guilty, aware of a personal failure, of a disorder which attacks one's whole personality. One detests oneself; one feels oneself to be punishable and realizes that the disorder should be repaired.

Upon a deeper analysis of these symptoms one will notice that sin, according to one's own conscience, does not only represent a fault against other people, against society at large, or even a feeling of unworthiness in one's own regard. It brings one to a realization that one is responsible to a Being: to a Person who completely sees through one and is perfectly just. And one has this consciousness even though it may be accompanied by the knowledge and the feeling that this same Person is ready to forgive and to reconcile one to Himself. The idea of sin is a religious concept: it is an act which touches the very kernel of man's personality, because and in so far as this act is connected with the highest, most infinitely perfect and holy Being, God.

What exactly do we understand by sin?

According to the general moral law sin is, in the first place, regarded as an act which we can describe following the classical definition, as *a conscious, voluntary transgression of God's law*. Original sin, which has already been discussed, is not now under consideration and we are concerned only with personal sin. It is the interior decision of the will which turns the scale. For instance, anyone who in his own mind voluntarily entertains the idea of repudiating his wife—even though circumstances would make such an act impossible—sins. God has imposed His will upon man's nature in the positive laws which He has, either directly or indirectly, given us. It is difficult to outline in words precisely what God has expressed in man's nature. By an immediate insight, by reflection, by instinctive preferences and antipathies, human nature in many cases reveals certain definite trends. It has, for instance, no difficulty in finding either blasphemy, or the killing of an innocent person, highly objectionable; it also has a certain respect for the property of other people, although it often fails in the concrete application of this principle.

It accepts that it must serve God, that it ought to practise charity, and to dominate the passions by the mind; but in ordinary, everyday life, positive laws will have to follow on and amplify these general principles, which are accepted by all normal people. It is for this reason that in the Old Testament God set out various laws, and at least in part formulated the natural law into those ten commandments which were later on perfected by Christ. Christ, followed by the Church, has therefore given us our general line of conduct, and by many precepts, set the standards by which we are to live the Christian life. Sin is a voluntary transgression of all these laws and commandments given to us by God; but the real essence of it remains that inward decision of the will regarding an action, a decision not in conformity with the mind of God, and therefore a deviation from our real aim, which is Himself.

Sin is an offence against Him. It may not be man's intention to offend God, but this very offence is implied by his act: for he turns away, either completely or in one instance, towards transitory things without pausing to take the will of God sufficiently into account.

The New Testament shows us yet another aspect of sin: it regards it as a denial of the light and a participation in the invisible works of darkness: it shows[2] that contemptuous indifference to the grace of being born of God which sin always indicates.[3] St. Paul begs the Ephesians not to distress God's Holy Spirit whose seal they bear,[4] and speaking of other sins he says that they crucify the Son of God a second time.[5] When we reflect upon such strong expressions as these we shall of course realize at once that not all sin could be described in this way. It is obvious that not all transgressions of the law of God are equally serious. Therefore the Church distinguishes between mortal and venial sin. This distinction we shall first find in the Bible which mentions sins for

[2] Eph. 5, 8-10. [3] I John 3, 9. [4] Eph. 4, 30. [5] Heb. 6, 6.

which the reward is death;[6] which bring doom and destruction in their train;[7] by reason of which those who live in such a way will not inherit God's Kingdom;[8] as well as many faults into which, as St. James says, we are, all of us, betrayed.[9]

Even a Christian who calls God by the name of Father, and is conscious of being His child, will still have to pray "forgive us our trespasses".

Mortal sins mean exactly what the word implies: a sin which kills. To sin mortally is to die as a child of God, for love is extinguished. When by our action, or by some interior decision of our will, we virtually express a complete contempt for God and His laws, and therefore in reality are sacrificing Him to some creature, to some selfish desire, to some passing enjoyment; then indeed we are speaking of mortal sin. This is a case of such a transgression of God's will that man simply sweeps aside His law, and the right order is completely reversed, the end being made subordinate to the means. One who commits mortal sin is in himself displeasing to God, for it means that he has withdrawn his subjection and rejected God's sovereignty. In the strict sense of the word he offends his Creator.

This is precisely what happens every time one of the important laws of God is transgressed either by a direct offence against Himself, or against our neighbour, or in connection with our own personal welfare. To injure either oneself or one's neighbour so that normal human duties become impossible of performance (i.e. suicide; total neglect of one's own spiritual welfare; theft or murder) are indeed mortal sins. Everything which is in direct conflict with God, and the glory and love of God, is a grave sin: such for instance is hatred of God or blasphemy. Except in these last cases, however, sins in this same category need not necessarily be so serious. A person who only slightly upsets general good order (for instance by a trifling theft, or a lie on a matter of no great importance) has not committed the sin in all its full completeness.

As we saw above, personal knowledge and conscience are the standards by which all actions should be judged, and therefore mortal sin always requires full consciousness that a serious sin is being committed, as well as full consent. On the other hand, we speak of venial sin when the following three

[6] Rom. 6, 21, 23. [7] II Pet. 2, 3. [8] Gal. 5, 21. [9] James 3, 2.

conditions, or any one of them is absent: when the actual matter of the transgression is not of sufficient gravity; when the person involved is blamelessly unaware of the fact of the wrongdoing; when the choice of the will was in any way obstructed or impeded. One who has committed mortal sin is, as we said before, displeasing to God in *himself*. But in the case of venial sin, he himself is not displeasing to God but only what he has done. By committing venial sin we do not completely sever our ties with God.

No wonder that the results are so different in the two cases. By mortal sin we lose sanctifying grace: that is to say, the intimate participation in the interior life of God, and the right to heaven. By venial sin our love of God is only weakened, so that we become more easily a prey to interior and exterior temptation, and thus the danger of falling into further sin is increased.

This distinction drawn between mortal and venial sin may seem strange to the non-Catholic. He will be more likely to characterize a whole attitude to life as sinful. In such a case, a man stands, as it were, with his back towards God. There are people who maintain that sin is our way of giving up God, and that the different forms of sins are only the results or the expression of this condition of ours. Roman Catholicism, however, does not see sin as a final judgment of God, but as a personal act which goes against the nature of man, now restored and elevated by Christ.

§ 2. *The Ten Commandments*

We will next deal with each commandment separately. In various passages of the Old Testament a summary of these commandments is given[10] which is called the decalogue (deca—ten). Although these ten commandments are an application of the natural law to the needs of the Jewish people living at that time, yet, even in such a form, they have a great value for us, because they are all a part of Revelation, and a monument to tradition. Although they are not a finished code of moral law, yet most of the books on moral theology follow the classification used in the decalogue in which (sometimes not without distortion) all possible kinds of sin are classed under the various commandments. We pro-

[10] Ex. 20, 2-17. Deut. 5, 6-12.

pose to adhere to this classification also, as far as possible without straining the sense unduly.

The more elaborate form of the decalogue, as it is set out in the Old Testament (and is learned by Protestant children), has been replaced in the Catholic Catechism by a summary which dates from St. Augustine. It reads as follows:

I am the Lord thy God, who brought thee out of the land of Egypt and out of the house of bondage.

1. Thou shalt not have strange gods before Me. Thou shalt not make to thyself any graven thing, nor the likeness of anything that is in heaven above, or in the earth beneath, nor of those things that are in the waters under the earth. Thou shalt not adore them nor serve them.
2. Thou shalt not take the name of the Lord thy God in vain.
3. Remember that thou keep holy the Sabbath-day.
4. Honour thy father and thy mother.
5. Thou shalt not kill.
6. Thou shalt not commit adultery.
7. Thou shalt not steal.
8. Thou shalt not bear false witness against thy neighbour.
9. Thou shalt not covet thy neighbour's wife.
10. Thou shalt not covet thy neighbour's goods.

Originally these laws were engraved upon stone. In Exodus chapter 24, verse 12, we read how God gave to Moses tablets of stone on which He had written down the law and the commandments. With regard to the division of the commandments we shall keep to the traditional rendering in which on the first tablet were engraved the commandments which deal with our relationship with God (the first three commandments) and upon the second one the remaining commandments which deal with our relationship with our neighbour.

A. *The first tablet of the Commandments* (the theological virtues)

In various parts of the Gospel Christ asks us to follow Him. "If any man has a mind to come my way, let him renounce himself, and take up his cross daily, and follow Me."[11] To follow Him means to become a child of God and to obey His will and His commandments with all one's heart and soul. By Baptism we are born of water and the Holy Ghost,[12] in the strict sense of the word, as children of God. God does then indeed live in our soul, and the fresh life which this bestows upon us is called by the Church Sanctifying Grace. Through this grace the soul experiences a new depth and an enrichment of spirit which elevates it above created life: it has a share in God's own nature and His own interior, divine existence. Through this grace there arises also a communion of life with Christ and, just as the branch must remain one with the vine in order to prevent it from dying, so also we must remain in Christ and bear fruit in Him. "If a man lives on in Me, and I in him, then he will yield abundant fruit; separated from Me you have no power to do anything."[13] This means that we must lead a Christian life.

Such a Christian life is in the first place lived interiorly, and we could describe it as an ever-increasing living of that which we now really are: that is, a living of this state of sanctifying grace: a continual unfolding of our attention and our love in the direction of God and of Christ. It is a growing realization of the presence of God in us which has its origin in the grace and love of Christ, but is nevertheless willed and practised by us.

How does this spiritual development take place? How does grace unfold all its activity, its force and its influence? How do we become more and more intensely and truly children of God?

We know that being raised to the supernatural order of life brings in its train a multiplicity of theological virtues and gifts, which, taken together with sanctifying grace, make up the whole supernatural structure.

The three theological virtues of faith, hope and charity are closely connected with grace; they are the active force and the organs of the new divine life in the soul. Just as the spirit of man expresses itself through the mind, which formulates his thoughts for him, and through the will which aspires and loves, so also the life of grace reveals itself through faith, hope and charity. So the child of God continually meets his Father

[11] Luke 9, 23. [12] John 3, 3-6. [13] John 15, 4-5.

and his Redeemer through the action of these three virtues which God has infused into him at Baptism.

Virtue is not in this instance to be understood as a habit acquired by personal activity, but rather as a God-given spiritual wealth which raises both understanding and will on to the supernatural plane. The intellect is then able to lift its own thoughts towards God, and to incline the will towards Him as towards that infinite perfection which is worth the utmost endeavour.

Faith, hope and charity are called theological virtues because they alone bring the soul into immediate contact with God. By means of them the unattainable God and His own interior life become attainable by us. In Him we then find our immediate and unfailing support and our resting-place. We are united to Him by love, and this union is the result of His infinite love for us.

The child of God unfolds its Christian life from the heart of these three virtues.

The virtue of faith is described by the Vatican Council as "a supernatural virtue by which we, with the inspiration and assistance of God's grace, believe those things to be true which He has revealed, not because our understanding with its natural enlightenment apprehends the interior truth of things, but on the authority of the revealing God Himself, who can neither deceive nor be deceived".

It is by faith that man first turns towards the Revelation of God and from this Revelation he learns divine secrets. For "none knows the Father truly except the Son, and those to whom it is the Son's good pleasure to reveal Him".[14] That which was hidden from man in the divine consciousness, God now unfolds to him: that is to say, the truths of our Faith which we have endeavoured to explain in the previous chapters.

The Faithful accept these truths simply and solely because they are guaranteed by the truth of God. There is no question here of human insight or understanding, only of the infallible authority of the Word of God itself. It is not given to man to fathom and fully comprehend the mysteries of the Deity, but by the operation of the Holy Ghost he arrives at the complete submission of the human understanding to the divine. The reason why the intellect is able by this act of

[14] Matt. 11, 27.

faith to express its agreement with something which it cannot fully understand, is because the authority for it is that of the God who reveals, and who can neither fail nor deceive. Faith is founded exclusively upon the authority of God.

But this faith has its origin in *grace*, from a free choice of the love of God to which we can either respond or not. It is an elevation of our whole nature; an inpouring of divine truth; a penetration of our understanding into the love and the decrees of God. "That is what I meant," said Christ to His disciples, "when I told you that nobody can come to Me unless he has received the gift from My Father,"[15] and St. Paul says explicitly to the Ephesians: "It was grace that saved you, with faith for its instruments; it did not come from yourselves, it was God's gift."[16]

Through the grace of faith then, we hear the voice of God speaking through Christ, and through His Church in which He still lives on. For only in the Church can Faith be sure of receiving God's word in all its fulness, and therefore obedience to its authority becomes the criterion of true faith.

This faith, however, should not be limited to the mere acceptance of truth: it must penetrate deeply into our life, and be its inspiration. If it only remains for us as a kind of rational phenomena, then in the end it is bound to lose all meaning, and the trend towards the truth engendered by faith will ultimately disappear also. To be effective an unconditional dedication of oneself to the Invisible must have its foundation, as well as its irradiance, in actual life.

That is because in Faith we meet a Truth which is a Being: God Himself. Between Him and myself there ensues a personal contact. It is me, personally, whom He calls—through Jesus Christ and through the Church. God even deigns to try and attract my attention by the wonders and the miracles of His Son; to reveal His presence to me by signs; to instruct me by His teaching.

Faith thus becomes a participation in the life of a Person, a participation in the living knowledge and the Spirit of Christ; a participation in His own personal contact with His Father.

And it is in this faith that the surrender of the whole man takes place. To believe may be difficult because it is not a matter of personally acquired knowledge, but of surrender.

[15] John 6, 65.

[16] Eph. 2, 8.

This surrender, being supernatural, must be constantly renewed if it is to retain its spiritual vitality and value.

It is never a waste of time and energy to absorb the truths of faith by means of religious instruction, and above all by the reading of the Bible. But if we do not also live daily in accordance with that belief, and so lead a truly Christian life, we shall weaken and finally lose that delicate sensitiveness to the things of the world of faith: to its demands, its practices and its prohibitions. The Church endeavours, therefore, to exert her influence in many different directions and to warn us of any danger: she warns us against books or writings which may be dangerous to faith and morals, and keeps an indexed list of unsuitable publications. She finds it infinitely better not so much to dispute over the Faith as to confess it openly, and so not to hide her light under a bushel.[17]

Any Catholic who intentionally neglects the carrying out of the laws of the Church, and takes no pains to increase his or her religious knowledge, sins against faith; the result is bound to be indifference and the following of an empty routine: Catholicism in name only, of which the inner content has long since been lost.

We are not living according to Christ if we deny our faith, keeping it inwardly, but outwardly speaking and acting as if we had nothing to do with it. "And whoever disowns me before men, before My Father in Heaven I too will disown him."[18] "And now, whoever acknowledges me before men, I too will acknowledge him before My Father who is in Heaven."[19]

It is a grave sin to reject the grace of faith contrary to one's better judgment, and obstinately to refuse to accept a truth which one knows that God has revealed and which the Church teaches; under the name of heresy this is called a sin against faith.

One must, however, make a clear distinction between doubts of faith which are voluntarily entertained, without sufficient cause, and genuine difficulties as to belief, when, for instance, one finds some contradiction between an article of the Faith and one's own ideas which it is impossible to resolve. In the former case it is one's duty simply to accept the divine truth; in the latter case one is perfectly justified in trying to find a solution.

[17] Matt. 5, 15. [18] Matt. 10, 33. [19] Matt. 10, 32.

Faith, which we possess as a precious gift from Jesus Christ[20] and which promises the enjoyment of eternal life,[21] should be most carefully watched over and guarded.

Through the theological virtue of *hope* we confidently expect from God all the means which are necessary to us in order that we may obtain eternal salvation. This virtue brings us into immediate contact with the omnipotence of God; makes us long for the happiness of contemplating His infinite Being; and fills us with the assurance of one day possessing Him as He is in Himself. Due to the working of hope in our soul we are able to enter the sphere of divine life; the happiness which it holds out to us is not merely a human happiness but the interior bliss of God; the help it offers is not so much a strengthening of our own will as a surrender to God's fatherly omnipotence; the desires and trust which it induces are entirely founded upon the merits of Jesus Christ who, according to St. Paul in his letter to Timothy, is our hope,[22] and upon the promises of God "who did not even spare His own Son, but gave Him up for us all; and must not that gift be accompanied by the gift of all else?"[23] Supported by this hope, therefore, we strive after God as our future happiness and our eternal life; we expect the resurrection of the body; and we count on all the graces and the means which we need to achieve our supernatural aim.

This supernatural virtue corresponds to a fundamental urge in man: that is, the continuous search for his own personal happiness, which he now finds in God. Therefore it is a force which can raise strength of will to its very peak, and as long as it is present the fundamental urge towards the ultimate goal will remain constant.

This supernatural hope should be surrounded with every care, because, although we are sure of God who, even if we play Him false remains true to His word,[24] we can never be sure of ourselves. A certain fear of the Lord is necessary. Grace never fails us, but grace alone is not sufficient; it depends for its action upon our co-operation. We are able to neglect God's graces; not to respond to His invitation and His love. The fear of personal disloyalty is based upon bitter experience, and upon the fact that we still suffer from the results of original sin. The danger that we shall drift away

[20] II Pet. 1, 1. [21] Tim. 1, 1. [22] John 6, 47.
[23] Rom. 8, 32. [24] II Tim. 2, 13 and 1, 12.

from God is a very real danger. Therefore our personal co-operation with grace needs human intelligence, reflection, some sort of method, or else actual experience. The folly of the Cross only asks us to turn away from the world when the world itself turns against God. We remain in a state of confidence and trust in God when, under the stress of temptation, adversity, or suffering, we still admit His omnipotence and goodness, and never demand that His Providence should justify Itself to us.

A twofold danger threatens this virtue: either that we should trust too much or trust too little.

It is just as impossible for man to have too much real trust in God as it would be for him to have too much love for Him. Hope should be limitless. But this expression is sometimes used to describe a state of mind in which we expect that God should grant us all our desires, even though they may clash with His wisdom and His holiness; in this case we begin to assert that God ought not to tolerate a particular state of affairs, or some injustice or other. It is really, we feel, His duty to interfere. In this frame of mind a man forgets that God's Providence achieves its aim by secret ways, and he misunderstands the Mystery which rules the world. The Gospel tells us of faith which, though only the size of a grain of mustard-seed, yet can move mountains,[25] but such faith is no guarantee against suffering and difficulties, neither does it permit of a reckless playing with the span of life allotted to each one of us. We must remember that the Gospel constantly speaks of personal effort and of that co-operation which goes with the grace of God.

On the other hand, a lack of faith and trust can express itself in many different ways: in a certain faint-heartedness for instance such as the apostles experienced when caught in the midnight storm upon the lake;[26] in a mood of dejection, as when we do not see how to rid ourselves of some bad habit, and think that there is no progress in our spiritual life; and finally, in actual despair, which is a total lack of trust in God, and the direct opposite of St. Paul's words: "Nothing is beyond my powers, thanks to the strength God gives me."[27] This despair can even develop to such a pitch that life ceases to have any meaning for us, and the function of the grace of God is thus entirely done away with.

[25] Matt. 17, 20. [26] Matt. 8, 26. [27] Phil. 4, 13.

But the greatest of all the theological virtues is *charity*, which inspires both faith and hope. "Meanwhile, faith, hope and charity persist, all three; but the greatest of them all is charity."[28] By this supernatural virtue, we love God above everything else, and our neighbour as ourselves for love of Him. "God is love," says St. John,[29] and everyone who loves, is born of God and knows God; and we know also that, according to the words of St. Paul: "the love of God has been poured out in our hearts by the Holy Spirit, whom we have received".[30]

This love is a gift of God which He offers us together with sanctifying grace. It is therefore a fruit of the Holy Ghost and unites us to Him. It raises in us a supernatural desire to love God, and at the same time a great joy because of God's eternal happiness. It consists in taking pleasure in Him, and this pleasure of ours finally expresses itself in deeds. Whoever possesses this love will perceive within his heart the longing to become perfect as the Heavenly Father is perfect: to do His will without ceasing; and to help to bring His Kingdom to others. One should not confuse this desire with mere sentimentality or a feeling of pity: it is the strong and steadfast will to serve God, wherever He may wish and because He asks it. "If you have any love for me, you must keep the commandments I give you."[31]

This love is in itself a command: "Thou shalt love the Lord thy God with the love of thy whole heart, and thy whole soul, and thy whole strength, and thy whole mind."[32]

In this love consists the whole of the Christian life, and from it rises an intimate and continuous life of prayer. In this love we shall find our trust in God increasing, fervour in fulfilling our daily duties, until we begin truly to keep the commandments. Again this love is unceasingly eager to spread God's Kingdom upon earth.

Christ frequently speaks about it in the Gospels, and from His account, it seems to us that it can best be described by the word "friendship". Whoever loves God becomes a friend of God, says St. Augustine. Gathered into the divine life by sanctifying grace, man meets with, and receives, God's infinite and disinterested love, and he can reply to this invitation by loving and serving God in return, for the sole reason

[28] I Cor. 13, 1. [29] I John 4, 8. [30] Rom. 5, 5.
[31] John 14, 15. [32] Luke 10, 27.

that He asks it, and just in the way in which He asks it. God will then take the predominant place in our existence. However, *the* proof of the love of God is to love one another: *charity*. This is the new commandment which Christ has given us: "You are to love one another; your love for one another is to be like the love I have borne you."[33] By this, men are to know that we are His disciples. St. John expresses it with a great deal of point in his first Epistle when he says: "If a man boasts of loving God, when he hates his own brother, he is a liar. He has seen his brother, and has no love for him; what love can he have for the God he has never seen?"[34]

In this love, we are taught by the Sermon on the Mount, all are to be included, friend as well as foe.[35] A man's attention is to be turned towards his neighbour, in his spiritual as well as in his temporal need; towards his eternal happiness and his ascent towards God; but the motive always remains God; it is for His sake that we love one another.

In his first Epistle to the Corinthians, St. Paul has enumerated the characteristics of love. "Charity is patient, is kind; charity feels no envy; charity is never perverse or proud, never insolent; does not claim its rights, cannot be provoked, does not brood over an injury; takes no pleasure in wrongdoing, but rejoices at the victory of truth; sustains, believes, hopes, endures, to the last."[36]

Every mortal sin committed banishes this love of God from the soul, and if the sin is followed by a systematic indifference, the love will gradually disappear altogether. "Being what thou art, lukewarm, neither cold nor hot, thou wilt make me vomit thee out of my mouth," says Christ.[37] It is usually by a lack of charity (especially by neglect of the seven last commandments) that the love of God is injured, languishes, and finally disappears.

By the practice of these three theological virtues the life of grace in the soul expands, and ultimately reaches its completion by the continuous operations of the Holy Ghost.

The first three commandments, which deal with our relationship with God, are closely connected with this action of the theological virtues.

[33] John 13, 34. [34] I John 4, 20-21. [35] Matt. 5, 44.
[36] Cor. 13. [37] Apoc. 3, 16.

We shall remember that the commandments are thus set out in the Catechism:

I am the Lord thy God, who brought thee out of the land of Egypt, and out of the house of bondage.

1. Thou shalt not have strange gods before Me. Thou shalt not make to thyself any graven thing, nor the likeness of anything that is in heaven above, or in the earth beneath, nor of those things that are in the waters under the earth. Thou shalt not adore them nor serve them.

2. Thou shalt not take the name of the Lord thy God in vain.

3. Remember that thou keep holy the Sabbath day.

These commandments are meant to express our correct attitude towards God.

The first commandment demands our absolute and implicit interior and exterior acknowledgment of Him. The exclusion of all other gods indicates the entire subjection of our whole mind to Him; the complete orientation of our heart towards His will. We may not place anything either next to Him or above Him; He is our Creator and our final end. We are totally dependent upon Him. Him only must we worship in spirit and in truth,[38] and Him only should we love above everything else.

In this connection we use the expressions interior and exterior adoration of God, or interior and exterior worship. The interior adoration or worship refers to our personal, inner dedication to God, and especially to our union with Him in faith, hope and charity. The exterior worship is the spontaneous result of this inner attitude of dependence and devotion, and expresses itself outwardly by words and gestures, by actions such as kneeling, singing, or sacrifices and offerings. This exterior worship derives its value from the force of the symbol, and from the interior attitude of the soul; folded hands, for instance, express deep concentration upon God, while the offering we make also includes the offering of ourselves to Him. This public worship takes place in the name of the Church and has at its very centre, the Mass.

Anyone who pays divine homage to a mere creature, attaching to either persons or things a supernatural power which they do not possess, sins against this first commandment. We still meet with many different forms of super-

[38] John 4, 24.

stition: the man who no longer believes often seeks, by other means, to come into contact with the spiritual world. By the use of mascots and charms he will try to give a favourable turn to a hopeless case; by fortune-telling he will try to discover the future which is known only to God; and by spiritism he will try to renew contact with the dead. In these cases it is difficult to draw a definite line between the powers of nature, of fraud, and of suggestion. The first commandment is only broken when one has recourse to a power which is hostile to God, or to forces which lie outside both nature and grace.

The second commandment insists that reverence for God should be preserved in our intercourse with other people; this commandment has a certain social aspect since it obliges everyone to use the names of God and of Jesus Christ reverently. These names represent the Person of God and must therefore never be used as expletives. Anyone who despises, mocks at, or curses God and His Church, or anything especially connected with them, is culpable of blasphemy by refusing God the reverence due to Him, if, that is to say, he realizes what he is doing.

Where cursing is genuinely used to call down evil from God either upon oneself or others, then, if seriously meant, it is a gross abuse which is a grave sin. Usually by swearing is understood the use of some coarse expression, and if this is directed towards another person in order to call down evil upon them, then it is also a definite breach of charity and of the fifth commandment.

On the other hand, the swearing of an oath or the making of a vow are considered to be a correct use of the Holy Name. When taking the oath, a man makes God his witness that he is speaking the truth or in the case of a vow, that he means to fulfil his promise. In this is also included an implicit act of faith, for he acknowledges that God is both omniscient and truthful, and that in the case of a lie, or the breaking of a promise, he will become subject to the justice of God. One must, however, never take an oath without a serious reason. Christ Himself said: "Let your word be Yes for Yes and No for No; whatever goes beyond this comes of evil."[39]

So long as men remain by nature unreliable and dishonest, and certainly as to their deeds and intentions is at times

[39] Matt. 5, 37.

absolutely necessary, this appeal to the omniscent God is permissible.

A vow is also an act of divine worship. Some piece of work, some project, some particular dedication, which in such concrete circumstances must be particularly pleasing to God, is formally promised and made a matter of serious obligation. Such a vow is more than the expression of a good intention, it is the expression of man's total dependence upon God and a homage rendered to His infinite majesty. Vows of this nature, after mature deliberation and much prayer and sound advice, can be made in the name of the Church, either publicly or privately, to some person in authority.

The third commandment concerns the execution of a social duty which rests upon the community in general. The Christian community as such, and as a creation of God, is obliged to worship and adore Him, and can only do so publicly according to definite and prescribed regulations. This commandment tells us of our obligation to set aside a certain part of our time for God, since otherwise in our busy daily life it would be easy for the consciousness of His presence to be lost. An individual, or a whole community, who no longer keep the holy-days as something sacred, soon lose their practical recognition of God, and then the Faith itself, and finally even the perfection of moral life.

The Church regulates which days are to be specially dedicated to God, and the manner in which they should be observed. The actual Lord's Day is the Sunday. We shall find one positive element in the celebration of this day, which is our obligatory presence at the Holy Sacrifice of the Mass; and one negative element, which is to rest from our work. The sanctification of the Sunday, and the resting from labour, belong together. As a minimum of prayer and worship of God, the Church requires us to take part in the Sacrifice of Christ, that is to say the Mass. A fervent Catholic will, of course, add to this, assistance at Benediction or other religious services. The Sunday-rest has a very beneficial effect upon man; he finds recollection in this leisure, free from the pressure of daily occupations, and can therefore direct his mind more easily towards the development of his whole personality: that is to say by indulging in reading, art, sport, play, friendship, or just simple homeliness, according to his disposition.

The Church realizes the value of this rest, but when making it of obligation her first intention is to produce favourable conditions for the raising of man's mind and heart to God. Therefore she forbids any kind of work unless it be necessary. The Sunday, however, is not intended to be kept as a day of mourning and penance, nor of silence and loneliness, since it is meant to be, as it were, a foretaste of our eternal joy. It should be a feast for both heart and mind.

Thus we see that these three commandments protect and assist the blossoming of the three theological virtues in the soul, and a life of faith and hope finds its completion in an eternal and joyous charity.

B. *The second tablet of the Commandments*

After having explained in the preceding chapters the consequences which flow from our attitude towards God, we shall try in the following pages to make a short survey of the general type of conduct which is required for the mutual relationship of men as fellow-members of the great supernatural human community.

A fact which should be carefully noted is that man does not stand face to face with God as an individual only. Naturally, as well as supernaturally (because of the Redemption), he lives in close relationship with a number of fellow-creatures. He cannot stand altogether apart from them since his affairs are too much involved with theirs. If we observe the purely natural course of man's life on earth, we shall immediately be struck by the fact that he is what is called a social being: that is to say, that he cannot live altogether without the assistance of other people, and that his natural instinct urges him to make himself useful to others. We both receive from the community, and give to the community: we need one another.

If God has created man thus, and not otherwise, then we shall naturally have to take into account this condition of His.

At the same time we must remember that that is not the whole story of man's present state. In actual fact something further has taken place since the Creation: the Redemption or the re-Creation. This regeneration through Christ means that the communal tie between men has been renewed and reinforced. We will not here repeat what has already been said in previous chapters as to the Kingdom of God, the Church, and the Mystical Body of Christ. But it may be useful to draw some conclusions from those chapters for practical application to daily life.

The ten commandments which were given in the Old Testament were in no way changed by Christ. He only perfected and drew attention to them by commenting on them and interpreting them. This also applies to the seven remaining commandments which regulate our relations with each other, as man to man, and our more general relationship with human society as a whole.

When Christ spoke of these commandments in the Sermon on the Mount, He made it quite clear that they were not to be looked upon as merely formal rules of behaviour, but as laws of existence which must be appreciated at their spiritual value and which, ultimately, are only variations of the single theme, which so constantly recurs in all Christian teaching upon our relationship with our neighbour: charity. Thus we can call charity the summing-up of the second tablet of the law, and with this thought in our mind may try to reach a clearer understanding of the contents and tendency of the following seven commandments, which we will now consider separately.

1. *Honour thy father and thy mother*

When, in the fourth commandment, we are told to honour father and mother, God is pointing out to us that we should show a fitting respect to our parents and others who are our spiritual and secular superiors. St. James in his Epistle, stresses the fact that all authority comes from God, and formulates the Christian idea that behind all true and legitimate authority, divine authority is to be recognized. St. Paul had evidently also come to the same conclusion when he wrote: "You who are children must show obedience in the Lord to your parents . . . you who are fathers . . . the training, the discipline in which you bring them up must come from the Lord. You who are slaves, give your human masters the obedience you owe to Christ."[40]

This respect, therefore, is founded upon love of men, and love of God whom one sees represented in men: it expresses

[40] Eph. 6, 1-9.

itself in respect and ready co-operation with those who are in authority. Of course, both obedience and co-operation can be shown without any love at all, e.g. for purely practical or disciplinary reasons. They assume a Christian and supernatural character only when we obey or co-operate in the spirit expressed by St. Paul when he says: "And you, children, be obedient *to the Lord* in your parents."

We ought not to find it surprising that in this fourth commandment, so much emphasis is laid on the reverence and love of children for their parents. Parental authority is of service to the family, and the family is the germ-cell of every other community. Parental authority thus fulfils an important function in regard to both Church and State.

According to the teaching of the Old Testament, children who honoured their parents were to be richly rewarded both in heaven and upon earth. And to-day even when children grow up, filial love and respect should still be expressed by gratitude for all that has been done for them. In certain circumstances this gratitude may even have to take a practical form, such as helping their parents in their spiritual or material needs, while they should of course at all times defend their father and mother if necessary; that is to say stand up for their rights, and protect their good name.

As regards the spiritual rulers of the Church, we are bound to obey them in all those matters upon which they have authority to judge, such as matters of faith and morals, church discipline, and also in affairs of a temporal nature which may, nevertheless, be closely related to those of a more spiritual and religious character. It need hardly be said that a Catholic sees far more in the Church Authorities than he would in just the members of some worldly committee. In Catholic circles an expression is used which clearly sums up the general attitude of Catholics to the Church; she is spoken of as "Our Holy Mother the Church" and loved as such. Reverence and obedience increase and flourish in this love for what is called the *sensus catholicus*: that is to say a sympathetic familiarity with all the traditions, the teaching and the general feeling of the Church. As Thomas Merton says: "*Sentire cum Ecclesia* is freedom."[41]

The secular authorities should also be obeyed and respected since Christ has told us that we should render to Cæsar that

[41] The Sign of Jonas, p. 299.

which is Cæsar's, and St. Paul also writes in the same sense. We must remember that worldly authorities are in charge of a community which has its definite rights: a community by which we also profit as citizens, and towards which, therefore, we have obligations. Added to this our own nation is composed of people who have a special right to our loyalty and regard because we are of the same stock. The government of the country should therefore be respected and its laws obeyed; anyone who fails in this duty is hampering that government and so harming the community as a whole.

The obedience of which we have been speaking is, however, never an absolute obedience. Ultimately and above all man owes his obedience to his own conscience, and he is therefore not bound to obey any Authority which tells him to do something which would be against his principles. In that case he can apply the answer of St. Peter and the apostles to himself: "God has more right to be obeyed than man."[42]

2. *Thou shalt not kill*

The rules of life which are set before us in the following six commandments do not imply any obligations towards particular people, but deal only with our general duty to our fellow-men. We certainly do not owe obedience to everyone, but the law of charity is universal and knows no exceptions. This law is founded upon the belief that—created by God and redeemed by Christ—all one's fellow-men have the right to an existence worthy of human beings, both naturally and supernaturally. The fifth commandment particularly emphasizes the right which every man possesses to life itself, whereas the other commandments define man's rights regarding those essential conditions necessary for an existence suited to both a human being and a child of God. Every man, for instance, has a right to his own property and goods, which enable him to live and conduce to his natural and supernatural well-being (seventh commandment). For the same reason the community in general has a right to demand that a man should behave responsibly when it comes to matters affecting the preservation of the race in general (sixth and ninth commandments).

The fifth commandment actually implies more than man's

[42] Acts 5, 29.

right to live. Let us listen to the words of Christ Himself in the Sermon on the Mount:

"You have heard that it was said to the men of old, Thou shalt do no murder; if a man commits murder, he must answer for it before the Court of Justice. But I tell you that any man who is angry with his brother must answer for it before the Court of Justice, and any man who says Raca to his brother must answer for it before the Council; and any man who says to his brother, Thou fool, must answer for it in hell fire. If thou art bringing thy gift, then, before the altar, and rememberest there that thy brother has some ground of complaint against thee, leave thy gift lying there before the altar, and go home; be reconciled with thy brother first, and then come back to offer thy gift. If any man has a claim against thee, come to terms there and then, while thou art walking in the road with him."[43]

It is clear that Christ's words are meant to draw attention to the primarily interior character of sin as well as virtue: charity is not only a matter of exterior actions, but first and foremost an inner orientation of the will. Sin is not confined to murder, but is also present in unreasonable anger, hatred, envy and jealousy. Words alone can injure our neighbour if, for instance, for ulterior motives we either insult him or jeer at him, or in any way pester and annoy him.

The fifth commandment therefore lays upon us a positive duty to respect both our own and our neighbour's spiritual and physical life and health. Our own life is just as dependent on God, and is just as much His creation, as the life of our fellow-man. Hence we have no right whatsoever to take our own life or in any way to injure ourselves physically. For the same reason we may not needlessly or recklessly endanger our life or health. There is a form of self-love which is not only justifiable but which Christ Himself used as a measure for charity: we must love our neighbours *as ourselves*. Apart from the law one may neither strike, injure nor kill one's neighbour, nor in any way intentionally shorten his life. Christ also showed clearly, by the words which we quoted, that one has no right to make the life of a fellow-man unbearable, or in any way embitter him by words or attitude.

A man's good name is essential to him, therefore both

[43] Matt. 5, 21-26.

slander and back-biting are to be condemned. It is true that they do not kill our neighbour or normally shorten his life, but either of them damages his general standing and that dignity to which he has a right.

To discuss with someone else the faults of another can only be useful in a case where the person to whom we speak will be enabled to help him, or should we ourselves be in need of advice as to how to assist him. An exception must of course be made in the case of persons who, for some reason or another, have a real right to be informed of any evil, and who exercise some function which concerns the good of the community in general. It may possibly even happen under such circumstances, that the interests of a particular fellow-man may have to be sacrificed to the interests of the community as a whole. By slandering someone (that is, speaking evil against him although we ourselves know that what we say is not true) we not only sin against the fifth but also against the eighth commandment, as we shall show later on.

We cannot but be struck by the strength with which Christ connected charity with his fundamental teaching. When, on the very eve of His Passion and death, He once again recapitulated His principal instructions and, among others, the parable of the Vine and the Branches to illustrate the living organism of His Church, He also made the meaning of charity quite clear: "I have bestowed my love upon you, just as my Father has bestowed His love upon me . . . You will live on in my love if you keep my commandments . . . This is my commandment that you should love one another as I have loved you. This is the greatest love a man can show, that he should lay down his life for his friends . . . These are the directions I give you, that you should love one another."[44]

The fifth commandment can only be understood in its full significance when it is considered in relation to the general law of charity.

In connection with the foregoing there are still two subjects which call for comment:

1. What view does the Catholic Church take of Abortion?
2. What is her attitude as regards war?

It is clear that both these questions are closely connected with the fifth commandment.

Abortion may be briefly described as the loss of a fœtal life.

[44] John 15, 9-18.

It may occur either by causing the fœtus to die, or by premature extraction of it. It will be easy to grasp the attitude which a Catholic should have towards such practices. The attitude of the Catholic Church itself, is on the whole, already sufficiently well known. As no individual has the right to end any life, Abortion falls inexorably under the general condemnation of the fifth commandment: Thou shalt not kill. Only the State itself can pronounce the Death Sentence, and even then only in the case of a profoundly guilty person and in the interests of the community at large. As with an unborn child this question of guilt cannot arise, not even the State has the power either to order or to approve Abortion. Therefore the Church unreservedly condemns all these practices which, used willingly and knowingly, have as intention either the direct killing or the removal of the fœtus. Apart from any question of danger to the life of the mother, Abortion cannot be viewed otherwise than as an attempt at murder.

We have used the words "direct killing". There is obviously a sharp distinction between an act directly meant to kill and an act which has no such primary intention, but which may—indirectly—cause death as its result. In such a case one can only say that the result—death—is voluntarily *permitted.* It is not easy to decide, either in principle or in practice, how to judge an action which may, in addition to one unfortunate and regretted result, have several other good ones. What is one to think, for instance, of an operation to be performed, where the fœtus itself is not touched, but which will most probably result in its death? There are many similar cases in which an action may have good as well as bad results, as in the example just given where the mother would probably live and the fœtus die.

We are not always prohibited from doing what is lawful in itself, although evil consequences may follow which we do not desire. The good effects of our acts are then directly intended, and the regretted evil consequences are only reluctantly permitted to follow because we cannot avoid them. The evil thus permitted is not imputed to us provided four conditions are verified, namely:

1. That the immediate effect be good in itself, and the act be not already, for some other cause, a bad or unlawful act.

2. That the evil be not made a means to obtain the good

effect; for this would be to do evil that good might come of it —a procedure never allowed.

3. That the act be in no circumstances performed in order to obtain the evil effects, but that we make all reasonable efforts to avoid them.

4. That the good effect be at least as important as the evil effect. There must be a very serious reason for performing the action and so voluntarily risking the evil effect.

This last condition is most vital and calls for a genuine application of the laws of common sense and prudence, and of a judgment which knows how to weigh the various values in question, one against the other.

As regards the problem of war the reproach is sometimes levelled at the Catholic Church that her attitude towards it is too casual. In view of the fifth commandment, she should express herself openly against every form of warfare, and forbid her members to take part in, or co-operate with, any war. It is well known that such a radical attitude has never been adopted by the Catholic Church. She regrets war, in company with all right-minded people, and with all who are interested in the destiny of human society. But she neither dares nor desires to forbid such people or communities as are unjustly attacked to put up a spirited defence. On the contrary, she believes it to be the duty of both the individual and the community to defend their rights against violation, and it is her opinion that self-defence may, in decisive moments, demand from a people both personal and communal heroism. Anyone is at liberty to defend themselves from someone who attacks them, especially if it concerns their actual existence. A community in general possesses this same right, and the lawful authorities who are responsible for the welfare of a nation, both may and should appeal to their subjects for co-operation in order to defeat any unlawful attack, to the best of their ability. In connection with this matter we would again refer the reader to what has been said in the section dealing with the fourth commandment, as to obedience to Civil Authority.

3. *Thou shalt not commit adultery*
Thou shalt not covet thy neighbour's wife

The reason why we should live chastely is primarily

because we may not use our bodily functions contrary to God's design for them and secondarily because our body is a member of Christ and a temple of the Holy Ghost.

Arising out of these two principles, the sixth commandment forbids all external sins, and the ninth commandment all internal sins of impurity. What exactly does this mean? Impurity in general we may define as the irregular desire for sexual pleasure. The sexual organs obviously play an important part in the whole of man's physical and psychic life. They are the natural instruments of reproduction, created by God, and dependent on the co-operation of husband and wife. How this human co-operation can come to full flowering in marriage has been dealt with already, earlier in the book. Sexual intercourse entails not only reproduction, but also the possibility of education for the offspring. If this is not the case, then one is using one's bodily functions contrary to God's design and flouting the interests of human society in general; in short, merely for one's own selfish ends.

This line of thought leads us to conclude that the sixth and ninth commandments protect the right of Society in general to existence. There appears an even deeper meaning, when we view Society, the Community, as a union of mankind with Christ: a supernatural union which is fundamental to mutual love. Viewed in this way, love can be a strong incentive to moderation and self-restraint for those who endeavour to live chastely. We have already spoken about external and internal sins of impurity, those namely, which are expressed in outward visible actions, and those which remain hidden within man, such as impure thoughts and desires. In the Sermon on the Mount, Christ emphasizes the guilt of internal sins. He says: "You have heard that it was said, Thou shalt not commit adultery. But I tell you that he who casts his eyes on a woman so as to lust after her has already committed adultery with her in his heart."[45] And in order to clearly indicate the seriousness of this matter He continues: "If thy right eye is the occasion of thy falling into sin, pluck it out and cast it away from thee; better to lose one part of thy body than to have the whole cast into Hell. And if thy right hand is an occasion of falling, cut it off and cast it away from thee; better to lose one of thy limbs than to have thy whole body cast into Hell."

[45] Matt. 5, 27, 28.

From this, it is plain that we must avoid not only direct acts of impurity, but also those actions, whether external or internal, which can easily lead to impurity as a consequence, and which are called in general, indecent or immodest. Under this heading are comprised looks, talks, reading, singing, shows or films which may lead to impurity because of their nature, or through particular circumstances they may exercise a strong provocative influence on our sexual passion. One should not delude oneself too easily, saying that one can "stand" it. Of course it goes without saying that modesty makes demands also on those who through their conduct, attitude or way of acting, are responsible for such unnecessary provocation. In the matter of dress, particularly for women and girls, the opposite sex should not be given occasion for sin. Naturally the surroundings in which one is, have an influence here. When bathing at the sea-side or swimming-pool, one dresses differently from when at home or when out shopping. It is here not a matter of measurement but of good taste, politeness, self-respect and sufficient fine feeling not to wish to hurt or give umbrage to one's fellow-men.

Certain actions can be in themselves good and useful, and yet lead to temptation (things like nursing, or medical examination). These actions come under the same principle enunciated under the fifth commandment, the principle of double effect; where one action results in both good and bad effects. According to this principle it follows that no action may be performed, outside of permissible sexual intercourse, in order that relief or stimulation may be the result.

For the rest, common sense and prudence should judge whether the usefulness of any action balances against the risk of consenting to sexual pleasure. Accordingly, it is for instance quite clear that one may perform actions which are good and useful for bodily cleanliness and health, although they may bring about indirectly and unsought for, some sexual stimulation.

Catholic teaching on married life has already been dealt with in the chapter on Matrimony.

Probably many readers will be interested in the question of courtship and engagement, and what is allowed by the sixth and ninth commandments. Such a more-than-friendly companionship between boys and girls is meant as a preparation for future marriage and married life. Therefore the intimacies of married life are not permitted; courtship serves to create the right atmosphere of generous and unselfish love, so that later on these intimacies can truly and worthily thrive. Sexual passion may not yet realize itself in loving physical surrender, because the conditions which guarantee the education of possible children have not yet been fulfilled, and because the unity intended by God, whereby these two wills will be one flesh, has not yet been entered into by the Sacrament of Marriage. Consequently, everything that might lead up to intimacy must be avoided by the engaged couple, as far as possible. They may and must show their love for each other, but they may not let themselves go in this at the risk of losing control of themselves. A great self-restraint is asked of them and particularly of the engaged girl a prudent modesty. In self-sacrificing love, they must help each other to avoid dangerous occasions and risky temptations. Not only do they develop unselfishness and will-power in this way but also what is even more important, they are already building strong foundations for a healthy and happy married life.

In conclusion one may say that the virtue of chastity demands the avoidance of all sexual intercourse outside of marriage; further, the avoidance of all preparatory acts to intercourse and of all things which intentionally, needlessly and uselessly can be used as an inducement to sexual pleasure.

No exaggerated prudence or fear is required, but honest care for the high value of Christian purity. Above all careless frivolity and dishonest self over-estimation are quite inimical.

4. *Thou shalt not steal*
Thou shalt not covet thy neighbour's house, nor his servant, nor his ox, nor his ass, nor anything that is his

The seventh and tenth commandments deal with our conduct as regards the goods and belongings of our fellow-men. Man has not only a right to live, but also a right to the necessary conditions which make life possible. To these conditions belong, amongst other things, the right to possess what he needs in the way of material goods, and—to ensure his quiet possession of them—the right of ownership which includes the right to dispose of them as he pleases. The virtue of justice sets definite standards for us in this matter, and the Catechism describes justice as "giving what is due to God, our neighbours, and ourselves". For ourselves and our neighbour this due certainly includes more than material things, so when we speak of justice in connection with the seventh and tenth commandments we must realize that we are only speaking of a part of that virtue.

The expression "what is due" suggests that individuals have a right to possess property, and the Church has always accepted that right. She is convinced that the material benefits and wealth of this world are primarily destined for the use of all men, that is for the use of the whole community, and in order to realize such an ideal she acknowledges the necessity of what is called private ownership. Every mentally efficient adult should be able to have his legitimate share of these material goods which form part of the immediate necessities of life. We are here, therefore, speaking of rights which belong to men as individuals. . . . This justice between man and man is called individual, particular, or commutative justice.

The right of the individual to own property is, however, neither unlimited nor absolute; the community as a whole has its rights also, and both the authority governing it and the members composing it must take those rights into account. The owner is free to sell, exchange or waste his property, even to destroy it, without sinning against commutative justice. But by doing so he may, at the same time, be sinning against other virtues in so far as he infringes the rights of the community (against general or legal justice), and puts on one side charity, piety, and consideration for his neighbour.

Every form of Socialism, including Communism, which does not adequately recognize this right to private property, is condemned by the Church. Every political system which, either in theory or practice, holds that the right to private property is unrestricted, or not sufficiently restricted, and selfishly exploits it, is also condemned by the Church. For this reason certain forms of capitalism find no favour with the Church.

A very topical problem at the moment is the relation between Capital and Labour, in short the whole social question. Special attention has been drawn to all these matters by Papal Encyclicals and pronouncements of the last few decades, and many of these offer wise and practical solutions.[46]

We will now explain what is forbidden by the seventh and tenth commandments in order to protect the rights of private property. In general it can be summarized by saying that anything is forbidden which infringes upon the rights of the owner beyond his reasonable will. We must here distinguish between theft, damage and destruction, idling, and so defrauding another of our work, usury and deception, the non-payment of debts, the withholding of just wages, and not returning things found or borrowed. The gravity of the sin is to be measured by the harm which is done either to the individual or to the community. When the loss or damage is equal to one day's cost of living for the injured party (and his family if he has one) theologians are inclined to speak of grave sin. It is, however, impossible to fix concrete figures in such cases, and conscience has to fill up the gaps. The standard of one day's cost of living is naturally liable to all kinds of variation—not only dependent upon the era in which one lives, but also upon the varying needs of different classes of people. Stealing from a millionaire will not be so grave a sin as stealing from some poor person; but it must nevertheless be recognized that there is a limit to injustice even towards a rich man, and that once one surpasses that limit, the sin is grave. There is no question of stealing a hundred pounds and only calling it a venial sin, because a hundred pounds has about the same value to him as, say, one pound to a poorer man. Were an elastic standard of that sort to be in common use the community in general would suffer. In these present days, a theft or damage caused up to the value of about six or eight pounds, should be recognized, by any person with a conscience, as a grave transgression.

Theft consists in taking away someone else's property against that person's reasonable will. This may be done by either taking the thing in order to keep it oneself, to sell it, or to use it in some other way.

It is not however called theft should, for instance, a servant give an alms which she knows that her mistress most certainly would not refuse: should a man help himself to something in extreme need, or in order to reimburse himself secretly, for

[46] See especially the Encyclicals Rerum Novarum and Quadragesimo Anno.

something which has been stolen from him, or of which he has been defrauded. In these cases the act is not performed against the reasonable will of the owner.

A so-called small theft can also be a grave sin, if the intention is to steal a large sum by means of many small sums, or if the thefts are committed in association with others thus amounting to a considerable value. It must also be regarded as mortal sin, if, even without premeditation or any definite plan, small thefts should end by amounting to a large theft, through the fact that either that which was stolen was not subsequently returned, or that the thefts followed each other in rapid succession.

We spoke earlier of the case of someone in "extreme need". These words must be applied literally, meaning that the absolute necessities of life are at stake. In such a case, where every other reasonable attempt has failed, one is justified in appropriating sufficient to alleviate that need. The reason is that individual ownership of the goods of this world, though according to the natural law, yields to the stronger and more sacred right conferred by natural law upon every man to avail himself of such things as are necessary for his own preservation. St. Thomas declares that (II—11 Q. lxvi, a. 7) in such straits what is taken becomes, because of the dire need experienced, one's very own, and so cannot be said to be stolen.

We also mentioned "secretly reimbursing". This is only permissible on the following conditions:

1. It must be absolutely certain that one is strictly entitled to whatever it is (i.e. if agreed wages have not been paid).

2. It must never be done at the cost of a third party (e.g. where they might be suspected of theft).

3. It must be the only way in which to get what is one's right (otherwise one offends against general justice, which includes the preservation of peace, and harmony among individuals, and the guaranteeing of the security of human society).

He who either steals, or damages, or is guilty of usury, is obliged to make restitution: he must give back that which he has stolen, or make good the damage. As, however, the impossible can never be a duty, one is not obliged to make restitution where it is manifestly beyond one's power, or impossible for some reason in connection with other persons concerned. One cannot get absolution in Confession from a sin against the seventh commandment if one refuses to fulfil this duty of restitution in so far as it is possible. Such a refusal is as sinful as the theft or damage itself. All damage, or at least all foreseen damage, must be repaired, and the compensation must, as far as possible, be such that from the point of view of the rightful owner it is as if the thing had never been stolen or damaged.

Anyone who, without just cause, demands interest at an exorbitant rate, for something which he has lent, is guilty of usury. There may, however, be special circumstances justifying a stipulation for a higher rate of interest, proportionate to the risk involved in the loan. If, however, no special circumstances exist, one is then obliged to set the matter right according to the rules given above regarding restitution.

There is another form of grave injustice which is not nearly so obvious, and which many people do not consider to be either wrong or sinful, namely idling. We are here considering the injustice to the community in general, or to an individual employer, of not spending the time of work for which we are paid, according to the manner agreed upon. It is true that in the Occupied Countries during the war, sabotage in certain factories and industries could be of the greatest service to one's country, and assist towards future victory, in which case it was not only allowable but often became even a duty. In normal circumstances, however, the situation is quite otherwise. No one is entitled, if he has agreed to work and receive wages for this work, either to "work to rule" or to "go slow".

5. *Thou shalt not bear false witness against thy neighbour*

By the eighth commandment the love of truth, or veracity, is protected. Not only does the bearing of false witness run counter to the virtue of truthfulness—but we can strain the truth by either lying, or mis-statement, and by being guilty of calumny or rash judgment.

In our intercourse with each other we make use of all sorts of signs and symbols, notably by speech and the written word. These signs are not only for the purpose of making something known to another, but may also be taken as an expression of our own feelings. We can, as a matter of fact, express ourselves without having the slightest intention of drawing other people's attention to us. We can, for instance, speak to ourselves; give vent to our feelings when alone; and a poet may write a poem which he does not mean to show to anyone else—or at all events without that intention being foremost in his mind. Words and other signs are called truthful when they concur with the reality which someone is trying to express. A person is called truthful, if, by the expressions which he uses, he *wants* to express the truth as far as possible.

We must not forget that men also use these modes of expression on occasion to convey something different from that which they are genuinely thinking, feeling or experiencing. Words can also serve to blur the truth and mislead. It is possible for someone to tell me a whole long story with the definite hope and intention that I shall not discover the truth about certain persons or events.

According to what standards must we judge of these things morally?

As a preparation it may be as well to consider lying. It does not appear to be very easy to define a lie accurately. Theologians give us different definitions, none of them entirely satisfactory. The difficulty is not only theoretical, but arises principally from the fact that one feels that not every untruth can be called a lie and a sin; sometimes it may be a good thing to withhold the truth from someone, and yet in many cases, in view of the circumstances, one cannot remain altogether silent. The words must therefore, in such an instance, fulfil their function, which is to keep the truth a secret. In default of a better description, we might perhaps define a lie for practical purposes as to withhold the truth, *to which he has a right,* from someone, or without very good grounds for such an action, to inform a person of something which is clearly untrue, or is thought by ourselves to be untrue.

One is never permitted, under any circumstances whatever, to tell a lie, even though by so doing one might prevent a great evil. Of itself lying is a venial sin, but if through the lie some other virtue is also gravely violated (justice, for instance, or charity) then of course it is a mortal sin.

What is called a jocose lie by which, teasingly or merely to enliven the conversation, one says things which do not tally with the truth, is no sin, so long as it is perfectly clear to any sensible person that one's words and gestures are not meant to convey the truth but to amuse the company.

To say something which is not true, or at any rate to keep the truth secret by means of one's words or actions, is sometimes allowable, but only in a case where the other person has no right to know the truth, and where there is some strong reason for withholding it.

The act of lying particularly violates the virtues of justice and charity in the case of calumny—which means the saying of what is not true about someone else, or at all events of what is not thought to be true by the speaker. Everyone has a right to his good reputation as long as he himself does not make it impossible for people to believe in it. By calumny this right is not only violated, but mendaciously violated, so that in such a sin one can discern a double evil. The gravity of the sin must be measured according to the harm which has been done to the reputation of the victim. One must bear in mind that loss of reputation can have very far-reaching consequences for both the spiritual and temporal prosperity of the person in question. One must always take this into account when judging a calumny.

Rash judgment has less serious consequences but, strictly speaking, is an evil on a par with calumny. As the words themselves indicate, rash judgment means to condemn, or think ill of, someone or something, without being sufficiently aware of what one is talking about. If this does not develop into calumny, that is to say if this condemnation is not communicated to others, it will not as a rule do much harm, and is not usually a mortal sin; justice and charity may, however, be violated in this case also, since everyone has a right to be well thought of unless they themselves make it impossible.

We must conclude with the remark that one can also commit a sin by telling the truth. We have already suggested the possibility. There may be two reasons which forbid us to tell the truth to someone else: these two reasons rest upon the person to whom we are speaking, and the person who has told us the truth. To hear the truth might be injurious to the person to whom we are speaking, or it might be harmful to others if that person came to know the truth. It may have been told us as something for our ears *alone*: as a secret. We shall know whether it was meant as a secret by the way in which it was told us, by the nature of the information itself, or by the nature of our own profession (e.g. that of a lawyer, doctor or confessor). In all these cases to speak the truth, which, in fact, would be the exposing of a secret, is nothing less than an abuse of trust, and a violation of that right which everyone has to the privacy of his secrets, and so a serious infringement of the law of charity to one's neighbour.

Apart from the secret of the confessional, there may be exceptions for certain other professional secrets, as well as for secrets which have been entrusted to us outside of our profession, or which we have discovered for ourselves. These exceptions are difficult to define. The professions themselves usually have their own rules. In general one can only say that there must be a very great benefit to be obtained on the one hand, or a very great evil to be avoided on the other, before it is allowable to communicate a serious secret without the permission of the person concerned.

With this the ten commandments of God have been dealt with in bold outlines. Faith, trust, reverence, justice, temperance and veracity, are the high values which these commandments are intended to preserve. It is not difficult to see why these values should stand in need of protection. Without them, charity would lack her solid foundation, her possibility of expression. She is protected by all these qualities, as they themselves are protected by the ten commandments. On the other hand, justice and truthfulness, fidelity and honesty, temperance and all the other virtues, are held together by charity, in what is called by St. Paul, "the bond of perfection".

§ 3. *The Six Precepts of the Church*

The Church received from Christ the power to bind and to loose here upon earth. She uses this power by issuing, among other things, general disciplinary laws which are recorded in her book of Ecclesiastical Laws, the *Codex Juris Canonici*.

Especially applicable to daily life and to the use of the Sacraments are what are commonly known as "the six precepts of the Church". These are:

1. To keep the Sunday and Holidays of Obligation holy by hearing Mass and resting from servile work.

2. To keep the days of fasting and abstinence appointed by the Church.
3. To go to Confession at least once a year.
4. To receive the Blessed Sacrament at least once a year and that at Easter or thereabouts.
5. To contribute to the support of our pastors.
6. Not to marry within certain degrees of kindred nor to solemnize marriage at the forbidden times.

We will add a short note on each of these, and we shall use the word precept when referring to the six precepts of the Church, and the word commandment when meaning the ten commandments of God.

1. The Holidays of Obligation are those days which have to be kept as if they were Sundays. In England they are: Christmas Day, the Circumcision, the Epiphany, the Ascension, Corpus Christi, the Feast of SS. Peter and Paul, the Assumption, and the Feast of All Saints. We do not mention those feasts which invariably fall on a Sunday, since they are already provided for. The precept for these feast-days does not put the Faithful under any other obligation than the obligation of keeping them as a Sunday.

2. The third commandment has already given us a description of the natural law which obliges us to honour God: the way in which God is most honoured is by the sanctification of His day. Keeping Sunday holy has just been dealt with so here we will only refer once more to the third commandment, which can be summarized briefly as enjoining (a) Sunday rest and (b) attendance at Holy Mass.

Sunday rest excludes all kinds of so-called servile work, that is, all work which demands more physical than mental energy and which is mainly done for material profit. The Church's law, however, does not bind where higher obligations (either the natural law or divine commandment) oblige us to perform such work on a Sunday.

Attending Mass with proper attention and devotion has the same reasonable conditions attached to it; whoever has other and overriding duties to fulfil is exempt from the obligation. For instance, anyone who is ill may not, according to divine commandment, risk either his life or his health in order to comply with the Church's law.

3. Fasting and abstinence are two different things, between

which even many Catholics do not sufficiently distinguish. Both are forms of physical mortification.

By the law of fasting the Church obliges all her subjects between the ages of 21 and 60 years of age, who have not been exempted on account of either sickness, manual labour, or any other valid cause, to take less food than ordinarily. One full meal per day, supplemented by a light meal in the morning and in the evening, according to the approved customs of the country or the district, have to suffice on days of fasting. These days of fasting are: all the days of Lent (from Ash Wednesday until midday on Easter Saturday) excepting Sundays; the Ember Days (at the beginning of the four seasons of the year) known as *quartuor tempora*; and the Vigils of the big feasts.[47]

The Church's laws of fasting do not prescribe what one should eat or not eat, neither has the Church stipulated anything as to *drinking* for example a cup of tea or coffee between meals. The aim of fasting is to enable us by penance and mortification, to turn with greater freedom and earnestness towards the thought of God and virtue, and so to reach the right attitude towards material things: further, to strengthen the will and to purify the spirit.

The same applies to abstinence. By the law of abstinence the Church forbids us to eat either meat, or soups made from meat, on certain days, which include all Fridays in the year, the ember days and the vigils, Ash Wednesday and Easter Saturday till noon. The law of abstinence is therefore a restriction of our liberty in the matter of food, which is not meant merely to transfer our choice to favourite dishes, but which has the same motive as fasting, and aims at a directly spiritual result.

4. The two following precepts are closely connected. The fourth precept is an indirect obligation to go to Confession once a year. It is an indirect obligation in this sense that (according to the explanation of theologians) this precept is only binding for those who, without confession, cannot meet their obligation to go once a year to Holy Communion. It is an act of sacrilege for anyone in a state of mortal sin to receive Holy Communion; he must first receive Absolution.

[47] By special dispensation for the British Isles, only four days of Fasting are of obligation during the year. The Vigils of Christmas, Easter, The Assumption of Our Lady and All Saints. [Editor.]

Because of this, for those who are consciously in a state of mortal sin, there arises the obligation to go to Confession in order to be able to make the required Communion at about Eastertime. In the chapter dealing with the Sacrament of Penance, as such, the reader will find set out when it is actually obligatory to receive this latter Sacrament.

5. The Church is conscious that the most precious thing which has been entrusted to her care is enclosed within the mystery of the Holy Eucharist. That is why she so constantly rouses her children to renewed reverence and gratitude for the Blessed Sacrament. The best way in which we can express our gratitude for a gift is by making use of it. To obey this precept means that at least once a year we shall express our gratitude by going to Holy Communion. But the Church advises the Faithful most particularly to do far more than is strictly obligatory. Frequent and, if possible, even daily communion is recommended to all who have the opportunity.

The obligation holds good for all who have come to the age of reason, which is generally considered to be at or about the age of seven. Paschaltide normally begins a week before Easter Day itself, and finishes upon the Octave of Trinity Sunday. Diocesan regulations may, however, lengthen this period in some cases.

Church laws and directions fall under what is called the Positive law, namely laws which do not follow from the actual nature of things, but are issued by some particular authority in order to promote or guarantee the observance of the natural law. Those who make these laws are not only empowered to promulgate their own laws, but may also abolish or modify them. So the Church has the right to use her legislative power at will. Her laws, however, are never of so compelling a nature as to leave room for no exceptions. She may always dispense from them for a good reason, and when circumstances either prevent, or make it morally impossible, to obey an ecclesiastical law, no one, even in the absence of a dispensation, is bound by it.

Positive divine law and the law of nature always take precedence over the precepts of the Church.

The Ecclesiastical Law for Books

The Church makes her laws regarding reading matter for Catholics upon the reasonable assumption that not all her members have at their command either sufficient judgment or knowledge to ensure a perfectly sound choice on all occasions. The Church regards us in truth as her children, for whom she is responsible to God, and whom it is her duty to keep unspotted for Him and in union with Him for our own happiness.

All those with any self-knowledge and humility, knowing their own human deficiency, and looking back on their own past mistakes, will be only too happy to avail themselves of the judgment and direction of the Church. Were there to be any feeling of mental opposition to such laws, it would be immediately overcome by the deep consciousness of personal insufficiency which is felt by every good Catholic and which, since there is no reason to be ashamed of it, should always be borne in mind.

Upon the very extensive list of books with which the world is for ever presenting us, the Church marks certain reading matter as definitely not suitable for Catholics, and other books as needing permission before they may be read. The Church excludes, for us all, any reading matter in which the evil is so frankly exhibited and promoted that it carries the danger of infection to every human conscience not already entirely corrupted. Any obscene writing or art, which lowers human standards of culture or honour, must be absolutely avoided. Concerning writings which deal with religion or morality, the Church often makes distinctions in those who may and may not read certain books. That which might be dangerous for one person, or for the masses indiscriminately, might be quite harmless to another, and even useful and necessary to them in their work.

That is why an express ecclesiastical permission is necessary in order to read:

1. Non-Catholic Bible translations and publications.

2. All books defending heresy or schism or attacking the foundations of religion or morality.

3. Books which in any way ridicule Catholic teaching; which try to subvert ecclesiastical discipline; which attack divine worship or ecclesiastical hierarchy; which offend the clerical or religious orders; or which commend any form of superstition.

All kinds of reading matter (including newspapers and magazines) are included under the heading books.

Anyone who asks and obtains a dispensation with regard to reading must not use it as a blindfold for his conscience, but must indeed use that conscience all the more watchfully in order to distinguish the false from the true in all that he reads.

CHAPTER XIV

SPIRITUAL GROWTH

THE TEN COMMANDMENTS and the precepts of the Church are a signpost to the road which man has to take if he is to live in the friendship of God. But the development of that friendship, and of his interior life, involves far more than is comprised in merely not transgressing the commandments: it means interior union with Christ by means of prayer and continual self-sacrifice. In this way the Christian grows in the perfection which Christ asks of him: "But you are to be perfect, as your heavenly Father is perfect."[1]

We will now deal successively with the life of prayer, mortification, and Christian perfection.

§ 1. *The Life of Prayer*

There are many Christians who look for a compromise in life: a half-way house between those who are for, and those who are against, Christ: and who find it in an existence which only differs from that of the pagans by a few exterior Church practices. Does anyone nowadays marvel, as did those heathens of the first few Christian centuries, exclaiming: How these Christians love one another; how wise they are in their social views; what courage they show in protesting against all the prevalent opinions and rules of conduct! "

It is easy enough to attribute this religious poverty of ours to the spirit of the times, which tends to make people impervious to the teaching of Christ: or to the use of outworn methods in regard to the care of souls: or to dull and slovenly church services.

But the real seat of the trouble, which has made the salt to lose its savour and the light which should have shone to be hidden under a bushel—the profound root cause—is the *conscious or unconscious neglect of prayer* in the personal life

[1] Matt. 5, 48.

of each individual: of that real and sincere prayer which endeavours, although perhaps not always easily, and often even amid the weariness of spiritual darkness and dryness, to meet God, and to give itself to Him in order that He, too, may give Himself in return.

Without prayer God's word does not become for us, as St. Paul describes it, "something alive, full of energy; something which can penetrate deeper than any two-edged sword, reaching the very division between soul and spirit, between joints and marrow, quick to distinguish every thought and design in our hearts".[2]

The Sacraments, also, without prayer remain partially ineffective, and do not, as they should, serve to intensify all our human activities.

Without the meeting of the soul with God, and without that frequent dilation of the spirit in contact with Him, we become petty and narrow in our judgment of the events, circumstances and trials of life.

Prayer gives poise to our personality; it gives us wider and more realistic views; in short, a noticeable increase of both supernatural and natural vitality.

Let us therefore now consider Christian prayer as a whole.

Christian Prayer

The Catechism teaches us that "Prayer is the raising up of the mind and heart to God". We notice the word "raise" in this definition; that is to say an uplifting: an orientation of our whole soul towards the goal for which we were created. The mind, which is necessarily and continuously occupied with the details of a busy and varied profession or career, thus has the opportunity to enter into communication with God; and the heart seeks to free itself for a space from the attractions and temptations of the company of our fellow-men and the world in which we live, and to rest instead in the certainty of God's love and sustaining power. Urged by His grace, our mind is raised towards Him while our whole personality longs for Him, and longs to lose itself in God in order the better to perform all its duties.

One can also perhaps describe prayer as an entering into

[2] Heb. 4, 12.

ourselves; as a retiring into the inmost centre of the soul, which is the dwelling-place of the Blessed Trinity; or again as a concentration of heart and mind on the presence of God. By thus concentrating on Him, who by sanctifying grace constantly lives and works in us, the courage and strength to perform our task in this complicated and restless modern civilization is maintained and steadily increased.

We attach too much importance to what we achieve for ourselves and other people, and too little importance to what we *are* to God. In prayer we touch the very essence of our existence: we know that dependence from out of which grows love.

For this reason prayer is not to be regarded as a kind of luxury: a pause in life: for between these two—living and praying—there exists an intimate and essential connection. Praying is just as necessary to us as breathing, and yet it remains a pure gift from God, although at the same time a duty and a habit, sometimes only acquired after much struggle. In this case practice and faith go hand in hand. The main theme is that God becomes the sphere in which we think, will and act: the very air which we breathe. In order to know how we should pray we can refer to the Gospels and find there the example of Jesus Christ: His whole existence consisted in this mutual movement of the Father towards Himself and of Himself towards the Father.

1. *Jesus Christ our Example*

At all times prayer has been the voice of man, but it was Christ who first actually taught us how to pray.

a. The Evangelists unanimously describe His life as *a life of prayer*. All the important incidents which occurred during it received their impetus from prayer and were hallowed by it: His miracles were the outcome of it; His whole redemptive work was nourished by this silent dialogue with the Father. When He was baptized, St. Luke tells us, heaven was opened as He prayed, and a voice answering Him, replied: "Thou art My beloved Son, in Thee I am well pleased."[3] How often we find Him retiring into the mountains to pray while, in the loneliness of the night, He centred His thoughts upon Him to whom He owed His life. We

[3] Luke 3, 21-23.

even read that one day (this happened but once only) while He prayed His whole countenance was transfigured, while His garments became white as snow, and a cloud enveloped Him from out of which spoke a Voice: "This is My beloved son; to Him, then, listen."[4] The seventeenth chapter of St. John's Gospel tells us how, at the Last Supper, Jesus prayed for Himself, for His apostles, and for all His faithful followers. In His prayer there was a constant interplay between His Godhead and His Manhood.

b. This prayer of Jesus was the most intimate act of His soul by which He expressed His own personal life and His unceasing awareness of what He was: both God and Man. He gave His uninterrupted attention to the one living God who is Lord of all; He continually showed His love for the Father by the fulfilment of His will; and all this He did in His own completely unique way. No man can imitate Him. He never included Himself with the rest of Creation. He spoke of "My Father", but did not join in the "Our Father" which He taught His disciples. In His prayer He expressed His own personal relationship with God, and that is not for us, but what we have learnt from Him is that His prayer was always directed towards *a Person*: a Person who lives; who is unendingly fruitful in Himself; who fathomed His own eternal glory and expressed it in one Word: that Word which in turn breathes Love. We must pray to the Father who created us; to the Son who became man in order to redeem us; to the Holy Ghost who consoles and guides us. And so we enter into contact with a God who listens, who always turns upon us His personal attention, although we do not always actually experience His answer. Still, we *believe* in that loving attention.

Prayer, in the case of Christ, was not just an accidental way of passing the time, dependent upon education or surroundings; neither was it a pious but automatic occupation, confirmed by habit but lacking all inner conviction. It was a profound and personal communion with the Father. It did not consist in any great flow of words: Simplicity was its chief characteristic but the whole point was that Christ *lived* His prayer.

c. A third characteristic of this prayer could be described by the words, *a pure intention*.

[4] Luke 9, 28-37. Also 6, 12; 9, 18; 11, 1.

The very centre of the prayer of Christ was the will of His Father: a conscious, implicit surrender to Him. And in that surrender there was nothing of resigned suffering or of a dull acceptance of unavoidable divine decisions. There was no human sighing or weeping; there was no mustering of courage followed by a sorrowful: "Lord, Thy will be done." But this prayer expressed, quietly and simply, Christ's total surrender to God.

Following Him, we too should pray: "Thy will be done on earth as it is in heaven." With this prayer we rise far above our own personal interests: for the moment we no longer have, as it were, any name of our own, any individual career, any family beyond the great family of God: suddenly we become, instead, just creatures in His presence. Our interest is concentrated upon the whole earth and its affairs: "Thy will be done on earth."

Jesus expressly told us that we should ask for the fulfilment of the divine will. "This then is to be your prayer . . . Thy will be done, on earth as it is in heaven."[5] This means that the accomplishment of the will of God is so important that we must even pray for it: we must ask for it, that is to say, by means of the highest, most supernatural action of which man is capable: with the greatest sincerity, attention and desire.

In what does the will of God consist? As a rule when we think of God's Will we think of the commandments, of the duties which are connected with our daily work, of our profession or of our family. But in reality this Will comprises everything which, by God's eternal decree, is real and exists anywhere in the universe. It comprises all the discoveries of His wisdom, the results of His omnipotence, the loving desires of His heart.

The will of God remains the foundation of all prayer. Even our prayer of petition, in which we ask for personal favours, is enclosed in this same truth; for we only try to obtain from God those things for which He wishes us to ask Him. Seen in this true light, prayer never fails, because all petitions are safely stored up in the will of God, and sooner or later, in time or eternity, receive their answer.

In this sense there is no place at all for those semi-serious

[5] Matt. 6, 9 etc.

attempts at a compromise with God in which some people are apt to indulge. We should never regard God as a kind of wealthy friend who is always ready to distribute presents and the good things of life. There is no room for bargaining in prayer. Neither is prayer a species of law-court proceeding, in which we ask God to give an account of His actions and explain His delays and refusals. Prayer is never to be regarded as a meeting of equals in which Man is to have the last word.

God's will remains the foundation of it. It asks for no reward, for it is its own reward. The omnipotence of prayer is indeed the omnipotence of God—on one condition: that man's will is God's will. God's will is all-important. This is the great characteristic of the prayer of Jesus which demands from us so much patience and self-conquest.

d. In three of His parables Our Lord has explained to us the new spirit with which all Christian prayer should be permeated.

A man may ask himself anxiously: Is God taking any notice of my prayer? Is He turning a deaf ear to my petitions? Was not everything already planned by Him long before the beginning of time; has He not already foreseen and decided everything? To all such questions Christ never gave a direct answer. That answer remains His secret: God's secret. The knowledge and belief that we can always rely upon the unfailing goodness and love of the Father should be sufficient for us. A parable will illustrate how ready God always is to hear us.[6]

"Let us suppose that one of you has a friend, to whom he goes at dead of night and asks him, lend me three loaves of bread, neighbour; a friend of mine has turned in to me after a journey, and I have nothing to offer him. And suppose the other answers, from within doors, Do not put me to such trouble; the door is locked, my children and I are in bed; I cannot bestir myself to grant thy request. I tell you, even if he will not bestir himself to grant it out of friendship, shameless asking will make him rise and give his friend all that he needs. And I say the same to you; ask, and the gift will come; seek, and you shall find; knock, and the door shall be opened to you. Everyone that asks, will receive; that seeks, will find; that knocks, will have the door opened to him. Among your-

[6] Luke 11, 5-14.

selves, if a father is asked by his son for bread, will he give him a stone? Or for a fish, will he give him a snake instead of a fish. Or if he is asked for an egg will he give him a scorpion? Why then, if you, evil as you are, know well enough how to give your children what is good for them, is not your Father much more ready to give, from heaven, His gracious spirit to those who ask Him?"

That is the parable. Jesus draws no conclusions. He does not say that God gives an order to be left in peace. But He teaches that persevering, repeated, insistent prayer is irresistible. Sometimes it almost seems as though God were pretending to be deaf in order to compel us to persevere in prayer. There is no doubt of it: prayer is answered.

Asking, seeking, knocking, persevering, trusting: these are the conditions. And what is this "gracious spirit" of which Christ speaks? He explains it further; it is the Holy Spirit. The Father will send the Holy Spirit, and this Holy Spirit will come to those who pray, and will inspire them more and more as they advance in prayer. By this in-pouring of the Spirit they will learn how to become happy and at peace in the fulfilment of the will of the Father.

Our Lord also related another parable about a judge and a widow, in order to illustrate how we ought to pray continually and never to be discouraged. The judge was an independent type of person: he had no fear of God and no regard for man; nevertheless he was conquered by the widow who, insignificant as she was, never ceased to worry him about her affairs.[7]

Faith and trust in God are the necessary conditions for prayer. The man who prays, *must trust*. "If someone says to this mountain, remove from thence, hither, and throw yourself into the sea, and if he does not doubt in his heart and believes that it will happen, then it does happen." One must believe in goodness. God is love. Trust in God is a quiet appeal to His heart—an acknowledgment of Him as Father; of Jesus, the Sacred Heart, as our brother and bridegroom. But this faith and trust go hand in hand with *humility and modesty*: with the realization that we are always dependent upon the grace of God, and that even the very prayers which we pray, are only the gift of His love. In the parable of the Pharisee and the Publican[8] Jesus has shown

[7] Luke 18, 1-9. [8] Luke 18, 9-14.

us this fundamental truth. The publican, a worldly man, usually immersed in his scales and his money-bags, who did not dare to lift his eyes towards heaven, yet humbly struck his breast, saying, "God, be merciful to me a sinner", was truly praying. But the Pharisee, who wore phylacteries and gave God a short résumé of his well-spent life, yet knew no prayer with which to touch His heart.

2. *Conditions and Methods of Prayer*

To attain to prayer there are certain conditions to which we should give our attention, for prayer requires preparation. One sometimes hears it said that prayer cannot be forced; that it must arise spontaneously from the soul; that it flows from an inexhaustible source; it is the heart which counts, the disposition, the inclination, otherwise it will be only a strained and hypocritical pretence.

It is quite true that prayer may often be the expression of our personal experience of God; it may arise from a sudden, interior need or urge. But the man who waits until he feels in the mood for prayer will seldom practise prayer seriously. In order to arrive at a genuine and regular life of prayer, time, real attention, and recollection are required.

Time. It should be done at certain definite times of the day: in the morning when getting up, at night before going to bed, before and after meals, when we are in Church, when we are beset by difficulties or temptations. One cannot give any more specific rules, since it depends upon our duties and our leisure, but the great thing is to be supremely conscious of the fact that prayer is worth while, and then we shall surely manage to make time for it daily.

Attention. Many people do not care for prayer because they find it difficult to occupy their mind with an invisible God, and because it never results—psychologically speaking—in a conversation. Therefore they think that they have no time for it, and make all sorts of excuses about being too busy in order to avoid it. Usually however it is not time which is lacking, but faith and courage. One of the laws of growth, which causes the entire personality to expand, is the law that we must give our whole attention to one thing at a time, to what we are doing at the present moment. This attention will have to ensure perseverance and the courage to battle against both boredom and distractions. It also needs recollection.

Recollection. This is the art of concentration upon the important occupation which we are about to undertake; it is an earnest search for the God who dwells in us, but secretly; it is a detachment from everything which is not prayer and has nothing to do with prayer. This concentration is not a gift, but can only be attained by long practice, and it is the result of a firm decision of the will which takes no notice of moods or circumstances. In prayer our whole attention should be given; we should try to avoid all contacts except the one; we should reject everything which either the senses or the imagination have to offer us. This is called recollection, and means the mental rejection of all that is unimportant or disturbing. A certain exterior quiet, the symbol of our interior surrender, is often helpful. To rest means to be able to live entirely in the present, to be quite simply oneself, and in this way a strong character seeks to give itself entirely to God. This rest is the fruit of activity, in a sense it is activity, and has the effect of enlarging all our understanding and releasing us from the dulling consequences of routine.

Silence, it is true, does not inevitably lead to prayer, nevertheless it remains the best exterior condition for it. It is always possible, of course, to raise the mind and heart to God even in the noisiest surroundings, but the natural approach will then be different. Great importance should be attached to the exterior attitude in prayer. There is necessarily a strong link between interior and exterior things. A weeping child becomes even sadder when it sees somebody else crying, but when it sees a laughing face it cheers up almost immediately. A quiet, reverent, and prayerful attitude produces and promotes the interior life and contact with God, although the former need not necessarily be the result of the latter. Kneeling, standing, folding the hands, do not only express this conscious life, but they actually arouse it.

The *method* of prayer has no absolute value in itself and remains only a means to an end. We can judge that a method is good when it actually effects contact with God: methods, being technical, prove their worth by results. Gradually we shall find that they disappear of themselves. An old man who had been sitting alone for a long time in an empty church was asked what he was waiting for, to which he replied: "I just sits and looks at 'Im and He just looks at me."

3. Forms of Prayer

There are many forms of prayer to be distinguished: vocal prayer, formal or prescribed prayer, mental prayer or meditation, and contemplation or mystical prayer.

We will now discuss the two forms which are important for our purpose, vocal prayer and that prayer which is a silent immersion in God.

a. Vocal Prayer

That which is passing interiorly is often shown by an expression of the face, a movement of the hands, an attitude of the body; but the clearest revelation of ourselves is to be found in the spoken word, and in that way we call prayer "speaking with God". Words are important, and it is incorrect to observe casually, "after all, what matters most is the sincere intention". The interior life unconsciously searches for the right word and, conversely, words have a strong influence on interior thoughts. From our youth onwards, we think in the words which we heard in our earliest surroundings; our inner life is unconsciously connected with them; we understand and meet other people through them. We receive and absorb words—words of prayer as well as others.

It is not necessary to prove that the words by which we personally thank God, entreat Him and ask His pardon, immediately become a prayer: for we do not pray in order to inform God how we are. In prayer we endeavour to live and to appear before Him as we really are, to associate with Him, and to receive from Him that which He is willing to give us. The words that most truly represent our selves are the best. If they do not come spontaneously to our lips, welling up from the fulness of the heart, then they will have to be laboriously acquired and at the same time still try to express all that is essential in the light of faith and understanding.

But our poverty may be so great that just the right word altogether escapes us. In that case the only thing to be done is to borrow from others who are better equipped than we.

It may be that their experience will act as an inspiration and enlarge the narrow groove of our thought. There are prayers given us by God Himself: these were written down in the Bible under the inspiration of the Holy Ghost. There are, for instance, the Psalms, the Magnificat,[9] the Benedictus,[10] and the Nunc Dimittis.[11] In the letters of St. Paul one can find hidden prayers galore. Christ Himself taught the apostles to say the "Our Father".[12] The child of God already lives in all these prayers, strengthened and enlightened by the Holy Ghost.

The liturgy still treasures those ancient texts by which the Early Church addressed itself to God.

As we said, it is important to find the exact word; it is often even more difficult to find the sincere, true and simple prayer. Much that is described as prayer is only too often meaningless, exaggerated and sentimental. There is also the danger that in using formal prayers we shall begin to repeat them superficially and thoughtlessly. Saying them only is not praying them. A prayer book if used should be such that it helps us to pray and then can be closed again at will. At this point our thoughts will naturally turn towards the Rosary. "When you are praying speak not as the heathens do for they think that in their much speaking they may be heard." Does this then imply a condemnation of continuous repetition of the same words and prayers? Our Lord was not reproving the number of repetitions but the idea that sheer numbers should weigh with God. Repetition in itself may be a psychological necessity. The composer repeats his theme over and over again, either just as it is or with variations, for his artistic emotion is not satisfied by only giving us the melody once. One finds this same tendency in poets. All that we feel and think is not necessarily expressed by those spoken words which so quickly "fleet to air". When addressing a petition to God, or when expressing contrition, we should be careful to have a pure intention and to be transparently sincere: words then become only the vehicle of the inner force which produces them.

There is also the type of prayer in which we do not actually say anything in particular to God but only wish to remain in His presence, and in this kind of prayer we shall unconsciously begin to use fewer and fewer words. There is still another

[9] Luke 1, 46-55. [10] Luke 1, 68-79. [11] Luke 2, 29-32. [12] Luke 11, 1-4.

way of praying quietly in the presence of God where the word becomes, as it were, the bed along which the prayer flows, and at the same time is the power which keeps it moving. In this case it is not necessary to be continually finding new words, but the same ones may be repeated. The very repetition gives this prayer its form, and has for its purpose to make our emotion at once fuller and calmer. The prayer of the Rosary exactly meets these requirements: by repetition of the "Hail Mary" we achieve a continuous resting in the presence of God while our prayer quietly progresses.

This type of prayer requires vivid faith and the constancy to meditate peacefully upon the fifteen incidents in the life of Our Lord especially connected with His holy Mother. We shall find that the effect of the reiterated words of the angel will be to sustain the flow of our meditation. This is a method, however, which only comes with practice, as it requires patience, concentration and a certain amount of time.

b. Mental Prayer

This method of prayer uses no words at all but is a silent attention to God and to the mysteries of the Faith. We now begin to seek for truth in order the better to contemplate it: we long to meet God Himself in our heart and to learn more of His infinite richness. We meditate upon the goal and the meaning of our own lives and destiny in the light of God's love and plan of creation. But contemplation itself is never the final end; either it is filled with the longing desires of love, or leads to union (sometimes even sensible union) with the Blessed Trinity dwelling in the soul. As this prayer increases it tends to become more and more simple; such adjuncts as composition of place, meditation, and good resolutions disappear. The number of our thoughts grows less, but the thoughts themselves will be deeper and more fruitful. In the end this prayer turns into a simple quiet regard fixed on God: a realization of His presence and of our union with Him.

The continual self-examination and self-analysis, which so often is no more than a kind of balance-sheet of progress or decline in virtue, also disappears. For present-day people, there is a certain danger of coming to regard prayer as merely another branch of psychology. This tendency hampers the growth of the spiritual life, for the development of which great receptivity is required: a receptivity towards God, as the flower receives light from the sun. When we consider ourselves instead of God, when we narrow down our thoughts and our hearts in order to take stock of our own spiritual condition and progress; when we begin praying in order to discover whether our prayer is satisfactory, and "leave our rest" as St. Francis de Sales says, "in order to see whether our prayer is truly restful", then we lose all the fruits of the spiritual life; we create disturbance rather than peace in the soul, and risk falling into every kind of delusion.

We do not mean, of course, to condemn all spiritual self-examination. If this is undertaken before God and in order genuinely to try to correct our failings, then it is even to be recommended. But when it is done merely to give ourselves the pleasure of the vain and foolish assurance that we are achieving sanctity by our own efforts, and that we have shown to what spiritual heights we are capable of rising, then it is positively pernicious. The soul to whom God draws near is the soul which is the most detached from self. The more the soul surrenders itself to God the more will His far-reaching care attend to the least details and circumstances of life.

Out of this contemplative prayer in time will grow that decisive rebirth—a conversion not only of our behaviour, but also of our views of life, our judgment, our appreciation of values, our ability to distinguish between substance and shadow. Then both heart and spirit will genuinely find their happiness in the joyous Gospel-message.

In souls which have reached this stage there will gradually develop a fully "Christian" conscience, that is to say a conscience which accepts as true the values of God's Revelation, and so accepts as good, beautiful, noble and excellent, everything that is seen to be so in the light of Faith. The content of Faith agrees with the content of their own concrete existence.

This contemplative prayer also requires *preparation*. We should make up our minds beforehand what is to be our subject of thought. But in the end contemplation rests upon Jesus Christ, just as He is described in the Gospels. He is the Way which leads from the Father to us, and again from us to the Father. He is the truth which guides us on that way. He is the divine Life in which we share through grace. Revelation must speak to us personally. A quiet and unhurried attitude of mind and body is of great importance for the practice of this prayer since it tends to produce the necessary concentration.

But whatever the subject we select or in whatever way we pray, the object, after all, is never either the attainment of knowledge or contemplation in itself, but only the attainment of contact with God. When by pondering over certain thoughts our heart is touched and moved, then prayer will result: we shall be satisfied with the consciousness of the reality and the holiness of God, and of the holiness which he holds within Him for us.

4. *Distractions*

One of the great difficulties of prayer is the persistence of distractions in various forms. Sometimes we find that our attention is vague, superficial and not directed to anything in particular: or again it may be divided: there will be that about which we *desire* to think, and simultaneously something else to which our thoughts keep automatically wandering, and which attracts and holds them against our will. It is also possible for our mind to be directed to one subject but at the same time to be subconsciously occupied with several other ideas and impressions.

For the person who is inclined to first dream a little, and then look round in search of some diversion, there is only one cure: to pray quietly but with great resolution. If, however, the distraction persists, we may be fairly sure that it is not our surroundings which are distracting our attention, but that our mind is occupied with all kinds of problems and worries of our own. There are two ways of dealing with this: either we can try to deal with these problems, and find a solution for them ourselves, or we can, as it were, build them in as part of our prayer. But the best way, as a rule, is quite simply to set them on one side and surrender ourselves instead to the will of God.

The question has often been asked as to whether, during distractions, one is still orientated towards God and therefore the prayer continues in spite of them. Here a distinction must be drawn between voluntary and involuntary distractions. In the case of voluntary distractions the contact between God and the soul is interrupted, because of our own free will instead of praying, we are thinking either of ourselves or of other matters. In the case of involuntary distractions the effect of the original intention, which was to pray, still continues; since the firm intention persists, the whole process of our thought continues virtually to be directed towards God. In that sense distractions are relatively unimportant because they do not touch the essence of the personality. Prayer is a matter of the will, the intention, the fundamental disposition, and those are infinitely more important than the mere accident of possible distractions. It is in the will that the obligation to be as attentive as possible to God resides. In order not to worry about involuntary distractions, however, a good deal of faith, confidence and trust in God are required. We must remember that if we make sheer concentration alone the goal, and consider it as the highest achievement of our prayer, then we are actually seeking not God but ourselves.

5. *The Catholic and non-Catholic way of Prayer*

A non-Catholic and particularly a Protestant non-Catholic, is often scandalized by the Catholic way of praying. He has been brought up to think that every word should be reflected upon. After repeating every sentence one should know what one has just prayed. The matter of his prayer is always quite clear in his mind and he is aware of every change of thought. He prays slowly and quietly and, in the case of vocal prayer, pronounces the words with great dignity. It is not really, as Catholics sometimes think, his intention to impress, but merely his way of speaking to God.

The Catholic attaches more value to his uninterrupted concentration upon God. His attention is not so much centred upon the words which he is pronouncing, or on the manner in which he is formulating his thoughts, as on the fact of trying to remain in the presence of God. His first pre-occupation is with his intention, his desire to be with God, his surrender to the will of God. His point of view is that God, after all, knows all about his intentions and his desires long before he expresses them in prayer, and so the words scarcely matter.

This attitude will explain why the Catholic does not appear to say his prayers with as much devotion and respect as the Protestant non-Catholic. He does not use any special tone of voice nor does he linger over the sentences. Often, indeed, the words are no more than an undercurrent holding undisturbed his contact with God. For this reason he will often pray during his work, and does not mind using the same words over and over again. The words are, in such a case, regarded as no more than a general framework for the real interior prayer.

However one should never pass judgment upon the life of prayer of either. That which the one attains by his loving attention to the Word of God, the other will achieve in a quiet moment spent before the Tabernacle. That which a Catholic experiences by following the prayers of the Mass, the Protestant will experience by uniting himself to the prayers of the preacher which fill his mind with rounded and well-chosen phrases.

For both equally the choice of time and place, the undivided attention, the recollection, and especially the will to pray and to be united with God who is present in both of them, remains the most important thing.

§ 2. *Christian Mortification*

Grace raises our life from a human to a divine level, but nevertheless this life remains self-active. It only grows by means of our own effort and as a result of our devoting ourselves to it completely.

In this connection we discover an altogether new aspect of Christian life which is so rich in God but yet bound up with a human nature on which original sin has left its scars.

If we are honest with ourselves we shall have to admit that there is in human nature a pervading egoism which is apt to expand in all directions and express itself in immoderate self-exaltation and sometimes in an irresistible urge for pleasure and self-satisfaction. Disorder is still rife in the depths of our being where God should dwell: the soul refuses to be subject to the influence of the Holy Ghost, while the flesh rebels against the spirit; blind instinct often obscures the clarity of our mental vision, and we realize that the original harmony of our nature has been lost. We wish to do good and nevertheless do evil: we hear the Word of God and continue to commit sin. Grace can only build up slowly and with difficulty; its first work has to be to cure and to restore. Somehow or other by the help of God's grace, we must regain this interior balance of ours, whatever the cost. In other words, we must practise the virtues which will help us; we must avoid sin, be watchful, fight, mortify and deny ourselves, learn to bear our sufferings patiently.

What exactly do we understand by "practising virtue"?

The Catechism mentions four virtues which regulate our conduct according to Christian principles: prudence, justice, fortitude and temperance—under which will also fall the virtues of humility, patience and obedience. The aim of these four virtues is to bring our life completely under the influence of the cardinal virtues, especially charity, and to create in us a harmony and balance by which our orientation towards God can be unostentatiously realized in all our thoughts and actions.

Who will deny that it is of inestimable value to know ourselves for what we are really worth? This is called humility, and it is the precise opposite of egoism, which seeks to make itself at once the goal and the centre of everything. Under the influence of humility, the intellect tries to regain its balance and to search for the proper means by which to right itself. It strives to acquire a sound judgment, seeks reality and avoids illusion, and thus gradually grows in a practical knowledge of the world in which is mingled reflection and a sense of duty.

The spirit should control the senses and instincts, and learn to use the energy of the latter for useful human purposes. The senses are not to be killed, or wholly suppressed, but merely controlled and guided by the mind. If in the spiritual life we practise sobriety and the required self-control, there is no need to deny our natural desires, but only to satisfy them reasonably and after due consideration. In this case, the spirit, enlightened by faith and directed by the laws of the Church, uses the will to govern the passions and so achieves balance and poise. This, however, is more or less a life's work, and will not be attained without increasing detachment from material things and obedience to those who, in this particular case, are directing us.

Our will must learn to practise patience and to accept life just as it is in all its monotony, simply trusting to the guidance and the love of God. This patience must even cover our own personality, our temperament and our habits. God will give us the strength in this way to acquire harmony and integration of the self, as well as the courage to begin the work and persevere steadily in it. This balance, acquired by steady and unwearied effort, will finally result for us in that inward peace which is the fruit of quiet action, but never of nervous and spasmodic activity in the matter of good resolutions or physical mortification.

If we regulate our spiritual life along these lines, we shall find a blossoming of both faith and love in our soul, and our relationship with our fellowmen will of itself improve as we realize, practically, that love of God seeks its most natural expression in love of our neighbour. Here we encounter once more the virtues which we have already briefly described above.

That this spiritual life is impossible of attainment, and that the love of God will surely languish, if purification, mortification and detachment are neglected, is clear in the case of all those among us who merely leave their spiritual life to chance, and do not expect to find their principal welfare in Catholic surroundings and with, if possible, a Catholic upbringing.

We have just mentioned mortification. By mortification is meant a certain habit of paying attention in our daily life to the things which will be most likely to promote our spiritual development and to see that we do our part towards ensuring a steady inflow of grace into the soul by removing anything likely to impede it. Mortification is by its nature a form of self-denial, and prevents us from blindly following our instinct or our inclinations, and so strengthens the will. Only a strong will is able to keep its spirit free and to serve God, and it is able to do this precisely because it does not allow itself to be influenced by the prevalent vice of self-love, and purifies its own soul and heart of any inordinate craving for consolation and pleasure.

It is in order that the spirit may rule over the flesh that the Church has prescribed fasting and abstinence. Thus the soul learns to obey God's will and ordinances, and concupiscence is checked and controlled. Practical mortification, expressing itself supernaturally in such matters as obedience, patience, charity, and the fulfilling of one's daily duties, is reacting continually against the tendency to make our own interest and enjoyment our principal aim in life, and it steadily rejects the ideal of the crowd, which is to amuse itself.

Mortification, however, must never be regarded as an end in itself, but only as a means and a preparation for a life lived in union with God. It should lead us directly to Him, and never be undertaken merely on account of a sense of duty, or as a matter of self-control and fancied perfection. If mortification gives rise to any sense of superiority, it will only end in pride and self-worship and so it will defeat its own object. It is also possible for our attention to become, in this way, altogether too centred upon self, so that all spontaneity disappears and a person deteriorates into a kind of automatic machine for carrying out its own will, or else a Pharisee. Let us repeat, it is most important to realize that mortification only serves a purpose. It teaches us self-control, and self-control is one of the conditions for surrender to God.

In connection with this we may also speak of detachment from sin, from the world, and from self, the whole aim being to attach ourselves to God instead; but, here again, only according to His will, in the way He wants, and which He indicates to us by the circumstances in which He places us.

Christ, who has enjoined this detachment on us all by the words: "How is a man the better for gaining the whole world, if he loses himself, if he pays the forfeit of himself?"[13] at the same time teaches us to bear our sufferings patiently and humbly.

Suffering plays an important part in the growth of the interior life.

The problem of the meaning of suffering has puzzled many people, and apart from religion, there is no answer to it. Those who listen to the voice of the Church know that it is a consequence of sin—a sad result of original sin and sometimes also of personal guilt.

But in spite of this, it has both meaning and sense.

Rightly used it can serve as a cure, because, if serenely borne, it strengthens the will, regulates the passions, and leads us inevitably to reflection and recollection, and so to God.

It is, in the eternal plan of God, the only way which will bring us to salvation. It has redemptive power when it is accepted and borne for the love of Christ. We are, after all, members of Christ's Body, and it is fitting that, since our Head, Jesus Christ, suffered upon earth, we also should suffer and sacrifice ourselves in union with Him.

Used in this way, it becomes fruitful for the entire Church and is a means for the conversion of sinners. St. Paul clearly regards it as an act of reparation when he says: "Even as I write I am glad of my sufferings on your behalf, as, in this

[13] Luke 9, 25.

mortal frame of mine, I help to pay off the debt which the afflictions of Christ leave still to be paid, for the sake of His Body, the Church."[14]

Those who accept their sufferings voluntarily, whatever form they may take, and put them at love's disposal, obtain salvation for others. To them the words of Our Lord can be applied: "This is the greatest love a man can show that he should lay down his life for his friends."[15] The Christian life develops in continuous interior activity. Man strives to become increasingly conformed to Christ and like to Him, by loving God with his whole heart, his whole mind, and his whole strength. On his own human level he longs to be perfect as the Heavenly Father is perfect.

§ 3. *Christian Perfection*

And so we come to the final question: which of us should strive after perfection, and in what way should we strive? Striving after perfection simply means to practise all the cardinal virtues, as well as the life of prayer, just described, according to the measure of grace given us. It means to serve God, to imitate Christ, and to co-operate with grace, in the particular *vocation* which we have chosen.

There are many different vocations in life: that of the priest, of the religious: to marriage, or to the single life in the world. The aim of them all is exactly the same, that is to say, the love of God and of one's neighbour, and it is only the means which differ.

Most people are called to live a Christian life in the world, to some special profession or occupation, and in addition either to look after a family or maybe only to look after themselves. In living out their life on earth, and in all the duties and events connected with it, they will continually meet with the will of God. It is in life itself that, for the most part, their faith and love can find both expression and nourishment. Whatever sufferings, difficulties and sacrifices life may involve, however much positive practice of virtue it demands of them, all will contribute to the harmonious integration of their personality.

The Church itself shows the way to a vocation which, in itself, is particularly adapted to the attainment of interior

[14] Col. 1, 24. [15] John 15, 13.

purification and harmony, and thus enables the soul to live only for God: the *religious life*.

This is a state of life which calls for the practice of the evangelical counsels: poverty, chastity and obedience.

When we speak of the "counsels" we mean a special call to perfection, and to the leaving of all in order to follow Christ, which is not generally binding on everyone. Such a vocation will show itself by a certain obvious suitability for the religious life, and in an attraction towards it. Christ Himself pointed out this way by His reply to the rich young man who had kept all the commandments from his youth up. Only one thing more was wanting: "Go home and sell all that belongs to thee; then come back and follow Me."[16] Elsewhere Christ also said somewhat cryptically, "There are some eunuchs who . . . have made themselves so for love of the Kingdom of Heaven; take this in, you whose hearts are large enough for it."[17]

These three counsels are designed to remove all obstacles to the full development of the love of God, and to make man free, both interiorly and exteriorly, from all attachment to earthly possessions, from the craving for pleasure, and from self-love and self-esteem.

They contain a negative element, that is to say the removal of all that impedes the upward flight of the soul, but this negative element serves to keep the way open for free intercourse with God. By means of voluntary poverty, which renounces the unrestricted possession and use of material things, both mind and heart remain at liberty to give themselves to God's work for souls. The vow of chastity excludes marriage, not for the purpose of escaping its burdens, but in order to be able to approach God unhampered by earthly ties, and to work unhindered in His service. "He who is unmarried," says St. Paul, "is concerned with God's claim, asking how he is to please God . . . So a woman who is free of wedlock, or a virgin, is concerned with the Lord's claim, intent on holiness, bodily and spiritual."[18]

By the vow of obedience independent decisions in all personal matters are renounced, the intention being instead to follow the will of Christ in everything. Those entering the cloister bind themselves by a vow to keep these evangelical counsels, which means that they give themselves in total

[16] Mark 10, 17-21. [17] Matt. 19, 12. [18] I Cor. 7, 32.

surrender to God, and are thus established in a state of life which is especially designed and regulated in order to keep the attention fixed upon the practice of the interior life. They voluntarily make these vows in the hands of the Church, which then accepts them officially, as it were, as members of the Order or Congregation which they have chosen and they are thus placed under the obligation of living *in community* according to the particular rule and constitutions governing it.

In addition to these regular Religious, there are others who, for love of Christ and His Kingdom, elect to embrace celibacy in order to dedicate themselves to some particular apostolate, to social work, or to labouring in the foreign missions.

Lately the Church has devoted a great deal of time and attention to this matter of the Secular Institutes. Many lay people are binding themselves by the three vows of religious, but at the same time are not living in community, in order to exercise their apostolate undisturbed and without too many restrictions. There are also a number of religious confraternities and sodalities, all designed to promote the spiritual life: the Children of Mary: the Knights of St. Columba, the Legion of Mary, and the Young Christian Workers, in addition to the well-known Third Orders. All are called to co-operate in the extension of Christ's Kingdom upon earth by their good example, by prayer and by supporting the work of re-Christianizing the world both at home and through the missions.

The Bishops are directing the Faithful with particular urgency in these days to co-operate for the welfare of souls under the guidance of priests and prelates. This work is generally referred to all in one as *Catholic Action*, which is really a participation, acknowledged and approved by the Church, in the apostolate of the Hierarchy.

But the spiritual life which should lie behind all activity still finds its most perfect blossoming and realization in the love of God and of our neighbour for His sake; and without this love all practice of perfection, all asceticism and mortification in every walk of life, only lose their meaning and significance. Here on earth, if all these things, Church, Sacraments, Dogma, virtues and abnegation of self, do not lead finally towards this love, then all our means of salvation are robbed of their actual intention and fecundity. Faith and hope shall pass away: only love remains.

PART IV

THE COMPLETION OF THE CHURCH

CHAPTER XV

THE FOUR LAST THINGS

SYNOPSIS

When this life is over, trouble and effort will have passed us by, and we know that our eternal life will be beginning. Christians live in the expectation of a happiness which will never end. They are convinced that eternity is boundless and illimitable. This certainty gives to the transitory existence of earth a wonderful perspective, which stretches out before them in unending support and consolation. Everything which they now possess will perish it is true, but perish only to return to them a thousand times glorified, while they themselves will know completion and fulfilment in the contemplation of the Blessed Trinity. We also know, however, that the moment of death is a moment of judgment: at that instant good will be separated from evil, and our eternal happiness will swing no longer in the balances of God.

This final fulfilment of our lives is the work of Jesus Christ. He who sowed in our souls the divine seed will bring it to fruition and to the test. Belief in this fulfilment must necessarily include belief in death which closes every earthly existence: in the judgment of God: in the resurrection of the body and everlasting life. Creation was also included in this ending and completion. Christ came, and judged, and bestowed upon man a share in His Resurrection and eternal life.

All this we refer to under the name of Eschatology, which deals with the doctrines of the four last things and the consummation of the world.

§ 1. *Death*

DEATH IS A MYSTERY and a secret: a secret which has however always been one of the principal preoccupations of man. Although amid the hurrying rush, and the succeeding joys and troubles of life, it is possible to keep the thought of the end of existence almost completely in the background yet there are bound to be moments when we cannot help asking ourselves the question: is death the end of everything, a final passing into the void? Or is it instead the triumphant entry into a new life and an eternal Hereafter? Is death a liberation, or a descent into the kingdom of the dead—a kingdom which may possibly include some reward for the good I have done, and retribution for the evil?

In the Old Testament a pessimistic conception of the future life almost entirely predominated. Good and evil were repaid here on earth, and beyond the grave there seemed to exist only a deeply hidden abyss called Sheol, where Jahve was no longer praised. In those days man's one hope was for a long life: he did not even pray for a happy death. It was only during the last two centuries before the Coming of Christ that belief in a Judgment belonging to another world began to grow; this is to be gathered from parts of the Book of Wisdom.

"But the souls of the just are in God's hands, and no torment, in death itself, has power to reach them. Dead? Fools think so; think their end loss, their leaving us, annihilation; but all is well with them."[1]

In the New Testament, on the other hand, whenever there is mention of death, it is only to speak of it as a conquest. For Christ Himself rose from the dead. He it was who said: "I am the Resurrection and life; he who believes in Me, though he is dead, will live on; and whoever has life, and has faith in Me, to all eternity cannot die."[2]

The gloomy prospect of an ending without hope or meaning thus vanished. Being a Christian brought with it the hope of an eternally happy future. Nevertheless that which Revelation teaches as to death has a sobering effect. It is shown as a separation of soul and body. The actual physical decay of the body is no more, of course, than a disintegration of corporeal elements which at last cease to be able to take in, and respond to, the life-force supplied by the spirit. At the beginning of the Bible, as we know, this fact is emphatically stated: "Dust thou art, and unto dust shalt thou return."[3] The Psalms, too, are full of musings upon the transitoriness of life. What is man? A flower in the field; a wind blows over it and it is gone. Life is as a cobweb which is shattered by a single sigh. Formed out of clay man's body soon withers away. The thought of death brought bitter words to the lips of Job: "It was Thy hand that made me, no part of me but is Thy fashioning; and wilt Thou cast me aside all in a moment? Thou the craftsman, though of clay Thy handiwork, and must all be ground to dust again? . . . Brief, brief,

[1] Wisdom 3, 1-3. [2] John 11, 25-26. [3] Gen. 3, 19.

is my span of days; for a little leave me to myself, to find some comfort in my misery. Soon I must go to a land whence there is no returning, a land of darkness, death's shadow over it; a land of gloomy night, where death's shadow lies over all, and no peace haunts it, only everlasting dread."[4]

Revelation tells us that originally this condition of things was removed by the action of God's almighty power, but returned soon after the Fall. In our present state death is a penalty. "If ever thou eatest of this (tree)" said God to Adam in the Garden of Eden, "thy doom is death"; and then, "Still, thou shalt earn thy bread with the sweat of thy brow until thou goest back into the ground from which thou wast taken; dust thou art, and unto dust shalt thou return."

That this original state of happiness was not forgotten, is evidenced by phrases to be found in the Book of Wisdom: "God, to be sure framed man for an immortal destiny, the created image of His own endless Being; but, since the devil's envy brought death into the world, they make him their model that take him for their master."[5]

"It was through one man that guilt came into the world; and, since death came owing to guilt, death was handed on to all mankind by one man."[6] It is clear therefore that all who participate in the original sin of Adam must undergo this death. Revelation still further points out that the moment of death will settle our destiny for ever. In the Christian conception of life, death stands for final, eternal decision. After death, no repentance can bring back to us the lost chance of everlasting life and happiness; any change of disposition on our part is absolutely impossible. The parables of Lazarus and the rich man and of the wise and foolish virgins all go to illustrate this implacable truth.

Finally, death comes like a thief in the night; it is unexpected. But death is also the birth of eternal life, and therefore holds no horror for the Christian. Extreme Unction has prepared him for the encounter with Christ, who already stands at the gate and knocks: As the soul passes into the agony of death it knows that the prayers of its family go with it, and as it leaves the body the words of the Church's Blessing are recited by the priest: "Go forth, O Christian soul, from this world, in the name of God the Father Almighty, who created thee, in the name of Jesus Christ, the

[4] Job 10, 8 and 21. [5] Wisdom 2, 23-25. [6] Rom. 5, 12.

Son of the living God, who suffered for thee; in the name of the Holy Ghost who sanctified thee . . . Eternal rest give to him, O Lord, and let perpetual light shine upon him."

§ 2. *Judgment*

"We shall all stand, one day, before the Judgment Seat of Christ . . . and so each of us will have to give an account of himself before God." Thus St. Paul writes to the Romans and the Corinthians.[7] "All of us have a scrutiny to undergo before Christ's Judgment Seat, for each to reap what his mortal life has earned, good or ill, according to his deeds."[8]

The Church now teaches universally that this Judgment takes place after death.

We ought not to visualize it with absurd surroundings. There is no question of a judge making his appearance, trying to assess the value of a life, and listening to charges and defence. This is not a case of the worldly administration of justice. In time it has no duration, and it takes place wordlessly in the silence of Eternity. It is a purely spiritual event: the meeting of God and the soul. Enlightenment suddenly pierces the soul and it receives a clear, inevitable knowledge of its own value: its worth or its worthlessness. In a flash it grasps the import of all its acts, and sees how it came to that one final act of life which either spoke of eternal love for God or of eternal resistance to His will. If it is turned away from God, it has yet to acknowledge His utter holiness and realizes to the full why it is doomed to hell. If it is not completely pure, it longs for purgatory as a necessary and desired purification. If its soul is immaculate, then it hears the voice of the Master: "Well done, My good and faithful servant, since thou hast been faithful over little things I have great things to commit to thy charge; come and share the joy of the Lord."[9] This judgment takes place at our deathbed, when all relationship between the body and space has been severed. Our conscience, which now acts as a warning to us, will then only serve to convince and condemn us.

§ 3. *Hell*

After our death, the Judgment: after the Judgment, Heaven, Hell or Purgatory. The word "hell" originally

[7] Rom. 14, 12. [8] II Cor. 5, 10. [9] Matt. 25, 23.

came from *helan* or *behelian* "to hide". In the New Testament the word "Gehenna" is used more frequently, which is another name for the "valley of the sons of Hinnom", situated to the south of Jerusalem, and now called Wadi er-rababi. It was notorious in earlier days as the scene of the worship of Moloch, and held in abomination by the Jews, who used the name of this valley to designate the abode of the damned. We also find many other names for it in the New Testament, such as abyss, place of torments, pool of fire, furnace of fire, unquenchable fire, exterior darkness, perdition and eternal destruction.

St. John briefly summarizes the state of the damned as follows: "Death and hell gave up the dead they imprisoned, and each man was judged according to his deeds, while death and hell were thrown into the lake of fire. This is the second death; everyone must be thrown into the lake of fire, unless his name was found written in the book of life."[10] God does not wish anyone to go to hell; it is a punishment for those who, of their own free will, reject the love of God and ignore His justice.

The Church, basing her teaching upon the Revelation of Christ, holds that this punishment is everlasting; that it consists in the terrible absence of God, and the torment of fire; and that it is not the same for everyone.

Eternal Punishment

It would be difficult to understand the words of Christ regarding the damned in any way which did not exclude all possibility of a return to God. All the parables recorded by St. Matthew point unmistakably to everlasting punishment. "Gather up the tares first, and tie them in bundles to be burned";[11] the man who had no wedding garment: "Cast him out into the darkness where there shall be weeping and gnashing of teeth";[12] the foolish virgins whom the Bridegroom would not recognize because they came too late;[13] and the unprofitable servant who is to have taken away from him even that which he calls his own: "And now cast the unprofitable servant into the darkness without where there shall be weeping and gnashing of teeth."[14]

[10] Apoc. 20, 14-15. [11] Matt. 13, 30. [12] Matt. 22, 11-13.
[13] Matt. 25, 12. [14] Matt. 25, 29.

After the solemn warning that it is "better for thee to enter life maimed, than to have two hands when thou goest into hell, into unquenchable fire",[15] Christ distinctly tells us that the King will say at the end of time to those who are upon His left-hand side: "Go far from Me, you that are accursed, into that eternal fire which has been prepared for the devil and his angels."[16] This eternal fire is clearly referred to at the end of His sermon as an eternal punishment.

Undoubtedly the early Christians also understood such a punishment in its severest sense. St. Paul, writing to the Thessalonians, says: "But that is for the day when the Lord Jesus appears from Heaven, with angels to proclaim His Power; with fire flaming about Him, as He pours out vengeance on those who do not acknowledge God, on those who refuse obedience to the Gospel of Our Lord Jesus Christ. The presence of the Lord, and the majesty of His power, will condemn them to eternal punishment."[17]

Privation of the contemplation of God

Nothing has been revealed to us concerning the interior state of those who undergo this punishment. We only know that they will never behold God, who alone could be their happiness. This complete absence means a complete absence also of their own personal and eternal happiness, and they realize that this is the fruit and result of their own action. The soul sees that it can never attain to its everlasting joy, and at the same time sees very clearly *why* it can never attain to it. Those words of the King in the Day of Judgment, just quoted, must be taken absolutely seriously and literally: "Go far from Me." They are excluded from the marriage-feast of the Bridegroom. He does not recognize them.[18]

The soul is aware that grace for conversion will never again be granted, and it despairs. Irresistibly and eternally attracted towards that happiness which had been reserved for it also, the soul is obliged to exist without it and without God, and all the time repeats to itself: through my own fault.

This deprivation of the vision of God appears to be accompanied by an agonizing torment, called in the Bible—70

[15] Mark 9, 43. [16] Matt. 25, 41. [17] II Thess. 1, 7-9.
[18] Matt. 25, 10-12 and 41.

times—by the name of *fire*. We do not know precisely how we are meant to understand this fire. All that we can imagine or invent about it is valueless. One might surmise that it is some form of created reality, which tortures both soul and body, binding and curtailing the liberty of the spirit which by its nature was destined to expand freely.

This Punishment is individual

The punishment is commensurate with the degree of guilt: the justice of God demands no less. Every sinner makes his own hell. But now arises the emphatic question: *which* sinners?

> What sin casts a man into hell?
> The Church replies: deadly sin. But then—*one* deadly sin?

Of its nature such a sin deserves hell. But nobody is damned for one single evil deed, unless that deed reflected the profound personality of the sinner, his decisive, permanent attitude towards God and life itself. God judges according to the whole of a life, and He does not lay snares for our feet. He weighs the soul itself, its state, its degree of responsibility, rather than the actual deed. God bestows His grace upon men. We should never judge or speculate as to whether a person is guilty or not before the Eternal Court of Judgment. "Believe me, the publicans and the harlots are further on the road to God's Kingdom than you," said Our Lord to the chief priests and elders.[19] And on the Cross Christ prayed, "Father, forgive them for they know not what they do." Jesus, who fathoms all hearts, knows better than we how some hereditary taint, deficiency of education, or force of custom may weaken the will; how the mind is constantly affected and reason obscured by conflicting influences. When diagnosing deadly sins the greatest hesitation and humility is necessary.

It is difficult indeed for the human mind to take in and accept this mystery of hell: by mere reflection it cannot grasp the necessity of eternal punishment. Yet it cannot deny the unequivocal pronouncement of Revelation. Sometimes it tries to escape from the reality by the thought that the good-

[19] Matt. 21, 28-31.

ness of God could never allow such everlasting suffering; but in doing so it forgets that an eternity of hell depends upon a will which, with full knowledge and choice, has preferred a life contrary to the will of God, and has not accepted the grace of repentance.

It forgets that the goodness of God goes hand in hand with His justice. God is kind and everlastingly merciful: at the same time God is everlastingly just. We are answerable for our acts according to the *exact* measure of our knowledge and strength. The rest is a secret. The love of God, the justice of God, are also secrets. We cannot understand either the existence or the nature of hell. We can do nothing but submit to the decrees of God's Revelation. We *believe* in its existence.

§ 4. *Purgatory*

The word purgatory is derived from purgation, which means purification as well as penance. It is consequently a state which purifies and cleanses the soul as with fire.

The Church teaches us that this is a place or condition of temporal punishment for those who, departing this life in God's grace, are yet not entirely free from venial faults, or have not fully paid the satisfaction due to their transgressions. The doctrine of the Church is that heaven itself is only open to those who are absolutely pure and holy, and that every sin must be forgiven and expiated before we can enter there.

We shall not find this expression purgatory in the Bible, although it teaches that there are sins for which "there is no forgiveness, either in this world or in the world to come",[20] and that it is "a holy and wholesome thought to pray for the dead, for their guilt's undoing".[21] The Church has always prayed for the dead for the remission of their sins.

We do not know precisely in what this purification of purgatory consists. A part of the punishment will surely be the delay in the beholding of the Beatific Vision. As purification progresses the soul will long more and more intensely for God, and feel this deprivation the more keenly. But the souls in purgatory have accepted it as their lot, and are completely surrendered to the will of God. The longing for God is

[20] Matt. 12, 32. [21] Machabees 12, 46.

moreover assuaged to a certain extent by the sure hope of the salvation which they await. This deep longing, accompanied by submission to the loving decrees of God and the unshakable certainty of ultimately possessing Him, produce, in spite of His absence, a certain happiness. Those who try to give a dreary interpretation to purgatory have not grasped what it means to belong for certain to the number of the Elect. But because payment is required for every debt,[22] we have to help these souls by our prayers. For they are allowed to participate with us in the spiritual riches of the Community of Saints. They are assisted by our prayer, our almsgiving and indulgences, by the Sacrifice of the Mass, and so are sooner able to behold the glory of God in Heaven.

§ 5. *Heaven*

Heaven means eternal life, God's greatest gift to us: our ultimate aim, our everlasting happiness.

Christ was the first to tell us explicitly about heaven: the House of His Father, from which He, the Son of Man, came down to us.[23] He tells us of it in such plain language that henceforth earthly existence has but one significance for the Christian: an ascent to the eternal Kingdom of God. He came into the world to lead men to it, to set them once more upon the road which leads to salvation. He told His disciples that He was returning to His Father, and then: "Do not let your heart be distressed; as you have faith in God, have faith in Me. There are many dwelling-places in my Father's House; otherwise, should I have said to you, I am going away to prepare a home for you? And though I do go away, to prepare you a home, I am coming back; and then I will take you to myself, so that you too may be where I am."[24]

With every kind of parable and simile He tries to picture to us that heaven in some degree. It is a marriage-feast to which we are invited;[25] a just wage for the labourer in His vineyard;[26] Before all, it is a place where we shall know God and His Son Jesus Christ, and have the eternal happiness of beholding them: "Eternal life is knowing Thee, who art the only true God, and Jesus Chrust, whom Thou hast sent."[27]

[22] Matt. 18, 24. [23] John 3, 13. [24] John 14, 1-4.
[25] Matt. 22, 1-14. [26] Matt. 20, 1-16. [27] John 17, 3.

To whom does this Kingdom of Heaven belong? To the poor in spirit; and to those who are willing to give everything in exchange for it, even an eye or a hand.[28] We are to lay up our treasure there. "Where your treasure-house is, there your heart is too."[29] Our Lord's disciples each tried to explain Christ's Revelation in his own way. St. John always emphasizes that we shall see God as He is. "But we know that when He comes we shall be like Him; we shall see Him, then, as He is."[30] And St. Paul says that he will then know, as he himself is known. In heaven faith will disappear, hope pass away, but love for ever remain. And beyond this he knows but little for, as he writes to the Corinthians: "things no eye has seen, no ear has heard, no human heart conceived, the welcome God has prepared for those who love Him."[31]

St. John alone describes what he has seen in a vision of the souls who are in the presence of the Lamb.[32]

It is no wonder that the Church is grave and temperate in her teaching about eternal salvation.

For those who die without being in a state of sin, heaven begins immediately after death, but for those who still have to be purified, only after purgatory.

This eternal happiness never passes away but—being the reward of a devout and conscientious life—it differs in intensity. God gives Himself completely to the soul of man, but not every soul returns that loving surrender in the same degree. That degree depends on the individual life of each of us on earth. According to the measure of our goodwill, and the more perfectly our will is tuned to the will of God, will our happiness in heaven be increased. Love is repaid by happiness: it is the reward of good works. But in exactly what does this happiness consist?

That which is of itself incomprehensible cannot obviously be described, but can only be indicated more or less in general terms. Theologians speak of a sanctifying contemplation, an ascent of the spirit into the illimitable richness of God's Being. The veil of the created world from behind which we now see God, will disappear; faith which accepts God's truth and draws near to Him in a dark and obscure

[28] Matt. 5.
[29] Matt. 6, 20-21.
[30] I John 3, 2.
[31] I Cor. 2, 9.
[32] Apoc. 21 and 22.

submission, and according to its pure human conceptions tries to stammer out something of His reality, will give place to the eternal Light in which we shall then behold Him face to face and forever. God will impart Himself immediately to our spirit, so that His endless perfection will become our unalloyed perfection and happiness too. The soul in heaven receives an interior power by which it intuitively contemplates God, and this contemplation is a participation in God's own inner divine life itself: the crown and the final blossoming of sanctifying grace. The mind will enjoy God in uninterrupted peace, and will know at last the eternal and triune Being of God; it will understand all the mysteries of faith, marvel over the ways of Divine Providence, and appreciate in all its beauty God's creation sustained and supported by His unending love and power. Christ, Our Lady, the saints, the angels—all are included in this heavenly knowledge.

From this contemplation there will flow into the will and into all the faculties of the soul the sweet satisfaction of love fulfilled. Love in heaven is endless enjoyment and eternal happiness.

This happiness in God knows no end; it knows neither change nor diminution. It is one eternal moment of complete absorption in everlasting life—it is one single moment which neither passes away nor continues. Growth and development lie far behind us: we remain stationary, unwearied, enjoying an eternal abundance and an utterly comprehensive wealth. Heaven is an imperishable, eternal life in Jesus Christ: the happy and harmonious completion of ourselves and all our possibilities in unmixed joy. Grace blooms at last in the full knowledge of the divine realities of which it is the seed.

Here on earth heaven is, as it were, a sealed book to the understanding: imagination must perforce keep silence. Faith alone gives us some vague inkling of that reality which it both accepts and awaits.

§ 6. *The Resurrection of the Body*

Scripture, properly speaking, does not teach the immortality of the soul, but lays great emphasis on the immortality of the whole man. Man continues to exist for ever as he is.

In this conception of immortality the body is therefore included.

Resurrection is one of the main doctrines of Christian belief. Christ, and following Him St. Paul, continually return to the point.

It was Christ who first revealed the fact of the Resurrection of the Body in its proper sense. It is true that the ancient prophets had suggested that the righteous who had departed this life were to participate in the great day of the coming of the Messiah. The Pharisees believed in it while the Sadducees rejected this dogma. But Christ, by virtue of His own power, rose up again in His glorified body three days after His death, as he had predicted. This was the sign of the prophet Jonas given as a sign to a wicked and unfaithful generation.[33] This was the temple which He had said that He would build up again three days after it was destroyed.[34] By this ressurrection He both revealed His Godhead and conquered death.

The Resurrection of Christ is still to be continued in the resurrection of the dead. For Christ came to make full reparation for the sin of Adam; He desired to repair *everything* which Adam had lost; to conquer sin and all its consequences, leaving nothing whatsoever to the power of the devil. Christ redeemed the *complete* man—both flesh and spirit, and consequently freed him from both sin and death. He has raised our souls already by baptism: our bodies will rise with Him at the Judgment Day.

St. Paul states quite simply that our faith is vain and his preaching of no value whatever without the Resurrection of Christ.[35] But if Christ rose from the dead how is it possible to pretend that we do not rise with Him? Death came into the world through one single man: and so also Resurrection comes to us through one alone, Christ. He even goes on to try and describe this Resurrection: it is sown in corruption but shall rise clothed with incorruptible life: it is sown in dishonour, it shall rise in glory; it is sown in weakness, it shall rise in power. "This corruptible nature of ours must be clothed with incorruptible life, this mortal nature with immortality." Only then is death swallowed up in victory. All this corresponds with the words of Christ spoken in His

[33] Matt. 12, 39. [34] Mark 14, 58 and John 2, 19-22.
[35] Cor. 15, 1-57.

farewell discourse after the Last Supper. "The man who eats my flesh and drinks my blood enjoys eternal life, and I will raise Him up at the last day."[36]

This glorification therefore grows out of the state of grace and from belief in Jesus Christ,[37] and it will be actually effected by means of the Holy Spirit.[38] To the question, when will the dead actually arise again, Scripture replies: at the coming of Christ. "It will happen in a moment," says St. Paul, "in the twinkling of an eye, when the last trumpet sounds. The trumpet will sound, and the dead will rise again, free from corruption."[39]

Exactly how the resurrection will take place; what will then happen; upon these points the Church has very little to go upon. She has, however, determined that all will rise from the dead with their own bodies, those bodies which once died. "The time is coming," says St. John, "when all those who are in their graves will hear His voice, and will come out of them; those whose actions have been good, rising to new life, and those whose doings have been evil, rising to meet their sentence."[40] Nothing further is explained by the Church. Theologians, however, say that the three characteristics, identity, entirety and immortality, will be common to all risen bodies, but the bodies of the saints will be distinguished by four transcendent endowments: impassibility, brightness, agility, and subtility.

All shall rise from the dead in their own, in their entire, and in immortal bodies, but the body will participate in the soul's more perfect and spiritual life to such an extent that it becomes itself like a spirit. Exactly how this glorified state is to be thought of or imagined is not clear. Christ definitely stated that, after the resurrection, there will be no marrying or giving in marriage, and that we shall be like angels in heaven. From the descriptions which we have of Our Lord's appearances to His disciples after His Resurrection, we are able to a certain extent to deduce the properties of this glorified state. As we have already said, the body will then be impervious to suffering, will be endowed with a clearness of vision which will make it, for the first time, completely itself, with agility by which it can penetrate everywhere with the utmost rapidity, and subtility by which the body becomes

[36] John 6, 55. [37] John 11, 24-26. [38] II Cor. 5, 5.
[39] I Cor. 15, 52-53. [40] John 5, 28-29.

subject to the absolute dominion of the soul. It is only with the greatest reserve that we should picture to ourselves these things, for revelation only gives us an inkling here and there in obviously figurative language. We believe profoundly in the resurrection, we humbly expect it, but we only understand it in part. The resurrection should be the greatest consolation to man, who so loves his body, and should respect it as the willing instrument of his soul.

CHAPTER XVI

THE END OF TIME

1. *The Coming of Christ*

THE GOSPELS are absolutely steeped in the thought of the final Coming of Christ. This marvellous event is described by every sort of image and figure of speech. The Son of Man is to come with the clouds of heaven.[1] All the tribes of the earth will mourn and see the Son of Man coming in the clouds of heaven with much power and majesty. Angels will be sent to gather together His elect from the four winds, "from earth's ends to heaven's". And the Son of Man will sit at the right hand of God's power.

This Second Coming is to be the revelation of the goodness and justice of God; the completion of Christ's work.

Christ says explicitly that the hour and the day of this awe-inspiring event remain unknown. "But as for that day and that hour you speak of, they are known to nobody, not even to the angels in Heaven, not even to the Son; only the Father knows them."[3] Although this coming is to be by surprise, as a thief in the night, yet one fancies one can find here and there signs in the Scriptures which point to the end of time. But many of these signs are already with us and rouse our attention. It is impossible to give any clear definition of it: they are texts of a prophetic character, which have but little relation to the succession of time, and it is far from plain which parts of the descriptions have to be taken literally and which merely figuratively. Among others may be mentioned the preaching of the Gospel to the whole world;[4] the conversion of the Jews to which St. Paul alludes somewhat vaguely in his Epistle to the Romans;[5] the destruction of Jerusalem which has already happened; finally "the champion of wickedness must appear first, destined to inherit perdition.

[1] Mark 14, 62. [2] [3] Mark 13, 32 and I Thess. 5, 1.
[4] Matt. 24, 14. [5] Rom. 11, 25-27.

This is the rebel who is to lift up his head above every divine name, above all that men hold in reverence, till at last he enthrones himself in God's temple and proclaims himself as God".[6] This sign has already appeared. "At present there is a power (you know what I mean) which holds him in check," says St. Paul, and gives no further explanation. A great apostasy is predicted, a general reduction of faith whereby the love of many people will grow cold.[7] Indeed Christ Himself once said: "When the Son of Man comes, will He find faith left on the earth?"[8] St. Matthew describes how then a new and terrible crisis will be reached throughout creation, "when the sun will be darkened, and the moon will refuse her light, and the stars will fall from heaven, and the powers of heaven will rock".[9]

2. *The Last Judgment*

This Last Judgment has been revealed to us in varying language and with the aid of many similes and images. Christ Himself revealed it to us as a reunion of the whole of mankind in the presence of His angels, whom He sends out to separate the tares from the wheat. He Himself will sit down upon the throne of His glory, and all nations will be gathered in His presence, where he will divide men one from the other, as the shepherd divides the sheep from the goats, setting the sheep on his right hand and the goats on his left. Then the King will say to those who are standing at His right hand: "Come, you that have received a blessing from My Father, take possession of the kingdom which has been prepared for you since the foundation of the world. For I was hungry and you gave Me food, thirsty, and you gave Me drink." Whereupon the just will answer, "Lord, when was it that we saw Thee hungry and fed Thee, or thirsty and gave Thee drink?" And the King will answer them, "Believe Me, when you did it to one of the least of My brethren here, you did it to Me."

But to those who are on His left hand He will say in their turn, "Go far from Me, you that are accursed, into that eternal fire which has been prepared for the devil and his angels. For I was hungry, and you never gave Me food, I was thirsty and you never gave Me drink." Whereupon they in

[6] II Thess. 2, 3-4. [7] Matt. 24, 4-13. [8] Luke 18. [9] Matt. 24, 29.

their turn will answer, "Lord, when was it that we saw Thee hungry, or thirsty, and did not minister to Thee?" And He will answer them: "Believe Me, when you refused it to one of the least of My brethren here, you refused it to Me."[10]

Elsewhere Our Lord describes this Judgment as a harvest. God is the owner of the land, the field is the world, the angels are the reapers, the furnace where the weeds are to be burnt is hell, and the barn into which the wheat is to be gathered is heaven.

The use of this metaphorical language places the actual Day of Judgment beyond the scope of our understanding and turns it into one of the mysteries of faith, a reality which altogether surpasses our comprehension. The actual manner and reason of it all remain God's secret enshrined in symbols and images.

But this much at least is clear. At this Judgment, Christ will be the Judge. He will judge us in the name of God, and in the light of this Judgment the whole of human life will be laid bare, with all the good and evil which each has committed, every secret, every influence, the fight against—and the fight in favour of—grace. In each case the final verdict will depend upon His decisive knowledge and understanding of the relationship of the whole to God, and to the ways of God's Providence.

The purpose of this Judgment is the honouring of Jesus Christ as Head of the human race. Everyone and everything is placed in order following Him as the supreme Head, and the righteousness, wisdom and love of God will be made clear as day, and all His decrees will be brought to light and understood.

Included, therefore, in the particular Judgment will be this more general revelation: how utterly fallen we were in Adam, how utterly redeemed by Christ, and in this Judgment we shall learn—one from the other—how this redemption worked for the glory of God and the salvation of souls; how the spirits formally separated themselves, the good from the evil. At the same time we shall see clearly how Christ is in the centre of everything, the Way, the Truth, and the Life. He will appear as the Redeemer and Monarch of the whole of Creation. All knowledge will lie open in the eternal light of God. Every soul will then either radiate as

[10] Matt. 25, 31-46.

a praise of the shining grace of God, or bear the sign of the disgrace earned by its own fault.

Beyond this almost everything about the Last Judgment is hidden from us: we can only believe by faith in the Coming of Christ and His glorious revelation.

3. *The New Creation*

"Then I saw a new heaven and a new earth. The old heaven, the old earth had vanished, and there was no more sea."[11]

The old universe passes away and a new one comes into being; the present world, as we know it, will disappear. St. Peter describes in his second Epistle how the world will perish: by fire.[12] Perhaps he is alluding to some purification of the world, since the world is not to perish in order to disappear, but in order to be renewed. Nature in its turn will be set free from the tyranny of corruption, to share in the glorious freedom of God's sons.[13] St. John saw this new Creation in a vision: "The holy city Jerusalem, as it came down, sent by God, from heaven, clothed in God's glory. The light that shone over it was bright as any precious stone, as the jasper when it is most like crystal . . . I saw no temple in it; its temple is the Lord God Almighty, its temple is the Lamb. Nor had the city any need of sun or moon to shew in it; the glory of God shone there and the Lamb gave it light, the nations will live and move in its radiance . . . Nothing that is unclean, no source of corruption or deceit can ever hope to find its way in; there is no entrance but for those whose names are written in the Lamb's Book of Life."[14]

With deep longing we look forward to this new harmony between man and creation. This is the fulfilment of the prayer taken from the "Our Father": Thy Kingdom come. It is the full and splendid fulfilment of God's work, the completion of the Church under one Head: Jesus Christ.

[11] Appoc. 21, 1. [12] II Pet. 3, 7-8. [13] Rom. 8, 19-23.
[14] Apoc. 21, 10-27.

SUMMARY OF THE TRIPTYCH OF THE KINGDOM OF GOD

The title of this book perhaps requires some explanation and therefore we will ask the question to begin with: What do we understand by the Triptych of the Kingdom of God?

By this Triptych we understand the three inter-related stages of the development of the Kingdom of God, that is to say:

The first panel: Preparation by the election of the Jews as the Chosen People and the prophecies of the prophets as to the Messiah and His Kingdom.

The second panel: The Messiah, Jesus Christ.

The third panel: His Kingdom, the Church.

These three stages represented by the three panels, necessarily belong to one another, and together work out God's intervention in the history of mankind.

PART I: THE FOUNDATION OF THE CHURCH

In the introductory chapter we suggested that man might have been more or less free to choose his own form of religion, and follow his own heart in that respect, *had not God intervened in a special way* in the history of mankind and particularly revealed in what manner He wished to be served.

This, however, He did, as will be shown in the following chapters.

Chapter I. Prehistoric Days

A book called the *Bible* exists which was, in part, written centuries and centuries before Christ, but of which a reliable text has been preserved. From this book it is possible to prove that a nation was chosen by God and that certain men received prophetic gifts in order to prepare the way for the future Messiah.

1. *What do we understand by the Chosen People?*

We understand the Jewish People, from among whom their ancestor, Abraham, was called by God from his surroundings in Mesopotamia to the land of Canaan which is the present Palestine.

God promised him innumerable descendants and that through him all the future generations of the earth should be blessed. In spite of everything, Abraham placed all his confidence in this promise.

The descendants of Abraham became very numerous and it was their mission to keep intact the Patriarch's belief in the particular mission of his People. After many adventures, all recounted in the Old Testament, we learn how the Jews succeeded in holding this belief.

An important share in the task was awarded to the prophets.

2. *What do we understand by the Prophets of the Old Testament?*

These prophets were men who, especially in troubled times, gave a spiritual lead to the people, kept their belief in God alive, threatened with punishments those who deviated from the way of God, and constantly impressed upon them the mission of the Jews in regard to the coming of the Messiah, and the promises of God connected with it.

The first prophecy regarding the Messiah is to be found in the first book of the Bible, where in somewhat vague terms the fight against evil is alluded to. The prophets later elaborated this picture. According to them the Messiah was to:

a. conquer evil;
b. for the good of all;
c. spring from the race of David and be born at Bethlehem;
d. be both teacher and prophet;
e. take upon Himself the Priesthood and sacrifice Himself by His death and Passion for mankind;
f. be born a King and found a spiritual Kingdom which should be everlasting.

Chapter II

Before showing that Christ could truly claim to be the Messiah, we shall try to prove the reliability of the books in which His life is described, that is to say the Gospels and all the other sources which mention His name.

Para. I. The Sources

3. *Which sources deal with Jesus Christ?*

To the non-Christian sources belong the Roman authors Tacitus, Suetonius and Pliny the Younger.

To the Christian sources belong particularly the four Gospels, the Acts of the Apostles, and St. Paul's Epistles.

The four Gospels originated out of the way of life of the first Christian communities which were formed as a result of the Apostolic preaching. Each Gospel has its own distinct characteristics.

The Gospel of St. Matthew was written between the years A.D. 50 and 55 for the Jewish Christians, and endeavours to prove—following the plan of grouping all the events round five sermons—that Jesus was the Messiah foretold by the Prophets.

St. Mark addressed himself in his Gospel (dating from between A.D. 55 and 62) especially to the Roman Christians who were converted pagans, and he particularly emphasizes the fact that Christ was the true Son of God.

St. Luke, St. Paul's travelling companion, completed his Gospel about the year A.D. 60 and probably intended it for converted pagans. It has a more general character.

St. John supposed the other Gospels to have been already read, and definitely set out to show us Christ from another angle. Above all he emphasized the divine nature of Christ. His Gospel first appeared about the year A.D. 100.

4. *On what evidence does the historical authenticity of the Gospels rest?*

Besides obvious inter-relation and a good deal of conformity, we yet find striking differences in some parts, which point to an old-established Christian tradition, to which the Evangelists kept faithfully, without troubling themselves about seeming contradictions. St. Matthew and St. John were eye-witnesses, and St. Luke and St. Mark pupils of eye-witnesses, and there is no evidence of any motive whatsoever for which they might have invented these stories. Had they done so, contemporaries would immediately have discovered the fraud.

In favour of their authenticity and reliability is the high morality of the doctrines set out, and the quiet, unprejudiced manner of presentation. Everything is connected with a certain definite historical milieu, of which the details given are repeatedly confirmed (by later studies, modern excavations, etc.).

That the Gospels were indeed written by the four authors mentioned is also confirmed by the witness of tradition: since the year A.D. 200 that conviction has been general. This tradition is further strengthened by the different character of the four Gospels. From the Gospel of St. Matthew there speaks the Jewish publican; from St. Mark the close companion of St. Peter; from St. Luke the assistant of St. Paul; and from St. John the beloved disciple of Christ.

The Gospels have come down to us undamaged, thus the age

of the manuscripts can be proved, some (fragments) even dating from the second century.

Para. II. Jesus Christ

We conclude that we have now proved the reliability of those who described the life of Christ, and that we may therefore accept their testimony as regards what follows.

Thus, Jesus Christ stands out from all other religious leaders (Buddha, Mahommed, etc.), in that He called Himself the Son of God and maintained that the age-long prophecies about the Messiah were fulfilled in Him.

If these assertions can indeed be proved then it means the collapse of the meaning of all non-Christian religions. For Christ has come and has founded a Kingdom to include all the nations of the world. It is therefore no longer possible to serve God according to some other religion, and one is obliged to join the Kingdom of Christ.

We will therefore now put this important question:

5. *How has Christ proved his Divine Mission?*

a. By the fact that the ancient prophecies of the prophets have indeed been fulfilled in Him.

b. By the miracles wrought by Him. These miracles were completely different from any magical or spiritualistic phenomena, because they had sense and meaning; their purpose was to prove that He was the prophesied Messiah, and they were also connected with the salvation of souls and the healing of the sick.

c. By His marvellous personality and high moral doctrine. He was full of wisdom, dominated His surroundings and governed Himself, lived solely for His high religious ideal, and exhibited a love until then unknown to mankind. Because of His high moral standing, the doctrine He preached and the miracles He performed, became in themselves trustworthy. From this it follows that we may quietly yield to His teaching and allow ourselves to learn about the Kingdom which He came to found.

Chapter III. The Kingdom of the Messiah

6. *What sort of a Kingdom did He preach?*

It was not a Kingdom of this earth; it was neither political nor national, but spiritual and wholly turned towards God; it was in fact the Kingdom of God. It also however assumed a certain visible form, although the spiritual element remained its kernel. Christ selected twelve men, and it grew more and more obvious that these men were destined first to extend, and then to rule, that Kingdom later on.

7. *How did this transfer of government take place?*

It took place at the moment when Christ was about to leave the earth and ascend to Heaven. The words were of paramount importance: "You, therefore, must go out, making disciples of all nations, and baptizing them in the name of the Father, and of the Son, and of the Holy Ghost, teaching them to observe all the commandments which I have given you. And behold I am with you all through the days that are coming, until the consummation of the world." (Matt. 28. 19-20). As these Apostles could not possibly reach all nations, and certainly would not live to see the consummation of the world, obviously Christ was here speaking also to their successors. He thus instituted and established a permanent doctrine which was to be taught to *all* nations of *all* Ages until the end of Time. The Apostles set out to begin their mission after ten days when they had received the Holy Ghost. (Whitsuntide.)

It is noticeable, however, that one among them, Simon Peter, evidently occupied a special position.

a. Although he was not the first to be called, he is mentioned first in all four Gospels;

b. By the special intervention of God, he was chosen to be the one to admit the Gentiles first into the Church;

c. It was he who spoke the final word at the meeting of the Apostles and disciples in Jerusalem. Consequently one is obliged to ask this further question:

8. *Did God give some special power and prerogative to St. Peter?*

He did. We can quote the well-known text: "And I tell thee that thou art Peter, and it is upon this rock that I will build my Church, and the gates of hell shall not prevail against it; and I will give to thee the keys of the Kingdom of Heaven."

From these words it is clear that the Church at that time, depended upon one man, Peter. We might even say that St. Peter was appointed as head of the Church and as a visible representative of Christ who always remains the essential Head.

From the comparison to a rock it is evident that Peter was never to waver, and that he might depend upon the special and infallible guidance of the Holy Ghost. The power of the keys symbolizes the supreme leadership in the Kingdom of Christ, who entrusted the keys to Peter.

We may now ask the further question:

9. *Was this power and this leadership given to St. Peter alone, or was it conferred permanently not only upon St. Peter but upon all his successors?*

If we understand rightly the figurative language used by Christ, we shall realize that the simile of a rock used to indicate the foundation of a Church against which the devil is never to prevail, is meant to represent an enduring institution. It is moreover evident from the tradition of the early Church that the successors of Peter, that is the Bishops of Rome, were always regarded as the heads of the Church.

10. *Was the power of the other Apostles also granted to their successors?*

From the Acts of the Apostles and also their Epistles, it is evident that they delegated the power of government to:
a. The Episcopate and the Presbyters who, by imposition of hands, were appointed as heads of one or more communities (e.g. Titus, Timothy, etc.);
b. deacons, of lower rank, to assist in practical administration and also to preach and baptize. From these the offices of bishop, priest and deacon later developed.

11. *What conclusion are we to draw from the fact that St. Peter and the other Apostles appointed successors?*

The important conclusion follows that the Church founded by Christ is to be found where those successors are to be found, i.e. where the Popes and Bishops can be proved to have ruled the Church since the apostolic days. *This is only the case in the Catholic Church.*

PART II: THE TEACHING OF THE CHURCH

Chapter IV. The Administration of the Church

The actual Revelation of God came to an end with the death of the last Apostle. The Church had the further task of preserving this Revelation intact and handing it down to future generations, not according to the "letter which kills" but as a treasure of the Christian Faith. All that was contained in it, in embryo, was later to come to maturity, by progressive stages, through the guidance of the Holy Ghost.

12. *Are all those governing the Church therefore safeguarded from the possibility of error?*

Although Popes, Bishops and ordinary Priests may rely on the special help of the Holy Ghost to assist them in their government, yet human error is not excluded so long as the Faith of the Church itself is not at stake. When, however, a pronouncement is made which is binding upon the whole Church, either by a General Council under the direction of His Holiness the Pope, or by the Pope himself, this pronouncement, made under the guidance of the Holy Ghost, is infallible. Were this not so, the entire Church might fall into error.

13. *In what does the power of the Pope consist?*

The Pope as a private person is fallible and not impeccable. In virtue of his office, however, he possesses:
a. The primacy, that is to say the highest teaching and governing functions in the Church, under which legislative powers are included:
b. under certain circumstances, infallibility.

14. *When is the Pope infallible?*

The Pope is infallible when he:
a. Acts in his capacity as head of the Church;
b. Makes a pronouncement as regards Faith or Morals;
c. Has the intention that the pronouncement should be accepted as infallible by the whole Church.

Such a pronouncement is called a *Dogma*, as also any other similar pronouncement made by a General Council of the Church. Anyone who deliberately denies such a Dogma becomes a heretic and places himself outside the Catholic Community.

Chapter V. The Traditional Teaching

15. *How must the Catholic obey the Church?*

The Catholic places himself, in all matters appertaining to Faith and Morals, under the guidance of the Church. This ought not to be done (in the case of converts) without due consideration or under any compulsion, but from a personal conviction that the authority of the Church is derived from Christ and that the Church is guided by the Holy Ghost. In the last resort, therefore, the Catholic obeys, not a human being, not even the Pope, but God.

His faith is likewise founded, not on human wisdom, but upon divine Revelation. And therefore the Authority from which he can be sure of obtaining the truth on all matters of Faith, is the contemporary living, teaching Authority. The power of this Authority is vested in the Congregation of the Holy Office. The further question may be asked:

16. *From what source does the Church obtain the teaching which she hands on to the Faithful?*

The source is divine Revelation, contained in:

a. The inspired writings, i.e. the Bible;

b. the infallible oral preaching.

We will examine both these points more closely.

17. *What does the Church teach about the Bible?*

a. Under the guidance of the Holy Ghost, the Church has compiled the list of the books which compose the Bible (the Canon of Scripture).

b. God is the actual Author of the whole Bible: that is to say the whole Bible is *inspired*.

He used as His instruments, however, men who wrote down these God-inspired truths according to their own individual temperament and culture and environment. One must therefore try to understand very thoroughly the meaning of the various authors. That which they present to us as the truth, *is* the truth: that which is only the contemporary framework should be regarded as such. The ordinary reader, as well as the theologian, can do no more than offer an opinion which is both human and fallible. The actual truth can only be reached by the aid of the following important rule:

c. the authentic, infallible explanation of the Word of God belongs exclusively to the Church under the guidance of the Holy Ghost.

The Bible, however, is not the only source of our Faith. The verbal preaching of Christ, and the infallible preaching of the Apostles have the same value. As, however, no inspired writing which records these discourses exists, we are justified in asking the following question:

18. *What are the principal records or monuments handed down to us by all this oral teaching?*

These are in particular:

a. the writings of the earliest Christian authors, who were disciples of the Apostles (the Apostolic Fathers);

b. the writings of the Fathers of the Church (the saintly, learned men of the first twelve centuries of Christianity);

c. the ancient liturgical books, confessions of Faith, Acts of the Martyrs, inscriptions, images, etc., etc., especially those preserved in the Catacombs.

19. *How can we be sure that the infallible preaching and teaching has been reliably handed down to us?*

Tradition is only completely reliable and a point of Faith when the Church, acting under the guidance of the Holy Ghost, has made an infallible pronouncement concerning it, or (without the official, infallible pronouncement of the highest Authority) if it is accepted by the entire Church as a sacred Truth: for the Church, as a whole, cannot err.

20. *What is the connection between Bible and Tradition?*

The Bible contains the revealed truth, inspired and set down in writing. Next to this comes revealed truth which has only been preached. The latter is sometimes figuratively called Tradition. Tradition in the real sense, however, is the infallible exposition of the whole revealed truth of the Church under the guidance of the Holy Ghost, handed down to the succeeding generations of the Faithful.

Once it is clear that the Church, acting under the guidance of the Holy Spirit, infallibly explains divine Revelation, then it only remains for us to ask the Church what She teaches. Once more, it is not forbidden, but on the other hand highly commendable, to reflect upon the Church's doctrine and the grounds upon which it is founded, and to trace this doctrine both in Holy Scripture and Tradition, penetrating deeply into the facts of Revelation. But for those who have accepted the infallible authority of the Church all is plain sailing: they have received the answer to the first two questions put at the beginning of this book. There only remains the third and final question:

WHAT IS THE TEACHING OF THE CATHOLIC CHURCH?

We will divide this question into a number of others, and thus make a systematic survey of the whole of Catholic teaching.

Chapter VI

21. *What is the mystery of the Blessed Trinity?*

God is a living Being with His own personal interior life which is realized in Three Persons.

The Father knows Himself from all eternity. This knowledge, the Word, is the Son, begotten from all eternity. The eternal love existing between Father and Son is the Holy Ghost.

Although there are thus Three Persons in God, yet there is only one divine Being, one divine nature.

This mystery of the blessed Trinity, the mystery of God's eternal, interior fecundity, we can only know because Christ Himself revealed it to us: this revelation was made the most plainly at

His Baptism in the Jordan, and when He sent His disciples in their turn to baptize " In the Name of the Father, and of the Son, and of the Holy Ghost ". This is the most precious revelation made to us by our Redeemer which we shall only understand fully in the life to come.

Chapter VII. The Creation

22. *What are angels and devils?*

From the Bible it is evident that there are individual spirits who:

a. adore and praise God;

b. are messengers from God to men (the Greek word " angelos " signifies messenger);

c. help men. Every man has his own particular spirit or guardian angel.

These spirits are called *angels.* They were created before man and are above him because they are pure spirits, not in any way bound by matter. But the angels also had their day of trial, during which a number of them fell as appears from the revelation of St. John, from the Gospels and I St. Peter.

The fallen angels are called *devils,* and are rejected by God for all eternity. As the spirits of evil they play a notable part in the life of the visible world; they are able to tempt man to evil, but by the help of God's grace, man is also able to resist.

The world and man

23. *What do we know of the creation of the world and of Man?*

Out of nothingness God brought the world into existence. We call this to create. God also keeps Creation continually in existence, for without Him it would again revert to the nothing from which He made it.

The highest motive of God's action is, and always must be, His own glory. In His love and wisdom He has, however, connected man's happiness with this glory.

The Bible story of creation need not be taken absolutely literally in all its details. The author adapted himself to the circumstances and language of his day. His actual purpose was to put before people important truths such as: God created the world: He created man after His own image and likeness: man at first lived in friendship with God, but lost this friendship by transgressing one of God's commandments, etc., etc. The intellectual believer accepts all these truths, but this does not prevent him from also examining the nature and existence of the world according to scientific methods.

Chapter VIII. The Fall and Redemption

Para. I. The Fall and Original Sin

24. *What is the Fall?*

Man was created in a state of happiness, with God in his heart and Creation at his feet. He was to enjoy God's friendship, and experience neither suffering nor death so long as he remained faithful to the commandment which God had given him. To this, however, he did not remain faithful. We know from the story of the Garden of Eden how the devil, under the guise of a serpent, tempted Eve (and Eve in turn tempted Adam) to transgress the commandment of the Lord. By this Fall they lost both God's friendship and all the supernatural gifts which went with it, especially their right to Heaven. They also lost the preternatural gifts (gifts which are not absolutely beyond the order of nature but are not customarily accorded) such as a clear intellect, a strong will, harmony between the higher and lower aspirations, exemption from suffering and death. They were therefore degraded from their original state of happiness, weakened in will and judgment, but still capable of some good: nevertheless with the absolute impossibility of restoring the friendship with God. Because Adam was the responsible head of the human race, that race in its entirety fell with him. All his descendants came into the world with this hereditary taint, weakened in mind and will, and delivered up to the interior conflict between good and evil, and liable to both suffering and death. The absolute core of this curse, however, the hereditary debt of original sin, was the loss of the supernatural friendship with God and, through it, of the right to heaven.

Para. II. The Incarnation and Redemption

This friendship could not be restored by man himself because the offence to the infinite greatness of God demanded an act of propitiation of equally infinite value. God could, of course, have forgiven sin without any human co-operation, but His wisdom and love required propitiation to be offered by a Mediator who, on the one hand could represent man, and on the other hand was capable of performing an act of infinite worth.

25. *In what way was the sin of Adam repaired?*

Jesus Christ as *one* Person united in Himself two natures: human nature by which He was able to represent mankind to God, and the divine nature by which His acts possessed infinite worth. This God-man, the second Person of the Blessed Trinity, offered a life which, concluded by His death on the Cross, was accepted by God as complete atonement for the sin of the first man and his descendants. This general (objective) Redemption enables everyone, by subjective participation in it, to obtain personal redemption. How this takes place will be explained later.

The second aim of the incarnation was to instruct us by word and example and to safeguard the fruits of the Redemption by establishing a community and a Church on earth. Everyone can share in these fruits, because, as St. Paul tells us, Christ died for all men.

Chapter IX. Grace

Because the fruits of Redemption are summed up under the general term of *grace,* and this conception plays a most important part in Christianity, we must go further into it. The term grace is a translation of the biblical word *charis* (Latin *gratia*) which means benefit of God, given to us without any merits on our part.

Usually it is used to indicate gifts which are above the order of created nature, and which are therefore called *supernatural.*

Two kinds of grace are to be distinguished: *Sanctifying grace and actual grace.*

26. *What is sanctifying grace?*

Christ has told us about sanctifying grace in His conversation with Nicodemus and in His discourse after the Last Supper. He describes it there as a re-birth, a new life which is a participation in the divine life, and a life of union with Himself. St. John speaks of the sonship of God by which we become heirs of Heaven. St. Paul contrasted the two: this new life in Christ and the sinful condition of man which is taken away by it.

St. Peter expressed this state as one in which we become participators in the nature of God.

All this can be briefly summarized as follows: sanctifying grace is a supernatural, permanent gift of God to the soul, by which we, in Christ, participate in the divine life.

27. *What is actual grace?*

Actual grace is a supernatural assistance from God by which our understanding is enlightened and our will strengthened. This grace incites us to good deeds and accompanies our accomplishment of them; without it we can do nothing in the supernatural order. We also need it in order to keep even the natural law in its entirety; to avoid committing mortal sin sooner or later, and also to obtain the grace of final perseverance. In dispensing grace God does not act according to a fixed plan but according to His own good pleasure. Everyone, however, may be sure of receiving sufficient grace to obtain his own salvation, and no one is lost except through his own fault.

28. *What do we understand by the merit of good works?*

Without grace we can do nothing, but that does not mean that we are led blindly by grace as Beings without freewill. It is essential that we should co-operate with grace, listen to its inspirations, and surrender to its secret urges. How the co-operation between grace and freewill takes place is a great mystery. But the whole of Scripture rests upon the principle that man is responsible and therefore free.

By thus co-operating with grace our works become meritorious in the supernatural order, that is to say, for Heaven. The Bible continually speaks of a reward, even of deserts according to merits; and the future happiness of Heaven will be in proportion to the good works performed on earth. We do not suggest, however, that it is a high moral principle to perform good works merely for the sake of the reward. Ultimately we should always act for the love of God, but in His wisdom and love He has graciously attached eternal happiness to these actions of ours.

The merit does not exclude grace, but is the fruit of it. Grace always precedes any act, and our merit is founded on the merits of Christ, without whom no good works are possible in the supernatural order. Good works, if performed in a state of mortal sin, are not meritorious for Heaven; yet they are not useless since they may pave the way for conversion.

Thus Revelation connects the following together: the state of being a sinner: faith: grace: perseverance in the fight: meritorious works and eternal reward.

Chapter X. The Communion of Saints

The grace of Christ did not remain ineffective. From the wounds of His Body the Church issued forth, and millions who died in a state of grace are awaiting eternal happiness, while millions have already entered upon it.

29. *What is the Communion of Saints?*

A living bond exists between all these members of the Church, and there is continuous prayer either to or for each other. They are all welded into a supernatural communion with Christ as their head, and this is called the *Communion of Saints*. Three separate groups are to be distinguished into which it is divided:

the Militant (here on earth); the suffering (in Purgatory); and the Church triumphant (in Heaven). We could therefore describe the Communion of Saints as the supernatural union which exists, in Christ, among the members of the Militant, Suffering and Triumphant Church.

Para. I.

30. *What do we understand by the Mystical Body of Christ?*

St. Paul's most usual simile for expressing the intimate union between Christ and His Church is that of Head and Body: Christ the Head of the Body which is the Church. In this simile we also see a representation of that organic unity bound together by the Hierarchy. Later in the history of the Church this simile began to be more carefully considered, and in 1943 Pope Pius XII gave a clear summary of the Church's teaching in his Encyclical on the Mystical Body. Stress is particularly laid upon the difference between an ordinary Society or corporate body, and the Mystical Body of the Church. This Mystical Body is founded upon a principle of its own, which really exists, and which wields its influence over the community in general as well as over each member separately. This governing principle is the Divine Spirit which pervades and unifies the Church. Just as we call Christ the Head and the Church the Body, so also we can consider the Holy Ghost as the soul of the Church.

Para. II. Veneration of the Saints

The veneration of the Saints is based upon Holy Scripture, in which we read that particular servants of God were accorded special reverence and credited with a particular power of intercession with God. That this veneration continued long after their death is again apparent from some passages in the Bible, although nowhere does it say that they were actually prayed to. But the latter became a practice in the Church as soon as martyrs had died for their Faith. Out of this practice the general veneration of the Saints developed.

31. *How does the Catholic get into contact with the Saints?*

Mainly in three ways:

1. By the actual cult, which may be separated into the *direct* cult which honours the person of the saint, and the *relative* cult which shows honour to something connected with the saint, such as a relic or a picture or statue, etc.

2. By asking their intercession with God. This intercession derives all its efficacy from the merits of Christ, the only Mediator;

3. By following their example, that is by seeing in them the way in which we should ourselves follow Christ.

Para. III. Devotion to Mary

The foundation for this devotion is also to be found in the Bible. It is founded upon the Scriptural parallel between Eve who paved the way for man's Fall, and Mary who paved the way for man's Redemption. Mary voluntarily consented to become the Mother of the Redeemer. Because of this she has a real, although completely subordinate share in the work of Redemption, and holds a very special place among the saints in the matter of intercession with Christ.

In the teaching of the Church about Mary we shall observe, even more than anywhere else, the development of Revelation under the guidance of the Holy Ghost.

32. *What privileges are ascribed to Mary?*

1. Mary is, in the real sense of the word, the *Mother of God* because one becomes the mother not of a nature but of a person, and there is in Christ only *one* (divine) Person.
2. Mary remained a Virgin before, during, and after the birth of Christ. The so-called "brethren and sisters" of Christ were in reality more distant relations.
3. Mary was immaculate from her conception; that is, because of the merits of Christ, she was already, even before actual existence, safeguarded from original sin.
4. It is also a dogma of the Church that Mary was assumed into Heaven.
5. It is accepted by many that all graces come to mankind through the hands of Mary.

Chapter XI. The Sacraments

Christ is not limited to only one way of distributing His graces. He can work and sanctify directly if He chooses. Nevertheless He has instituted certain means, by which in a particular manner we can receive these graces, namely the Sacraments.

Para. I.

33. *What is a Sacrament?*

Christ instituted visible signs or symbols which represent the invisible working of grace in the soul. In this way Baptism is a visible cleansing by water which symbolizes an invisible cleansing (from sin). The remarkable thing about these symbols, however, is that they do not only signify a working in the soul but actually effect it: through the cleansing at Baptism the soul is really purified from Sin. Accordingly one can define a Sacrament as certain holy ceremonies and words instituted by Christ to convey the grace which they symbolize.

This grace is not given because of either the faith or the sanctity of the one who administers the Sacrament, but solely because of the redemptive power of Christ which He Himself conveys by means of the Sacrament.

There are seven Sacraments, each of which brings with it actual grace, and together they promote the birth, growth, renewal and continuation of the supernatural life in the soul. In addition to this, some can convey sanctifying grace (Baptism and Confession). If one is already in possession of this, which is necessary in order to receive the other Sacraments, it is further increased by the reception of each separate Sacrament. (The Sacrament of Extreme Unction can convey sanctifying grace in the case of unconscious persons.)

For the validity of a Sacrament certain requirements must first be fulfilled. (This will be dealt with later.)

If these conditions are fulfilled, grace is always given, unless (apart from Baptism and Confession) one receives the Sacrament in a state of mortal sin, that is to say unworthily. In such a case one commits the mortal sin of sacrilege.

Baptism, Confirmation and Holy Orders are Sacraments which can only be received once because they impress upon the soul an indelible mark.

Para. II. Baptism

In the Gospels we read of the Baptism of John which was a symbol of penance and of a will to amend one's life. But the new Baptism, to which John alluded, we encounter for the first time in the conversation of Our Lord with Nicodemus. This is a true rebirth: by water and the Holy Ghost a new life is engendered. After His Resurrection Christ charged His Apostles to Baptize all "in the Name of the Father, and of the Son, and of the Holy Ghost". This Baptism is a Sacrament. Here the symbolism resides in the outward cleansing with water which symbolizes the inward cleansing from sin. Both body and soul are purified and become clean.

34. *How is this Sacrament administered and what are the the results?*

The normal minister of Baptism is the priest; it can however be performed by anyone in case of necessity. Usually the cleansing is effected by pouring the water three times over the head while at the same time repeating the words, "I baptize thee in the Name of the Father, and of the Son, and of the Holy Ghost." The godfather and (or) godmother are present either personally or by proxy and take upon themselves the duty of watching over the godchild as far as possible.

The results of Baptism are:

1. Infusion of sanctifying grace and supernatural virtues by means of which one becomes a child of God and capable of performing supernatural actions.
2. The wiping out of original sin as well as personal sins (provided these latter are accompanied by sincere contrition).
3. The leaving of an indelible mark upon the soul by which we become members of the Catholic Church and receive actual grace to lead a Christian life.

Para. III. Confirmation

Through Baptism one receives sanctifying grace, through the supplementary sacrament of Confirmation one receives the Holy Ghost in a special manner. The Apostles received this Sacrament at Pentecost, after which they administered it to those of the Faithful who were already baptized. This took place—as recorded in the Bible—by means of the imposition of hands and prayer.

35. *How is the Sacrament of Confirmation administered and what are the results?*

The usual minister of Confirmation is the Bishop, but in danger of death the parish priest. To the imposition of hands and prayer the Church has added unction with blessed chrism, during which the Bishop says these words: I sign thee with the sign of the Cross and strengthen thee with the chrism of Salvation in the Name of the Father, and of the Son, and of the Holy Ghost. In the case of Confirmation also a godfather and (or) godmother are present.

The *results* are:

1. the outward form symbolizes the descent of the Holy Ghost into the soul so that it is imbued with a special strength to confess the Faith steadfastly.
2. This Sacrament leaves an indelible mark on the soul through which we participate more closely in Christ's priesthood; are hallmarked as His fellow soldiers, and are able to take part in certain forms of the Christian Apostolate.
3. We receive an increase of sanctifying grace.

Through Baptism and Confirmation one becomes a Christian but not as yet a saint; and the weak man, who succumbs to mortal sin, may thus lose his sanctifying grace.

Christ in His mercy has, however, foreseen this, and through His Apostles He gave yet another Sacrament to the Church: "Receive the Holy Ghost. Whose sins you shall forgive, they are forgiven; whose sins you shall retain, they are retained." This power presupposes that the Apostles and their successors are to *judge*, and this in turn presupposes a confession. The form of this Confession has altered somewhat in the course of the centuries. But the outward symbolism of the administration of justice will always require some form or another.

36. *What is required of the penitent in the Sacrament of Penance?*

1. *Contrition.* Without contrition and a firm purpose of amendment to shun the occasions of sin, one will never receive the forgiveness of God.

Perfect and imperfect contrition are distinguished by the motive of contrition: on the one hand the love of God because of His intrinsic goodness, and on the other hand the less worthy motive of fear of punishment, etc., etc.

This imperfect contrition is, however, sufficient for Confession and Absolution. Through perfect contrition the sins are already forgiven even before Confession; nevertheless they must be confessed at the following Confession.

2. *Confession* of all mortal sins committed since the last good confession, together with the number of them, so far as one can remember, and any circumstances by which the nature of a sin may be changed from a lesser into a greater kind, or vice versa. For instance the theft of a chalice from the altar also becomes a sin of sacrilege: the sin of unchastity committed by or with a married person becomes adultery, etc., etc.

There is no obligation to confess venial sins, although it is very desirable to do so. Sins which one forgets to confess by inadvertence are forgiven together with the others. If however one later remembers them, one is obliged to confess them at the next Confession.

3. *Satisfaction.* To this symbolism of the administration of justice there also belongs the imposition of a penance for the sins committed. This penance is imposed by the priest and serves to reduce the temporary punishments which may still remain after the forgiveness of sin. The eternal punishments are always remitted through a good confession.

37. *What is the Priest's task in Confession?*

The priest administers justice in the name of God, just as does a worldly judge in the name of the king. He forgives (that is gives Absolution) if he finds that the penitent is in the right frame of mind; he has however the right either to refuse or to postpone Absolution if real contrition is lacking in the penitent. As a Confessor he is absolutely bound by the secrecy of the Confessional which *knows no exceptions whatsoever*. Nevertheless he is not only a judge, but also a physician and father, who will always know how to give kindly advice and direction.

Para. V.

38. *What are Indulgences?*

The punishments which may remain after the forgiveness of sins, can be expiated by every form of good work: prayers, the reception of the Sacraments, suffering patiently borne, alms-giving etc., etc. A special power is ascribed to what are called Indulgences: an application of the infinite satisfaction made by Jesus Christ, and of the abundant satisfaction offered to God by the saints since then. These Indulgences are attached by the Church to the performance of certain good works and the recitation of certain prayers. "That which you shall loose upon earth shall also be loosed in Heaven."

The convert to Catholicism should note carefully that Indulgences can never forgive sins, and that it is very strictly forbidden by the Church to sell them for money.

Para. VI. Holy Eucharist

Holy Eucharist is the Sacrament in which Christ makes Himself present under the appearances of Bread and Wine in order to perpetuate the Sacrifice of the Cross, both mystically and in reality, and to be consumed by both Priest and Faithful as a sacrificial food.

39. *Where is this Sacrament mentioned in the New Testament?*

1. In the sixth chapter of the Gospel of St. John we read that Christ promises eternal life to all those who eat His Flesh and drink His Blood. From the reaction of the Jews, His Apostles and disciples, we can be certain that He meant this literally.
2. In company with the other three Evangelists we are told by St. John how the evening before His Death, Christ instituted this Sacrament with the words uttered at the breaking of the Bread: "This is My Body", and at the offering of the Wine: "This is My Blood".

3. St. Paul also repeats these words and testifies that he has received them from the Lord.

In the case of this Sacrament we must distinguish between the Sacrifice (Holy Mass) and the sacramental partaking of the sacrificial food (Holy Communion).

40. *What do we mean by Holy Mass as a Sacrifice?*

In the New Testament we read of only one Sacrifice, namely Christ's sacrifice upon the Cross in which He offered Himself to the Father as expiation for our sins. This unique Sacrifice of the Cross is perpetuated in a mystical but real way in the Catholic Church through a visible Rite: (the Rite of the Last Supper which Christ Himself instituted). Round this centre of the Sacrifice, other prayers and ceremonies have grown up during the course of history. This Rite is called Holy Mass. It is not a case of a *new* Sacrifice but of an unbloody perpetuation of the unique Sacrifice of the Cross. "Do this in commemoration of Me." Christ remains the sole Offerer and Priest in the full sense of the words. Ordinary priests perform the exterior Rite, and through the power of that Rite the Sacrifice of the Cross is perpetuated. Holy Mass has a symbolical meaning; Christ's Body is represented by the Bread, and His Blood by the Wine, and the separation between the Body and Blood symbolizes the death on the Cross. Because it is a sacramental symbol, that which is symbolized becomes a reality—the death on the Cross.

41. *What do we mean by Holy Communion?*

By virtue of the sacramental words of the Priest: "This is My Body", "This is My Blood", Christ becomes really present. This happens through transubstantiation which means that the essence of bread and wine are changed into the essence of Christ's Body and Blood, while the appearances (accidents) of bread and wine, such as colour, taste, volume, etc., still remain. Christ is not present in virtue of His extension, so that He is completely present in every part. Because He is completely present under the appearance of bread as well as under the appearance of wine, it is possible to go to Holy Communion under one appearance only, which for practical reasons has been adopted in the case of the Faithful.

Christ becomes really present, but in a mystical way, and accordingly those who partake of the appearances of bread and (or) of wine, partake of the Body and Blood of Christ, as He is now, glorified in Heaven.

This Sacrament effects in us a very special union with Christ, which is the pledge of our future resurrection. We may only receive it in a state of grace, and therefore anyone with mortal sin upon his conscience, must first go to Confession. In other cases Confession is not necessary. The Church prescribes that, out of respect for this Sacrament, one must be fasting (water not included) from twelve midnight. One is in duty bound to go to Holy Communion at least once a year, or when in danger of death.

Para. VII. Holy Orders

42. *What is meant by the Sacrament of Holy Orders?*

Christ, the eternal High Priest, has communicated His Priesthood to the Church. During His public life He collected round Him a group of twelve Apostles, to whom He promised power over the Kingdom of God, and to whom He bequeathed the mission of preaching that Kingdom. They received the Holy Ghost, the power to baptize and to forgive sins, and the mandate to continue the Celebration of the Last Supper in memory of Him.

The Apostles in their turn appointed bishops, priests and deacons, by the imposition of hands, to continue their task to the end of Time. This imposition of hands is the Sacramental sign of the Priesthood: it confers a lasting union with the Priesthood of Christ, and gives the power to say Mass and to administer the Sacraments. It is accompanied by the grace to perform this responsible task well.

Para. VIII. Matrimony

The main purpose of matrimony is the perpetuation of the human race; the urge given to man by nature leads to the creation of the child.

But bound up in this Institution is also the personal happiness of husband and wife; the state of matrimony offers the most favourable conditions for the all-round development of human personality. The mutual complement of the man and the woman only finds its true realization in love, which is built up on lifelong fidelity and the willingness to sacrifice.

43. *What is the Sacrament of Matrimony?*

This State of life was raised to the dignity of a Sacrament by Christ. The first chapter of the Bible tells us all about the *purpose* of natural marriage (Go and multiply) while the second chapter deals with the complement of man and woman by means of love. (Therefore shall a man leave father and mother and cling to his wife and they two shall become one flesh).

St. Paul, in his Epistle to the Ephesians, enlarges upon this subject. He raises marriage to the supernatural sphere of Christ and His Church, while he points to the protection of the virtue of the individual which such a union offers. In this case the symbol of the Sacrament is to be found in the mutual consent of husband and wife; in the free will to realize the purpose of marriage. Thus they administer the Sacrament to one another and receive the grace to fulfil all the duties of the married state perfectly. By the will of Christ Marriage is indissoluble so long as both the partners to it are alive.

The Church, however, has the power to loosen the bond of matrimony in some cases. In the same way actually living together can be suspended for valid reasons, without however either party having the right to re-marry.

44. *What does the Church lay down about Marriage?*

1. For the validity of a marriage between two baptized Catholics it is necessary that it should be contracted in the presence of one's own Parish Priest and two witnesses, but the Parish Priest can appoint another priest to act instead of him.
2. The Church has fixed certain impediments which render a marriage invalid; or in some cases not invalid but only unlawful.

Para. IX. Extreme Unction

In the last decisive battle at the end of life the Church assists the soul with a separate Sacrament: Extreme Unction.

45. *What is the Sacrament of Extreme Unction?*

In his Epistle St. James speaks of the prayer of the priests of the Church over the sick, and of unction with oil from which follows consolation, healing and the forgiveness of sins. This is therefore an exterior sign (Unction as the symbol of the oldest way of healing) which conveys an interior grace (the healing of the soul). The form of this Sacrament has been defined by the Church in detail. The Sacrament conveys:

1. Forgiveness of venial sin and the punishment due to sin: forgiveness of mortal sins only if one is unable to go to Confession—for instance if unconscious. This presupposes however that one has contrition, and the intention of receiving the Sacrament of Extreme Unction. (A good Catholic should bear this in mind from time to time).
2. Sometimes physical recovery, but always the strength to accept suffering and death patiently at the hands of God.

Para. X. Sacramentals

Although the value of Sacramentals is small in comparison with that of the Sacraments themselves, they are sometimes considered by non-Catholics to be the most important expression of the mind of the Church. It is therefore necessary to note the following points:

46. *What are Sacramentals?*

They are exterior signs (actions such as for instance a blessing, a gesture, a Rite; or such objects as a statue, a medal, Holy Water, etc.) which, in contrast with the Sacraments, neither possess nor convey supernatural power in themselves. That which conveys the power in this case is the prayer of the Church which accompanies such actions or is attached to such objects.

Sacramentals were not instituted by Christ Himself but by the Church. Anyone who ascribes to them greater power than is intended by the Church, is guilty of superstition.

PART III: LIFE IN THE CHURCH

Chapter XII. Liturgy and the Liturgical Life of the Church

We do not propose to summarize this Chapter fully but will confine ourselves to the following question:

47. *How has Liturgy developed from the Rite of the Last Supper into the present form of the Mass?*

1. At the Last Supper the Sacrament of the Altar was enacted for the first time, with its solemn words and gestures. There is a definite exterior frame within which is contained the essence of this sacrament.

(1) *The Offertory:* "Jesus took bread". . . . "And taking the chalice". . . .
(2) *The Consecration:* "This is My Body". . . . "This is My Blood".
(3) *Holy Communion:* He gave it to His disciples.

2. *In Apostolic times* Christians still took part in the religious ceremonies of the Jews in their temple and synagogues. From the very beginning, however, they only assisted at the "breaking of bread" in strict privacy. This intimate ceremony had the outward form of a Supper, usually partaken of in the house of one of the disciples. From St. Paul we learn of certain excesses, and of the necessity of serious reflection upon the meaning of this

holy Mystery. Everyone took part in the ceremony of the Offering which was also connected with charitable poor relief (Love-feasts).
3. *In the later and post-Apostolic times* different liturgies gradually came into being. Each Christian community adopted its own particular manner of celebrating the Lord's Supper and the commemoration of the Passion of Christ. Veneration for the Mystery was greatly enhanced by the secret character of this ceremony. Despite the absence of any rigid liturgical laws, there grew to be a close similarity between the various forms. The different Churches came into contact with each other and the spiritual centre was Rome. Definite liturgies began to develop such as those of Antioch, Alexandria, Byzantium, Milan and Rome, which by their variety augmented the splendour of religious worship.
4. From the fifth century onwards the Roman Liturgy obtained a predominant position in the slowly Christianizing northern and western Europe. At the present day it is by far the most widely used of all the Liturgies of the Church.

Chapter XIII. Moral Law

Para. I. Principles

Not every human act falls under the law of Morality: we must therefore ask the question:

48. *What is necessary in order to make a human act moral (or immoral)?*

It is necessary that the action should be performed with both knowledge and freewill.

a. Knowledge of the moral value

One is responsible for an act in so far as one knows that it is good or bad, and for the consequences in so far as one ought to have foreseen them. It is assumed that there is no *culpable* ignorance involved.

b. Freedom when performing an action

Interior freedom is greatly decreased by both passion and habit. Responsibility is also diminished in the same degree if one is not intentionally culpable and desires to break the habit.

49. *What do we understand by conscience?*

Conscience is one's interior judgment as to whether an act which one is about to perform is permissible or not.

This judgment may be clear but it may also leave room for doubt.

What should one do in such a case?

One is then free to choose on the following conditions:
1. It must involve a *serious* doubt which one is unable to solve (e.g. by taking advice);
2. It must concern the fact of whether an action be permissible only, not whether it be valid;
3. In no case must it involve the violation of the rights of another.

50. *What is sin?*

According to Catholic Moral Law sin is not so much regarded as a condition in which the whole of mankind is involved owing to the consequences of Adam's fall, but rather as a personal act by which one deliberately and consciously transgresses God's law.

Thus it is possible to speak of sins in the plural: one can, so to speak, count them. One should, however, note that a sinful act need not necessarily be visible, but that voluntary thoughts and desires, and the neglect of one's duty, also fall under the heading of sin. God sees the heart.

We understand by God's law the natural law which God has put into the hearts of men, as well as that positive law imposed by Christ and the Church, and those laws imposed by any other human Institution clothed with the authority of God—the State, the head of a family, etc. It is very important to distinguish the difference in sin in the case of:
1. An actual sin in which one deliberately turns away from God towards the creature. By committing such a sin one loses the *supernatural* life and the friendship of God. It is called *mortal sin.* For this it is necessary that one should transgress God's law in a serious matter, deliberately, and fully conscious of the evil of one's action. Such serious matters are further described in the ten commandments.
2. Those faults which but slightly affect general moral well-being (either because of the slightness of the transgression, or because of either a lack of consciousness or of liberty). In this case one does not deliberately put the creature before God, and would never commit the act if one realized that by doing so one were losing His friendship. These are the faults into which most people fall daily. It is called *venial sin.*

Para. II. The Decalogue

A. *The first tablet of the Commandments*

The theological virtues

The theological virtues enable the understanding and the will to focus themselves directly upon God as their supernatural and final end.

51. *Which are the theological virtues?*

1. *The virtue of Faith*

This is a supernatural gift of God by which the understanding subjects itself to the truths revealed by God *because* God has revealed them and not because of the understanding of the mind.

Through this Faith man hears the voice of God in the voice of Christ and by means of the teaching Authority of the Church. In order that this Faith may be alive and active, it must go hand in hand with the two other theological virtues. St. James tells us that Faith without works is a dead Faith. The main sins committed against this virtue are:
a. rejecting the Faith. This rarely happens suddenly, but the way has been paved for it by careless exposure to danger (unwise reading, meetings, etc.). First one begins to doubt and then voluntarily entertains these doubts. (Involuntary doubts, arising through no fault of one's own, are not sinful). Finally the Faith is entirely lost.
b. by practising one's Faith with indifference and out of mere routine.

2. *The virtue of Hope*

This is a supernatural gift by which we expect with firm confidence that God will grant us eternal salvation and all the means which are necessary in order to attain to it. This hope is founded upon the omnipotence of God which is *able* to give, and upon God's promise which will give. It meets man's infinite craving for happiness. This virtue is threatened by a twofold danger, that is, that one had so little trust in God that one despairs, or that one trusts too easily and so hopes to obtain eternal salvation without any co-operation.

3. *The virtue of Charity*

This is a supernatural gift by which we love God for His own sake and above everything, and love our neighbour and ourselves because of our love for Him. This, according to Christ's own words, is the chief among all the commandments. It embraces God and all men, even our enemies. This virtue is lost by every mortal sin.

52. *What is the virtue of Piety?*

Closely connected with the three theological virtues is another, which is not one of the theological virtues but a so-called moral virtue: the virtue of piety. It is not addressed directly to God but to the service of God. One can consider the first Table of the

Decalogue as a commandment of this virtue, and we will briefly sum up the principal ways in which it can be transgressed.

1. By different forms of idolatry and superstition: neglect of prayer and sacrilege are also opposed to the true worship of God.

2. Opposed to the reverent use of the name of God are blasphemy, cursing, and the thoughtless taking of an oath, or, worse still, actual perjury.

3. Opposed to the sanctification of the Sunday are doing unnecessary servile work on that day and not attending Holy Mass. The latter falls partly under the Precepts of the Church and will be dealt with again later.

B. *The second table of the commandments*

These commandments concern man's attitude towards himself and the community in general. The virtues required are called *moral virtues*.

53. *What is the meaning of the fourth commandment?*

The fourth commandment deals with our attitude towards all who are in authority over us, and requires:

a. that we show our parents respect, love and obedience;

b. that we submit to the spiritual authority of the Church, in all matters which fall under her jurisdiction, or are concerned with the government of the Church.

c. that we show a reasonable obedience towards the State authorities and willingness to contribute to the general welfare.

The virtue of obedience can, however, never bind us to perform actions which are genuinely contrary to our conscience.

54. *What do we mean by the fifth commandment?*

The fifth commandment protects man's right to existence and forbids, in virtue of justice and charity, every unlawful attack upon his life. Christ emphasizes strongly the inner meaning of this commandment in His Sermon on the Mount, and enlarges it to include charity in general, by which slander is also condemned. Slander is in reality an attack upon life because it can rob a man of his good name which he needs in order to lead a respectable life. *Abortion*, which is the direct killing of the yet unborn foetus also comes under this commandment, and is nothing less than the killing of the innocent and defenceless. In the case of indirect killing (i.e. an action which is not meant to kill but which may result in death) one must consider the rules which Catholic morality lays down for actions which may have either good or bad results:

a. the action must not be unlawful on some other account;
b. the good result must not be achieved only on account of the evil;
c. the bad result must not be wilfully and primarily intended;
d. there must be a reason which must be important enough to justify the performance of the action in spite of its bad result.

War is always regretted by the Catholic Church but is not always condemned.

It may be the duty of the individual and the community to defend their rights against violation, and in decisive moments heroism may even be asked of a nation in order to protect its well-being and existence.

55. *What is the meaning of the eighth commandment?*

The eighth commandment forbids everything which is contrary to the virtue of truthfulness.

We call a person truthful when, by his mode of expression, he is honestly seeking to convey the truth as far as possible. Such modes of expression (words, gestures, etc.) can also be used to hide the truth. This is only permissible when it is genuinely better to keep something secret from another person.

1. To lie is to keep the truth, to which a person has a right, from him—or without sufficient reason to communicate something to another which is untrue, it is never permissible to lie.
2. Calumny is to speak evil of another which is either not true or is exaggerated. The gravity of this sin must be measured according to the harm which is done to the victim of the slanderous statement.
3. Rash judgment has less serious consequences because the unfavourable judgment is not communicated to others.

56. *What is the meaning of the sixth and ninth commandments?*

The sixth and ninth commandments regulate the virtue of chastity and safeguard the right of both the supernatural and human community to continue to exist.

This commandment is broken by any sexual relationship outside that ordained by God, or by any provocation of sexuality. If in this matter one makes it difficult either for oneself or others to practise the virtue of chastity, by reason of exterior acts or interior thoughts and imaginations, one sins against the virtue of modesty.

For actions which might be dangerous to chastity but which might also have good results, the same rules apply as were mentioned above in the case of the fifth commandment. Courtship and engagement are the normal preparations for marriage. To secure the best preparation, self-restraint and prudence are necessary side by side with the growth and development of love. Certain Catholic usages and customs in this matter should be regarded as the standard to be observed; *all* must avoid what might be dangerous for *many*.

57. *What is the meaning of the seventh and tenth commandments?*

The seventh and tenth commandments regulate our attitude towards the material possessions of our fellowmen who have a right to enjoy certain material conditions of life. From this right is derived the right to private property, which however, is not to be taken in an unlimited sense, because the goods of this earth were primarily intended for the use of all men.

One infringes the rights of private property and commutative justice by:

a. theft or damage;
b. usury;
c. idling.

Para. III. The Precepts of the Church

58. *What are the principal Precepts of the Church?*

1. To keep Sundays and Holydays of Obligation holy by attending at Mass and resting from servile work.
2. To keep the days of fasting and abstinence appointed by the Church.
3. To go to Confession at least once a year.
4. To receive Holy Communion at least once a year, and that at Easter or thereabouts.
5. To contribute to the support of our pastors.
6. Not to marry within certain degrees of affinity, nor to solemnize marriage at the forbidden seasons.

PART IV. THE COMPLETION OF THE CHURCH

Chapter XV. The Extremes of Man

Immediately after death the judgment of God upon man takes place: and that man will be for all eternity where his state at the moment of death places him.

59. *Where do the souls of the deceased go?*

Nothing is known with absolute certainty as to the final destination of unbaptized children, but for other men:

1. Those who die without sanctifying grace (consequently in a state of mortal sin) remain for ever separated from the vision of God, tormented by a punishment which Christ repeatedly refers to as *fire*. This punishment is undergone in hell but is not equal for all who go there.

2. Those who die in the grace of God go to everlasting happiness.

a. If all the penalties of sin have not been expiated, the soul is purified by fire in a place called *Purgatory* (the existence of fire is not a formal point of doctrine).

b. If the soul is already purified, and free from all penalties, or has never been subject to them (as in the case of a small child) it is admitted directly to the contemplation of God as He is in Himself. This contemplation of God confers perfect happiness, leaving no unsatisfied desire and lasting for ever. This is called Heaven.

60. *What will happen at the end of Time?*

Christ redeemed us wholly, that is soul and body, the complete man. Therefore the complete man will also participate either in final bliss or final condemnation, according to whether he had part in that Redemption or not. From this it follows that the body will also rise as the Body of Christ rose from the dead.

This will happen at the end of Time, when the world is destroyed by fire and mankind ceases to exist on this earth. Then Christ will come as King to make a final judgment of men; the unfaithful servants will be rejected while the faithful will take their place in His Kingdom.

Thus, after Resurrection and the Last Judgment, The Church will begin a new life, for ever triumphant under her Head, Jesus Christ.

INDEX

LIST OF BOOKS FOR FURTHER READING

General Reference Books

There are several translations of the Bible. The one used in this book is that of Monsignor R. Knox. This is a modern English translation. Another accepted translation is the Douai Version.

The Teaching of the Catholic Church. (2 Vols.) Edited by Dr. G. D. Smith.
The Spirit of Catholicism – Karl Adam.
Everyman's Catholic Church – A. Reynolds.
Letters from Rush Green – J. C. Heenan.
The Collected works of Abbot Vonier. (3 Vols.)

Apologetics

Map of life – F. J. Sheed.
Theology and Sanity – F. J. Sheed.
The Third Day – A. Lunn.
The Lord, my Light – Rickaby.

A Selection of individual Apologias.

Apologia pro vita sua – J. H. Newman.
Road to Damascus. (2 Vols.)
From Faith to Faith – Dr. Orchard.
One Lord, One Faith – Vernon Johnson.
I believed – Douglas Hyde.
Elected Silence – Thomas Merton.

God

The Unknown God – A. Noyes.
God, His existence and Nature – Garrigou–Lagrange.

The Chosen People

The redemption of Israel – Friedman.

Messianic Prophecy

The Incarnation – Cambridge Summer School Papers.

HISTORICAL TRUTH OF THE GOSPELS
Gospels in slow motion – R. KNOX.
The Catholic Students "aids" to the Bible – H. POPE O.P.
The Third Day – A. LUNN.

JESUS OF NAZARETH
A short life of Our Lord – CREAN.
The Life and teaching of Jesus Christ – LEBRETON.
The Public Life of Our Lord Jesus Christ – A. GOODIER S.J.
The Life of Jesus – G. RICCIOTTI.

The life of Christ viewed from the theological standpoint.
The Christ of Catholicism – AELRED GRAHAM.
Christ Our Brother – K. ADAM.
The Son of God – K. ADAM.
The Incarnation – Cambridge Summer School Papers.

THE CHURCH
The Church in the New Testament – BULLOUGH.
Religion of the plain man – R. H. BENSON.
Infallibility – V. MCNABB.
One Lord, One Faith – V. JOHNSON.
Studies on the early Papacy – CHAPMAN.

THE BIBLE AND REVELATION
Back to the Bible – C. LATTEY.
The Bible and the early history of mankind – HUMPHREY T. JOHNSON.
The Religion of the Scriptures – LATTEY.
Revelation – LATTEY. (Catholic Truth Society pamphlet.)

ORIGINAL SIN AND REDEMPTION
Incarnation and Redemption. (Vol. I.) Collected works of ABBOT VONIER.
Original Sin – O'CONNOR. (Catholic Truth Society pamphlet.)
The fall of man – MILLER.

GRACE
Supernatural Life – VASSAL–PHILLIPS. (C.T.S. pamphlet.)
Catholic doctrine of grace – JOYCE.
God within us – R. PLUS S.J.

COMMUNION OF SAINTS; THE MYSTICAL BODY
Christ in the Church – BENSON.
The Whole Christ – E. MERSCH.
The doctrine of the Mystical Body – ANGER.

Our Lady

The Mary Book – F. J. Sheed.
The glorious Assumption – J. Duhr S.J.
Mary in the documents of the Church – Paul F. Palmer.
New Testament witness to Our Lady – McNabb.
Cult of Mary – Gerrard.

The Sacraments

Sacraments in daily life – Kelly.
Sacramental system – Martindale.
Spirit of Catholicism – K. Adam.

Baptism and Confirmation

Why be baptized? – P. E. Hallett. (C.T.S. pamphlet.)
Teaching of the Catholic Church – Edited by G. D. Smith.

Eucharist and Sacrifice of the Mass

Catholic Faith in the Holy Eucharist – Cambridge Summer School.
The Holy Eucharist – Hedley.
Key to the doctrine of the Eucharist – Vonier.
Essays on the Eucharist – Wiseman.
Mass in slow motion – R. Knox.
Breaking of bread – Coventry S.J.
Mind of the Missal – Martindale.

Confession and Extreme Unction

Confession – Shine. (C.T.S.)
Confessional – Burke. (C.T.S.)
Extreme Unction – Jagger S.J.

Indulgences

Indulgences – H. Pope. (C.T.S.)
Indulgences for sale – Thurston. (C.T.S.)

Marriage

Christian Marriage – Joyce.
Nullity of marriage – F. J. Sheed.
Two in one Flesh – Messenger. (3 Vols.)
Happiness in Marriage – By a priest and a doctor.

Liturgy

Splendour of the Liturgy – M. Zundel.
Liturgica Historica – Bishop.
The Mass of the Roman Rite – Fortescue.

Spiritual Life

Christ the life of the soul – Marmion.
Seeds of contemplation – Merton.
Inward Vision – R. H. Steuart S.J.
Two Voices – R. H. Steuart.
Prayer for all times – Charles.
Path of prayer – McNabb.

The Last Things

What becomes of the dead – Arendzen.
Purgatory – Graham. (C.T.S.)